PRIVATE FOREIGN INVESTMENT IN DEVELOPING COUNTRIES

Published for the Development Centre of the

ORGANIZATION FOR ECONOMIC
CO-OPERATION AND DEVELOPMENT

Paris

The Organization for Economic Co-operation and Development was set up under a Convention signed in Paris on 14 December 1960 by the Member countries of the Organization for European Economic Co-operation and by Canada and the United States. This Convention provides that the O.E.C.D. shall promote policies designed:

> to achieve the highest sustainable economic growth and employment and a rising standard of living in Member countries, while maintaining financial stability, and thus to contribute to the world economy;
> to contribute to sound economic expansion in Member as well as non-member countries in the process of economic development;
> to contribute to the expansion of world trade on a multilateral, non-discriminatory basis in accordance with international obligations.

The legal personality possessed by the Organization for European Economic Co-operation continues in the O.E.C.D. which came into being on 30 September 1961.

The members of O.E.C.D. are Australia, Austria, Belgium, Canada, Denmark, Finland, France, the Federal Republic of Germany, Greece, Iceland, Ireland, Italy, Japan, Luxembourg, the Netherlands, New Zealand, Norway, Portugal, Spain, Sweden, Switzerland, Turkey, the United Kingdom, and the United States.

The Development Centre of the Organization for Economic Co-operation and Development was established by decision of the O.E.C.D. Council on 23 October 1962.

The purpose of the Centre is to bring together the knowledge and experience available in Member countries of both economic development and the formulation and execution of general policies of economic aid; to adapt such knowledge and experience to the actual needs of countries or regions in the process of development and to put the results at the disposal of the countries by appropriate means.

The Centre has a special and autonomous position within the O.E.C.D. which enables it to enjoy scientific independence in the execution of its task. Nevertheless, the Centre can draw upon the experience and knowledge available in the O.E.C.D. in the development field.

TABLE OF CONTENTS

PREFACE

This study is the result of research undertaken by the Netherlands Economic Institute, Division Balanced International Growth, Rotterdam, under the auspices of the O.E.C.D. Development Centre. In the division of labour agreed with professor Grant L. Reuber, who directed a parallel study under the auspices of the Centre[1], the N.E.I. research deals with the evaluation of economic effects of private foreign investment in developing countries. The effects studied are confined to macro-economic effects which are quantifiable. The lack of a satisfactory methodology for the assessment of these effects seemed to justify this limitation in the approach to the evaluation of private foreign investment.

The study is organized as follows. Part I reviews briefly and critically the literature about the evaluation of private foreign investment and suggests the need for an appropriate macro-economic methodology. Part II develops the principles and techniques for such a methodology which is applied empirically to data for five developing countries in Part III. While Parts II and III are concerned with the effects of aggregated volumes of private foreign investment, Part IV considers, independently of the previous parts, the appraisal of projects financed through foreign investment and discusses the special features of social benefit-cost analysis of such projects.

Parts I and IV were prepared by Martin Sanders, M.A., senior economist of the N.E.I., Carlo Secchi, now associate professor at the Faculty of Economics of the University of Trento and of Luigi Bocconi University, Milan (Italy), developed the methodology of Part II and carried out the applications of Part III. In the empirical work he was assisted by Mrs M. Hulsman-Vejsová, M.A., of the N.E.I. and by J. Kol, M.A., and H. B. H. Visscher, M.A., of the Centre of Development Planning of the Netherlands School of Economics. Professor H. C. Bos, director of the N.E.I., directed the study and is responsible for the final result.

The authors wish to acknowledge gratefully the indispensable cooperation received from the research institutes and persons who provided the data for

1 *Private Foreign Investment in Development*, Clarendon Press, Oxford 1973.

the country studies in Part III. In organizing the collection of these data the Secretariat of the O.E.C.D. Development Centre has also given helpful assistance.

Miss I. Bovenkerk and Mrs B. Elderson typed the various drafts of the manuscript with great patience.

The study was financed by the Government of the Netherlands through a grant to the O.E.C.D. Development Centre.

The study was concluded in the summer of 1972 and does not take account of later developments.

Rotterdam, September 1973

Netherlands Economic Institute
Division Balanced International Growth
H. C. BOS

PART I

EVALUATION OF PRIVATE FOREIGN INVESTMENT
A CRITICAL SURVEY OF CURRENT APPROACHES

TABLE OF CONTENTS

CHAPTER I

GENERAL INTRODUCTION

1.1. INTRODUCTION

This part is concerned with the methodology for the macro-economic evaluation of some effects of private foreign investments (PFI) in less developed countries (LDC's).

Subsequent extentions of the methodology are possible, in order to get a more realistic picture of a LDC's economy through a sectoral breakdown. Still, the model which will be discussed in the following pages, and the underlying assumptions and economic rationale, should be considered as the hard core of the complete methodological framework.

In this part of the research, the main concern is in the effects of the total volume of PFI, instead of an evaluation at the project level.

Chapter II presents the mathematical model on which the analysis of the effects of PFI is based.

Chapter III introduces the main economic effects of PFI, relevant for the present macro-economic analysis, while Chapter IV concentrates on some other economic effects, not taken into account.

Chapter V deals with the quantification of the effects of PFI, concentrating on four of them, and points out their interdependence – simultaneous and over time.

Chapter VI analyses the 'cumulative' effects of PFI, derived by comparing in time t the actual situation with PFI with the 'alternative' situation which would occur without PFI. The effects will be then formulated on the basis of the model.

Chapter VII deals with the 'marginal' effects of PFI, defined as the changes in some variables, from t to $t+1$, which occur as a consequence of the presence of PFI. The model will again provide the starting point for the quantification of these effects.

Chapter VIII compares the two approaches, and their practical applicability. A numerical exercise will illustrate the possibilities offered by this approach.

Chapter IX shows how the model can be disaggregated into sectors, and discusses the possibility of introducing input-output analysis.

Arguments in favour of or against direct private foreign investment are of relatively recent date. In classical economic theory international capital movements were generally considered to benefit both the host and the investing country. In the traditional approach international capital movements imply a flow of investment funds from countries where capital is relatively abundant to countries where capital is relatively scarce; in other words it moves from countries with low marginal productivity to countries with high marginal productivity of capital. The host country in this situation benefits from the foreign investment to the extent that the productivity of the investment, the income created, is higher than what the foreign investor takes out in the form of profits and interest.

The investor country benefits to the extent that the rate of return on its foreign investment, through profit and interest receipts, exceeds the rate of return on domestic investment. In this approach international capital movements are to the benefit of the world economy, and also to all of the individual parties participating [1].

It is curious to note that to a large extent recent official and semi-official views on the benefits of private foreign investment are still based on the classical notion of mutual benefits, despite the fact that in the traditional approach foreign investment stands for *loan* investment rather than *equity* investment, which latter gives rise to far more complicated analytical problems. The views have not been unchallenged, however. In recent years the classical theory of the distribution of gains between recipient and donor countries of foreign private investment has increasingly be questioned on several grounds. The discussion has not been restricted to welfare considerations for investing countries and host countries, but in addition a number of other topics have attracted considerable attention, foremost of which has been the balance of payments effect of private foreign investment.

Among the first economists who took exception to the classical approach was H. W. Singer, who, in his well-known study reached the conclusion that by and large direct private investments have been very beneficial to investing countries, but have had no effects, or even more likely, negative effects on the host countries [2].

This conclusion is reached mainly through a terms of trade argument, and

[1] The last couple of sentences do not do complete justice to the classical theory. Indeed the impression we give is a very crude one and omits several aspects, as e.g. the adjustments in the terms of trade. Nor should we like to create the impression that all classical economists fully believed in the benefits of foreign investment.

[2] H. W. Singer, 'The distribution of gains between investing and borrowing countries', *American Economic Review*, 1950, p. 473-485.

in addition through the argument that, at least until recently, foreign investments were not really integrated in the structure of the host country's economy, and consequently were in an economic sense domestic investment on the part of the industrial countries.

Singer's analysis leads to the conclusion that the classical presumption about mutual benefits can only be reached on the basis of static comparative advantage, which may not be appropriate with respect to private foreign investment. What is needed according to him is a dynamic approach, which in Singer's analysis shows that the benefits of private foreign investment have accrued to the investor countries, mainly because rising productivity gains have been passed on to the investor country, rather than having accrued to the host country [3].

Singer's article has given rise to a lively discussion on the benefits of PFI. MacDougall concludes in his 1960 article on lines slightly different from Singer, that unlimited PFI may not be in the selfinterest of the recipient country [4]. Other authors, such as Balogh and Streeten [5], Kemp [6], Frankel [7], take an opposite view from that reached by Singer by pointing out that foreign investment abroad, if proceeding at high rates, may be harmful for the investing countries. Concern with the effect of PFI on the position of the investing country, and more in particular its balance of payments consequences, was the origin of the Hufbauer/Adler study [8], and the Reddaway report [9], the former directed towards an empirical investigation of the effect on the U.S. balance of payments of manufacturing investment abroad, the latter concerned with the effects of U.K. foreign investment.

It is outside the scope of the present report to discuss the consequences of PFI for the investor countries. Neither is it our intention to give a complete survey of the existing literature on the impact of PFI on the economies of the

3 It is worthwhile to note that Singer's analysis refers primarily, if not only, to private foreign investment in the extractive industries.

4 G. D. A. MacDougall, "The Benefits and Costs of Private Investments from Abroad: a Theoretical Approach', *Bulletin of the Oxford University Institute of Statistics*, August 1960.

5 T. Balogh and P. P. Streeten, 'Domestic vs Foreign Investment', *Bulletin of the Oxford University Institute of Statistics*, August 1960.

6 M. C. Kemp, 'Foreign Investment and the National Advantage', *Economic Record*, March 1962.

7 M. Frankel, 'Home vs Foreign Investment: A Case Against Capital Export', *Kyklos*, No. 3, 1965.

8 G. C. Hufbauer and F. M. Adler, *Overseas Manufacturing Investment and the Balance of Payments*, U.S. Treasury Department, 1968.

9 W. B. Reddaway, *Effects of U.K. Direct Investment Overseas*, Cambridge 1967, 1968.

developing countries. The preceding paragraphs were mainly intended as an illustration that, unless one accepts the framework of the classical economists, there is certainly room for debate on the subject [10].

This debate has now been going on for quite some time, becoming more intense in recent years, with diverging views ranging from the position that PFI has been exceptionally beneficial to the developing countries to the opposite extreme that PFI is nothing but a means for the exploitation of the Third World. It would be impossible even to try to give a survey of the current debate, and consequently this will not be attempted. However, some of the more important arguments put forward in favour of or against PFI in developing countries will be presented in the chapters below, in connection with the discussion on the effects of PFI.

1.2. SCOPE OF THE STUDY

The present part of the study aims at giving a critical summary of the attempts to evaluate the impact of PFI on the economies of the LDC's as can be found in the literature, restricting ourselves to the main arguments only. As the debate on the effects of PFI has in recent years tended to become increasingly chaotic and confused, an effort is made to create at least some order in the debate by giving first of all a schematic presentation of the effects on the host country's economy. This is done in Chapter II, where also the question of alternatives to PFI is discussed and criteria for the measurement of the effects of PFI are derived.

Chapter III discusses the effect of PFI on GNP. Starting with a survey of the aspects relevant in this connection, the arguments put forward by different authors concerning the income effect of PFI are subjected to a critical examination.

In Chapter IV the same procedure is followed with regard to the balance of payments effect of PFI.

Chapter V deals with effects of PFI other than the income and balance of payments effect. In addition attention is paid to a limited number of other issues raised in the debate on PFI.

Whereas in the Chapters III, IV and V the evaluation of PFI is approached in a partial analysis, in the final chapter of this part of the study, Chapter VI,

10 A cautious note may be relevant here. Although classical theory generally led to the conclusion that capital transfers (implicitely loan capital) had positive effects on both the host country and the investing country, there was no unanimity as to the path through which this conclusion was reached. Nor can it be maintained that the classical position was adhered to by all classical economists.

the need for a comprehensive approach is stressed and in this light the recent work by UNCTAD on PFI is reviewed.

Throughout this part of the study emphasis is put on a critical evaluation of the arguments in favour of or against PFI put forward by others. In addition the discussion is of a qualitative rather than a quantitative nature.

CHAPTER II

PROBLEMS IN AND CRITERIA FOR EVALUATING THE IMPACT OF PFI

2.1. INTRODUCTION

As was said already in Chapter I, the aim of this part of the study is to evaluate the major arguments put forward in the literature concerning the effects of PFI on the economies of the developing countries. In order to be able to do so in a systematic manner, and also in order to make a distinction between arguments which are relevant and arguments which are not relevant within the context of the NEI study on PFI, it is first of all necessary to make a schematic classification of the possible effects of PFI.

This is done in Section 2.2. As it is not feasible to extend the discussion to all possible effects, a choice has to be made between effects to be dealt with in this survey and effects which have to be omitted. This problem is dealt with in Section 2.3. In addition criteria have to be derived for the measurement of the effects of PFI. Section 2.4 pays attention to this question, and in addition raises the question of alternatives to PFI, as this latter question may be of importance for the determination of the appropriate criterion.

The question of whether the measurement of the effects of PFI should take place at an aggregate or at a project level is discussed in Section 2.5.

2.2. THE EFFECTS OF PFI, A SCHEMATIC CLASSIFICATION

In principle one could make a very extensive list of possible effects of PFI on the host country's welfare in the widest sense. Such a list would, however, be of little value for the question of evaluating the impact of PFI, as one would get lost in a large number of different arguments. For an evaluation to be at all possible a choice has to be made between those effects to be taken into account for the purpose of evaluation and those which are irrelevant or have to be excluded for other reasons. As a first step in this screening procedure a classification of possible effects of PFI may prove helpful.

The effects of PFI can be classified as follows:

(a) a distinction can be made between effects which can be verified and those which are non-verifiable, meaning, that in this latter case the occurrence of the effect can neither be proved nor disproved;

(b) a distinction can be made between effects of a socio-economic character and effects which are of a different nature;

(c) a further distinction can be made between effects which are measurable and effects which are unmeasurable;

(d) a final distinction can be made between direct effects and indirect effects.

Ad a: Verifiable vs Non-Verifiable Effects

As will be obvious there is little to be gained in discussing possible effects of PFI if these cannot be verified. Therefore an evaluation of PFI has, irrespective of its focus, to be limited to those effects for which the occurrence can be verified.

Ad b: Socio-Economic vs Other Effects

The socio-economic effects of PFI contain a limited number of well-known categories, such as the GNP, the balance of payments, employment and income distribution.

The category 'other effects' contains a wide variety of effects among which the political seem to attract most attention. An example of such a political effect might be the supposed or real loss of political freedom as a result of political pressure by the foreign investor's country of origin. A different effect of PFI belonging to the category 'others' could be the introduction, through private foreign investors, of ways of life alien to the national culture [1]. As a third example one could think of the effect of PFI on national self-esteem, a hazy concept, no doubt, but not irrelevant for policy-makers.

In principle the list of non-socio-economic effects of PFI could be extended almost without limit. This is not attempted here, nor would it serve any useful purpose. What should be obvious from the small sample given above, is that, no matter how important they may be in an overall sense, the economist's tool-box does not contain the equipment necessary to integrate these effects in his analysis. Partly this is due to the fact that some of these effects are non-verifiable and have therefore to be excluded. But even if this is not the case the economist has to exclude them from his analysis as he is not competent to deal with political, cultural and other non-economic aspects. These aspects have to be evaluated by the host country, and not by outside economists.

[1] To the extent that this effect takes the form of changing consumption habits, this cultural effect is at the same time a socio-economic effect through its influence on total consumption expenditure.

Ad c: Measurable Effects vs Non-Measurable Effects

Not all effects, even if they can be verified, lend themselves to measurement. The examples of non-economic effects given above are also examples of effects which cannot be quantified in a conventional way. This does not mean that these effects are for that reason less relevant. To the extent that they otherwise qualify for the list of relevant effects they should be taken into account. Since, however, it is difficult to do so in a systematic and correct way for an economist, they can best be taken into account on top of the considerations brought forward by the economist.

Ad d: Direct and Indirect Effects

The distinction between direct and indirect effects is well-known and need not be elaborated upon here. What is important, however, is that an economic analysis which limits itself to direct effects is not complete and may even be grossly misleading if there are significant effects of the indirect variety. Consequently, both direct and indirect effects of PFI should be taken into account.

2.3. THE EFFECTS RELEVANT FOR THIS STUDY

The classification of effects presented in Section 2.2 and the comments made imply that a number of effects can be neglected, either because they are non-verifiable, or because they are outside the economist's area of competence. In addition a case could be made to treat non-measurable effects separately. This leaves as a relevant class of effects the socio-economic effects of PFI, both direct as well as indirect, and to the extent that they are measurable. This still leaves a wide area within the scope of the present study; in all likelihood too wide an area. As some of the effects to be included on the basis of the discussion in Section 2.2 may be of secondary importance only, a more limited list of effects to be included may be desirable. In order to arrive at this, it is useful to go back to the more fundamental question of the focus of the present study.

The current debate on the consequences of PFI for the economies of the less-developed countries is not a purely academic debate in the sense that it is in the first place an analytically interesting problem. Without denying that also from a theoretical point of view it is an interesting problem, it is obvious that the prime importance of the topic lays elsewhere. The major relevance of a study on the effects of PFI derives from the fact that it is assigned an important role in the efforts to increase the financial transfers to the developing countries in order to promote economic development. In other words,

PFI has to be considered as an instrument of international economic policy aimed at economic development in the less developed countries. Approaching PFI in this way, e.g. as an instrument of international economic policy, the distinction between relevant and irrelevant effects can be solved by looking at the aims of economic development of the LDC's. For an appraisal of PFI these aims of economic development are the relevant factors. In other words, considering PFI as an instrument of international economic policy aimed at economic development in the Third World, one can measure its effects by analysing the contribution made to the aims of economic development of the LDC's, such as GNP, employment, a greater income equality, an improvement in the balance of payments, etc., as laid down in national as well as international development strategies.

2.4. CRITERIA FOR MEASURING THE EFFECTS OF PFI AND THE QUESTION OF ALTERNATIVES

In order to be able to determine the socio-economic impact of PFI, criteria are needed for the appraisal of the socio-economic effects considered relevant for the analysis. These criteria may be simple and straighforward, or they may be rather complex, depending on the nature of the investigation. In appraising individual PFI projects rather complex criteria as are used in social cost-benefit analysis will be appropriate. In aggregate macro-economic investigations these refined criteria are of less operational value, and consequently simple and straighforward criteria may be applied.

Even in situations where very simple criteria are appropriate, there is one further question which complicates the analysis, however. This is the question whether the criterion to be applied should be an *absolute* one or a *relative* one. These two options correspond with different analytical questions. For the absolute criterion the relevant question is: what are the consequences, in terms of such socio-economic categories as GNP, employment and balance of payments position, of a given volume of PFI ? For the relative criterion one has in addition to ask the question of how the consequences of a given volume of PFI compare with those that could possibly be obtained through the application of other instruments.

This is an important question in that the outcome of the analysis may be seriously affected by the choice between an absolute and a relative criterion. Therefore the choice of criterion should always be made explicitly. This is not to say that the decision whether an absolute or a relative criterion is appropriate is a simple affair. Indeed no clear-cut solution to the problem presents itself. To some extent the decision will depend on whether one has to do with short-term or with longer-term perspectives. In the first case one may assume that the extent to which other instruments of international development can be utilized is fixed, in other words, that the total amount of, for instance, official development assistance is given, and that the only choice is between having more or less PFI. In that case the absolute contribution of PFI to the aims of economic development is the appropriate yardstick for measuring its effects.

In the case of a medium or long-term analysis the assumption of given levels of official development assistance and other instruments of international economic policy would seem less appropriate, and in that case relative contributions to the aims of economic development would seem more appropriate.

Apart from considerations related to the availability of instruments of international economic policy, the question of whether absolute or relative criteria are appropriate may also depend on the availability of possible other alternatives to PFI. If, for whatever reason, these are not available, the absolute contribution to the aims of economic development is always the appropriate yardstick. However, in cases where alternatives do exist, the relative criterion may be more relevant. It is therefore important to investigate what possible alternatives to PFI may be available.

In a recent study Paul Streeten gives the following five alternatives:

(i) raising the capital and other resources domestically and setting up an indigenous plant;

(ii) borrowing money abroad, hiring engineers and managers and buying the know-how through a licensing agreement;

(iii) any partial combination of (i) and (ii), including joint ventures with foreign firms, management contracts etc.;

(iv) importing the finished product;

(v) not carrying out the investment nor importing the product, but doing without it for the time being.[2, 3]

One may question to which extent Streeten's alternative (v) is a real alternative. It is certainly true that governments sometimes do approve invest-

2 UNCTAD, *The Flow of Financial Resources, Some Aspects of the Balance of-Payments Effects of Private Foreign Investment*, Study prepared by Paul Streeten. Document TD/B/C.3/79/Add. 1 dated 21 May 1970.

3 Sen has amended this list by pointing out that in case the commodity concerned is to be exported, alternatives (iv) and (v) should be read as: foregoing the export opportunities. UNCTAD, *The Flow of Financial Resources, Methods of Evaluating the Economic Effects of Private Foreign Investments,* Report prepared by Prof. Amartya K. Sen. Document TD/B/C.3/94Add. 1 dated 20 August 1971.

ment proposals which lead to unviable projects because of a lack of demand for the commodities concerned. However, provided one assumes, as would seem to be reasonable on a priori grounds, that foreign investors willing to undertake an investment, do so because they want to make a profit, it is utterly unlikely that they invest unless there is a demand for the commodities to be produced. Therefore, to do without the product concerned would generally not be a real alternative. The only exception to this would be if a government, judging that there is no need for the commodity concerned from a social point of view, would find it feasible to prohibit its import. Although it is conceded that this may sometimes be the case, we do not think that this will be a frequent occurrence.[4]

The alternatives to PFI listed above are not always available, especially those mentioned under (i), (ii) and (iii). It is useful to make a distinction here between PFI whose primary contribution is that it makes available production techniques that could not be obtained otherwise, and PFI which technically could be replaced by a domestic investment because know-how is either avaliable or could be obtained through licensing agreements. In the latter case the contribution of PFI is mainly a financial one. Alternatives, other than importing the product concerned, do not present themselves in those cases where know-how cannot be obtained in another way than through a direct investment by a foreign firm. Consequently in this case, in order to determine the effects of PFI it is sufficient to use an absolute criterion.

As will be obvious, a detailed and precise scrutiny of available alternatives can only take place at a project level. Studies aimed at tracing the effects of PFI at a macro-economic level have to make assumptions in this respect, which should preferably take into account whatever concrete information is available concerning the availability of alternatives to PFI. Even then the assumptions made in a macro-economic study cannot be more than plausible approximations of reality, however, as a theoretically correct approach would require that first of all the consequences of all possible alternatives are determined, and that in a second stage a comparison is made between PFI and the most promising alternative.

In the absence of alternatives other than of importing the commodity

4 We leave aside here the difficult problem of whether a government is able to decide whether certain consumption items have to be considered wasteful or even harmful. Although almost everybody will consider certain consumption items as wasteful, it would seem difficult to reach a social consensus on the items to be prohibited. On top of that governments tend to be notoriously inefficient in prohibiting certain forms of consumption, even through a ban on imports. High taxes on these de-merit goods are normally a better solution.

concerned, the determination of the effects of PFI is relatively easy, at least conceptually, provided the necessary data are available. The determination of the consequences of PFI in terms of contributions to the aims of economic development can be obtained in a rather straightforward comparison between a situation with and a situation without PFI, in which latter case the commodity will have to be imported, or in case of export commodities, not to be exported. In situations where alternatives to PFI do present themselves the analysis tends to become much more complicated, for not only does one then have to make a comparison with the effects of alternative ways of realising the investment, such as the alternatives (i), (ii) and (iii) given by Streeten, but also, in cases where the alternative requires domestic investment expenditure, one has to take into account the opportunity costs of domestic investment expenditure. It is especially this latter element, as we shall see in the following chapters of this study, that complicates an analysis of the effects of PFI severely.

2.5. AGGREGATE VS PROJECT APPROACH

Before concluding this chapter a few lines have to be spent on whether a study on the impact of PFI should use an aggregate over-all approach, or whether the investigation should take place at a project level, using social cost-benefit techniques. In our opinion there is no need to make a choice between these two approaches, as they serve largely different purposes, and for that reason are complementary to each other rather than being alternatives, let alone substitutes. Whereas social cost-benefit analysis aims at appraising the contribution of individual investment proposals to the aims of economic policy, aggregate studies aim at a more general appraisal of the impact of PFI on the economies of the developing countries. Only in the case of a large and representative sample of PFI projects would it be possible, at least to some extent, to generalize from individual case studies. Therefore studies concerning the over-all socio-economic impact of PFI should not be based on social cost-benefit analysis but should use more aggregate approaches. This does not mean that social cost-benefit analysis is irrelevant for studies concerning the impact of PFI. Indeed, as in the end investment policies are realized through investment decisions at the project level, social cost-benefit analysis is a necessary complement to more aggregate approaches. For this reason a separate volume dealing with the appraisal of individual PFI projects is presented as a separate part of the NEI research on PFI.[5] At present, however, emphasis will be on more general and aggregate approaches.

[5] *Part IV, The Appraisal of Private Foreign Investment Projects – A Social Cost-Benefit Approach.*

CHAPTER III

THE CONTRIBUTION TO GNP

3.1. OUTLINE

As an increase in per capita income ranks very high in the list of aims of economic development, an evaluation of the literature on the effects of PFI should in first instance be directed towards bringing together a sample of the arguments, and if available, evidence presented in the literature concerning the contribution of PFI to GNP.

As will become evident in the following pages, surprisingly little reliable factual evidence is available concerning the effect of PFI in this respect.[1] Both proponents and critics of PFI have tended to base their conclusions on broad general statements, often without theoretical basis, rather than on empirical evidence. Moreover, arguments have been presented in an unsystematic and often chaotic way, making it extremely difficult to judge their relevance.

Before turning to the literature it is therefore essential to come to a framework for the discussion. Making the usual distinction between direct and indirect effects, we shall first discuss the direct effects. This is done in Section 3.2. A systematic procedure for estimating the direct effects requires that one first establishes the income created by PFI in the form of wages, profits accruing to domestic parties, royalties, taxes, etc. In cases where alternatives to PFI are relevant one has subsequently to make a comparison with the alternative situation. Under perfect competition a discussion of the direct effects could stop here. However, as perfect market conditions do not in reality prevail, one may have to make further corrections. As a second step the indirect effects have to be taken into account. Arguments based on these indirect effects are presented in Section 3.3. In Section 3.4 other considerations presented in the literature, basically of a financial character but having implications for the income effect are discussed. In Section 3.5 some attention will be paid to the profitability of PFI to the parent companies. Although this topic is less directly of relevance to the discussion of the income effect in a narrow sense, it is nevertheless included here as arguments concern-

1 The same is true for all other aspects, unfortunately.

ing profits made are often found in connection with a discussion concerning the income effect.

3.2. THE DIRECT INCOME EFFECT

3.2.1. *Positive Contributions to GNP*

As was mentioned earlier surprisingly little empirical evidence has been brought forward concerning the contribution to GNP in the form of wages, taxes, royalties *etc*. The Pearson report might serve as an illustration of this lack of evidence. While acknowledging that in the absence of detailed empirical studies it is difficult to come to definite evidence concerning the contribution PFI has made to GNP, the report jumps to the conclusion that "in our judgment, available facts do suggest that direct foreign investment has added substantially to the real national income of developing countries".[2] The only evidence presented to support this statement are the, no doubt impressive, amounts of royalties and taxes paid by foreign-owned oil companies to the main oil-producing countries of the Middle East, to Libya and to Venezuela, leaving aside the consideration that the oil industry, although a major sector in which PFI takes place, can for many reasons not be accepted as a typical example representing PFI in general.

A direct, but unsuccessful, attempt to measure the contribution of PFI to national income was made by Herbert K. May in his report for the Council for Latin America, Inc.[3]

This report comes to the conclusion that in 1966 alone, US-owned PFI generated an income of US $ 12 885 mln., or 13.7% of the GDP of the region. These findings have to be rejected, however, as May equates total sales by US affiliates with contribution to GDP.[4] As is obvious, total sales volume is not an adequate approximation for the contribution to GDP. For this latter what is relevant is the value added created in the form of wages and taxes paid as well as profits, to the extent that they do accrue to domestic participants. Thus calculated the figure for contribution to GDP is bound to be much lower than the one given by May. As no detailed breakdown of production costs is presented in the May report, it is not possible to come to a

2 Lester F. Pearson *et al.*, *Partners in Development*, London 1969, p. 104.

3 *The Contributions of US Private Investment to Latin America's Growth.* A Report by Herbert K. May for the Council for Latin America, Inc. January 1970.

4 *Ibid.* page 3 and 4. As May elsewhere brings in indirect effects as defense for his figures, one may assume that he was aware of the fact that there is a difference between sales volume and contribution to GDP.

corrected estimate of income generated through PFI in Latin America, however.

It should be noted that in the last paragraph we used the words 'income *generated through* PFI' and not 'income *due to* PFI'. A distinction between these two expressions is needed because it is questionable whether evidence presented on income generated through PFI, even if the data are fully correct, is acceptable as evidence of income due to PFI. This latter would only be appropriate if the productivity of factors of production employed in PFI would have had a zero productivity in the absence of PFI. In other words it would require that all labour and capital (and perhaps land) used in the PFI sector would have been idle in the absence of PFI. If this is not the case the opportunity costs of factors of production employed in the PFI sector have to be deducted from the value added generated in the PFI sector in order to obtain the contribution made to GNP.

Apart from the critical remarks made in the preceding paragraph there remains the further question of the appropriate criterion. May assumes, and implicitly the Pearson report does the same, that no alternatives other than importing the commodities concerned are available to PFI. If this assumption holds then indeed all income due to PFI should be considered as a contribution of PFI. As was discussed in Chapter II, this need not necessarily be the case if there is a domestic alternative to PFI. Then it could be argued, and indeed is argued frequently, that in order to establish the income effect of PFI one has to make a comparison with the income which would have been created through domestic investment.

In this case the income effect due to PFI would be the absolute contribution of PFI minus the contribution the domestic alternative would make.

Whether absolute contributions are relevant or whether relative contributions to income have to be considered is of course an empirical question, dependent upon the availability of alternatives to PFI. May's implicit assumption of no alternatives other than importing may be a reasonable one for a number of PFI activities; to make this assumption for all PFI activities in Latin America, however, is not defensible. Indeed, inspecting rather detailed lists of US PFI activities in Latin America one cannot but conclude that, whereas some of the activities may belong to the category for which know-how cannot be obtained in other ways, a substantial part of the PFI activities could have been realised by way of domestic investment, provided the necessary investment funds could have been raised.

If it is assumed that domestic alternatives to PFI are available the conclusion concerning the direct income effect of PFI will differ from the conclusion reached so far on the assumption of no alternatives. One may then even, and without introducing new arguments, come to the conclusion of a negative income effect. This is for instance the case with Kidron[5] who in a well-documented case study on India arrives at the conclusion that the income effects of PFI in India are negative partly because of the high costs of capital servicing in the form of profits and technical fees which compare very unfavourable with the interest costs of foreign public debt.

In order to avoid misunderstanding it should be mentioned that Kidron's negative conclusion derives from a number of arguments and not only depends upon the question of alternatives. Nor does he argue that in the presence of a domestic alternative to PFI the income effect of PFI tends to be negative solely because the profits accruing to the foreign investor from a national economic cost which would not be incurred in case of domestic investment. This latter argument which is occasionally heard in discussions, would be incomplete, if not incorrect, as it neglects the opportunity costs of domestic investment funds. An example of this neglect of opportunity costs can be found in a recent UNCTAD study.[6]

3.2.2. *Negative Contributions to GNP*

In this section attention is paid to a number of arguments introduced in the discussion on PFI which aim at providing evidence that PFI may have a negative income effect. This category of arguments is most frequently found in connection with discussions on the balance of payments effect, which will be discussed in Chapter IV. At this place attention will only be given to those aspects of the discussion which pertain to the direct income effect, postponing a discussion of the arguments based on indirect effects to Section 3.3.

In its sharpest form opponents to PFI have sometimes argued that PFI is of an exploitative nature in that the additional income created through PFI is smaller than what foreign investors tend to appropriate in the form of profits. Proponents of PFI have been quick to point out that this type of reasoning is at fault with economic theory. According to them a foreign investor may appropriate a large share of the income generated through PFI, in some cases perhaps all of it, but never more than that. This attack on the argument that foreign investors take out more in the form of profits and other payments than their investments contribute to national income is correct in the sense that in conventional economics one expects that factors of production get

5 Michael Kidron, *Foreign Investment in India*, Oxford 1965, p. 229-314.

6 UNCTAD, *Balance-of-Payments Effects of Private Foreign Investment: Case Studies of Jamaïca and Kenya* – Study prepared by L. Needleman, S. Lace, R. Lacey, L. Seagrave – TD/B/C.3/79 Add. 2 – May 1970. This study will be discussed in Chapter VI.

paid according to their marginal productivity and that moreover the factors of production together can never obtain more than they produce. In such a situation the foreign investor, even if he were a monopolist, could never obtain more than the income created through his investment. However, as is shown below a number of arguments can be given to show that factual conditions do not reflect the world of conventional economics. Limiting ourselves for the moment to the direct income effects, the arguments relevant have to do with price distortions, payment for labour and depletion of natural resources.

3.2.2.1. *Price distortion* The argument that foreign investors cannot take out more than the income created through PFI pertains to a situation in which prices are reflecting real scarcity. In reality, in a large number of developing countries prices are seriously distorted. This is obvious in the case of foreign exchange rates which often do not reflect real scarcity. It is also true for commodity prices, especially for industrial products, which may, due to protection, be much above world market prices. Other commodities and services are perhaps subsidized, in order to stimulate industrialization, etc. In such a situation it is conceivable that foreign investors take out more than the income created through the foreign investment valued at international prices. It remains true that commercial profits can never be more than the value added at domestic market prices, but here one has to take into account that the commercial profitability may well exceed social profitability. Furthermore the foreign investor may exchange his domestic currency earnings at an unrealistic exchange rate so that in real terms he obtains payment in excess of his commercial profits. The charge that foreign investors take more out in the form of profits than they create in the form of income is therefore at least correct as a possibility and, one would expect, in view of the often serious price distortions in developing countries, also in fact. To this should be added, however, that no empirical evidence on this question is at present available.

Moreover, it should be borne in mind that the possibility of making profits over and above what is warranted on the basis of national economic profitability is not limited to foreign investment; it also pertains to domestic investment [7], the only difference being that foreign firms can take out their profits

7 In an interesting study on Pakistan, Soligo and Stern found that in a number of industrial sectors value added measured at world market prices was negative, despite a considerable positive value added at domestic market prices. R. Soligo and J. Stern, 'Some Comments on the Export Bonus, Export Promotion and Investment Criteria' in *Pakistan Development Review*, Spring 1966, pp. 38-56.

whereas domestic investment cannot normally, at least legally, convert its earnings in undervalued foreign exchange.

On the basis of the above analysis one cannot but agree that at least in principle the argument is valid. In the absence of empirical evidence one cannot go further than admitting that under a situation of serious price distortion the hypothesis that PFI may get payment in excess of the contribution made to GDP measured at shadow prices is at least plausible. As we have seen, however, also with domestic investment price distortions tend to lead to profit distortions, although to a lesser extent because of difficulties in converting domestic currency in foreign exchange. The question should therefore be raised whether it is appropriate to use the existing price distortions as an argument against PFI, or whether one should blame the host countries for pursuing economic policies leading to such price distortions.

One further remark on the question of price distortion should be made. It is implicit in the paragraphs above that PFI is not to be blamed for the possibilities offered by serious price distortions. An exception to this has to be made, however, if the foreign investor enjoys a position which enables him to apply over- and under-invoicing practices, and also in cases where he is able to exert sufficient pressure on the host country to further distort pricing through granting of excessive protection or through subsidies. Unfortunately, also here one is faced with serious problems of measurement.

3.2.2.2. *Payment to labour* An argument occasionally used in support of the exploitation argument is that foreign investors make excessive profits because of paying extremely low wages to the labour force employed, which is made possible by the existence of large scale unemployment in a large number of developing countries. We here have to do with an argument which is correct in one sense and incorrect in another. It is correct in the sense that in a specific plant the marginal productivity of labour may be high, due to a high capital intensity, whereas the wage rate is low because of a low marginal productivity of labour in the rest of the economy. In this sense exploitation is possible.

The argument is incorrect, however, at a macro-economic level, as in this case what is relevant is not the marginal productivity of labour employed in PFI but the marginal productivity of labour in the absence of PFI, in other words, its opportunity cost. In this sense, in situations of massive unemployment, low wage levels reflect a low marginal productivity of labour. As this is in accordance with economic theory, one cannot argue, from an economic point of view, that it is a sign of exploitation. Indeed, quite the reverse might be true in many developing countries where wage rates are fixed, for institutional and social reasons, well above what would be warranted on grounds of marginal productivity alone. In those cases it is not completely incorrect, on strict economic grounds, to argue that the labour force obtains more than it is entitled to[8].

3.2.2.3. *Depletion of natural resources.* A final argument concerning the existence of exploitation to be discussed under the heading of direct income effects is concerned with the depletion of natural resources, such as oil and minerals, against payment of royalties *etc.* well below the value of these resources. The argument here is that the use of a country's national resources by foreign investors is not necessarily better than to postpone their exploitation to a later period when the country is in a position to exploit these resources without foreign participation. In order to solve this question a comparison is needed between the opportunity cost of the resources and the return offered by exploitation now through foreign investment. Such a comparison can only be made for specific projects, and consequently it is impossible to come to general conclusions. To this should be added that it is indeed not difficult to find some cases, both in the past and in present times, where the social return to the host country was in all likelihood below the opportunity costs of the natural resources. There is no evidence, however, that this is generally the case at present. Without denying that exploitation of this nature can, and probably does, take place in certain instances, it is only fair to admit that compared with the past developing countries have been able to improve their bargaining position in such a way that they now can insist upon obtaining a considerable higher share of the profits made in the exploitation of natural resources. The trade union of oil producing countries, the OPEC, would seem to be a particularly forceful, although a typical, example of this.

3.3. INDIRECT INCOME EFFECTS

3.3.1. *Forward and Backward Linkages*

The questions of the forward and backward linkages of PFI is, in the literature, mainly discussed in relation with transfer of technology. For that reason the question of the existence of these linkages will in this study be discussed in Chapter V. For reasons of consistency and completeness, however, a few words on this type of indirect effects have to be included also at this place.

[8] In order to avoid misunderstanding, this statement does not imply that we are against payments of wages in excess of marginal productivity. Indeed, for welfare and social justice reasons, we would be in favour of it.

In a situation where all prices are equilibrium prices there is no need to pay attention to the effects of PFI on the level of activity in other production units in the same production column, as these indirect income benefits are fully reflected in the commodity prices concerned. As we noticed, however, market prices in developing countries do not generally reflect scarcity values, and for that reason PFI may lead to income effects elsewhere in the economy.

3.3.2. *The Terms of Trade*

A deterioration in the terms of trade because of the behaviour of foreign investors and the countries from which they originate has in a number of cases been brought forward as a specific way in which PFI could lead to exploitation. A good example of this is the famous article by Singer[9]. This article gives an impressive argumentation pointing out that indeed in the earlier stages of PFI, concentrated as it was in extractive industries, exploitation through terms of trade deterioration may be expected to have occurred. This was made easy by the deliberate way in which foreign mining and plantation industries could, by means of their dominant market position, appropriate the proceeds of increased productivity. In Singer's opinion, however, this terms of trade argument was less, if at all, relevant for PFI in manufacturing industries. Subsequent students of the subject have been somewhat more critical in this respect. Their arguments are, in summary fashion, well stated by Vernon:

> . . . the terms of trade by which the less developed countries exchange their goods with the advanced countries and acquire their foreign exchange are adverse, both in the static and in the dynamic sense. Because of high import restrictions in the advanced countries, the less developed areas are obliged to accept poor prices for their exports. And the terms of trade grow progressively worse for all the familiar reasons that have been associated with Raul Prebisch and the Economic Commission for Latin America (ECLA). Accordingly, the servicing of foreign claims proves more and more costly in real terms as the years progress.[10]

We leave aside here the empirical question of whether the terms of trade do indeed grow progressively worse, on which there is no general agreement. There is furthermore no reason not to agree with the statement that developed countries do indeed apply high import restrictions on goods, especially

9 H. W. Singer, 'The distribution of gains between investing and borrowing countries', *American Economic Review*, 1950, p. 473-485.

10 Raymond Vernon, 'Foreign-Owned Enterprise in the Developing Countries', in James D. Theberge (ed.), *Economies of Trade and Development*, New York, p. 450.

manufactured goods, from less developed countries. What would seem to be a relevant point in a discussion on PFI is the question whether possible deteriorating terms of trade are a result of PFI. To this question the answer should be negative in almost all respects. Admitting that in the past foreign investors may have been powerful enough to dictate world market prices for certain commodities, this is no longer the general case at present, though it is agreed that there are cases where foreign investors are able to dictate export prices, especially if they are subsidiaries of importing companies in developed countries, and thereby to influence the terms of trade. Changes in the terms of trade do take place for a variety of often complex reasons quite independent of PFI, and consequently PFI cannot be charged with sole responsibility for terms of trade deterioration.

3.3.3. *Pre-Emption of Investment Opportunities*

Finally, some attention has to be given to the argument that PFI tends to pre-empt the good investment opportunities, leaving only the marginal projects to domestic enterprise. This argument can take two different forms. In the first place one can think of foreign firms being in a stronger bargaining position *vis-à-vis* domestic firms which enables them to lay claims on the more profitable investment opportunities. As a second possibility one can think of pre-empting the most profitable investment opportunities because of the fact that foreign firms are leaders in the field of technology. Thus it would be possible that a foreign firm pre-empts good investment possibilities by investing in an activity, for which there would in future be a domestic alternative.

The argument that PFI may pre-empt good investment possibilities is a sensible one, and needs to be taken seriously. It does not automatically follow, however, that PFI has because of this to be rejected. This depends upon more detailed scrutiny in which in particular the spread between the internal rate of interest of such a good investment opportunity and the opportunity costs of domestic investment is important. In fact, the proper way to deal with this problem is the one suggested earlier for measuring the income effect of PFI in cases where there is a domestic alternative. Only by proceeding along those lines can one obtain a quantitative estimate of the relevance of the argument. Without such a quantitative scrutiny one cannot go further than the rather vague statement that the argument raised will be more serious if the difference in return between good and marginal projects is large then in cases where they only differ by a few percentage points.

Note that the pre-empting argument here does not imply that PFI is taking out more than it brought in, but depends on whether it brings in sufficiently to compensate for potential social profits which could have been obtained through domestic investment.

3.4. OTHER CONSIDERATIONS

The arguments discussed in Sections 3.2 and 3.3 have not allowed to reach firm conclusions concerning the income effect of PFI. The only conclusion which one arrives at from what was said so far is that the question of the income effect is an extremely complex one, which cannot be answered unless much more empirical research is undertaken. Nevertheless, the treatment we have so far given to the problem is over-simplified in that it does not take into account a number of related factors which might be of crucial importance. Two of these problems, the question of take-overs and the question of financing PFI will be discussed in this section.

3.4.1. *Take-Overs*

We have thus far treated PFI as if it were always creating new productive capacity. This is not necessarily correct. Raúl Prebisch, in his report to the Inter-American Development Bank, shows to be much concerned with the fact that domestic firms are rather frequently bought up by foreign-owned enterprises [11]. Leaving aside at this moment the political and psychological implications of such take-overs, as well as arguments in the field of technology transfer, it is obvious that these take-overs are not in all cases beneficial to the host country. As far as the income effect is concerned, this could in the case of buying up domestic enterprises, only be positive if the price paid for these domestic enterprises could subsequently be invested in more profitable activities than those sold to foreign firms. On a priori grounds this does not seem to be generally plausible, the less so as Prebisch points out that one of the reasons for local firms to pass into foreign hands is the want for enough domestic credit to finance their current operations [12].

3.4.2. *Financing PFI*

PFI normally brings in from abroad only part of the investment funds requir-

11 Raúl Prebisch, *Change and Development, Latin America's Great Task*, report submitted to the Inter-American Development Bank, Washington, July 1970, p. 155, 156.

12 Raúl Prebisch, *op.cit.*, p. 156. In this connection it might be of some use to cite the following sentences, also given on p. 156 of the said report: "Another motive of concern is the infiltration of foreign take-overs of banks which used to be in national hands. The foreign bank or its branch office has a specific and limited function when it is linked to external investment and trade operations."

ed. Vernon, whose support of PFI can hardly be doubted, gives the following illustration of this:

In 1964, for example, the equity interest of United States private foreign direct investment in their subsidiaries, affiliates, and branches in Latin America, Asia, and Africa increased by $ 3.3 billion; yet the added funds coming from the United States amounted to only $ 565 million, the rest of the increase coming out of the net income and depreciation reserves of the subsidiary firms and from non-United States capital sources. Thus, the argument goes, less-developed countries contributed to the growth of foreign claims largely out of local savings and local resources. [13]

Also other authors draw attention to the fact that foreign investors raise a large amount of their investment requirements in the host country, both in the form of loan capital and through domestic participation in the form of joint ventures. This latter, participation in the form of joint ventures, has not generally been criticized. Indeed it has quite often been applauded. Nevertheless, it would seem to complicate the analysis of contribution of PFI to GNP, if directly or indirectly the earnings are unevenly divided between the partners in the joint venture. Far more important problems are raised, however, in the case of loan capital. Here the consequences for the income effect of PFI depend on the interest paid on this loan capital in relation to the opportunity costs of domestic investment. To the extent that the former is lower than the latter, which is not at all unlikely, loan capital employed in PFI has a negative income effect.

Although it is difficult to quantify the difference between interest rates and the opportunity costs, it is obviously clear that the interest rate is below the productivity of this loan capital in the private foreign firm. Were this not the case, the foreign investor would not attract loan capital. Indeed, a frequently heard accusation against private foreign investors is that they typically undercapitalize in order to take maximum advantage of the low interest prevailing in the developing countries, which allows them, due to the gearing effect, to increase the rate of return on their investments.

3.5. THE QUESTION OF PROFITS MADE BY FOREIGN INVESTORS

Thus far we have not discussed the profitability of PFI to the foreign investor. Nor was there any serious need for this, as in our approach we looked

13 Raymond Vernon, 'Foreign-Owned Enterprise in the Developing Countries', in James D. Theberge (ed.), *Economics of Trade and Development*, New York, n.d. p. 448-449. No breakdown is available for 'non-United States capital sources' in capital originating in the advanced countries and capital generated in the less-developed countries. Vernon's guess is that such capital is largely raised in the host countries.

directly into the profitability of the foreign investments for the host country. In this approach the profits made by foreign companies can only be of secondary importance, that is to the extent that, as is often maintained, profits by foreign investors are extremely high. The question at stake here, in other words, is not whether PFI leads to a positive income effect in the host country, but whether the earnings are not divided in a way unnecessarily favourable to the investor.

Unfortunately, no detailed and reliable data are available concerning profits made. Whatever data are available are rough and subject to restrictions as will be noted further on in this section. Before giving data, however, it is of some use to try and define what would be reasonable profits, as only this can give us a yardstick to judge whether profits made are unreasonably high, or just adequate. One of the few authors who went into this question is Stikker in his 1968 report to UNCTAD [14]. While acknowledging that it is not possible to give a precise quantitative definition of 'reasonable profits', Stikker argues that it might be possible to come to a generally valid concept of reasonable profits by defining them as "the minimum profits required to attract investors to a project in the particular circumstances, present and future, applying or judged to apply to that project". This type of approximation is given contents by quoting subsequently, and as is clear in the context of the Stikker report, with approval, Lord Campbell in a publication by the Overseas Development Institute:

> A critical factor in mutual acceptability is a consensus of opinion about what constitutes a reasonable profit. I would take – one year with another, and over a normal commercial business as a whole – 10% after tax on capital employed. I would justify that, with conscious over-simplification, on the grounds that a business project with all its capital subscribed by ordinary shareholders, would need to pay them at least 5% per annum dividend, and put an equal sum of money each year to reserves. But the risk involved is an important consideration. We all know what danger-money is; the greater the real risk in any investment, the more attractive, in a literal sense, the financial return must be. A hard fact of economic life, whether we like it or not, is that unless an acceptable return on capital invested is forthcoming, big business will not be able to raise the capital they need for development. And there are many cases where the hazards of development expenditure is so great that 10% will simply not be enough to attract investment and to accumulate reserves adequate to carry a project through lean and difficult years. [15]

[14] Dirk U. Stikker, *The Role of Private Enterprise in Investment and Promotion of Exports in Developing Countries.* United Nations, New York 1968, E. 68.II.D.9, p. 11, 12.

[15] Sir John Campbell, *Investment and Development*, London, ODI, 1965 as quoted by Stikker, *op. cit.*, p. 12.

Accepting this 10% as a point of reference, without however accepting it as an objective criterion, what can be said about the level of profits realized? Stikker, in a somewhat vague way, estimates the average after tax profits at 9.4% Reddaway finds for the years 1956-1964 an average annual rate of return on U.K. non-oil investments of 12.3%, somewhat above the 10% Campbell deems necessary.

Interesting information is contained in the September 1967 issue of the U.S. Survey of Current Business [16], which shows that the yield of PFI in total, including both that in developed as well as that in developing countries, and expressed as a percentage of the value of investment at the start of the year, declined continuously from about 17% in the early 1950's to 11.5% in 1966. These percentages almost certainly underestimate the profitability of international investment. As it is pointed out in the Survey:

> ... the earnings on the foreign investments as measured for balance of payments purposes are not necessarily a complete measure of the income derived by American firms as a result of these investments. Such income can also accrue to U.S. parent companies through additional exports, imports at costs lower than the prices that would have to be paid to independent producers of the imported goods, receipts of royalties, management fees, and benefits resulting from the assumption of other costs, such as research and development expenditures, by foreign subsidiaries.

Of course, it is impossible to quantify the underestimation of real profits made as practices such as non-arm-length pricing do not lend themselves to precise measurement. On management fees and royalties some more information can be obtained. The Survey estimates that in 1957 royalties and fees amounted to 10% of the total investment income of US $ 2.5 billion, whereas in 1966 the combined receipts from foreign investment had increased to US $ 5.1 billion, of which more than 20% represented royalties and fees. Therefore, without being able to measure the real profits made by US investors abroad, it would seem obvious that the official profits contain a considerable downward bias. Moreover, these profit data pertain to all US investment abroad, not just to investment in developing countries. In these latter countries profits were, according to the Survey, much higher, 17.3% of total investment in 1965 an 17% in 1966. These percentages, together with the underestimates they contain, would surely indicate profits to be much above the level considered 'reasonable' by Lord Campbell.

The short survey of profit ratios is far from conclusive. Looking only at the official profits there would not generally be a case for stating that foreign firms investing in developing countries make unduly high profits. The Survey

16 Walter Lederer and Frederick Cutler, 'International Investments of the United States in 1966', in *Survey of Current Business*, September 1967.

of Current Business data show, however, profit ratios well above those which can be considered reasonable. To some extent this can perhaps be due to high risk premiums for investment in developing countries, but then the risk premium is very high indeed.

What is the significance of these high profit ratios? According to the Pearson Committee high profits are not to be frowned upon. In the words of the Pearson Committee "... unless it is assumed that profits derive from monopoly, or from distorted prices, high profits imply that such investment is particularly efficient." [17] This statement, while true in a sense, and only for the short run, does not seem to be of much practical relevance. As we have seen, price distortions do exist, and so do monopolies. A more important criticism to be raised, however, is that the Pearson Report does not pay attention to the most typical aspect of PFI, e.g. that it is foreign. It is this aspect which is responsible for some of the deviations between nominal profits and real profits. The multinational enterprise aims, as it should, at maximizing global profits; hence the temptation for applying a system of non-arm-length pricing, letting profits, from a bookkeeping point of view, accrue there where taxes are lowest. The developing countries pay a price for this in the form of lower tax receipts. This does not mean that excessive profits lead to negative income effects; it does mean, however, that the developing countries get less out of PFI than they otherwise could have obtained.

17 Pearson *et al., op. cit.*, p. 101.

CHAPTER IV

THE BALANCE OF PAYMENTS EFFECT OF PFI

4.1. INTRODUCTION

In the discussions concerning the impact of PFI the balance of payments consequences of PFI is by far the most discussed, and also the most controversial aspect. The discussion has essentially centred around four arguments which are discussed below. In Section 4.2 arguments pertaining to a direct comparison of capital inflow and profit outflow are reviewed. Section 4.3 deals with arguments based on direct as well as indirect balance of payments consequences of PFI. In Section 4.4 attention is paid to the possible consequences of the availability of alternatives to PFI on the estimation of its balance of payments impact. In Section 4.5 a limited number of other arguments referring to the behaviour of foreign firms are briefly mentioned. Finally in Section 4.6 the need for a more comprehensive approach with respect to estimating the balance of payments consequences of PFI is stressed.

4.2. A COMPARISON OF CAPITAL INFLOWS AND PROFIT OUTFLOWS

One of the ways, and admittedly a crude one, to measure the balance of payments effect of PFI is to make a comparison between capital inflows and the outflows of profits. The yardstick for measuring the balance of payments effect of PFI is applied by a large number of authors. As an example, we may refer to Griffin, who after giving a large number of theoretical arguments,

PFI–Investment flows and repatriated profits (in US $ mln.)

	1965	1966	1967	1968	1969
1. New Investments[a]	2 207	2 188	2 118	2 899	2 566
2. Outflow of Profits	3 489	4 095	4 286	5 006	5 380

a Including reinvested earnings.

Sources: OECD Development Assistance Review, various issues
UNCTAD, The outflow of financial resources from developing countries, TD/B/C.3/92 Rev.

refers to the balance of payment data, showing that only in exceptional cases the inflow of capital in the form of new PFI in LDC's exceeds repatriated profits.[1]

The correctness of his findings can be illustrated with more recent statistical data as presented in the table on page 31. These data confirm that the profit transfers do exceed the flow of new investment. This is often, by Griffin as well as others, seen as evidence that PFI leads to negative balance of payments effects, which negative effect equals the outflow of profits minus the new investment inflows. As is shown below, for a number of reasons the correctness of this conclusion may well be doubted.

4.3. DIRECT AND INDIRECT EFFECTS

The approach to the balance of payments effect of PFI as sketched in Section 4.2. has been criticised as being extremely crude and irrelevant. A clear example of this criticism can be found in the Pearson Report, where it is argued that attempts to measure the balance of payments impact of PFI by comparing net capital inflows with the total profits of the accumulated PFI in the country are based on a misunderstanding:

> Such a comparison neglects to take into account the reinvestment of profits by foreign investors in the host country and fails to note the impact of foreign investment on export promotion and import-saving. It does not make sense, for example, to evaluate the balance of payments effect of foreign investment in the oil-producing countries of the Middle East by a simple comparison of capital inflows with profit-remittances, neglecting oil exports. The correct way to look at the balance of payments effects of foreign investment is to ask what the balance of payments would have been like in its absence.[2]

An effort to measure the balance of payments effect of PFI using this approach can be found in Herbert K. May's report for the Council for Latin America, Inc.[3]

According to May, "during the period 1965-1968, U.S. private investment bolstered Latin America's balance of payments by an average of $ 8.55 billion a year". This amount is arrived at in the following way. Exports effected through U.S. companies amounted to some $ 4.5 billion, all of which is treated as a balance of payments gain[4]. In addition the U.S. affiliates produced

1 Keith Griffin, *Underdevelopment in Spanish America*, London 1967, p. 142-147.
2 Pearson *et al.*, *Partners in Development*, London, 1969, p. 100-101.
3 The Council For Latin America, Inc., *The Contributions of U.S. Private Investment to Latin America's Growth.* A report by Herbert K. May.
4 Note that no allowance is made for the import content of these exports.

about \$ 8 billion for the domestic market, which is estimated to have resulted in a balance of payments gain of at least \$ 4790 mln. annually (this figure is arrived at through an estimate of additional imports which would have taken place without U.S. investment, \$ 6110 mln., from which is subtracted the imports on behalf of the U.S. affiliates). These two figures, \$ 4.5 billion and \$ 4790 mln. together with a capital investment of \$ 700 million minus \$ 1440 million of profits remitted, lead to a balance of payments effect of approximately \$ 8.55 billion per year.

The position taken here by the Council for Latin America is an extreme one. Moreover, it is also an exaggeration in the sense that no allowance is made for the import content of exports. Even after a suitable correction for this obvious mistake some questions remain regarding the degree of realism of the entire calculation, as it would seem that it is based on the assumption that on the one hand no alternatives exist for the PFI whereas on the other hand the total level of demand in the absence of PFI is assumed to be the same.

4.4. ALLOWING FOR ALTERNATIVES TO PFI

The approach to the balance of payments effect of PFI used in the Pearson Report has been criticized as being of little practical value because of measurement problems. Moreover, it has been argued that the procedure outlined in the Pearson Report is correct only to the extent that no domestic alternatives to PFI are available. An example of this type of criticism can be found in a recent study by Paul Streeten on behalf of UNCTAD.[5]

According to Streeten, the view that the contribution of PFI to the balance of payments is equal to all additional sales made possible by the investment project, minus the imported inputs on behalf of the project, would be true:

> only if all resources employed in the project were previously unemployed, all sales were either exports or import substitutes, and all additional income were saved, or if the marginal propensity to import were zero or if fiscal policy kept consumption constant. Otherwise, there will be some reduction in the maximum foreign exchange earnings and savings depending on the amount of extra imports or reduced exports. A difficulty in the approach outlined . . . is that such indirect effects emerge from any investment, and not merely from foreign private investment. The characteristic peculiar to the latter, as distinct from domestic investment, is that privately owned foreign exchange first flows in for the construction of the project and later flows back in the form of remitted profits.

5 Paul Streeten, *Some Aspects of the Balance-of-Payments Effects of Private Foreign Investment*, UNCTAD TD/B/C.3/79 Add. 1, dated 21-5-'71.

After having pointed out what possible alternatives to PFI may be available, and after having analysed the impact of the existence of alternatives on the effects of PFI, Streeten concludes that

> the analysis which runs in terms of capital inflow and profit outflow, crude though it is, has stronger logical validity and operational use than the analysis based on 'indirect' effects in cases where alternative investment schemes are available. On the other hand, the analysis based on 'indirect' effects is more appropriate in cases where in the absence of foreign private firms, no investment for and production of a specific commodity would have taken place.

Whereas this last conclusion is correct, as will be seen below, the first conclusion presented is somewhat more difficult to accept.

4.5. ARGUMENTS BASED ON THE BEHAVIOUR OF FOREIGN FIRMS

Arguments relevant under this heading have mainly centered around the import and export behaviour of PFI. Often one finds the argument that private foreign firms import more raw materials and semi-manufactured goods than is required, whereas at the same time they do not sufficiently promote, or may even restrict, exports of finished products. Although, here again, difficulties of measurement make it impossible to reach definite conclusions, it would not seem to be correct to completely reject this accusation. Concerning the import argument one could point at a substantial amount of PFI in manufacturing industry which was made in order 'to jump the tariff'. With high tariffs on final products and low tariffs on intermediate inputs foreign firms may be induced, in order to secure a market, to put up factories of an assembly type, which operate through imported intermediate products either because no local substitutes are available, or because of a technological bias not warranted on economic grounds, or because it offers prospects of gains to the parent company through means of non-arm-length pricing practices.

On the export side of the argument there is evidence that in a number of cases parent firms do restrict exports, even to the extent of forbidding them in the licence contracts, in order to avoid a situation whereby subsidiaries are effectively competing with the parent company.

It is impossible, at least within a macro-economic framework to quantify the extent to which these import and export practices do occur, and consequently it is also impossible to measure the impact of these practices on the balance of payments. All one can, on the basis of a priori reasoning, conclude is that these practices tend to depress the balance of payments contribution of PFI. Of course this does not necessarily mean that this leads to a negative balance of payments effect.

4.6. THE NEED FOR A MORE COMPREHENSIVE APPROACH

On the basis of the above discussion, what can one say about the balance of payments effect of PFI ? Not very much indeed. The arguments given in the Pearson Report are not complete and, moreover, do not lend themselves to easy computations. Also the crude measure of comparing capital inflows and profit outflows does not give us much guidance. Apart from the objections raised by the Pearson Report, the yardstick is also deficient in another and fundamental sense, namely that it adds up, or more properly deducts from each other, streams which have a different time dimension. Whereas capital inflows are 'one time shots', profit outflows have a more permanent character, and are not dependent on capital inflows in the same period. The two are logically unrelated, with profits related to investments in an earlier period, and may therefore not be compared with each other. An appropriate way to compare inflows of capital and the profit outflows would be to express the latter as the capitalized outflows due to a capital inflow, all related to the year the investment occurred. But this procedure would certainly be too complicated for practical purposes, even if one abstracts from the problem of finding the appropriate discount rate.

Nor indeed is there reason to be surprised that so little can be said, in a more or less definite way, about the balance of payments consequences of PFI on the basis of the arguments presented. The arguments put forward are defective in the sense that they either implicitly or explicitly try to estimate changes in the balance of payments as a result of PFI in isolation, that is without reference to what happens to national income. Since, in the end the balance of payments depends basically on what happens with changes in income, consumption and investment, one should, for a proper treatment of the balance of payments consequences of PFI look at the consequences of PFI on other macro-economic variables such as gross domestic product, consumption and investment in order to be able to derive the balance of payments effect to the host country.

A discussion of efforts made in this direction, such as the recent UNCTAD study[6], will be postponed to Chapter VI. Here it should be noted that unless an appropriate comprehensive approach is used, little reliable information on the balance of payments effect can be obtained.

6 UNCTAD, *Balance-of-Payments Effects of Private Foreign Investment: Case Studies of Jamaica and Kenya* – Study prepared by L. Needleman, S. Lace, R. Lacey, and J. Seagrave – TD/B/C.3/79 Add. 2 – 21 May 1970.

CHAPTER V

ISSUES CONCERNING OTHER EFFECTS OF PFI

5.1. INTRODUCTION

In the preceding chapters the discussion was limited to arguments relevant for the income effect and the balance of payments effect of PFI. Arguments put forward in the literature on the impact of PFI are, however, by no means limited to these two aspects, but also pay attention to possible contributions made to transfer of technology and training of the labour force, secondary effects through backward and forward linkages and other externalities. Arguments concerning these aspects will be reviewed in the present chapter. In addition some attention will be given to possible incompatibilities between the behaviour of foreign firms and planning priorities.

5.2. TRANSFER OF TECHNOLOGY

Arguments concerning the question of transfer of technology play an important role in the debate on PFI. Sometimes the contribution of PFI in this respect is even considered as its major benefit to the LDC's. In a companion volume to the present studies, Professor Grant Reuber pays specific attention to the various issues involved, and therefore the discussion at this place can be limited to some general reflections on the subject.

There can be no doubt that the problem of technology is indeed a very serious one for the developing countries. Leaving out China, it is estimated that at present almost all of the global expenditure on Research and Development is incurred in the rich countries, which in itself is a clear indication that as far as modern technology is concerned the developing countries are dependent upon the rich countries. However, it does not follow that a transfer of Western technology to the developing countries would solve the problems of the Third World in this respect. On the contrary, it might well be that a transfer of this technology tends to aggravate rather than to solve the development problems. The Research and Development work done in the Western world is based upon Western requirements, and not upon the requirements relevant for the LDC's. This may not have been a very serious aspect before the Second World War, but at present it certainly is, if only because of the fact that the new developments in Western technology are all of a very capital-intensive nature, whereas the relative factor proportions of the LDC's would require a labour-intensive or at least an intermediate technology. Apart from being too capital-intensive, there is the problem that a substantial part of the Research and Development is not relevant for the LDC's. In the developing countries new technological innovations are most needed in fields like agriculture. In these areas, with the exception of the work financed by the Rockefeller Foundation, the Ford Foundation and some other organizations, no new technologies are developed in the rich countries. Because of this bias the potential relevance of new technology developed in the rich countries for the developing countries is limited to the so-called modern sector, especially to the manufacturing industry. And even in this limited field the technologies available may be irrelevant, and sometimes harmful, to the developing countries, as they are based on the factor proportions of the rich countries, and not on those of the developing countries. The transfer of technology may, therefore, well lead to too capitalintensive production methods and hence, less additional employment opportunities than would have been possible if the technologies developed had been based on the factor proportions pertaining in LDC's.

Leaving aside now the question of whether the technology available in the rich countries is relevant to the developing countries, we may next turn to the question of how to transplant technology. One of the ways open to developing countries is to buy technical know-how through licensing agreements. This option is often used by the developing countries, and sometimes quite successfully. On the other hand, the market for buying know-how is a restricted one, in the sense that it is not generally possible to buy the know-how, whereas sometimes the strings attached to licensing agreements are such as to make them unacceptable. Sometimes know-how may be obtained through technical assistance programs of multilateral and bilateral donors, but here, too, the possibilities are clearly restricted.

Another way for the developing countries to obtain technology is, and this is relevant in the context of our review, to import new technology by means of PFI. This is then what is normally called the transfer of technology due to PFI. Although PFI certainly has introduced a large number of production processes in LDC's that could not have taken place without PFI, it is our impression that the word 'transfer' suggests more than might be appropriate. The new technology is 'transferred' in the sense that, through the PFI, it becomes available in a different country. This does not necessarily mean, however, that the technology is transferred in the sense that it becomes part and parcel of the economy where the investment is made. Quite to the contrary, the new technology may well remain an element alien to the domestic economy, if it is kept under the complete control of the foreign firm and its expatriate staff. Of course, there is a tendency to employ more and more local employees in staff functions, and to the extent that this occurs citizens of the host country may make themselves familiar with new technologies, or at least with parts of it. Even then it would, however, seem at least premature to speak about a transfer of technology, as the benefits of the technology applied may remain internal to the foreign firm. This may happen either because knowledge about the key elements of the technology is not made available to the local staff, or because the foreign firm is able, through the level of salaries paid, to avoid that local employees leave the firm for a job in domestically owned enterprise.

The reflections given above are far too general for allowing any firm conclusions concerning the transfer of technology due to PFI. For this to be possible a much deeper analysis would be required. It does indicate, however, that a large part of what is normally referred to as 'transfer of technology' is in reality only a transfer between firms belonging to the same multinational concern.

Thusfar we have approached the question of transfer of technology in a narrow sense. One could argue, that what is relevant is not in the first place the availability and spread of new techniques, but the introduction of modern ways of producing and organizing. Indeed one of the positive effects of PFI might well be to make society familiar with these essential prerequisites for sustained development, and to the extent that this occurs the effect of PFI might be more positive than in the more restricted definition of technology. In addition to this argument one should allow for the possibility that foreign firms may give technical and organizational guidance to firms elsewhere in the production column, that is to local suppliers and local purchasers. There is some evidence that this does indeed occur, and to the extent that this is the case PFI makes a positive contribution to the transfer of technology.

As will by now be obvious, analytically the question of transfer of technology is a difficult one. It is, unfortunately, an even much more difficult question in an empirical sense. Indeed, we have not come across empirical evidence indicating that transfer of technology has or has not occurred as a result of PFI. Helen Hughes and You Poh Seng, for instance, in their book on foreign investment in Singapore, list transfer of technology as one of the most important effects of PFI, but admit that they have not been able to find empirical proof that a transfer of technology has indeed occurred.[1] The

[1] Helen Hughes and You Poh Seng, *Foreign Investment and Industrialization in Singapore,* Madison, Wisconsin, 1969.

reason for the absence of empirical evidence may well be that serious problems of measurement are involved; perhaps even, transfer of technology has to be regarded as unmeasurable.

5.3. TRAINING OF THE LABOUR FORCE

Concerning the contribution towards training of the labour force we can, after the discussion concerning transfer of technology, be very short, as a number of arguments put forward in Section 5.2 also apply in this case. Also in terms of training of industrial skills we are dealing with effects which are in the first place internal to the firm. Indeed, because of the higher wages, industrial workers do not generally leave the foreign firm on a voluntary basis, and consequently the benefits of additional skills remain by and large within the firm. Indeed, PFI may tend to create a small elite of well-paid skilled industrial labour in a general setting of misery and unemployment. There is no doubt a somewhat higher mobility of skilled labour than of technology, but in view of the wage differentials, including fringe benefits, labour mobility may still be expected to be very low. Consequently, no significant external effects in the form of skill formation can be expected.

5.4. FORWARD AND BACKWARD LINKAGES

PFI may indirectly contribute to economic development because of forward and backward linkages. The argument here is that PFI induces changes elsewhere in the economy by providing new opportunities for domestic enterprise to invest, either because they are suppliers to the foreign firm, or because the products of the foreign firm provide possibilities for undertaking new activities. In principle, these indirect effects could occur with any investment and therefore are not due to PFI per se. However, there are instances where positive effects due to PFI in the form of forward and backward linkages can be discovered which were induced not so much by the creation of the new industry as by the efforts made by the foreign entrepreneur. A well-documented example is the Sears, Roebuck experience in Mexico. This enterprise, which originally distributed American merchandise in Mexico, through an active policy of providing financial and technical assistance to Mexican enterprises has succeeded in activating Mexican enterprises as suppliers to its department stores in a very fundamental way. Not only do Sears, Roebuck now market mainly Mexican products in their Mexican enterprises, they have also provided an important export market for these Mexican products.[2]

The existence of forward and backward linkages is not always an important consideration. Especially in the older literature one finds many examples of 'enclave' type of foreign investments, which operate almost without links with the economy of the host country. This type of investment, for which backward and forward linkages are not important, was predominant in mining and plantation agriculture, but is by no means limited to these sectors. Also in manufacturing and in service industries 'enclave' type of industries may occur, at least as far as backward linkages are concerned. In all cases where foreign firms have unduly high propensities to import, a case which we discussed in the last chapter, one can reasonably conclude that the backward linkages of PFI are largely absent. An extreme example of this 'enclave' type of foreign investment can be noticed in some of the international luxury hotels which import almost all consumables, even those which are abundantly, and at much lower costs, in the host country.

5.5. OTHER EXTERNALITIES

In addition to the indirect effects mentioned so far, a large number of other externalities; positive as well as negative, are mentioned in the literature. To mention but a few of them, PFI may assist in opening up export markets because of its knowledge of these markets, it may implant better management and organizational techniques in the host country, it may contribute to social and physical infrastructure, or contrarily it may benefit from the available infrastructure without contributing to it, it may assist the modernization process, whatever may be meant by that, or the behaviour of expatriates employed in foreign firms may effect social life in a positive or negative way.

Within this survey of arguments no detailed scrutiny can be given to these arguments. We therefore propose to leave them undiscussed.

5.6. BEHAVIOUR OF FOREIGN FIRMS AND PLANNING PRIORITIES

A further argument worth mentioning in this survey has to do with the behaviour of multinational firms, which may interfere with planning priorities. Multinational firms, so the argument goes, do not adhere to the planning priorities of the host country, because the role of the subsidiary is determined by the global strategy of the parent company. Indeed one would expect that the multinational firm aims at promoting its own goals, rather

2 For details see: National Planning Association, *United States Business Performance Abroad, the Case Study of Sears, Roebuck de Mexico*, S.A., 1956.

than those of the host country. But so does all private enterprise, whether it is foreign owned or domestically owned. So the argument should not be raised against PFI but against all private enterprise.

In addition, the argument is an exaggeration of reality. The government cannot decide what private enterprise should do, but it certainly can influence the private sector. To which extent this can be done depends largely upon the institutional framework in which development planning is taking place. In some cases a government may not have more powers than to allow or forbid certain investment activities, in other cases there may be scope for more detailed interference. In all cases it means that although the government can to a certain extent influence developments in the private sector, it can never completely assure that private enterprise adheres to the national planning priorities. Whether private enterprise is domestically or foreign owned does not make much difference in this connection, unless, of course, the foreign firms are supposed to be strong enough to form a pressure group dictating government economic policies.

CHAPTER VI

THE UNCTAD STUDY ON PFI

6.1. LIMITATIONS OF A PARTIAL APPROACH

A major shortcoming revealed by the review of arguments pro and contra foreign investment is that most of the available studies are based on a partial approach. Such an approach is only appropriate if one can treat different effects in isolation, assuming that with the exception of the effect studied, all other things remain equal. For a study of PFI this is obviously misleading since this would imply the absence of interrelationships in the economy, whereas it is rather clear that the interrelationships tend to be of paramount importance for an analysis of the effects of PFI. In other words, for a study on PFI to be useful a comprehensive approach paying due attention to the interrelationships within the economy is required.

6.2. THE UNCTAD STUDY

Recently an effort was made to come to such a comprehensive macro-economic approach in a study by Needleman *et al.* under auspices of UNCTAD, aimed at determining the balance of payments implications of PFI through case studies for Jamaica and Kenya.[1]

In that study detailed information is collected from a small sample of foreign firms operating in Jamaica and Kenya which are considered to be representative for PFI in general. The data obtained from these firms are subsequently applied to a macro-economic analysis of the balance of payments and income effect of PFI.

According to the UNCTAD study (par. 103)[2] in order to estimate the total effect of PFI on the host country's balance of payment two different positions must be compared – the actual situation, i.e. the actual inflows and outflows associated with a PFI in its investment period (IP) and operations

1 UNCTAD, *Balance-of-Payments Effects of Private Foreign Investment: Case Studies of Jamaica and Kenya* – Study prepared by L. Needleman, S. Lace, R. Lacey, and J. Seagrave – TD/B/C.3/79 Add. 2 – 21 May 1970.

2 References refer to the relevant paragraph in the study mentioned in Footnote (1).

period (OP)[3], and the alternative position, that is what the balance of payment would have been if PFI had not taken place.

The UNCTAD study, as to the 'alternative position', introduces the following assumptions:

(1) For each firm in the sample (i.e. each PFI), the alternative situation is taken to be that the particular firm under investigation was not established, while the rest of PFI in the country remains unchanged. This is justified by the fact that, otherwise, considering the complete absence of PFI, the economy of the two countries of the study (Kenya and Jamaica) would be completely altered (par. 104).

(2) The replacement of any PFI by another PFI is ruled out from the consideration of the alternative situation. Such replacement, either by expanding PFI's domestic sales or by establishing a new plant, would be, according to the UNCTAD study, the most probable alternative, but, for the purposes of the study, it would end up in a comparison of two PFI's operating in identical circumstances (par. 105).

(3) The total domestic sales of the goods produced by the foreign firm would be the same in the absence of that firm, the assumption being that the gap would be completely filled by indigenous producers, or by imports, or both. It is further assumed that the Government of the host country would allow any extra imports without additional restrictions, and that, in general, the tariff position would remain unchanged (par. 106).

(4) Given the impossibility to estimate the price at which local production or imports would replace domestic sales of PFI, a unit elasticity of demand with respect to price for all products sold by PFI under consideration is assumed. This implies that expenditure remains constant even if prices alter (par. 107).

(5) Advertising is assumed to have, on the whole, not a significant effect when replacing the sales of PFI considered absent (par. 108).

(6) No general assumptions are made about the extent to which domestic sales of foreign firms would be replaced by local production, but the situation of each individual firm is examined (par. 109). This is quite important in order to establish how much would be produced internally and how much would be imported.

(7) In most cases it is assumed that local producers partially or wholly replacing a foreign firm would use much the same techniques of production

[3] For reasons of comparison with Part III of the NEI studies, we will use the NEI terminology. The UNCTAD study refers to a foreign firm's investment and production. In the NEI terminology this corresponds to the Investment period (IP) and to the Operations period (OP), respectively.

as the foreign firm, and would have the same ratio of imported current costs to sales, and of imported capital equipment to sales as the PFI (par. 110).

(8) At least in the short run, it is thought that the scope for profitable substitution of labour for capital and local materials for imports is small. The social benefits might be substantial, but usually there is no net private benefit to the firm (par. 111).

(9) A certain degree of 'neutrality' from the Government is assumed, at least the assumption is that the Government policy would remain unchanged, without affecting the PFI activities' effects on aggregate domestic demand and on the balance of payments (par. 112, 113).

Subsequently the UNCTAD study develops a simple model in which a distinction is made between 'capital' and 'current' effects of PFI on the balance of payments.

Capital effects are those effects associated with long-term financial inflows and outflows, and with purchases of fixed assets. Expenditure on fixed assets is not strictly a capital item, since the main purpose of most capital inflows is to finance such expenditures, it makes sense, according to the UNCTAD study, to consider the categories together (par. 115).
Current effects are the remaining effects on the balance of payments of the changes in output and income arising from PFI.
On the assumption that:

– the marginal changes in output that are examined can occur without any changes in internal prices, and that

– exchange rates and interest rates are kept constant,

the capital effect of PFI on the balance of payments in any one year will be equal to the net capital inflow of the foreign firm, plus the net capital outflow that would have occurred in the absence of PFI (the major item being imports of capital equipment by the indigenous replacing firm), less the extra imports of goods and services bought out of the total increase in national income generated by the foreign capital inflow. The immediate increase in national income is equal to the immediate increase in domestic spending that occurs as a result of the improvement of the balance of payments. This increase in spending will lead to the employment of prèviously unemployed resources, and thus will result in a further increase in income. And so on. Using the Keynesian multiplier, the total increase in income is equal to the original increase times the reciprocal of the savings ratio (par. 118).

The capital effect is expressed by two equations:

(i) $$\Delta B_K = T_N + K_I - m \Delta Y_K$$

(ii) $$\Delta Y_K = \frac{1}{s}(B_K - T_{GS} - Z),$$

where

ΔB_K = capital effects in the balance of payments of the host country

T_N = net capital inflow of the foreign firm

K_I = purchase of capital equipment abroad that would have occurred in the absence of the foreign firm

m = marginal propensity to import

s = marginal propensity to save

ΔY_K = overall change in income as a consequence of the capital inflow

T_{GS} = share of the gross capital inflow of the foreign firm which is saved

Z = increase in other savings which occurs in the host country as an immediate consequence of PFI taking place (see also par. 118).

The current effect (par. 121 and ff.) is equal to the net inflow of foreign exchange as a result of the current operations of the foreign firm, less the net inflow that would have occurred in the absence of the foreign firm, less the extra imports of goods and services arising from the increase in income caused by PFI in OP. Part of the net inflow in the absence of PFI will be a proportion of the tariff revenue yielded by imports of goods, where these partially or wholly replace the domestic sales of PFI. The current effect is also expressed by two equations:

(iii) $$\Delta B_C = V - R - m \Delta Y_C$$

(iv) $$\Delta Y_C = \frac{1}{s} \Delta B_C.$$

The new symbols stand for

ΔV = local value added of PFI less the local value added that would have occurred in its absence

R = tariff revenue obtained by the Government of the host country from imports of goods, where these partially replace the domestic sales of PFI

The subscript C stands for current effect on B and Y.

6.3. SHORTCOMINGS OF THE UNCTAD MODEL

The UNCTAD model is interesting in that it makes a first effort to estimate the impact of PFI in a systematic quantitative way. Unfortunately the methodology applied would seem to have some serious shortcomings.

First of all, the assumptions made establish a static, short-run framework, while the analysis of the effects of PFI should be done in a dynamic, long-run context as static economic analysis is of little relevance in general and is quite unacceptable in the case of investment analysis, which typically belongs to dynamic economics.

In the second place, the implicit assumption that capital is not scarce affects the analysis in at least two ways. In the first place in dealing with the possibilities of domestic investment as an alternative to foreign investment, no allowance is made for the opportunity cost of capital. Clearly this has to be taken into account if one wants to come to a meaningful analysis of the impact of PFI. The neglect of the opportunity cost of capital tends to understate the benefits of PFI. In the second place multiplier effects are introduced into the analysis. For developing countries the introduction of Keynesian multiplier analysis would seem to be of little relevance, to say the least.

A further important question relates to the treatment of profit remittances. The UNCTAD model is unclear in this respect. One would expect to find an expression for profit remittances in the equations dealing with the current effects of PFI (Equations (iii) and (iv)). Not only is this not the case in the model presented, but also there is no indication how they are dealt with. Unless profit remittances are dealt with explicitly it is impossible to judge the appropriateness of the analysis.

There are a number of other points to be made, such as the way the distinction between the capital and current account is worked out (probably a distinction between effects occurring in the investment period, respectively operation period would be preferable), the way these effects, which have a different time dimension, are added, etc. In comparison with the main issues, the scarcity of investment funds and the treatment of profit remittances, they are, however, of secondary importance only.

The shortcomings mentioned here make it difficult to accept the methodology applied in the UNCTAD study. In the next part of the NEI studies on PFI a different type of model will be introduced which avoids, or so it is intended, the pitfalls of the UNCTAD model.

PART II

A MACRO-ECONOMIC METHODOLOGY FOR THE APPRAISAL OF THE EFFECTS OF PRIVATE FOREIGN INVESTMENTS IN LESS DEVELOPED COUNTRIES

TABLE OF CONTENTS

SUMMARY OF PART II

This part of the research concentrates on the macro-economic methodology, indicating also how it can be used both for decision making (Chapter XI) and for empirical applications (Chapter XII). The methodological framework presented is not considered to be complete, both because some problems still need a more satisfactory solution, and because some extentions are possible in order to get a better analysis (Chapter IX, in particular).

The introduction points out how the approach is meant first of all to be analytical, i.e. limited to the analysis of the effects of PFI, leaving any decision about their acceptibility to the policy makers themselves, for whom it is hoped that the methodology would provide a useful starting point and a base for their decisions (Section 1.2).

Furthermore, the approach is meant to be at a macro-economic (sectoral) level, and not a project level.

The purpose of the methodology is to quantify the economic effects of PFI in LDC's. A number of such effects is discussed in Chapter III. Attention is given to the more quantifiable ones, and consequently the list may not be complete. Some other economic effects of PFI, not taken into account by the model, are discussed in Chapter IV.

The methodology is based on a multi-sectoral dynamic model. A two-sector version of this model is given in Chapter II. Two sectors are considered: the 'PFI sector', and the 'rest of the economy' sector. Attention is given to the relations which are more relevant in a study about the effects of PFI; moreover, it is shown how the model could be extended to take into account employment (Section 2.9) and to take into account other ways of financing an investment project from abroad than through PFI (Section 2.11).

The formulation of some equations may raise some questions; Section 2.10 discusses briefly why certain specific formulations have been choosen. Finally, in Chapter IX it is pointed out how the model can be extended to become a multi-sectoral one.

The purpose of the model presented in Chapter II is not to get a set of full solutions for the endogenous variables it considers, but to provide a starting point for the quantification of the economic effects of PFI. The model is needed in order to have a detailed and consistent picture of a LDC's economy, with special reference to what happens to some key variables as a consequence of the presence of PFI. Starting from the model, it will then be possible to get some quantified expressions for the economic effects of PFI, which are consistent with each other, and which take into account direct and indirect effects.

In order to estimate the effects of PFI, the approach proposed is to compare (by difference) a situation *with* PFI and a situation *without* PFI, using the model as a basis to get the relations referring to the various effects.

Two sets of effects, corresponding to two different approaches, are distinguished in the report. In the NEI terminology, they are called, respectively, the *cumulative* and the *marginal* effects of PFI.

The *cumulative* effects (Chapters V and VI) are obtained by difference, comparing, for various variables corresponding to various effects, from time 0 to time *t*, a situation where PFI is always present, and a situation where PFI is always absent. Since the effects of PFI on some variables 'cumulate' from year to year, this particular terminology was choosen.

This can be seen considering, e.g. the cumulative effect on income. Since the increase in GDP from 0 to *t* is determined by the investments, through the capital-output ratio, the effects of PFI on domestic investments for every year will be present in the cumulative effect referring to time *t*. And since all other effects are also related to income, this same situation applies also to them. Moreover, for the balance of payments effect (b.o.p.) one must also consider the effects on it in the previous years, which are assumed to represent the debt effect of PFI [1]. Consequently, using this approach, it is also possible to point out how the effects of PFI are interdependent simultaneously and over time (Chapter V). The analysis of both cumulative (Chapter VI) and marginal (Chapter VII) effects mainly concentrates on four of them (income, private savings, public savings, and b.o.p.). However, in the report it is also pointed out how it is possible to extend the analysis to some other effects, like the one on employment (Section 8.5) the one on the distribution of income (Section 8.4) and the substitution effect (Section 8.6). The report discusses also how it is possible to take into consideration various practical situations different from the model given in Chapter II, like, e.g., different ways of financing an investment project from abroad, or joint ventures, or also different structural parameters for the two sectors (as it is the case when the Government wants to provide incentives or disincentives to PFI). Chapter X further points out how these various practical situations can be incorporated into the model changing some of the parameters, or introducing

1 For the foreign debt, the model assumes that its annual increase corresponds to the deficit of the b.o.p., equal to the foreign capital inflow (under the assumption of no variations in reserves etc.).

some new variables, and how the formulations of both cumulative and marginal effects can be modified accordingly.

The interdependence – simultaneously and over time – of the cumulative effects of PFI has been mentioned above. This makes the practical solution of the system which expresses them rather difficult. A general solution could be obtained in terms of a system of difference equations (Section 6.4), while an approximate solution, much more operational for its simplicity, can be obtained considering the rate of growth of the cumulative effects. It is proved that the latter is approximated by the rate of growth of the PFI capital stock (or gross value added), and consequently it is possible to arrive at a solution for the main effects considered (Section 6.5).

Such a solution is given as a system of four linear equations, where the four effects are the unknowns. Substituting the value of the parameters, and of the PFI gross value added in a given time t, it is possible to solve it, and to get the numerical value of the four effects.

Since, in practice, both for lack of data for a reasonably long period of time, or because the LDC's economy or the PFI capital stock do not behave exactly according to the assumptions of the model, it might be difficult to apply the cumulative approach, also a simpler one has been developed, called the 'marginal' approach.

Under the assumption that the situation in time t is given and that one is simply interested in finding out what happens from time t to time $t+1$ as a consequence of the presence of PFI on some variables, the *marginal* effects are defined as the variation in these variables from t to $t+1$ imputable to the presence of PFI. This approach is obviously quite different from the cumulative one. The two are compared in Section 8.1, where the reader may also find a useful picture, showing the cumulative and marginal effects on income.

The formulation of the marginal effects still involves the presence of lagged endogenous variables. However, it is possible to prove that the rate of growth of these effects is exactly the same as the rate of growth of the PFI capital stock (or gross value added), and consequently it is possible to eliminate the lags.

Also the marginal effects are given as a system of four equations, where the four main effects considered are the unknowns and which can be solved once the parameters and the gross value added of the PFI sector in t are given (Section 7.8).

The basic difference between the two effects is that the cumulative effects refer to the effects of PFI on certain variables from time 0 to time t, while the marginal effects simply point out the effect imputable to PFI in the development of the economy from time t to time $t+1$. These different concepts point out also the different practical possible uses of the two approaches (Chapter VIII). If detailed information is available for a long period of time, and if the economy and the PFI sector behave according to the relations of the model, then it is possible to use the cumulative approach. If, on the contrary, only data for one or two years are available, it is possible to use the marginal one. The former gives a more complete answer to the question of the economic effects of PFI; if it is not possible to apply it, then the latter can still provide some useful answers.

A numerical exercise is given in Section 8.3, with reference to both cumulative and marginal effects. First, a general solution is obtained giving some arbitrary values to the parameters. Then some variations are studied. The exercise proves quite useful both to compare different practical situations reflected in the various alternative values given to some of the parameters, and to get some insights in how the model reacts to some variations in its parameters.

As it was said at the beginning of this summary, the last chapters discuss the use of the methodological approach for decision making (Chapter XI) and its use for practical investigations (Chapter XII).

CHAPTER I

GENERAL INTRODUCTION

1.1. INTRODUCTION

In recent years there has been a significant increase in the interest of economists, social scientists and others in the subject of the impact of direct private foreign investment (PFI) on the economies of less developed countries (LDC's). To a certain extent the increasing interest in the effects of PFI can be explained by the quantitative importance of PFI. In recent years the flow of PFI capital to LDC's has amounted to around US $ 4 billion annually, or about 20% of the total net flow of financial resources to LDC's. In all likelihood, however, the present discussion on the impact of PFI is not primarily due to the actual flow of direct investment funds to the developing countries but rather to the fact that bilateral as well as multilateral donors increasingly consider PFI as an instrument to counteract the sluggish trend in official aid flows. As the divergence between the funds needed to realize the objectives of economic and social development and the flow of funds made available by the rich countries increased, both international agencies and individual countries have felt an increasingly pressing need for finding other avenues to bridge the gap between what is needed and what is available. It is because of this reason that the potential availability of private funds for direct investment has attracted serious attention as a potentially very important means for narrowing the gap between the required flow of resources on the one hand and the existing flow in the form of development assistance on the other hand.

Not surprisingly, the role PFI can play as an instrument of international economic policy has generated, in developed as well as in developing countries, serious and sometimes even heated debates, the main reason for this being that before PFI can be accepted as an efficient means towards economic development the effects of PFI have to be measured and analysed. As will be shown in this study, at the roots of the present discussion concerning the impact of PFI is the problem of disagreement between authors about the criteria to be applied in measuring the effects, and consequently the contribution to development, of PFI. It is to this question, the question of the evaluation of PFI, that the present part of the study addresses itself.

Chapter X points out how it is possible to take into consideration, introducing just a few variations, various practical situations which might arise.

Chapter XI deals with the possibility to use the methodological approach as a basis for decision making, while Chapter XII discusses its use in a subsequent empirical study.

1.2. THE APPRAISAL OF THE EFFECTS OF PFI

The purpose of this research is to analyse the economic effects of PFI in LDC's. However, it is necessary first to point out what is meant by 'measuring the effects of PFI'.

Various approaches could be proposed. The one adopted here is to compare a situation *with PFI* with a situation *without PFI*, and see what is the difference, for certain variables, between the presence and the absence of PFI.

This approach, carried out with the help of a mathematical model which 'explains' the whole economy, allows also a comparison between alternative ways of financing a given investment project, and it is also realistic enough to appraise the effects of additional PFI in a given situation, where some other PFI might already exist, along with some foreign capital of different nature.

In order to reach such a comparison, a distinction can be made between three different time periods:

(a) 'Before the Investment Period (BIP)'; this period concerns the situation in a given economy, with its characteristics and macro-variables, and also with some existing PFI and foreign indebtedness;

(b) 'The Investment Period (IP)'; for this period the effects of a given PFI project during the phase of its construction can be studied. In this stage a PFI is considered as a component of demand, characterized, on the real side, by imports of capital goods and by purchases of capital goods in the domestic market and, on the financial side, by a foreign capital inflow and by the absorption of a share of the domestic financial resources available for investments;

(c) 'The Operations Period (OP)'; the purpose is to study the effects of a PFI in its operations period, where it is considered as an addition to the existing capacity; furthermore, this period is characterized, on the financial side, by an outflow of profits and by the absorption of a given share of domestic financial resources to finance partially or in total its annual additions.

The methodological framework which will be presented and discussed in the following pages will concentrate on the OP; but it is easy to derive from it the BIP (putting some variables equal to zero) and the IP (introducing a few modifications in the model).

Once the various relations are quantitatively formulated, they should provide a framework to serve both for an empirical stüdy and as a basis for decision making. These policy decisions should aim at certain general targets for the economy as a whole. Consequently, the final evalution of PFI should be given only in the light of such general policy goals. This may also require a certain degree of trade-off between various targets, since one cannot expect a positive contribution to all target variables. Since policy objectives may vary from country to country, this study will concentrate on the *analytical* aspects of the effects of PFI which are quantifiable, leaving the *normative* stage for the decision makers themselves, on the basis of their value judgments.

As for the empirical appraisal of the effects of PFI in LDC's, it will be shown how it is possible to use the proposed approach for such an evaluation, according also to the data available.

1.3. THE QUANTITATIVE APPROACH IN GENERAL

The effects of PFI in LDC's are studied in the framework of a quantitative approach, i.e. with the help of a mathematical model. Its main characteristics are:

(a) it is a *dynamic model*; this means that time and the time behaviour of the various variables play a crucial role;

(b) it is a *multi-sector model*; in this simplified version, only two sectors are considered: the PFI sector (variables with superscript h) and the 'rest of the economy' sector (variables with superscript 0). If desired, the model could be extended to consider n sectors for the economy as a whole (of which m manufacturing sub-sectors) and a number ($\leqslant m$) of PFI manufacturing sub-sectors, for a maximum total of $n+m$ sectors. Together with this sectoral breakdown, input-output analysis could be introduced.

(c) it considers *constant prices*. The reason for this simplifying assumption is that detailed price information might be very difficult to obtain with sufficient accuracy, and, when using the methodology for practical purposes the introduction of price equations might make it too complicated.

(d) *the purpose of the model* is not to get a numerical solution for all the variables considered, but to reach some general and simplified formulations about the effects of PFI on some variables considered as relevant. As stated in the previous section, the appraisal of the effects of PFI will be made considering the difference between a situation with PFI and one without PFI.

(e) finally, as pointed out before, the model is intended to be *analytical*, although yielding results which should provide the starting point for subsequent decision making.

The model has some implicit limits, as it will also be easy to see from the description of its various assumptions given in Chapter II. However, these should be seen in the context of the analysis it is meant for.

No attempt, e.g., is made to differentiate the model from country to country, although it is possible to take into account, with little modifications, various practical situations. Furthermore, the various relations of the model do not derive from an econometric analysis of the empirical situation in various LDC's, but are taken from economic theory and from some general studies on the economic reality in LDC's. Some relations are oversimplified, and could be specified in a more satisfactory way. Some indications in this respect will be given in the text.

However, as it was said above, the methodological framework should be seen in the context of the purpose of the analysis of this research, together with the practical possibility that exists nowadays of applying such analytical approach to empirical data.

CHAPTER II

A MODEL OF LDC'S ECONOMY WITH SPECIAL REFERENCE TO PFI

2.1. INTRODUCTION

The model which will be presented is a two-sector growth model, and it could be subsequently disaggregated in the ways pointed out in Chapter IX. This chapter will discuss the various equations of the model. They are numbered from (1) to (38), and they are presented all together in Appendix 3 (pp. 76 ff.). Other equations are without any number, because they are relevant only indirectly for the analysis developed in this study. They are not included in Appendix 3.

Two other appendices are given at the end of this chapter. Appendix 1 (p. 74) explains the terminology and the abbrevations used, and Appendix 2 (p. 74 ff.) gives a list of the symbols standing for the variables and the parameters.

The various equations of the PFI sectors are explained in Section 2.2. Section 2.3 deals with the external sector of the rest of the economy, and, using some of the relations of the previous section, formulates the balance of payments (b.o.p.) for the total economy. Private savings are considered in Section 2.4, while Section 2.5 considers public current revenue and expenditure, to arrive at public savings. It is then possible, in Section 2.6, to establish the domestic investments formulation. Section 2.7 presents the function formulating the development of total income for the whole economy. The next two sections consider some relations not explicitly taken into account by the model: private consumption and employment. Finally, some alternative formulations of some of the equations are discussed in Section 2.10, while the last section shows how the model can take into consideration alternative ways of financing investments from abroad.

2.2. THE PFI SECTOR

The behaviour of the PFI sector is fully determined:

(a) its direct contribution to income Y_t^h is given by a simple production function with a given constant capital-output ratio:

$$Y_t^h = \frac{K_{t-1}^h}{k^h} \; ; \qquad (1)$$

(b) the capital stock (K_t^h) grows at a constant rate, assuming that PFI (I_t^h) grows in proportion to its capital stock (K_t^h):

$$K_t^h = K_0^h (1 + \alpha)^t \qquad (2)$$

$$I_t^h = \alpha K_{t-1}^h . \qquad (3)$$

Equation (2) follows simply from (3) and from the definition:

$$K_t^h = K_{t-1}^h + I_t^h \; ;$$

(c) profits reinvested (R_t^h) are a residual given by total profits (P_t^h), profits transferred abroad (Q_t^h), and direct taxes on PFI profits (T_{Pt}^h):

$$P_t^h = \pi^h K_{t-1}^h \qquad (4)$$

$$Q_t^h = \rho K_{t-1}^h \qquad (5)$$

$$R_t^h = P_t^h - Q_t^h - T_{Pt}^h \; ; \qquad (6)$$

(d) consequently, the annual addition to PFI (I_t^h) is partly domestically financed (F_{Dt}):

$$F_{Dt} = I_t^h - R_t^h . \qquad (7)$$

This implies that PFI is assumed to substitute domestic investments in the utilization of available financial resources. This crucial assumption will be dealt with in more detail later (see also Equation (37));

(e) in the external sector, PFI in OP promotes exports and/or substitutes imports of goods in a quantity proportional to its value added:

$$E_{Ct}^h = \varphi_e Y_t^h \qquad (8)$$

and it requires imports given by:

$$M_{Ct}^h = \varphi_m Y_t^h . \qquad (9)$$

Besides exports and imports of goods, PFI in OP affects also exports and imports of services in the following manner:

$$E^h_{Zt} = e^h E^h_{Ct} \tag{10}$$

$$M^h_{Zt} = m^h M^h_{Ct}. \tag{11}$$

Exports and imports of goods are kept separate from exports and imports of services, because it is assumed that PFI affects first of all the former, and then, indirectly, the latter. The formulation of Equations (10) and (11) establishes a time behaviour for E^h_{Zt} and M^h_{Zt} identical to that of E^h_{Ct} and M^h_{Ct}, respectively. Still, it is considered relevant to keep the two items split. In a subsequent version of the model, Equations (10) and (11) could, anyhow, be defined, if necessary, in a more realistic way. Apart from the fact, as it will be pointed out later, that Equations (8) and (9) are meant to be sectoral, while (10) and (11) are meant to be kept aggregate.

(f) If one wishes, it is possible also to take into account payments to abroad for royalties, technical fees, licenses, etc. i.e. the so-called 'know-how' payments. To do so, the following equation must be added:

$$N^h_t = \lambda K^h_{t-1} \tag{11 bis}$$

where N is the total payments to abroad for know-how in year t, while λ relates such item to the b.o.p. to PFI capital stock at the beginning of the period considered. This 'know-how' payment becomes then an item of the b.o.p. of Equation 25. In case it does not exist, then it is enough to put $\lambda = 0$. This point is particularly relevant with respect to the analysis of alternative ways of financing a PFI project from abroad, as it will be seen later in Section 2.11.

A short explanation is necessary about the numbering of this equation. Instead of (11 bis), it could have been Equation (12), changing all the others accordingly. It was left as Equation (11 bis), to underline the fact that it may not be there in some times, especially when all 'know-how' payments are included into profit remitted abroad. In such a case $N^h_t = 0$, because $\lambda = 0$. By putting the know-how parameter equal to zero, this component of the effects of PFI disappears as well from the quantitative formulations of the effects which will be given in Chapters V, VI and VII (b.o.p. effect).

(g) total wages and salaries paid by PFI in OP (W^h_t) are assumed to be a fixed proportion of its value added. This relation is important to get the contribution of PFI to public revenue.

$$W_t^h = w^h Y_t^h, \tag{12}$$

where w^h is the share of wages and salaries in PFI value added.

(h) As for the public sector, in OP PFI contributes to public current revenue, and requires certain public expenditure. On the expenditure side, public expenditure related to PFI (G_t^h) is assumed to be a given share g^h of the existing PFI capital stock:

$$G_t^h = g^h K_{t-1}^h. \tag{13}$$

On the revenue side, the total contribution to public revenue is given by:

$$T_t^h = T_{Pt}^h + T_{Wt}^h + T_{\text{IND}t}^h + T_{Et}^h + T_{Mt}^h + \bar{T}_{\text{OTH}t}^h \tag{14}$$

Direct taxes on PFI profits (T_{Pt}^h) are given by total PFI profits (P_t^h) and by the taxation coefficient on profits:

$$T_{Pt}^h = \tau_P P_t^h \tag{15}$$

Direct taxes on PFI wages and salaries (T_{Wt}^h) are given by total PFI wages and salaries, (W_t^h) and by the taxation coefficient:

$$T_{Wt}^h = \tau_W W_t^h. \tag{16}$$

Indirect taxes are given by PFI value added and by the indirect taxation coefficient:

$$T_{\text{IND}t}^h = \tau_{\text{IND}} Y_t^h. \tag{17}$$

Taxes on exports of goods and services are given by the total amount of PFI goods and services exported, and by the taxation coefficient:

$$T_{Et}^h = \tau_E (E_{Ct}^h + E_{Zt}^h). \tag{18}$$

Taxes on imports of goods and services (T_{Mt}^h) are given by the total amount of goods and services imported by PFI, and by the taxation coefficient:

$$T_{Mt}^h = \tau_M (M_{Ct}^h + M_{Zt}). \tag{19}$$

Other direct taxes (apart from taxes on wages and salaries, and on profits) and other current public revenue (T^h_{OTHt}) are assumed to be given:

$$T^h_{OTHt} = \text{given}.$$

2.3. THE EXTERNAL SECTOR OF THE REST OF THE ECONOMY AND THE B.O.P.

Imports of goods are given by the marginal propensity to import and by the increase in income:

$$M^0_{Ct} = M^0_{C0} + \mu(Y_t - Y_0) \tag{20}$$

while exports of goods are assumed to grow at a constant rate with respect to the base-year situation:

$$E^0_{Ct} = E^0_{C0}(1+\epsilon)^t. \tag{21}$$

Exports and imports of goods could be further disaggregated. This has little relevance here, and will be left, if necessary, for a later stage.

Again, as for the PFI sector, imports and exports of goods are kept separate from imports and exports of services, since it is assumed that the former have a definite time behaviour, while the latter indirectly adjust to it. Similarly to Equations (10) and (11), then:

$$M^0_{Zt} = m^0 M^0_{Ct} \tag{22}$$

$$E^0_{Zt} = e^0 E^0_{Ct}. \tag{23}$$

Again, the above formulation establishes a time behaviour for imports and exports of services identical to that for imports and exports of goods, respectively. Still, it is considered relevant to keep the two items split, since, as it was said for the PFI sector, Equations (20) and (21), like Equations (8) and (9), will, if the model becomes multisectoral, be split into the various PFI and domestic sectors, while Equations (22) and (23), like Equations (10 and (11), will still be considered at an aggregate level.

There is a certain foreign debt (H_t), which increases every year by an amount (B_i) corresponding to the deficit of the b.o.p. of the previous year, assumed to represent the net foreign capital inflow:

$$H_t = H_0 + \sum_{i=0}^{t-1} B_i \tag{24}$$

on which interests must be paid at a given annual rate θ.

The role played by Equation (24) in the model will be further discussed in Section 2.11, when dealing with alternative ways of financing an investment project.

Finally, factor income payments *from* abroad should be considered. They are assumed to be exogenous: J_t = given.

Consequently, the deficit of the balance of payments is fully determined by its various items previously considered (Equations (5), (8), (9), (10), (11), (11 bis), (20), (21), (22), (23), (24)):

$$B_t = M^0_{Ct} + M^0_{Zt} - E^0_{Ct} - E^0_{Zt} - \bar{J}_t + M^h_{Ct} + M^h_{Zt} - E^h_{Ct} -$$

$$- E^h_{Zt} + \theta H_t + Q^h_t + N^h_t. \tag{25}$$

The deficit is free to vary ('open b.o.p.' assumption); alternative assumptions will be dealt with in Section 2.10.

2.4. PRIVATE SAVINGS

Private savings (S_{Pt}) are obtained from the increase in income, through the marginal propensity to save:

$$S_{Pt} = S_{P0} + \sigma(Y_t - Y_0). \tag{26}$$

2.5. THE PUBLIC SECTOR

Similarly to what was done above for the PFI sector, it is necessary to introduce aggregate wages and profits for the rest of the economy, in order to determine, subsequently, direct taxation.

Profits for the rest of the economy P^0_t are given by their share in value added:

$$P^0_t = \pi^0(Y_t - Y^h_t). \tag{27}$$

In a similar manner, wages and salaries for the rest of the economy (W^0_t) are given by their share in value added:

$$W_t^0 = w^0 (Y_t - Y_t^h). \tag{28}$$

Government revenue and expenditure directly related with PFI were dealt with above in Section 2.2. Similarly, for the rest of the economy the following situation is assumed.

Government current expenditure is assumed to grow at a constant rate with respect to the base year situation:

$$G_t^0 = G_0^0 (1 + \gamma)^t. \tag{29}$$

Total Government current revenue for the rest of the economy is given by:

$$T_t^0 = T_{Pt}^0 + T_{Wt}^0 + T_{\mathrm{IND}t}^0 + T_{Et}^0 + T_{Mt}^0 + \bar{T}_{\mathrm{OTH}t}^0. \tag{30}$$

It is further assumed that the same taxation coefficients as for PFI hold also for the rest of the economy. Consequently, the various items of Equation (30) are explained as follows:

$$T_{Pt}^0 = \tau_P P_t^0 \tag{31}$$

$$T_{Wt}^0 = \tau_W W_t^0 \tag{32}$$

$$T_{\mathrm{IND}t}^0 = \tau_{\mathrm{IND}} (Y_t - Y_t^h) \tag{33}$$

$$T_{Et}^0 = \tau_E (E_{Ct}^0 + E_{Zt}^0) \tag{34}$$

$$T_{Mt}^0 = \tau_M (M_{Ct}^0 + M_{Zt}^0) \tag{35}$$

$$T_{\mathrm{OTH}t}^0 = \text{given}$$

So, public savings, taking into account both the PFI sector and the rest of the economy, are given by:

$$S_{Gt} = T_t^0 + T_t^h - G_t^0 - G_t^h \tag{36}$$

and they accrue to total financial resources available for investments.

An alternative formulation of public savings will be considered in Section 2.10.

2.6. INVESTMENTS IN THE REST OF THE ECONOMY

Domestic investments are assumed to be limited by total financial resources available (private savings, public savings, and foreign capital inflow equal to the deficit of the balance of payment) *less* the share which goes to finance part of the addition of PFI (Equation (7)):

$$I_t^0 = (S_{Pt} + S_{Gt} + B_t) - F_{Dt}. \qquad (37)$$

Alternative assumptions about the formulation of Equation (37) will be examined in Section 2.10.

2.7. INCOME FOR THE TOTAL ECONOMY

In the present two-sector formulation of the model, income for the whole economy is supposed to be given by the summation of income produced by the 'rest of the economy' and of the one produced by PFI:

$$Y_t = Y_t^0 + Y_t^h.$$

Similarly to what was done for PFI, income from the'rest of the economy' is supposed to be produced by investments, considered here as gross total. Assuming a fixed capital-output ratio, and given the level of income in $t = 0$, the increase in income for the 'rest of the economy' will be determined by the summation of investments from 0 to $t-1$, in order to take into account a one-year lag.

The capital-output ratios for the two sectors are assumed to be different, and, strictly speaking, the one of the 'rest of the economy' is an incremental capital-output ratio, while the one of the 'PFI sector' is an average capital-output ratio.

The second component of total income (PFI sector) was already established by Equation (1). Consequently, starting from the formulation given above, income for the whole economy is given by:

$$Y_t = Y_0 + \frac{\sum_{i=0}^{t-1} I_i^0}{k^0} + \frac{K_0^h (1 + \alpha)^{t-1}}{k^h}. \qquad (38)$$

2.8. DEMAND

Apart from government expenditure, the foreign sector (still at an aggregate level) and investments (also still aggregate, being considered as gross total) demand is not yet fully analysed. In particular, private consumption would come as a residual, since marginal propensity to save was already introduced:

$$C_t = Y_t - (I_t^0 + I_t^h + G_t^0 + G_t^h + E_{Ct}^0 + E_{Zt}^0 + E_{Ct}^h + E_{Zt}^h +$$

$$+ \bar{J}_t - N_t^h - M_{Ct}^0 - M_{Zt}^0 - M_{Ct}^h - M_{Zt}^h - \theta H_t - Q_t^h$$

$$= Y_t - (G_t^0 + G_t^h) - (S_{Pt} + S_{Gt} + R_t^h)$$

or,

$$= Y_t - (T_t^0 + T_t^h) - (S_{Pt} + R_t^h).$$

That is to say, private consumption equals the difference between income and savings (private, public and PFI savings) and government expenditure, or, alternatively, it equals the difference between income, total taxes, and total private savings including PFI savings given by profits reinvested (R_t^h).

2.9. EMPLOYMENT

Employment is not directly taken into account by the model, but it can be easily introduced, using labour-output ratios.

Total employment is given by employment in the two sectors:

$$L_t = L_t^0 + L_t^h.$$

Employment in the PFI sector is given by the PFI labour-output ratio:

$$L_t^h = \eta^h Y_t^h.$$

Employment in the rest of the economy is given by the labour-output ratio for that sector:

$$L_t^0 = \eta^0 (Y_t - Y_t^h).$$

2.10. ALTERNATIVE FORMULATIONS OF SOME EQUATIONS

In presenting the model, it was said how different assumptions could have been introduced, especially concerning the PFI sector, the domestic investments, the deficit of the b.o.p. and the public sector. Some possible alternative formulations and their implications, will be considered below.

(i) *The PFI Sector*

In the model, PFI is considered partly as a net addition to total investments and partly absorbing available financial resources, which, otherwise, would increase domestic investments. The two possible extreme alternatives are:

PFI is fully additional, or

PFI is fully financed from available domestic financial resources and thus it is fully a substitute for domestic investments.

The model considers an intermediate situation, but, with little variations, both such extreme cases could be taken into account, without affecting its mechanism. The effect of such different assumptions would come through the domestic investments Equation (37), via the b.o.p. deficit and F_{Dt}. This last variable would be, in the two extreme cases above discussed respectively, either = 0, or $= I_t^h$ (Equation (7)).

Another crucial assumption is that the PFI capital stock grows at a given compound rate, and accordingly it affects the growth of income. If, on the contrary, it stays constant, it will have no such direct effect on the growth of income, although it would still affect income indirectly, as it will be seen later.

(ii) *Investments for the Rest of the Economy*

Domestic investments are considered as given by available financial resources, taking into account the share absorbed by PFI (Equations (7) and (37)). Various alternative formulations would be possible, such as:

(a) an investment demand equation related to profits, etc.; besides complicating the analysis, it would determine savings (and consequently private consumption) as a residual, and this does not seem to be too realistic;

(b) an investment demand equation related to production; apart from the above objections, this would become, in the mechanism of the model, a duplicate of the production function;

(c) investments growing at a certain compound rate; although this would again determine savings as a residual, it is also rejected on the basis that it assumes domestic investments to be limited by the absorptive capacity of the economy, instead of by the total financial resources available.

(iii) *The b.o.p. Deficit*

So far, the b.o.p. deficit (B_t) was considered as determined endogenously by its components, fully specified by the model. Furthermore, it was assumed to correspond to the foreign capital inflow, assuming that (in the long run) there would be no variations in reserves, etc. While still keeping this last assumption, the former could be changed by:

(a) fixing the deficit of the b.o.p. at a given level; alternatively

(b) relating the deficit to some variable, or establishing for it an independent time behaviour.

Both for (a) and (b) the first problem which arises is that, if B_t is not the algebraic sum of its items, then one item of the b.o.p. should come as a residual; otherwise, the model would be overdetermined. In case (a), furthermore, it would be necessary to determine the yearly variation of B_t, which directly affects the growth of domestic investments. For example, if the deficit is constant ($\Delta B_t = 0$), it would have no effect on the growth of domestic investments. For case (b), two formulations could be:

$$B_t = b\,Y_t$$

or

$$B_t = B_0\,(1 + \beta)^t.$$

Apart from the complications that the introduction of one item of B_t as a residual would cause, any of the above formulations could be accepted both from a theoretical point of view, and considering the situation in many LDC's. So, for the purpose of the present methodological framework, an answer to this problem can come only from considering what is the relevance of B_t in the study of the effects of PFI.

If the deficit of the b.o.p. is not determined from a summation of its components, which are directly or indirectly influenced by PFI, then the effect of PFI on B_t would come not from a comparison between B_t with PFI and B_t without PFI, but from an analysis of the adjustments which have to take place among the various items, once a PFI is there, under the constraint of a B_t independently (with respect to its items) determined. It seems, then, that the assumption of an open deficit of the b.o.p. would allow a better appraisal of the effects of PFI. Furthermore, in the present methodological framework, B_t and the effect of PFI on it, are supposed to represent the increase (or decrease) in the LDC's dependence upon foreign capital inflow as a consequence of PFI.

In other words, if one considers that, ultimately, the model is supposed to yield results not in absolute levels, but in terms of differences between a situation with and one without PFI, then the assumption of an open deficit seems the most acceptable one.

There is one danger. Since B_t affects total income (Equation (38)) through the domestic investments Equation (37), then the bigger the deficit, the greater the rate of growth of income. But, again, since we are interested in comparing two different situations, also this possible objection can be rejected.

(iv) *The Public Sector*

It would be possible to introduce also a different assumption about the public sector. In the actual set-up of the model, the surplus or deficit of the public sector is determined by its various items. In the case the Government wishes to fix the deficit or the surplus to a given amount, this will imply a constant S_{Gt} (negative, or positive, respectively), and one of the items of the public sector will have to come as a residual. This can be T_{OTH}, which will represent, in such a case, if positive, extra taxes, and if negative, extra expenditure necessary in order to achieve a given level of S_{Gt}. Obviously, in the case of a fixed S_{Gt}, its contribution to the growth of domestic investments would be zero, as it can be seen from Equation (37). However, in the context of the analysis of the effects of PFI, it seems better, as for the b.o.p., to let the surplùs or deficit of the public sector free to vary in order to get as a result the exact effect of the presence of PFI.

2.11. ALTERNATIVE WAYS OF FINANCING INVESTMENTS FROM ABROAD

The model allows to compare alternative ways of financing from abroad a project, introducing little modifications.

In the arguments over the usefulness of PFI, as compared with alternative ways of financing, one main point often underlined is the transfer of 'know-how' connected with a PFI.

The model considers both the real aspects of PFI (domestically produced component and imported component) and the financial side (capital inflow and use of domestic savings), and can include the transfer of know-how (Equation (11 bis)). If 'know-how' is introduced, in the IP the composition of a PFI (K_0^h) is as follows:

$$K_0^h = K_{M0}^h + K_{D0}^h + N_0^h .$$

On the right-hand side, the first two variables stand, respectively, for the import component of the new PFI and for the part domestically produced. In the case of a project financed through a PFI, the know-how variable can either be considered included in the PFI itself, or be explicitly given. This variable becomes much more relevant if alternative ways of financing are used, and it is given by the foreign managerial costs, consulting fees, patents, etc. necessary to realize a project.

In the OP, in the case of PFI, the annual costs of know-how can be zero, under the assumption that they are included in total profits on PFI, or be explicitly given. In the case of alternative ways of financing, these costs are always there, and are given by the annual foreign management fees, royalties on patents, etc. Such items affect obviously the b.o.p. deficit.

In this way, the handling of the problem of the transfer of know-how connected with PFI is simplified. It must not be forgotten, however, that the main objective is not to analyze fully the 'know-how effects' of PFI, but simply to give a quantitative expression of this variable in the study of alternative ways of financing investments. So, in other words, the difference between PFI and other external ways of financing is that PFI influences in the OP the economy through the behaviour of profits, remitted or reinvested, and the absorption of a share of financial resources otherwise available for domestic investments, while other external ways of financing affect the economy through an increased amount of interests paid on the foreign debt and the yearly payments to abroad for know-how.

In connection with this point, a specification is necessary with regard to the foreign debt service.

The model, since it explicitly considers only the current account of the b.o.p., includes, as one of its items, interest paid on the foreign debt. In the analysis of alternative ways of financing an investment from abroad this can be considered as equivalent to the transfer of profits on PFI.

On the capital account, of course, as a consequence of the existing foreign debt, there will be annual repayments of principal to abroad. In the analysis of alternative ways of financing, this is equivalent to considering, always in the capital account, capital repayments to abroad on PFI.

If the b.o.p. current account is in a deficit position, this will require, according to the assumptions of the model, a net capital inflow of a corresponding amount. In the situation discussed above (repayments of principal or capital repayments to abroad) this will mean an increase in the capital inflow, in order to cover such increased capital outflow, and yield the required net capital inflow (equivalent to B_t).

The difference between the two situations, along with the 'know-how' variables, will represent the effect of different ways of financing from abroad.

Without too many modifications, it is also possible to take into account various other practical situations. This question will be further considered in Chapter X.

APPENDIX 1: TERMINOLOGY AND ABBREVATIONS

Domestic:	refers to the rest of the economy (not PFI)
Foreign:	refers to the PFI sector
Total:	refers to all the economy
b.o.p.	balance of payments current account
PFI	private foreign investments
BIP	Before the Investment Period
IP	Investment Period
OP	Operations Period
t	time; For *stock* variables it refers to the situation in instant t at the end of period t; for *flow* variables it refers to the period t (from $t-1$ to t).
$t = 0$	base year
LDC	less developed countries

APPENDIX 2: LIST OF SYMBOLS

Latin capital letters are used to indicate all variables of the models. There is no distinction between values and volumes.

The *superscripts* used are the following:

$h =$ PFI sector

$0 =$ 'rest of the economy' sector

A symbol with no superscript refers to all the economy.

In the analysis of the effects of PFI, two other superscripts are used: * refers to the cumulative effects, while = refers to the marginal effects.

Two sets of *subscripts* are used:

The first subscript, capital letter(s), refers to a specification of the variable or the parameter. It may not be there in many cases.

The second subscript refers to time.

Endogenous Variables

(All base year variables are assumed to be given)

B	b.o.p. deficit
C	private consumption
E	exports of goods and services
E_C	exports of goods
E_Z	exports of services
F_D	share of PFI not financed out of reinvested profits
F_M	share of PFI financed from abroad
G	Government current expenditure
H	foreign debt
K	capital stock
I	gross total investments
L	employment
M	imports of goods and services
M_C	imports of goods
M_Z	imports of services
N	payments for know-how
P	gross total profits
Q	profits of PFI transferred abroad
R	profits of PFI reinvested
S_G	Government savings
S_P	private savings
T	Government current revenue
T_P	direct taxes on profits
T_W	direct taxes on wages and salaries
T_{IND}	indirect taxes
T_E	taxes on exports of goods and services
T_M	taxes on imports of goods and services
W	wages and salaries
Y	GDP at market prices

Exogenous variables

(Apart from all base year variables which are assumed to be given)

T_{OTH}	Other direct taxes (apart from taxes on wages and salaries and on profits) and other public current revenue
J	Factor income payments from abroad

Parameters

α	rate of growth of PFI
γ	rate of growth of public current expenditure for the rest of the economy
g^h	share of public current expenditure for PFI, with respect to the PFI capital stock existing at the beginning of each period
ϵ	rate of growth of exports of goods for the rest of the economy
e	share of exports of services with respect to exports of goods
θ	rate of interest on the foreign debt
k	capital-output ratio
μ	marginal propensity to import goods for the rest of the economy
m	share of imports of services with respect to imports of goods
λ	rate of payments for know-how
η	labour-output ratio
π^0	rate of profit for the rest of the economy with respect to value added
π^h	rate of profit for the PFI sector with respect to the existing PFI capital stock at the beginning of each period
ρ	required rate of transfer of PFI profits with respect to the existing PFI capital stock at the beginning of each period
σ	marginal propensity to save
φ_m	imports requirements (of goods) for PFI in OP with respect to its value added
φ_e	exports and import substitution (of goods) of PFI in OP with respect to its value added
τ_W	direct taxation coefficient on wages and salaries
τ_P	direct taxation coefficient on profits
τ_{IND}	indirect taxation coefficient with respect to GDP
τ_E	taxation coefficient on exports of goods and services
τ_M	taxation coefficient on imports of goods and services
w	share of wages and salaries in value added

APPENDIX 3: THE MODEL

(a) *The PFI Sector*

$$Y_t^h = \frac{K_{t-1}^h}{k^h} \tag{1}$$

$$K_t^h = (1+\alpha)^t K_0^h \tag{2}$$

$$I_t^h = \alpha K_{t-1}^h \tag{3}$$

$$P_t^h = \pi^h K_{t-1}^h \tag{4}$$

$$Q_t^h = \rho K_{t-1}^h \tag{5}$$

$$R_t^h = P_t^h - Q_t^h - T_{Pt}^h \tag{6}$$

$$F_{Dt} = I_t^h - R_t^h \tag{7}$$

$$E_{Ct}^h = \varphi_e Y_t^h \tag{8}$$

$$M_{Ct}^h = \varphi_m Y_t^h \tag{9}$$

$$E_{Zt}^h = e^h E_{Ct}^h \tag{10}$$

$$M_{Zt}^h = m^h M_{Ct}^h \tag{11}$$

$$N_t^h = \lambda K_{t-1}^h \tag{11 bis}$$

$$W_t^h = w^h Y_t^h \tag{12}$$

$$G_t^h = g^h K_{t-1}^h \tag{13}$$

$$T_t^h = T_{Pt}^h + T_{Wt}^h + T_{\text{IND}t}^h + T_{Et}^h + T_{Mt}^h + \overline{T}_{\text{OTH}t}^h \tag{14}$$

$$T_{Pt}^h = \tau_P P_t^h \tag{15}$$

$$T_{Wt}^h = \tau_W W_t^h \tag{16}$$

$$T_{\text{IND}t}^h = \tau_{\text{IND}} Y_t^h \tag{17}$$

$$T_{Et}^h = \tau_E (E_{Ct}^h + E_{Zt}^h) \tag{18}$$

$$T_{Mt}^h = \tau_M (M_{Ct}^h + M_{Zt}^h) \tag{19}$$

(b) *The Rest of the Economy and the Total Economy*

$$M_{Ct}^0 = M_{C0}^0 + \mu(Y_t - Y_0) \tag{20}$$

$$E_{Ct}^0 = (1 + \epsilon)^t E_{C0}^0 \tag{21}$$

$$M_{Zt}^0 = m^0 M_{Ct}^0 \tag{22}$$

$$E^0_{Zt} = e^0 E^0_{Ct} \tag{23}$$

$$H_t = H_0 + \sum_{i=0}^{t-1} B_i \tag{24}$$

$$B_t = M^0_{Ct} + M^0_{Zt} - E^0_{Ct} - E^0_{Zt} + M^h_{Ct} + M^h_{Zt} - E^h_{Ct} - E^h_{Zt} + N^h_t$$
$$+ \theta H_t + Q^h_t - \bar{J}_t \tag{25}$$

$$S_{Pt} = S_{P0} + \sigma(Y_t - Y_0) \tag{26}$$

$$P^0_t = \pi^0 (Y_t - Y^h_t) \tag{27}$$

$$W^0_t = w^0 (Y_t - Y^h_t) \tag{28}$$

$$G^0_t = G^0_0 (1 + \gamma)^t \tag{29}$$

$$T^0_t = T^0_{Pt} + T^0_{Wt} + T^0_{\mathrm{IND}t} + T^0_{Et} + T^0_{Mt} + \bar{T}^0_{\mathrm{OTH}t} \tag{30}$$

$$T^0_{Pt} = \tau_p P^0_t \tag{31}$$

$$T^0_{Wt} = \tau_W W^0_t \tag{32}$$

$$T^0_{\mathrm{IND}t} = \tau_{\mathrm{IND}} (Y_t - Y^h_t) \tag{33}$$

$$T^0_{Et} = \tau_E (E^0_{Ct} + E^0_{Zt}) \tag{34}$$

$$T^0_{Mt} = \tau_M (M^0_{Ct} + M^0_{Zt}) \tag{35}$$

$$S_{Gt} = T^0_t + T^h_t - G^0_t - G^h_t \tag{36}$$

$$I^0_t = (S_{Pt} + S_{Gt} + B_t) - F_{Dt} \tag{37}$$

$$Y_t = Y_0 + \frac{\sum_{i=0}^{t-1} I^0_i}{k^0} + \frac{(1 + \alpha)^{t-1} K^h_0}{k^h} \tag{38}$$

CHAPTER III

THE ECONOMIC EFFECTS OF PFI

3.1. INTRODUCTION

The methodological framework presented in Chapter II allows to point out in a quantitative way some of the economic effects of PFI, also if it is kept in that simplified formulation, with only two sectors. Obviously, the analysis could be more accurate if the model were disaggregated into more sectors, as it will be seen in Chapter IX.

The following pages will discuss some of the economic effects of PFI, mainly on a general basis, in order to point out how it is possible to use the model for this purpose. A quantification of some of these effects will be attempted after the next chapter and in the following ones.

Attention will be given to the OP, but, with little modifications, the same procedure can be extended to the analysis of the effects of PFI in the IP.

3.2. THE EFFECTS ON INVESTMENT IN THE REST OF THE ECONOMY AND ON THE GROWTH OF INCOME

In the model presented in the previous chapter, PFI is assumed to be partly substitute and partly additional, with respect to domestic investments. Both extreme cases could be taken into account, as pointed out in Section 2.10, but what is relevant is the assumption that the degree to which PFI substitutes domestic investments in the utilization of available financial resources depends upon the PFI itself, and precisely upon the 'required rate of transfer of profits to abroad (ρ)'.

Assuming that the rate of growth of domestic investments in t is x_t, then the rate of growth of income r_t is given by:

$$r_t = \frac{\dfrac{x_t I_t^0}{k^0} + \dfrac{\alpha I_t^h}{k^h}}{\dfrac{I_t^0}{k^0} + \dfrac{I_t^h}{k^h}}$$

that is to say, it is a weighted average between the rate of growth of domestic investments (x) and of PFI (α).

An expression for x_t can be derived from the model:

$$x_t = \frac{\sigma}{k^0} + \frac{\Delta B_t}{I_t^0} + \frac{\Delta S_{Gt}}{I_t^0} - \frac{\alpha F_{Dt}}{I_t^0}.$$

Similarly, it is possible to derive the effect of PFI on the level of income in This will have to take into account, apart from the direct contribution of PFI (Y_t^h), the indirect effects of PFI on the level of domestic investments, through its effects on private savings, public savings, the b.o.p. deficit, and the absorption of domestic financial resources (Equation (37)).

This will be explicitly pointed out in Chapter V and in the following ones.

3.3. THE EFFECTS ON THE B.O.P.

The effects of PFI on the b.o.p. take place through its direct effects, given by Equations (5), (8), (9), (10), (11), (11 bis), and through its secondary effects due to the increase in income. If Y_t^* is the increase in income imputable to PFI, and if the secondary effect can be measured through the marginal propensity to import, then the cumulated effect of PFI on the b.o.p. is:

$$B_t^* = M_{Ct}^h + M_{Zt}^h - E_{Zt}^h - E_{Ct}^h + \mu Y_t^* + m^0 \mu Y_t^* + Q_t^h + \theta H_t^* - \bar{J}_t^* + N_t^h.$$

A star denotes the effects of PFI on a given variable. The various items of B_t^* will be explicitly considered in Chapter V and following, particularly for what regards the debt effect (H_t^*).

This way of quantifying the b.o.p. effect derives directly from the assumption introduced about an open deficit of the b.o.p., and discussed at length in Section 2.10.

In this context, the deficit is free to vary, and it has a growth effect, as it was pointed out there, justified, in the case of the b.o.p. effect, also by the fact that the latter stands for capital inflow imputable to PFI.

It is interesting, however, to point out what would happen in the alternative situation of a fixed deficit. The b.o.p. effect would again be obtained in the way seen above, but the 'rest of the economy' would then have to adapt to the difference between the fixed deficit and the share caused by PFI. This would require a mechanism of adjustment, which would go through a curtailment of imports. If this can be done by cutting imports not necessary for the production of income (i.e. consumer goods, instead of intermediate or capital goods V, then this would result in a reassessment of internal consumption. In the opposite case, also the level of income would be affected, and would diminish. Also this way of looking at the problem, then, must be kept in mind in interpreting the scope of the methodological set-up, and the results which will be given in Part III with reference to a number of empirical case studies.

3.4. IMPORT SUBSTITUTION AND EXPORT PROMOTION

In the debate over the effects of PFI in LDC's, one main point concerns the beneficial effects PFI may have in increasing the exports or curtailing the imports of the country concerned, with respect to what would have happened in its absence. In setting up the foreign trade equations for PFI (Section 2.2, Equations (8) and (9)) it was explicitly mentioned how the export coefficient (with respect to PFI value added) φ_e was meant to include, apart from the amount of exports promoted by PFI, also its import substitution effect.

It was felt necessary to stress again this point when dealing about the economic effects of PFI. In the case there is empirical evidence that PFI does substitute imports, this can be taken fully into account by the model in the parameter of Equation (8), expressing the amount of imports saved with reference to PFI value added in the period considered.

Moreover, in the case PFI competes with exports of the 'rest of the economy' sector, although this seems to be a rather extreme case, it is also possible to take it into account, either increasing the import coefficient of Equation (9), or decreasing the export coefficient of Equation (8). And this is also much simpler than introducing any modification in Equation (21) (exports for the rest of the economy) in case this export-curtailment effect happens in practice.

3.5. THE EFFECTS ON WAGES, PROFITS AND EMPLOYMENT

The model already considers, at an aggregate level, wages and salaries, and profits both for the PFI sector and the rest of the economy. This was introduced mainly to derive direct taxation.

It is also possible (Section 2.9) to introduce employment, at an aggregate (two sector) level.

The effects of PFI on wages and employment can be better studied after the model is disaggregated into sectors, introducing labour-output ratios, and average wage rates, and relating the analysis to the sectoral levels of value added, which would include the effects of PFI. The effect on unemployment could then very crudely be obtained by difference, considering the time evolution of the labour force, related to the rate of growth of population.

Similarly, the effect of PFI on sectoral domestic profits, could be obtained from its effects on sectoral value added.

3.6. THE EFFECTS ON THE DISTRIBUTION OF INCOME

The question of the effects of PFI on the distribution of income is not an easy one to handle, especially if one wants not to complicate the analysis too much (as it is the case here) and if the methodological framework which serves as a starting point has some implicit limits, as again it is the case here. Moreover, the kind of data one can expect for any empirical use exclude even the possibility of using some tradional measurements, like the Lorentz curve and the Gini coefficient.

Here an attempt will be made to give a solution to the problem, which can be handled with the two-sector model considered so far, as well as with a more detailed sectoral breakdown. The proposed approach is rather simple, and it might not be quite satisfactory. But it gives at least an idea of how the problem could be seen in the context of the analysis of the effects of PFI.

A useful starting point can be the analysis developed by G. M. Meier [1] and by G. D. A. MacDougall [2].

According to Meier, as long as PFI raises productivity, and this increase is not wholly appropriated by the investor, it follows that the greater product must be shared with others, and there must be some direct benefits to other groups. The benefit can accrue to:

- domestic labour in the form of higher real wages;
- consumer by way of lower prices;
- the government, through expanded revenue.

In addition, and of great importance in many cases, there are likely to be indirect gains through the realization of external economies.

MacDougall has shown how an inflow of foreign capital may be a major influence in raising labour's marginal productivity and increasing total real wages.

1 See Meier, G. M., *The international economics of development*, New York, Harper and Row, 1968, pp. 138–139.

2 See MacDougall, G. D. A., 'The benefits and costs of private investment from abroad', *Economic Record*, March 1960.

Assuming two factors of production – capital and labour – and assuming that profits per unit of capital equal the marginal product of capital, and that the total capital stock is domestically owned, an addition to it through a PFI lowers the marginal productivity of capital and expands real output [3].

Consequently, following this argument, one could propose the following rough estimate of income distribution

$$\frac{\text{wages}}{\text{profits}}$$

In the context of the appraisal of the effects of PFI, this one on the distribution of income could be measured comparing the ratio in the presence of PFI, with the one in the absence of PFI, and this can be done directly using the information of the model, which already gives wages and profits both for the PFI sector and for the rest of the economy.

But apart from this advantage, this approach seems rather simplified.

The argument put forward by MacDougall may be more relevant for developed countries, than for LDC's. As a matter of act, his concern was with what happens in Australia.

Besides, the proposed ratio leaves out completely the non-wage sector, the independent workers, etc., that is to say almost all the agricultural sector and a good share of the tertiary sector as well. However, since our main interest is in PFI in the manufacturing sector, where wages and profits really matter, this objection may be overcome. It must be borne in mind, anyhow, that once the situation with PFI and the one without PFI are compared to get a measurement of income distribution using the proposed ratio, there will also be the implicit assumption that nothing changes in the non-wage sectors. This might be too restrictive; if PFI promotes employment, one can expect that it would come from the non-wage sectors (e.g. agriculture), raising their productivity, with an effect on their real incomes.

Another objection to the proposed solution may be more relevant.

Following MacDougall's argument, the model should explicitly take into account the marginal productivity of labour and capital, and how it is modified by the increase in the foreign-owned capital stock. Consequently, the wage rate (w) and the rate of profit (π) should be modified accordingly.

This is not possible in the model set up in Chapter II, where a greater income to wage earners comes from a higher value added in some sectors (rest of the economy: Equation (28): PFI sector: Equation (12))and a greater in-

3 However, it has been pointed out how the analysis that leads to the conclusion of diminishing marginal returns to capital in the host country is based on static assumptions and does not take into account complementary demands for capital and other factors.

come to profit earners comes from an expansion of production (rest of the economy: Equation (27)) or an expansion of the capital stock (PFI sector: Equation (4)).

The implicit assumption is that wage rates and profit rates stay constant, although they are different from sector to sector, and particularly, in the two-sector case, from the PFI sector to the rest of the economy sector.

But anyhow, given the fact that it would not be so easy to relate specifically labour and capital productivity to the capital stock, the assumption of their constancy seems the most reasonable one, and the proposed measurement of income distribution

$$\frac{\text{wages}}{\text{profits}}$$

can be accepted, although it should be clear that any improvement or deterioration of this ratio will come not through a variation in the sectoral productivities, but from a different relative importance of the various PFI and domestic sectors, and their different structural parameters (wage rate and profit rate).

3.7. THE EFFECTS ON GOVERNMENT REVENUE AND EXPENDITURE

The model takes into account also the public sector, both for PFI and for the rest of the economy.

The primary direct effect of PFI on Government revenue and expenditure is given in OP by Equations (13) and (14), and the direct effect of PFI on public savings is given by:

$$T_t^h - G_t^h .$$

As for the cumulated effects of PFI, which should take also into account the secondary effect due to the increase in income caused by PFI, no effect is given by the model on public current expenditure, which grows at a constant rate, while a study of such effects on public revenue is possible considering the increase in those items which are affected by PFI. This will be done in Section 5.5.

3.8. THE EFFECTS ON PRIVATE SAVINGS

PFI, apart from its effect on the b.o.p. and on Government savings, and from the fact that its profits reinvested constitute a net addition to total savings, as pointed out in Section 2.8, has also secondary effect on private savings, due to the increase in income directly imputable to it, and it is measured through the marginal propensity to save.

3.9. SUBSTITUTION EFFECTS

The substitution effects of PFI can be seen from two points of view:

(a) substitution between productive processes, due to a difference in efficiency and in comparative costs;

(b) substitution between commodities, due to differences in prices, to the effects of sales promotion and advertising, and to variations in preferences, connected also with the increase in incomes.

The two are interrelated, because a different pattern of production will affect the pattern of demand; on the other hand, a different pattern of demand will have a feed-back effect on production.

On the production side, the model already assumes that PFI has an advantage on domestic investments, since the latter are a residual between total financial resources available and the share which goes to finance PFI. This implies that a firm set up by foreigners is preferred to a domestic one in the utilization of financial resources, and consequently, up to a given point, PFI is a full substitute for domestic investments.

But, apart from this substitution effect through investment, it is necessary to point out what happens to the level of output of the already existing domestic firms, once a PFI is there. Also in this case substitution might take place. The opposite case (i.e. domestic firms substituting PFI) should not hold, since PFI would not be set up at all.

However, while the question of substitution between PFI and new firms, at least on a simplified basis, can be considered as incorporated in the model, the same does not apply to substitution between PFI and existing domestic firms. So the problem arises with the already existing capacity in year 0, when the PFI is made. The production of PFI may be all additional, or it may substitute part of the domestic production.

Demand is taken into account in all its items, except private consumption, which in Section 2.8 was derived as a residual from the total level of income. But, since the latter is given by Equation (38), this means that, according to the model, demand adapts automatically to the level of production. This mechanism excludes the possibility of substitution between PFI and domestic firms, apart from the already mentioned effect through investments.

If there is evidence that existing firms are substituted by PFI, then the *full capacity utilization production function* of Equation (38) does not hold any longer, because the new level of income will be somewhat lower.

Moreover, the problem is complicated by the fact that there are some implicit limits of the model in handling the problem of substitution. In the two-sector model, from the point of view of substitution, it is assumed that only one commodity, (i.e. GDP) is produced both by domestic and by PFI firms.

Once the model becomes multisectoral, the implicit assumption will be that n commodities will be produced, of which m manufacturing commodities, that is one by each sector.

If there is also a number ($\leq m$) of PFI manufacturing sub-sectors, the same number of commodities will be introduced, and they will be all additional, or partly substitute the corresponding domestic commodities.

A first case in which PFI is all additional is the one where the corresponding domestic manufacturing sub-sector is 'empty'. But, given the limited number of sectors considered, this does not seem to be a very likely case.

Since the model, also in its multisectoral version, considers a 'fixed coefficients world' [4], any variation in any item of demand, not directly reflected in a variation of the conversion coefficients, would cause no variation in one or more specific sectors, but a general increase or decrease in all sectors.

This applies also to the substitution effect through new investments, in the sense that when a new PFI is made, its substitution effect on new domestic firms, through its effect on domestic investments, will come not through a direct decrease of the corresponding domestic manufacturing sub-sector, but from a general and proportional decrease in *all* domestic sectors.

Consequently, the substitution effect already taken into account by the model implicitly relies on the assumption that there is no direct effect from a PFI sub-sector on the corresponding domestic sub-sector, but a general effect on the whole economy.

But, also assuming that the substitution effect is properly taken into account, being the production functions of the fixed coefficients type, there will be no substitution between capital and labour within the sectors, but only a utilization of the existing domestic capital stock below the full capacity level, a consequent decrease in output, and a decrease in employment in the sector which is affected. There follows that a different utilization of the factors of production will be not at a sectoral level, where the relative importance of each factor will remain constant, but at the level of the whole economy. Here a different relative share of each sector in gross value added

4 I.e. fixed capital-output and labour-output ratios.

(or gross production) due to the presence of PFI, with respect to a situation without PFI, given the fact that the different sectors have different structural parameters (capital-output and labour-output ratios), will point out the substitution effect of PFI on the allocation of resources.

The analysis of the substitution effects of PFI will be based on the restrictive assumption that substitution takes place (if it does at all) *only* between the PFI manufacturing sub-sector (or commodity) under consideration, and the corresponding domestic manufacturing sub-sector (or commodity) [5].

This means that PFI does not affect the level of production of the other firms in the other $(n-1)$ domestic sectors, which produce the other $(n-1)$ commodities, apart from the investments effect already considered.

Given the limited number of sectors, this assumption seems quite reasonable, while it would not be so if the sectoral breakdown were much larger.

Assuming that the model is multisectoral, and that we are in BIP (no PFI), total gross value added is produced by the n sectors according to some fixed coefficients:

$$y_1, \ldots, y_n \qquad (\Sigma y_i = 1).$$

New domestic investments are split into the various sectors according to their capital coefficient (k_i^0), weighted by their share in gross value added (y_i), so that the structure of production remains the same, as income increases.

Mutatis mutandis, a similar situation will hold if input-output analysis is used. For simplicity, the following analysis will be limited to the case of sectoral breakdown without input-output.

Given this situation, let's see what happens once a PFI is there.

A certain PFI manufacturing sub-sector is introduced in the economy, and it produces y^h per cent of gross value added.

In such a context, there are three possibilities.

(a) the commodity produced by PFI is a net addition to total output. The PFI sector then becomes, in a sense, a new sector, and total output will be

$$Y^0 + y^h Y^0 = Y.$$

All the coefficients have to be reweighted, so that they still add up to one.

(b) the commodity produced by PFI is a net substitute of the one produced by the corresponding domestic manufacturing sub-sector. Consequently, the share in value added of the latter becomes:

5 Substitution will be considered only from a supply point of view, with the assumption that demand adapts to it. A demand-oriented analysis would be in contrast with the one developed so far.

$$y_i - y^h.$$

Total output, at least in time 0, remains the same. In a dynamic context, domestic investment funds (which include the PFI investments effect), will be allocated to the various domestic sectors, taking into account the above depicted effect of PFI on the corresponding manufacturing sub-sector.

The time behaviour of the economy will thus include all substitution effects, and the other effects of PFI will be affected accordingly.

In the case of a two-sector model, this would simply mean that Equation (38), while in case (a) still holds as it is, in case (b) becomes:

$$Y_t = (Y_0 - \overline{Y}_s) + \frac{\sum_{i=0}^{t-1} I_i^0}{k^0} + Y_t^h,$$

where Y_s (exogenous) stands for the substitution of PFI in 0, and in case (b) is given by Y_0^h.

(c) For an intermediate case, the same reasoning ad (b) would apply, with the difference that $\overline{Y}_s$ would be less than Y_0^h.

The capacity (of rest of the economy) which will be unutilized as a consequence of the presence of PFI can be derived considering the capital-output ratio of the sector which is affected:

$$K_s = \overline{Y}_s \cdot k_i^0$$

The approach developed above implies that the substitution effect takes place only in the first year of the establishment of a PFI. However, as PFI grows, it may continue to substitute domestic firms. If this is the case, then the level of output which is substituted can be expressed in the following way:

$$\overline{Y}_{st} = \overline{Y}_{s0}(1 + \alpha')^t$$

where

$$\alpha' = f(\alpha)$$

and should also be exogenously given.

The solution of the substitution problem outlined above has the advantage of including all substitution effects of PFI, and of better explaining the substitution effect through investments, without requiring any basic change in the model and in the formulation of the effects[6], but it requires *exogenous*

6 This will be considered later in Section 8.6.

information about the degree up to which the PFI production substitutes the one of the corresponding domestic sub-sector.

This fact, however, does not seem to be very relevant for the analysis of the effects of PFI, since it seems quite difficult to be able to establish endogenously, and thus in a way that holds more or less for all LDC's, a simple formula explaining substitution between PFI and domestic firms, which seems to vary to quite an extent from case to case.

CHAPTER IV

OTHER ECONOMIC EFFECTS OF PFI NOT CONSIDERED BY THE MODEL

4.1. INTRODUCTION

Apart from the economic effects of PFI considered in the previous chapter, which can be more or less explicitly taken into account by the methodological framework outlined in Chapter II, there are obviously others which have not been considered, due to the general set-up of the model.

In particular, the assumption of constant prices does not allow to introduce price variables into the analysis, and consequently to study the effects PFI has on them, although they might be quite relevant, since they might cause some structural changes, a different allocation of resources, etc.

So, while still keeping, for simplicity's sake and for lack of data for any practical use, the assumption of constant prices introduced in Section 1.3, it might be useful to spend some words to illustrate the possible effects of PFI on the main price variables. Of these, it seems important to consider the exchange rate, the internal price system and the terms of trade. This chapter will then consider other questions not directly related to the price variables, like the external effects of PFI, the effect on the savings rate, and the demonstration effects in general.

4.2. THE EXCHANGE RATE

The exchange rate is one of the most important variables; among other things, relative prices of domestic products and imports depend on it.

So this particular variable has a main influence on the other two, and it can well introduce the whole topic of price variables.

The analysis can start quoting some remarks by F. Ginor[1], who is particularly concerned to study what happens as a consequence of PFI to the exchange rate. According to her, apart from official exchange rates, tariff systems and import restrictions, the capital import itself decisively affects the exchange rate. Even if there are no import restrictions of any kind and no

1 Ginor, F., 'The Impact of Capital Imports on the Structure of Developing Countries', *Kyklos,* 1969, pp. 104–120.

tariffs, the foreign exchange rate will be determined from the supply side by the supply of foreign currency in the form of unrequited transfers, foreign investments, and foreign loans on favourable conditions.

Relatively large capital imports over a prolonged period will cause an especially low rate of exchange, and this will seriously limit the quantity of goods and services that can profitably be produced at home in the absence of protective tariffs and import restrictions.

Goods and services which can enter foreign trade (tradable goods) are profitable to produce only when their costs of production can compete with international prices, including the cost of transportation.

If there is a relatively large import surplus with the consequent low exchange rate, the share of tradable goods and services in GNP tends to be relatively low, since they can be imported from the cheapest foreign source without the necessity to pay for all of them with exports. Capital imports also provide means for investment without the necessity to save from income and to curtail consumption[2]. The result is that the structure of the economy developing under conditions of capital imports, becomes dependent on an import surplus.

The structure of the economy would be different in a situation in which the international accounts are balanced, as compared with a situation in which there is a persistent import surplus. I.e., if there were no persistent import surplus, and the foreign exchange rate were higher, more labour and capital would be allocated to the production of tradable goods and services.

The transition from an import surplus to the balancing of international accounts would require the diversion of production factors from the production of non-tradable goods and services to the production of tradable goods and services with declining comparative advantage, so that more and more non-tradable goods and services would have to be given up for every additional unit of tradable goods and services.

So, a sudden curtailment of imports to the level of exports would, in cases of a sizeable import surplus, drastically reduce the national product, creating large-scale unemployment as a consequence of the lack of imported raw materials and the decline in investments.

This argument can be summarized as follows.

An inflow of foreign capital allows an import surplus which causes an exchange rate lower than the equilibrium one would be. This affects the internal price system and the allocation of resources, shifting the economy

2 This refers also to the relationship between foreign capital inflow and the propensity to save. (See, e.g., T. Haavelmo, in *The Econometric Approach to Development Planning*, North Holland Publishing Company, 1965, p. 1062.)

from producing to importing 'tradable goods', according to the comparative advantage which derives from the new level of the exchange rate.

4.3. THE INTERNAL PRICE SYSTEM

The effect of PFI on the exchange rate has also an impact on the internal price system, as a consequence of the fact that imports become cheaper and the price of exports (in local currency) as given by the world market must be re-weighted to take into account the undervaluation of the exchange rate.

Besides, PFI can also influence relative prices in various ways, and particularly:

– through the price paid for domestic inputs, which may be higher than the existing price, or lower if PFI is in a monopsonistic position;

– through the price obtained for its output, which may be lower than the previous market price due to greater technical and economic efficiency, or higher if PFI is in a monopolistic position;

– through the increase in income (and in demand) caused indirectly and directly (higher real wages, etc.);

– through external economies provided to the economy as a whole, as well as through bottlenecks and shortages eventually caused by PFI.

4.4. THE TERMS OF TRADE

The effects of PFI on the terms of trade are usually associated with the transfer problem. They tend to improve with an inflow of capital, then tend to worsen when there is, subsequently, a return of capital (transfers and remittances). These effects should be considered as a part of the broader problem of the adjustment of the b.o.p.[3].

Aside from these effects, PFI may also affect the terms of trade through structural changes in the economy. These can be analysed both from the side of imports and from the side of exports.

The price index of imports will vary according to various effects. Imports, expressed in local currency, will become cheaper (through the exchange rate effect). This may cause an increase in demand, and thus an increase in prices (expressed in foreign currency). A general increase in imports, with similar price effects, may also be expected from the increase in income. Besides, PFI might require costly intermediate and capital goods, with negative consequences on the price index.

3 See Meier, G. M., *The International Economics of Development*, Harper & Row, New York, 1968, pp. 144–145.

Finally, one should also take into account the imports substituted by PFI, and their prices, as compared with the general imports price index of the economy.

The price index of exports, assuming constant and dependent upon world demand the existing price index previous to PFI, will vary according to the goods exported by PFI. If their price, both in the short and in the long run, has a favourable trend, the price index of exports should improve (and otherwise, in the opposite situation).

4.5. THE EXTERNAL EFFECTS

The model of Chapter II does not take into account the external effects of PFI, either positive or negative. It seems useful to spend a few lines also on this point, which is a rather important one, and one often stressed in the debate over the effects of PFI, as it was pointed out in Part I of this study. This topic can be covered quoting what G. M. Meier had to say about it in his *International Economics of Development*[4] :

From the standpoint of contributing to the development process, the major benefits from PFI are likely to arise in the form of external economies. Besides bringing to the recipient country physical and financial capital, PFI also includes nonmonetary transfers of other resources – technological knowledge, market information, managerial and supervisory personnel, organizational experience, and innovations in products and production techniques – all of which are in short supply. By being a carrier of technological and organizational change, PFI may be highly significant in providing 'private technical assistance' and 'demonstration effects' that are of benefit elsewhere in the economy. New techniques accompany the inflow of private capital, and by the example they set, foreign firms promote the diffusion of technological advance in the economy. Technical assistance may also be provided to suppliers and customers of the foreign enterprise. In addition, PFI frequently leads to the training of labor in new skills, and the knowledge gained by these workers can be transmitted to other members of the labor force, or the newly trained workers might be later employed by local firms.

PFI can also stimulate additional domestic investment in the recipient country. If PFI is in one industry, it may still encourage domestic investment by reducing costs in other industries; profits may then rise and lead to expansion in the other industries. Since there are so many specific scarcities in a poor country, it is common for investment to be of a cost-saving character by breaking bottlenecks in production. This stimulates expansion by raising profits in all underutilized productive capacity and by allowing the exploitation of economies of scale that had previously been restricted.

There is also considerable scope for the initial PFI to create external investment incentives by raising the demand for the output of other industries. The PFI in the first industry can give rise to profits in industries that supply inputs to the first industry, or that produce complementary products, or that produce goods bought by the factor-

4 See Meier, G. M., *op. cit.*, pp. 141–143.

owners who now have higher real incomes as a result of the inflow of foreign capital. A PFI that is product-improving or product-innovating may also have similar effects. A whole series of domestic investments may thus be linked to the PFI.

These external effects raise production outside the foreign enterprise, but the foreign investor cannot appropriate this additional output. The spill-over goes unpriced and constitutes an uncompensated service. To the extent that the foreign investment yields an external economy, the marginal social net product of the foreign capital is greater than its marginal private net product.

G. M. Meier concludes then that, on the basis of the discussion given above, and "according to the criterion of national economic benefit, the case for governmental encouragement of PFI is then strong"[5].

Such a conclusion is obviously questionable, especially on the grounds that also all the other effects must be taken into account before arriving at any policy recommendation. There is also, as for the external effects of PFI, 'another side of the picture', which will be taken up in the next section.

4.6. THE DEMONSTRATION EFFECTS

The arguments presented in the previous section concerned those external effects of PFI which are in general positive, although to varying degrees. It is possible now to turn the attention to the negative ones, which have been grouped, for simplicity, under the heading 'demonstration effects'. Some of the latter, may be positive, and they were mentioned in the previous section.

One argument often quoted to support the idea that PFI has an adverse impact on a LDC's economy concerns the question of 'expatriates', i.e. of foreign people coming to a LDC to work in PFI industries. The experience of many LDC's, especially of the ones at a lower level of development, shows that these people, due to the fact that they, in general, receive much higher wages than local employees, and that they are not willing to give up their habits and tastes, affect the pattern of consumption of that country, promoting the introduction of new goods that often have to be imported, at the expense of other more useful ones, from the point of view of the national advantage.

In so much as this refers to an increase in imports, this can be taken into account in the import coefficient itself of PFI (φ_m Equation (9), Section 2.2)). However, the impact that this has by altering the pattern of consumption is much more difficult to be taken into account, although one should mention it in judging about the effects of PFI.

5 Meier, G. M., *op. cit.*, p. 143.

This negative demonstration effect can be conceived also at the level of PFI. It may introduce the use of certain practices (expensive advertisements, public relations, etc.) which might not be appropriate given the level of development of a particular LDC. This consequently causes a misallocation of the available scarce resources, which could be better used for other purposes.

4.7. THE SAVINGS RATE

As it is well-known, following a paper by W. Leontief[6] during the 'Study Week on the Econometric Approach Development Planning', at the Vatican City, from 7–13 October, 1963, T. Haavelmo[7] raised a very interesting point concerning the relationship between capital inflow and internal savings:

> ... investment in the region is a fraction of regional income including what they get from abroad. I think we see the possible implications, it means that domestic savings could be negative if *H* (i.e. capital transfer from developed to underdeveloped areas) is very large.

That is, T. Haavelmo put forwards the opinion that there is an inverse relationship between foreign capital inflow and the savings rate of a country This relationship has been tested, and several times found true[8]. As a matter of fact, it seems quite logical, since a foreign capital inflow, providing additional financial resources, in a sense slackens the pressure put by any development program for a savings rate as high as possible.

In building a methodological framework for the appraisal of the effects of PFI, the explicit introduction of a relationship between PFI and the internal savings rate would have required an analysis much more sophisticated than the one set up; something similar to what follows here should have been done to Equation (26) (Section 2.4):

$$S_{Pt} = S_{P0} + \sigma^*(Y_t - Y_0)$$

$$\sigma^* = f(K^h_{t-1}).$$

6 See: Leontief, W., 'The Rates of Long-Run Economic Growth and Capital Transfer from Developed to Underdeveloped Areas' in *The Econometric Approach to Development Planning,* Amsterdam, North Holland Publishing Co., 1965, pp. 1039–1056.

7 See, Haavelmo, T., *op. cit.*, p. 1062.

8 (See, e.g., Boudhayan Chattopadhyay, *Domestic Savings Effect and Foreign Capital Inflow in Selected Countries of the ECAFE Region,* mimeo, 1971, United Nations Asian Institute for Economic Development and Planning).

Apart from theoretical complications, there would also have been the problem of finding empirical data for a practical exercise. All this suggested to keep the marginal propensity to save constant, as it is in Equation (26), although is was useful to cover also this point while considering some other economic effects of PFI *not* taken into account by the methodological framework.

CHAPTER V

THE INTERDEPENDENCE–SIMULTANEOUS AND OVER TIME–OF THE EFFECTS OF PFI

5.1. INTRODUCTION

Chapter III considered some of the major effects of PFI. Here, four effects will be explicitly quantified, in order to point out how the model can be used to yield the quantitative effects of PFI previously discussed, and also to point out their interdependence.

In this and in the next chapters the effects of PTI on a certain variable will mainly on the effects on income, b.o.p., private savings, and public savings. However, later, it will be shown how the analytical framework, although still at a simplified level, can be used to quantify the effects of PFI on wages and profits (and income distribution) and the effects on employment.

In this and in the next chapters the effects of PFI on a certain variable will be defined as the difference between a situation with PFI from 0 to t (the real one), and a situation without PFI from 0 to t (the alternative situation which would occur in the absence of PFI). The effects will be denoted by a star; e.g.:

$$Y_t^* = Y_t \text{ (with PFI)} - Y_t \text{ (without PFI)}.$$

5.2. THE INCOME EFFECT

Income in t is given by Equation (38), but the difference between Y_t without PFI and Y_t with PFI (i.e. Y_t^*) is not given by the last item of the right-hand-side term (which corresponds to Y_t^h of Equation (1)), because I_i^0 is influenced by PFI (also in the previous years) through B, F_D, S_P and S_G. The increase in income caused by the presence of PFI can be derived as follows:

$$\text{without PFI} \qquad Y_t = Y_0 + \frac{\sum_{i=0}^{t-1} I_i^0}{k^0} \qquad \text{(i)}$$

$$\text{with PFI} \qquad Y_t = Y_0 + \frac{\sum_{i=0}^{t-1} I_i^{0\prime}}{k^0} + Y_t^h, \qquad \text{(ii)}$$

where:

$$I_i^0 \text{ in (i)} \neq I_i^{0\prime} \text{ in (ii)}.$$

Consequently:

$$Y_t^* = \text{(ii)} - \text{(i)} = Y_t^h + \frac{\sum_{i=0}^{t-1} I_i^{0*}}{k^0} \quad \text{and,}$$

from Equation (37):

$$Y_t^* = Y_t^h + \frac{\sum_{i=0}^{t-1} (S_{Pi}^* + S_{Gi}^* + B_i^* - F_{Di})}{k^0} .$$

S_{Pi}^* is the *private savings effect* of PFI (Section 5.4).

S_{Gi}^* is the *effect on Government savings* of PFI and it will be dealt with in Section 5.5.

B_i^* is the *b.o.p. effect* of PFI and it will be analysed in Section 5.3.

F_{Di} is directly given by the model (Equation (7)).

5.3. THE B.O.P. EFFECT

From Section 3.3 the b.o.p. effect is:

$$B_t^* = M_{Ct}^h + M_{Zt}^h - E_{Ct}^h - E_{Zt}^h + \mu Y_t^* + m^0 \mu Y_t^* + Q_t^h - \bar{J}_t^* +$$

$$+ N_t^h + \theta \sum_{i=0}^{t-1} B_i^*$$

the last term on the right-hand-side includes the effect of PFI on the foreign debt in the previous years (equal to the deficit of the b.o.p. previously caused by PFI). The above expression excludes the effect on exports for the rest of the economy, due to the formulation of Equations (21) and (23).

B_t^* is a function of Y_t^*, and vice versa. Besides, B_t^* is also a (linear) function of the deficit of the previous years, included in the foreign debt effect.

5.4. THE PRIVATE SAVINGS EFFECT

The effect on private savings is given by the increase in income imputable to PFI, and by the marginal propensity to save:

$$S^*_{Pt} = \sigma Y^*_t .$$

5.5. THE PUBLIC SAVINGS EFFECT

Government savings are given by Equation (36). The direct contribution of PFI is clearly established by the model.

It is also possible to derive from the model the indirect effect of PFI on the rest of the economy.

G^0_t has an independent time behaviour (Equation (29)), while, in order to obtain the effect on revenue for the rest of the economy it is necessary to establish:

– the effect on *profits* for the rest of the economy (Equation (27)):

$$P^{0*}_t = \pi^0 (Y^*_t - Y^h_t) .$$

– the effect on *wages* for the rest of the economy (Equation (28)):

$$W^{0*}_t = w^0 (Y^*_t - Y^h_t) .$$

– the effect on *imports* of goods and services for the rest of the economy (eqs. 20 and 22); exports are not affected (Equations (21) and (23)), as it was noticed when dealing with the b.o.p. effect:

$$M^{0*}_t = \mu(1 + m^0) Y^*_t .$$

The effect on indirect taxation for the rest of the economy is given by Equation (33):

$$T^*_{\mathrm{IND}t} = \tau_{\mathrm{IND}} (Y^*_t - Y^h_t) .$$

The effect on taxes on profits for the rest of the economy is given by Equation (31):

$$T^{0*}_{Pt} = \tau_P \pi^0 (Y^*_t - Y^h_t) .$$

The effect on taxes on wages for the rest of the economy is given by Equation (32):

$$T_{Wt}^{0*} = \tau_W w^0 (Y_t^* - Y_t^h).$$

The effects on taxes on imports for the rest of the economy is given by Equation (35):

$$T_{Mt}^{0*} = \tau_M \mu(1 + m^0) Y_t^*.$$

The effect on the exogenous component of taxation is assumed to be given:

$$T_{\text{OTH}t}^{0*} = \text{given}.$$

Consequently, the effect of PFI on public savings is given by:

$$S_{Gt}^* = T_t^h - G_t^h + T_{\text{IND}t}^{0*} + T_{Pt}^{0*} + T_{Wt}^{0*} + T_{Mt}^{0*} + \overline{T}_{\text{OTH}t}^{0*}.$$

As it was said, T_t^h (Equation (14)) and G_t^h (Equation (13)) are given by the model, while all the other terms, apart from the exogenous component, are expressed as a function of Y_t^h (directly given by the model) and of Y_t^*. This last item, in turn, is a function of S_{Gt}^*.

5.6. THE INTERDEPENDENCE OF THE EFFECTS OF PFI

In the preceeding pages it was pointed out how our basic effects of PFI (income, b.o.p., private savings, public savings) can be obtained from the model only simultaneously.

For each year, from t=0 to t, the four effects are obtained from a system of four simultaneous equations, which looks as follows:

$$Y_i^* = f_Y \left(\sum_{j=0}^{i-1} B_j^*, \sum_{j=0}^{i-1} S_{Pj}^*, \sum_{j=0}^{i-1} S_{Gj}^* \right)$$

$$B_i^* = f_B \left(Y_i^*, \sum_{j=0}^{i-1} B_j^* \right)$$

$$S_{Pi}^* = f_{SP}(Y_i^*) \qquad (i = 0, \ldots, t)$$

$$S_{Gi}^* = f_{SG}(Y_i^*).$$

All equations are linear in the four variables with a star, and they also include other terms directly given by the model as it was seen above.

The next chapter will deal with the solution of this problem.

CHAPTER VI

THE 'CUMULATIVE' EFFECTS OF PFI

6.1. INTRODUCTION

The effects of PFI considered in the previous chapter will be called 'cumulative' effects, to point out that they refer to the effect on a given variable in t under the assumption that they are obtained by difference, considering two alternative situations, one with PFI from 0 to t, and the other without PFI from 0 to t.

This terminology, although not very precise from a strictly mathematical point of view, will also allow to distinguish them from the "marginal" effects of PFI, which will be considered in the next chapter.

At the end of the previous chapter, it was pointed out how the four cumulative effects considered formed a system of linear equations, characterized by the presence of lagged endogenous variables.

In this chapter, after having written explicitly the four effects, the question of the solution will be tackled. Unless one wants to solve the system year by year, it is necessary to find a general way to get the cumulative effects in t, on the basis of the model from which they were derived.

6.2. THE FORMULATION OF THE CUMULATIVE EFFECTS

In the previous chapters the four cumulative effects were given in Sections 5.2, 5.3, 5.4 and 5.5.

Under the assumptions that

$$J_t^* = 0$$

$$T_{\mathrm{OTH}t}^* = 0,$$

i.e. that the cumulative effects on factor income payments from abroad and on other current revenue are zero, in order to avoid further complications, it is possible to formulate the four effects as a function of gross value added of the PFI sector (Y_t^h), of the various parameters, and of each other, obtaining a system of four linear equations, with the effects as unknowns.

$$Y_t^* = Y_t^h - \left[\alpha - (\pi^h - \rho - \pi^h \tau_P)\right]\frac{k^h}{k^0} \cdot \frac{(1+\alpha)^t - 1}{\alpha(1+\alpha)^t}\, Y_t^h +$$

$$+ \frac{\sum_{i=0}^{t-1} (S_{Pi}^* + S_{Gi}^* + B_i^*)}{k^0}$$

$$B_t^* = \left[\varphi_m (1 + m^h) - \varphi_e (1 + e^h) + \rho k^h + \lambda k^h\right] Y_t^h +$$

$$+ \mu\,(1 + m^0)\, Y_t^* + \theta \sum_{i=0}^{t-1} B_i^*$$

$$S_{Pt}^* = \sigma Y_t^*$$

$$S_{tG}^* = Y_t^h \left[\tau_P \pi^h k^h + \tau_W w^h + \tau_{\mathrm{IND}} + \tau_M \varphi_m (1 + m^h) +\right.$$

$$\left. + \tau_E \varphi_e (1 + e^h) - g^h k^h\right] +$$

$$+ \left[\tau_{\mathrm{IND}} + \tau_P \pi^0 + \tau_W w^0\right] (Y_t^* - Y_t^h) +$$

$$+ \tau_M \mu (1 + m^0)\, Y_t^*.$$

The problem which remains is the one of lagged endogenous variables in the first and second expression after the summation signs. This question will be tackled in the next sections, first offering a general solution in terms of a system of difference equations, and then trying to solve directly the above expressions, introducing certain assumptions about the growth of the cumulative effects.

Before doing this, the four cumulative effects will be briefly commented, to point out their economic meaning.

6.3. ECONOMIC INTERPRETATION OF THE CUMULATIVE EFFECTS

The cumulative effect on income (Y_t^*) is given by the PFI sector gross value added (Y_t^h), less the effect through domestic investments given by the cumulated share taken from domestic financial resources to finance part of the annual addition to the PFI capital stock $(\Sigma_{i=0}^{t-1} F_{Di})$, plus the cumulated effect on the other three determinants of domestic investments. The last two terms are weighted by the domestic capital-output ratio. Three determinants of domestic investments are unknown, being, in turn, cumulative effects; they are explained by the other three expressions.

The cumulative effect on the deficit of the b.o.p. (B_t^*) is given by three additive components. The first one refers to the direct effect of the PFI sector (import requirements, export promotion and/or import substitution, and profit transfers). The second is the indirect effect which comes through the income effect and the marginal propensity to import. The third term refers to the cumulative debt effect, since

$$H_t^* = \sum_{i=0}^{t-1} B_i^* \,.$$

The cumulative effect on private savings (S_{Pt}^*) is readily understandable, being directly related to income through the marginal propensity to save.

The cumulative effect on public savings (S_{Gt}^*) is given by the direct effect imputable to the PFI sector, plus the indirect effect on indirect taxation, on taxes on profits, on taxes on wages, and on taxes on imports (last item).

More could be said about the role played by the various parameters, specially in the income effect. This would be quite similar to what will be done in Section 7.8 about the marginal effects, to which the reader is referred.

The crucial element which will determine the numerical value of the four effects is the level of PFI gross value added (Y_t^h), together with its rate of growth.

Moreover, in solving the system, it is possible to take into account various modifications in the parameters referring to the two sectors, along with some modifications in the formulation of some of the relations of the model. This point will be further discussed in Chapter X.

6.4. A GENERAL SOLUTION FOR THE CUMULATIVE EFFECTS

The system given in Section 6.2 can be reformulated in terms of difference equations, reintroducing H_t^*, as the cumulative debt effect of PFI.

It is possible to substitute in Y_t^* the formulations of S_{Pt}^*, S_{Gt}^*, and B_t^*; instead of writing all the parameters, the formulation of this system of difference equations will be given just in order to point out what the relationships among the unknowns are.

$$Y_{t+1}^* - Y_t^* = a\, Y_t^h + b\, Y_t^* + \theta H_t^* \,, \tag{1}$$

where a is the combination of parameters related to Y_t^h, and b the combination of parameters related to Y_t^*.

$$H_{t+1}^* - H_t^* = B_t^* \tag{2}$$

$$B_{t+1}^* - B_t^* = c\,\alpha\,Y_t^h + d\,(Y_{t+1}^* - Y_t^*) + \theta\,B_t^*\,, \tag{3}$$

where in (3) c is the combination of parameters related to αY_t^h, and d is the combination of parameters related to $(Y_{t+1}^* - Y_t^*)$.

Besides these three difference equations, there are the two Equations (4) and (5) giving the private and public savings effect:

$$S_{Pt}^* \quad \text{and} \quad S_{Gt}^*\,.$$

Their value is directly obtainable once the system is solved, and their formulation is the same as in Section 6.2.

The system composed by the first three difference equations can be solved by ordinary methods; it is possible to get a general solution in terms of the parameters (assuming Y_t^h given), and then study its behaviour, given certain numerical values to the parameters.

Such a solution will be omitted here, also because in the next section it will be seen how it is possible to find an easier one, although with some approximations.

6.5. A SOLUTION IN TERMS OF THE GROWTH OF THE CUMULATIVE EFFECTS

The general solution considered in the previous section is not very easy to handle in practice. Consequently, it seems useful to look for a simpler way of solving the system of Section 6.2. The complication is given by the presence of lagged endogenous variables, either related to Y_i^* or to B_i^*. If it were possible to get the rate of growth of the income cumulative effect, and of the balance of payments cumulative effect, then the system would be easily solvable.

The rate of growth of Y_t^h is given by the model, and it is equal to α.

$$Y_{t+1}^h = (1 + \alpha)\,Y_t^h$$

consequently

$$\sum_{i=0}^{t-1} Y_i^h = Y_t^h \frac{(1+\alpha)^t - 1}{\alpha(1+\alpha)^t}\ .$$

The following assumptions will be introduced:

$$Y_{t+1}^* = (1+\xi)\, Y_t^*$$

and

$$B_{t+1}^* = (1+\zeta)\, B_t^*\ .$$

Consequently

$$\sum_{i=0}^{t-1} Y_i^* = Y_t^* \frac{(1+\xi)^t - 1}{\xi\,(1+\xi)^t}$$

and

$$\sum_{i=0}^{t-1} B_i^* = B_t^* \frac{(1+\zeta)^t - 1}{\zeta\,(1+\zeta)^t}\ .$$

Since the various items of B_i^* from 0 to t are either related to Y_i^* or to Y_i^h (including thus the debt item), it follows that ζ is a weighted average between α and ξ.

Consequently, the b.o.p. effect becomes:

$$B_t^* = \frac{a\, Y_t^h + b\, Y_t^*}{1 - \theta \left[\dfrac{(1+\zeta)^t - 1}{\zeta(1+\zeta)^t}\right]}$$

and it is possible to write the income effect in the following way:

$$Y_t^* = c_t\, Y_t^h + d_t\, Y_t^*\ .$$

a and c include all parameters related to Y_t^h; similarly, b and d include all parameters related to Y_t^*. Moreover, since c and d include also some summations of geometric series, with common ratios depending upon a rate of growth which is either α or ξ, or a weighted average between the two (ζ), time must be taken into account.

It follows that:

$$Y^*_{t+1} = (1+\xi)\,Y^*_t = (1+\alpha)\,c_{t+1}\,Y^h_t + (1+\xi)\,d_{t+1}\,Y^*_t$$

and from the above expression it follows that *approximately*[1]

$$\alpha \simeq \xi$$

and

$$\alpha \simeq \zeta\,.$$

Thus, it has been proved that the rate of growth of the b.o.p. cumulative effect and of the income cumulative effect is approximated by the rate of growth of PFI gross value added. This allows to give an *approximate solution* to the system giving the cumulative effects, where all items with a summation sign are geometric series, whose common ratio is approximated by $(1+\alpha)^{-1}$. The solution is given below.

The 'cumulative' effects of PFI *as a function of* Y^h_t *and t*

$$Y^*_t = Y^h_t\left\{1 - (\alpha - (\pi^h - \rho - \pi^h\tau_P))\,\frac{k^h}{k^0}\,\frac{(1+\alpha)^t - 1}{\alpha(1+\alpha)^t}\right\} + \frac{S^*_{Pt} + S^*_{Gt} + B^*_t}{k^0}\,\frac{(1+\alpha)^t - 1}{\alpha(1+\alpha)^t} \qquad \text{(i')}$$

$$B^*_t = \frac{\left\{\varphi_m(1+m^h) - \varphi_e(1+e^h) + \rho k^h + \lambda k^h\right\}Y^h_t + \mu(1+m^0)\,Y^*_t}{1 - \theta\left[\dfrac{(1+\alpha)^t - 1}{\alpha(1+\alpha)^t}\right]} \qquad \text{(ii')}$$

$$S^*_{Pt} = \sigma\,Y^*_t \qquad \text{(iii')}$$

1 An idea of the degree of approximation can be seen comparing

$$\sum_{i=0}^{t-1} Y^h_i \quad \text{and} \quad \sum_{i=0}^{t} Y^h_i\,.$$

The ratio between the latter and the former, instead of being equal to $(1+\alpha)$, as it should be if α were the exact rate of growth of the cumulative effects, is given by

$$\frac{(1+\alpha)^{t+1} - 1}{(1+\alpha)^t - 1} = (1+\alpha)\,\frac{(1+\alpha)^t - \dfrac{1}{(1+\alpha)}}{(1+\alpha)^t - 1} > (1+\alpha)\,.$$

However, since some items of the cumulative effects do grow at the rate α, the degree of approximation is even closer to α.

$$S^*_{Gt} = Y^h_t \left\{ \tau_P \pi^h k^h + \tau_W w^h + \tau_{\text{IND}} + \tau_M \varphi_m (1 + m^h) + \right.$$

$$\left. + \tau_E \varphi_e (1 + e^h) - g^h k^h \right\} + (\tau_{\text{IND}} + \tau_P \pi^0 + \tau_W w^0)$$

$$(Y^*_t - Y^h_t) + \tau_M \mu (1 + m^0) Y^* . \qquad \text{(iv')}$$

The approximation between the rate of growth of the PFI capital stock (or gross value added) and the one of the cumulative effects seems quite reasonable; since the PFI capital stock grows at a rate α, it can be expected, as a consequence, that the rate of growth of its cumulative effects is also α.

In the system given above it would have been possible to substitute (ii'), (iii') and (iv') into (i') and get directly the formulation of the income cumulative effect in t; the system was left with all four equations in order to point out the interdependence which exists among the four effects.

CHAPTER VII

THE 'MARGINAL' EFFECTS OF PFI

7.1. INTRODUCTION

The approach developed in the previous pages requires, for its practical applications, that the LDC's economy and its two sectors (including the PFI sector) behave exactly according to the model of Chapter II. Since some assumptions are quite crucial, like the rate of growth of the PFI capital stock (and gross value added) constant over time, it might be useful to look for a simpler approach.

This will be done in this chapter. Although, generally speaking, the 'cumulative' effects give a better answer to the question of the economic effects of PFI, the 'marginal' approach which will be developed here and which will be explained in the next section might prove useful in many practical situations, with little data availability, or an irregular behaviour of the PFI sector.

Again, the analysis will concentrate on the same four effects as in the previous chapters, although it could be extended to the income distribution effect (through the effect on wages and profits), to the effect on employment, and to the substitution effect. These points will be reconsidered in Chapter VIII.

7.2. A 'MARGINAL' APPROACH AND THE RELATED PROBLEMS

A simplification, with respect to the cumulative approach previously developed, consists in considering the changes in the endogenous variables corresponding to the four effects (Y_t, S_{Pt}, S_{Gt}, B_t) which occur in a given time period (i.e. from t to t+1) as a consequence of PFI, assuming that it was present up to time t, and that one is simply interested in finding out the changes which occur in those variable as a consequence of the presence of PFI from t to t+1.

This is quite different from what was done in the two previous chapters. There PFI was considered once present from 0 to t, and once absent from 0 to t, while here the interest is in the 'marginal' effects, with respect to a given situation in t (i.e. the changes from t to t+1), assuming that PFI is already there in t[1].

The marginal income effect, $\overline{Y}_t$, would still be determined by the marginal effects of PFI on S_P, S_G and B in the previous time period, due to the lag of domestic investments in the production function (Equation (38)) and of the debt term in the b.o.p. effect. Consequently, developing this approach, the result would be:

$$\overline{\overline{Y}}_t = f_Y(\overline{\overline{S}}_{Pt-1}, \overline{\overline{S}}_{Gt-1}, \overline{\overline{B}}_{t-1})$$
$$\overline{\overline{B}}_t = f_B(\overline{\overline{Y}}_t, \overline{\overline{B}}_{t-1})$$
$$\overline{\overline{S}}_{Pt} = f_{Sp}(\overline{\overline{Y}}_t)$$
$$\overline{\overline{S}}_{Gt} = f_{Sg}(\overline{\overline{Y}}_t).$$

This (linear) system would still include other terms (base-year variables and parameters) given by the model, which are omitted here. In order to avoid the presence of lagged endogenous variables, two approaches could be followed:

(a) to stick strictly to the assumption of this 'marginal' approach, and assume that all variables in t are given, including S_{Pt}, S_{Gt}, B_t, without looking for the effect of PFI on them in the previous period; this would lead to:

$$\overline{\overline{Y}}_t = \text{fully given}$$
$$\overline{\overline{B}}_t = f_B(\overline{\overline{Y}}_t)$$
$$\overline{\overline{S}}_{Pt} = f_{Sp}(\overline{\overline{Y}}_t)$$
$$\overline{\overline{S}}_{Gt} = f_{Sg}(\overline{\overline{Y}}_t)$$

in this case, much of the relevance of the analysis would be lost;

(b) to find some way of eliminating the time lag, in order to arrive to;

$$\overline{\overline{Y}}_t = f_Y(\overline{\overline{S}}_{Pt}, \overline{\overline{S}}_{Gt}, \overline{\overline{B}}_t)$$
$$\overline{\overline{B}}_t = f_B(\overline{\overline{Y}}_t, \overline{\overline{B}}_t)$$
$$\overline{\overline{S}}_{Pt} = f_{Sp}(\overline{\overline{Y}}_t)$$
$$\overline{\overline{S}}_{Gt} = f_{Sg}(\overline{\overline{Y}}_t)$$

1 The marginal effect on a given variable from t to t+1 will be denoted by = E.g.: $\overline{\overline{Y}}_t$.
A comparison between the two approaches will be given in Chapter VIII. The reader might also find it useful to refer to the figure given in Section 8.1.

This second approach, aiming at getting the four effects in a system of linear equations without any time lag, will be attempted here.

Similarly to what was done for the cumulative effects, one could investigate the relations between the effects of one year, and the ones of the previous year, and thus eliminate the time lag.

In order to do this first the marginal effects on the b.o.p. and private and public savings in t, assuming $\bar{\bar{Y}}_t$ given, will be studied. Then $\bar{\bar{Y}}_t$ will be established, after having found the time behaviour of the marginal effects of PFI.

7.3. THE MARGINAL EFFECT ON THE B.O.P.

From Equation (25), and taking into account what was said in Chapter V about the debt effect, the marginal effect on the b.o.p. is given by:

$$\bar{\bar{B}}_t = (M^h_{Ct+1} - M^h_{Ct}) + (M^h_{Zt+1} - M^h_{Zt}) - (E^h_{Ct+1} - E^h_{Ct}) - $$
$$- (E^h_{Zt+1} - E^h_{Zt}) + (N^h_{t+1} - N^h_t) + (Q^h_{t+1} - Q^h_t) +$$
$$+ \mu(1 + m^0)\bar{\bar{Y}}_t + \theta\bar{\bar{B}}_{t-1}$$

The last term stands for the increase in the foreign debt due to PFI in the previous year. Assuming that there is a fixed relationship between $\bar{\bar{B}}_t$ and $\bar{\bar{B}}_{t-1}$ of the type:

$$\bar{\bar{B}}_t = (1 + \zeta)\bar{\bar{B}}_{t-1}$$

the last item can be expressed in terms of $\bar{\bar{B}}_t$.

A further assumption is that there is no variation in J_t (factor income payments from abroad) as a consequence of PFI.

In terms of $\bar{\bar{Y}}_t$, Y^h_t, and parameters, the marginal effect on the b.o.p. is:

$$\bar{\bar{B}}_t = \frac{\left[\varphi_m(1 + m^h) - \varphi_e(1 + e^h) + \rho k^h + \lambda k^h\right]\alpha Y^h_t}{1 - \dfrac{\theta}{1 + \zeta}} +$$
$$+ \frac{\mu(1 + m^0)\bar{\bar{Y}}_t}{1 - \dfrac{\theta}{1 + \zeta}}. \qquad \text{(ii)}$$

7.4. THE MARGINAL EFFECT ON PRIVATE SAVINGS

From Equation (26), it follows:

$$\bar{\bar{S}}_{Pt} = \sigma \bar{\bar{Y}}_t \,. \tag{iii}$$

7.5. THE MARGINAL EFFECT ON PUBLIC SAVINGS

Something similar to what was done in Chapter V, has to be done here, in order to get the marginal effect of PFI on taxation.

The marginal effect on *profits* for the rest of the economy is:

$$\bar{\bar{P}}_t^0 = \pi^0 \, (\bar{\bar{Y}}_t - \alpha Y_t^h) \,.$$

The marginal effect on *wages and salaries* for the rest of the economy is:

$$\bar{\bar{W}}_t^0 = w^0 \, (\bar{\bar{Y}}_t - \alpha Y_t^h) \,.$$

The marginal effect on *imports of goods and services* for the rest of the economy is:

$$\bar{\bar{M}}_t^0 = (1 + m^0) \, \mu \, \bar{\bar{Y}}_t \,.$$

It is now possible to get the marginal effect of PFI on the single items of current revenue for the rest of the economy.

The marginal effect on *indirect taxation* for the rest of the economy is:

$$\bar{\bar{T}}_{\mathrm{IND}t} = \tau_{\mathrm{IND}} \, (\bar{\bar{Y}}_t - \alpha Y_t^h).$$

The marginal effect on *taxes on profits* for the rest of the economy is:

$$\bar{\bar{T}}_{Pt}^{\,0} = \tau_P \, \pi^0 \, (\bar{\bar{Y}}_t - \alpha Y_t^h) \,.$$

The marginal effect on *taxes on wages and salaries* for the rest of the economy is:

$$\bar{\bar{T}}_{Wt}^0 = \tau_W w^0 \, (\bar{\bar{Y}}_t - \alpha \bar{\bar{Y}}_t^h) \,.$$

The marginal effect on *taxes on imports* for the rest of the economy is:

$$\bar{\bar{T}}_{Mt}^0 = \tau_M \, \mu (1 + m^0) \, \bar{\bar{Y}}_t \,.$$

The marginal effect on the *exogenous component of taxation* is assumed to be zero:

$$\overline{\overline{T}}^0_{\mathrm{OTH}t} = 0 \,.$$

As for government *expenditure*, there is no effect on expenditure for the rest of the economy (Equation (29)), while, of course, expenditure in the PFI sector is affected (Equation (13)).

Consequently, the *marginal effect of PFI on public savings* (Equation (37)) is given by:

$$\overline{\overline{S}}_{Gt} = \overline{\overline{T}}^0_t - \overline{\overline{G}}^0_t + (T^h_{t+1} - T^h_t) - (G^h_{t+1} - G^h_t)\,,$$

where:

$T^h_{t+1} - T^h_t$ is easily obtainable from the model (with the assumption that $\overline{\overline{T}}^h_{\mathrm{OTH}t} = 0$);

$G^h_{t+1} - G^h_t$ is also easily obtainable from the model (Equation (13));

$\overline{\overline{T}}^0_t = \overline{\overline{T}}^0_{\mathrm{IND}t} + \overline{\overline{T}}^0_{Pt} + \overline{\overline{T}}^0_{Wt} + \overline{\overline{T}}^0_{Mt}$;

$\overline{\overline{G}}^0_t = 0$.

Working out the above expressions, it is possible to get the marginal effect on public savings in terms of parameters, Y^h_t, and $\overline{\overline{Y}}_t$:

$$\begin{aligned}\overline{\overline{S}}_{Gt} = \alpha Y^h_t \Big[& \tau_P \pi^h k^h + \tau_W w^h + \tau_M \varphi_m (1 + m^h) + \tau_E \varphi_e \times \\ & \times (1 + e^h) + \tau_{\mathrm{IND}} - g^h k^h \Big] + \Big[\tau_{\mathrm{IND}} + \tau_P \pi^0 + \tau_W w^0\Big] \times \\ & \times (\overline{\overline{Y}}_t - \alpha Y^h_t) + \tau_M \mu (1 + m^0)\, \overline{\overline{Y}}_t \,. \qquad \text{(iv)}\end{aligned}$$

7.6. THE TIME BEHAVIOUR OF THE MARGINAL EFFECTS

Let's assume that there exists the following relation:

$$\overline{\overline{Y}}_{t+1} = (1 + \xi)\, \overline{\overline{Y}}_t \,,$$

where

$$\bar{\bar{Y}}_t = \alpha Y_t^h - \frac{F_{Dt}}{k^0} + \frac{\bar{\bar{S}}_{Pt-1} + \bar{\bar{S}}_{Gt-1} + \bar{\bar{B}}_{t-1}}{k^0}$$

$$\bar{\bar{Y}}_{t+1} = \alpha Y_{t+1}^h - \frac{F_{Dt+1}}{k^0} + \frac{\bar{\bar{S}}_{Pt} + \bar{\bar{S}}_{Gt} + \bar{\bar{B}}_t}{k^0} .$$

The derivation of the above expressions, although quite evident from what has been done so far, will be given in the next section.

Since:

$$Y_{t+1}^h = (1 + \alpha)\, Y_t^h$$

$$F_{Dt+1} = (1 + \alpha) F_{Dt}$$

$$\bar{\bar{S}}_{Pt} = (1 + \xi) \bar{\bar{S}}_{Pt-1}$$

$$\bar{\bar{S}}_{Gt} = a\,(1 + \alpha) + b\,(1 + \xi) \quad \text{where} \quad a + b = \bar{\bar{S}}_{Gt-1}$$

$$\bar{\bar{B}}_t = c\,(1 + \alpha) + d\,(1 + \xi) \quad \text{where} \quad c + d = \bar{\bar{B}}_{t-1}$$ [2] .

It is possible, now, to add up this various items, in a proper way, in order to get:

$$\bar{\bar{Y}}_{t+1} = e\,(1 + \alpha) + f(1 + \xi) \quad \text{where} \quad e + f = \bar{\bar{Y}}_t .$$

Since α is fixed, it follows that

$$\alpha = \xi$$

furthermore, for the b.o.p. marginal effect, it follows that:

$$\alpha = \zeta .$$

2 In Section 7.3 it was assumed that there exists a relationship between $\bar{\bar{B}}_t$ and $\bar{\bar{B}}_{t-1}$ of the following nature:

$$\bar{\bar{B}}_t = (1 + \zeta)\, \bar{\bar{B}}_{t-1}$$

It can be proved similarly to what was done for the cumulative effects in 6.5 that ζ is a weighted average between α and ξ and consequently, considering the additive nature of the various items of $\bar{\bar{B}}_t$ with respect to either $\bar{\bar{Y}}_t$ or Y_t^h, it is correct to assume that the marginal effect on the deficit of the b.o.p. is composed of two items, whose rate of growth is, respectively, α and ξ, as it was done above in the text.

Thus, a way to solve the time-lag problem has been found, and also it has been proved that the marginal effects of PFI grow at the same compound rate as the PFI capital stock.

7.7. THE MARGINAL EFFECT ON INCOME

On the basis of what has been proved in the previous section, the following relations hold:

$$\bar{\bar{S}}_{Pt} = (1 + \alpha)\bar{\bar{S}}_{Pt-1}$$

$$\bar{\bar{S}}_{Gt} = (1 + \alpha)\bar{\bar{S}}_{Gt-1}$$

$$\bar{\bar{B}}_t = (1 + \alpha)\bar{\bar{B}}_{t-1} .$$

Consequently, it is possible to calculate the marginal effect of PFI on income. The overall increase in income is:

$$\Delta Y_t = \Delta Y_t^h + \frac{S_{Pt} + S_{Gt} + B_t - F_{Dt}}{k^0}$$

in the last item, the components of I_t^0 have been already substituted. The increase in income imputable to the rest of the economy is given by:

$$\frac{(S_{Pt} - \bar{\bar{S}}_{Pt-1}) + (B_t - \bar{\bar{B}}_{t-1}) + (S_{Gt} - \bar{\bar{S}}_{Gt-1})}{k^0}$$

since from private and public savings, and from the foreign capital inflow (equal to the deficit of the b.o.p.) one must deduct the share imputable, from $t-1$ to t, to PFI. This is given by the marginal effects of PFI on the three variables in $t-1$.

Consequently, the marginal effect on income is given by:

$$\bar{\bar{Y}}_t = \alpha Y_t^h - \frac{F_{Dt}}{k^0} + \frac{\bar{\bar{S}}_{Pt-1} + \bar{\bar{S}}_{Gt-1} + \bar{\bar{B}}_{t-1}}{k^0} .$$

Taking into consideration the relations given above, the effect, in terms of Y_t^h, and the other three effects, without any lag, is:

$$\overline{\overline{Y}}_t = \alpha Y_t^h - \left[\alpha - (\pi - \rho - \tau_P \pi_t^h\right] Y_t^h \frac{k^h}{k^0} + \frac{\overline{\overline{S}}_{Pt} + \overline{\overline{S}}_{Gt} + \overline{\overline{B}}_t}{k^0 (1+\alpha)} . \qquad \text{(i)}$$

7.8. THE FORMULATION OF THE FOUR MARGINAL EFFECTS AND THEIR ECONOMIC INTERPRETATION

$$\overline{\overline{Y}}_t = \alpha Y_t^h - \left[\alpha - (\pi^h - \rho - \tau_P \pi^h)\right] Y_t^h \frac{k^h}{k^0} + \frac{\overline{\overline{S}}_{Pt} + \overline{\overline{S}}_{Gt} + B_t}{k^0 (1+\alpha)} \qquad \text{(i)}$$

$$\overline{\overline{B}}_t = \frac{\left[\varphi_m (1 + m^h) - \varphi_e (1 + e^h) + \rho k^h + \lambda k^h\right] \alpha Y_t^h}{1 - \dfrac{\theta}{1+\alpha}} +$$

$$+ \frac{\mu (1 + m^0) \overline{\overline{Y}}_t}{1 - \dfrac{\theta}{1+\alpha}} \qquad \text{(ii)}$$

$$\overline{\overline{S}}_{Pt} = \sigma \overline{\overline{Y}}_t \qquad \text{(iii)}$$

$$\overline{\overline{S}}_{Gt} = \alpha Y_t^h \left[\tau_P \pi^h k^h + \tau_W w^h + \tau_{\text{IND}} + \tau_M \varphi_m (1 + m^h) + \right.$$

$$\left. + \tau_E \varphi_e (1 + e^h) - g^h k^h\right] + \left[\tau_{\text{IND}} + \tau_P \pi^0 + \tau_W w^0\right] \times$$

$$\times (\overline{\overline{Y}}_t - \alpha Y_t^h) + \tau_M \mu (1 + m^0) \overline{\overline{Y}}_t . \qquad \text{(iv)}$$

The four marginal effects, as a function of each other, of the PFI gross value added in t (Y_t^h), and of the parameters are given above. This system of four linear equations can be solved, and its solution would give all four effects simultaneously.

Similarly to what was done for the cumulative effects, it is possible to comment briefly upon the economic relevance of the above formulations.

The marginal effect on income (Equation (i)) is given by three additive terms. The first one is easily interpretable. It is, out of the total marginal effect, the share given by the increase in PFI gross value added from t to t+1.

The second term stands for the decrease in financial availabilities for domestic investments caused by the share absorbed by PFI (F_{Dt}). Being a decrease in domestic investments, its influence on the marginal effect on income comes through the domestic capital-output ratio (k^0).

Also the PFI capital-output ratio is present, since F_{Dt} is related to K^h_{t-1}, and not to Y^h_t. The parameters of this second term stand for the difference between the increase in the PFI capital stock and the share of PFI profits reinvested. The latter is given by total PFI profits (determined by π^h), minus taxes ($\tau_p \pi^h$), minus the share transferred abroad (ρ). This second term affects negatively the marginal income effect. However, its influence may become positive, provided that

$$(\pi^h - \rho - \tau_p \pi^h) > \alpha,$$

i.e., that the share of profits reinvested is larger that the addition to the PFI capital stock, and consequently it accrues to total availabilities for domestic investments.

This does not seem to be a very likely case; it would mean an increase in private foreign portfolio investments in other domestic firms, or an increase in private foreign deposits in domestic banks.

At the most, it seems that an equality might hold, meaning that the increase in the PFI capital stock is exactly financed by PFI profit reinvested ($F_{Dt} = 0$)[3].

The third term giving the marginal income effect stands for the increase in domestic investments (weighted by the domestic capital-output ratio), split into its three components. These are, in turn, marginal effects given by the other three equations. Since there is a one-year lag, and since their time behaviour is known, they are corrected in order to take this into account.

The marginal effect on the b.o.p. (Equation (ii)) is given by a ratio. In the denominator there appears a correction, to take into account the debt effect, and to eliminate any lag.

The two additive terms in the numerator stand, respectively, for the PFI sector marginal effects on the b.o.p. (through its import requirements, export promotion and import substitution, and transfer of profits) and for the indirect effect, through the increase in income caused by PFI ($\bar{\bar{Y}}_t$) and the marginal propensity to import.

3 This point, connected with the assumptions of the model on the financial mechanism for the annual additions to PFI, will be further commented in Section 8.7.

The marginal effect on private savings (Equation (iii)) is directly related to the marginal income effect, and it is quite easily interpretable.

The marginal effect on public savings (Equation (iv)) is given by three additive terms.

The first one represents the direct effect of the PFI sector, i.e. the increase in taxes on profits and wages, indirect taxes, taxes on imports, taxes on exports, and increase in public expenditure directly related to PFI.

The second term gives the indirect effect of PFI for the rest of the economy on indirect taxation, on taxes on profits, and on taxes on wages, while the third gives the indirect effect on taxes on imports.

Also here, as for the cumulative effects, it would be possible to introduce some variations, to take into account various practical situations. This point will be discussed in Chapter X.

CHAPTER VIII

CUMULATIVE AND MARGINAL EFFECTS COMPARED

8.1. CUMULATIVE VS MARGINAL EFFECTS

The solution given for the cumulative effects is based on the fact that they have an approximate constant rate of growth when the PFI capital stock (or gross value added) behaves in accordance with the model, i.e. it grows at a constant rate.

Before considering the practical applicability of the two approaches it is possible to compare the solution for the cumulative effects (Section 6.5) with the solution for the marginal effects (Section 7.8).[1]

The simplest relation which might be expected is

$$Y_t^* = \sum_{i=0}^{t-1} \bar{\bar{Y}}_i$$

or

$$Y_{t+1}^* - Y_t^* = \bar{\bar{Y}}_t$$

for the income effect, and for the other three effects.

A first problem is created by B_t^* (Equation (ii')), since the correction for the debt is different from the one in $\bar{\bar{B}}_t$ (Equation (ii)). The former has to take into consideration all previous *cumulative* b.o.p. effects, while the latter takes into consideration only the previous marginal b.o.p. effect.

Apart from this, a relation between the two effects like the one discussed above would hold for Equations (ii) and (ii'), (iii) and (iii'), (iv) and (iv'), if it were valid for (i) and (i'), i.e. for the income effect. But this is not true, for a similar reason as for the b.o.p. effect.

This point can better be seen considering the two income effects formulation (the cumulative in terms of increases):

1 Both sets of solutions are numbered with roman numbers. The cumulative effects equations have, however, the mark' to distinguish them from the corresponding marginal effects equations.

$$(1)\qquad Y^*_{t+1} - Y^*_t = \alpha Y^h_t - \frac{F_{Dt}}{k^0} + \frac{S^*_{Pt} + S^*_{Gt} + B^*_t}{k^0}$$

$$(2)\qquad \bar{\bar{Y}}_t = \alpha Y^h_t - \frac{F_{Dt}}{k^0} + \frac{\bar{\bar{S}}_{Pt} + \bar{\bar{S}}_{Gt} + \bar{\bar{B}}_t}{k^0(1+\alpha)} .$$

But since

$$\frac{S^*_{Pt} + S^*_{Gt} + B^*_t}{k^0} \neq \frac{\bar{\bar{S}}_{Pt} + \bar{\bar{S}}_{Gt} + \bar{\bar{B}}_t}{k^0(1+\alpha)}$$

it follows that

$$(1) \neq (2) .$$

Consequently, the relation assumed between the cumulative and marginal effects does not hold. If a relation exists, it is different, and it cannot be formulated in a simple way, like the one analysed above.

Figure 1 below gives a graphical representation of the two income effects.

The *cumulative effect* in time t is given by AC, since C is income in t with PFI from 0 to t, and A is income in t without PFI from 0 to t.

The *marginal effect* is given by DE, since E is income in t+1 with PFI from

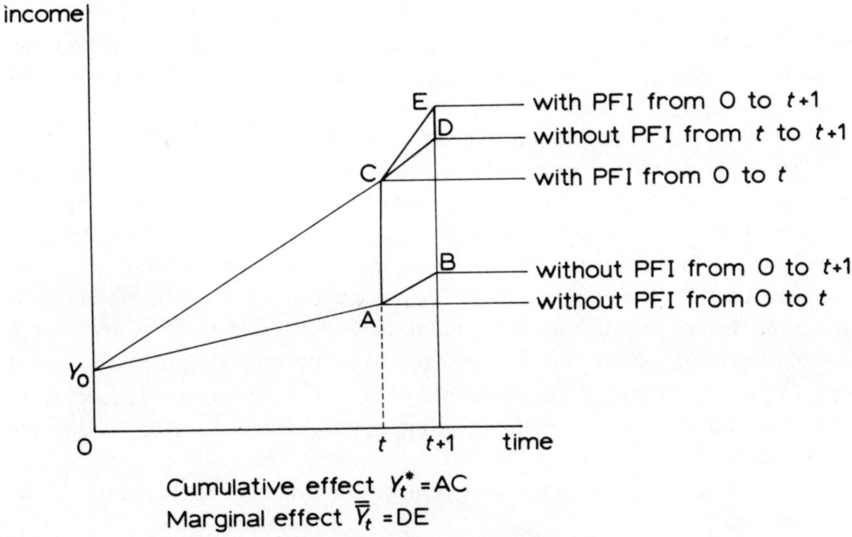

Fig. 1. The 'marginal' and 'cumulative' effects.

0 to t+1, while D is income in t+1 considering PFI absent from t to t+1.

The relation assumed at the beginning of this section would hold if $AC = BD$, where B is income in t+1 without PFI from 0 to t+1. But, again, this relation is rejected, since it is possible to show that

$$DE \neq (EB - AC)$$

which means that

$$BD \neq AC.$$

This is so because DE (income marginal effect) is affected only by the marginal effects on private and public savings, and on the b.o.p., apart from the other items given by the model, while $BE - AC$ (increase in the cumulative effect) is affected by the cumulative effects on private and public savings, and on the b.o.p. which are different, by definition, from the marginal ones.

8.2. PRACTICAL APPLICATIONS OF CUMULATIVE AND MARGINAL EFFECTS

As for the empirical use of the model, the definitions and the assumptions underlying the two different approaches point out their different practical use.

The *cumulative effects* give the total effects of PFI in t on the economy, and are obtained by difference considering two situations, one with PFI from 0 to t and one without PFI from 0 to t. The formulas given in Section 6.5 are applicable only if the rate of growth of the PFI capital stock (and gross value added) is constant. Otherwise, the cumulative effects can be obtained only by applying year by year their original formulations.

Moreover, t must be explicitly given.

The *marginal effects* refer only to the effects imputable to PFI in a given period (i.e. from t to $t + 1$), assuming that PFI is present in t, and comparing the two alternative increases which would take place in the variable standing for a given effect from t to t+1 under the assumptions of the presence and of the absence, for that period, of PFI. Consequently, it is not necessary that the time behaviour of the PFI capital stock (or gross value added) has a constant rate of growth, but it is enough to know the PFI gross value added in t (Y_t^h), and its rate of growth from t–1 to t, and from t to t+1, apart from the structural parameters of the economy, and of the two sectors, if they are different.

From these considerations there follows the practical applicability of the two approaches.

If the PFI capital stock behaves in accordance with the model, then the cumulative approach can be applied. Otherwise, if only data for one or two years are given, the marginal approach can be used.

8.3. A NUMERICAL EXERCISE AND SOME VARIATIONS FOR THE MARGINAL AND THE CUMULATIVE EFFECTS

The various alternatives considered are summarized in the table on pages 122 and 123, which also gives the results for the four marginal and cumulative effects.

Alternative 1 is the basic alternative; in the others only the numerical values of the parameters which change are given, while all the others remain the same as in alternative 1.[2]

Y_t^h is assumed to be 100; consequently, the results can also be interpreted as percentages of the PFI gross value added in t.

The parameter t (time) applies obviously only to the case of the cumulative effects. As it was explained on the previous pages, and with reference to this particular case, the time consideration for the two sets of exercises is as follows:

- the *marginal effects* point out what happens as a consequence of the presence of PFI *from* t *to* $t+1$ to the increase of the four variables corresponding to the effects from t to $t+1$;
- the *cumulative effects* point out what happens as a consequence of the presence of PFI *from* $t-5$ *to* t, to the four variables corresponding to the effects, and considered in time t;

in both cases the 'alternative situation' is established on the basis of the methodological framework set up in the previous chapters. The main purpose of this exercise is to give an idea of what, under various circumstances, the marginal and cumulative effects are in practice; furthermore, it is useful to provide an appraisal of the sensitivity of the results of the model when some of the parameters change.

Although it is possible to compare the variations in the case of the marginal effects with the ones in the case of the cumulative effects, one must keep in mind what was said in Section 8.1 about the former *vis-à-vis* the latter, and that there is no straightforward correspondence between the two.

2 Alternative 3 needs a further explanation. Since PFI profits are related to the PFI capital stock, a higher capital-output ratio implies higher profits, with respect to PFI gross value added. Consequently, the share going to wages and salaries was assumed to be less than in the basic alternative. In this case profits become 70% of Y_t^h, while, in all other alternatives, they are 50%. The share of wages, usually 50%, is consequently decreased to 30%.

Marginal and cumulative effects for alternative values of the parameters

Parameters	Alternatives 1	2	3	4	5
Y_t^h	100				
α	0.05			0.02	0.08
π^h	0.20				
ρ	0.10				
λ	0.02				
τ_P	0.40				
k^h	2.5		3.5		
k^0	3	4			
φ_m	0.20				
$(1+m^h)$	1.20				
φ_e	0.25				
$(1+e^h)$	1.20				
μ	0.12				
$(1+m^0)$	1.20				
θ	0.06				
σ	0.12				
τ_W	0.10				
w^h	0.50		0.30		
τ_{IND}	0.05				
τ_M	0.15				
τ_E	0.10				
g^h	0.05				
π^0	0.30				
w^0	0.70				
t	5				
Marginal effects	**1**	**2**	**3**	**4**	**5**
$\bar{\bar{Y}}_t$	3.50	3.93	2.65	2.62	4.35
$\bar{\bar{B}}_t$	1.81	1.87	2.31	0.91	2.69
$\bar{\bar{S}}_{Pt}$	0.42	0.47	0.32	0.31	0.52
$\bar{\bar{S}}_{Gt}$	0.92	1.03	1.01	0.68	1.16
Cumulative effects	**1**	**2**	**3**	**4**	**5**
Y_t^*	749.07	328.78	885.86	1482.97	482.97
B_t^*	178.14	95.90	219.11	328.45	122.47
S_{Pt}^*	89.89	39.45	106.30	177.96	57.95
S_{Gt}^*	189.23	83.51	229.63	373.82	122.28

Alternatives							
6	7	8	9	10	11	12	13
0.12	0.07						
			0	0			0.04
		0.30					
				0.40			
			0.40				
					0.16	0.08	
		0.05					
		0.08					
		0					
							0

6	7	8	9	10	11	12	13
1.60	6.34	5.35	3.06	3.92	3.55	3.45	3.84
1.78	1.84	2.09	0.52	2.87	1.81	1.79	2.12
0.19	0.76	0.64	0.37	0.47	0.57	0.28	0.46
0.44	1.64	1.01	0.88	1.22	0.93	0.91	1.63

6	7	8	9	10	11	12	13
754.20	720.02	695.60	509.64	955.50	1075.87	564.56	890.57
184.79	161.31	167.03	99.75	242.57	240.14	141.42	211.12
90.50	86.40	83.47	61.16	114.66	172.14	45.17	106.87
190.52	181.92	164.70	130.44	243.07	271.42	142.82	237.32

Finally, before analysing the results for the various alternatives, one other point should be considered.

In appraising the effects of PFI, it was stressed above how one should take into account the direct and indirect effects simultaneously. Since $Y_t^h = 100$, it is possible to point out here the direct effect in the two cases, and then, in each of the alternatives given below, to check this direct effect with the overall income effect, in order to find out the share imputable to the indirect effects.

In the case of the marginal effects, the direct income effect is given by αY_t^h. This is 5 in all cases, except alternative 4 ($\alpha Y_t^h = 2$) and alternative 5 ($\alpha Y_t^h = 8$).

In the case of the cumulative effects, the direct income effect is given by Y_t^h, which equals 100 in all cases.

In both sets of calculations the level of α measuring the rate of growth of the stock of PFI, will be one of the crucial elements in determining the overall results. In the case of the *marginal effects* one can notice, how, *ceteris paribus*, the lower α, the higher the indirect effects. This can be seen considering alternative 1, 4 and 5, and confronting the income effect with the direct effect of PFI on income as given by αY_t^h. This is explained mainly by the way the financial mechanism for the annual additions to PFI works, and this point will be discussed at length in the following pages (see also Section 8.7). The reasoning for the income effect applies also to the other ones, which depend upon it.

In the case of the *cumulative effects*, one can notice again that there is an inverse relationship between α and the results for the income effect. This can be seen, again, looking at alternatives 1, 4 and 5. This is also partly explained by the way the financial mechanism of the model operates, as well as by the fact that the higher α, the smaller the indirect effects which 'accumulate' over the previous years. And this also applies to the other three cumulative effects.

Alternative 1 is the basic alternative, and, as it was said before, provides the basic solution.

Alternative 2 assumes a higher capital-output ratio for the domestic sector. The income marginal effect is directly affected, and, consequently, also the others. The income marginal effect is higher because, *ceteris paribus*, as a consequence of a higher capital-output ratio, the decrease in domestic investments which occurs as a consequence of a partial domestic financing of PFI (F_{Dt}) affects less the growth of income.

The opposite happens in the case of the cumulative effects, which become smaller due to the fact that, given certain indirect effects on investments for the 'rest of the economy', a higher k^0 means that the resulting income effect will be smaller. The other three effects are then affected accordingly.

Alternative 3 assumes a higher capital-output ratio for the PFI sector. Due to the formulation of the model, PFI investments have a lower productivity, but yield higher profits (and this is the reason why wages are assumed to be less with respect to Y_t^h). The marginal income effect becomes much lower, the private savings effect derives accordingly, while the b.o.p. and public savings effects are relatively higher.

The cumulative effects are affected to a minor extent, and they become larger with respect to the basic solution, due also to the fact that now the indirect (negative) contribution to income, imputable to the financial mechanism, is smaller, although now the (positive) share imputable to the other indirect effects (last term of Equation (i')), (Section 6.5) is also smaller.

Alternative 4 assumes a lower rate of growth of the PFI capital stock. It can, as a consequence, be expected that all marginal effects become smaller, although, following the reasoning given above on this point, the indirect effects become positive, while in the basic solution they were negative. What was said above about the cumulative effects can be seen here, where they become much larger, with respect to the basic solution, due to the inverse relationship between α and the level of the results.

Alternative 5 assumes a higher rate of growth of the PFI capital stock. Contrary to what happened above, all marginal effects become larger, with respect to the basic solution, although now the indirect effects are much less, following, again, the discussion given about the relations between the level of α and the level of the results. The same happens for the cumulative results, which, for the reasons seen above, are now much less, with respect to the basic solution.

Alternative 6 assumes that the required rate of transfer of profits to abroad is higher. The whole addition to the PFI capital stock is financed from domestic sources (i.e. all PFI profits after taxes are transferred abroad). Consequently, financial resources available for domestic investments become much less, and income growth is much less. The b.o.p. is affected by the higher transfer of profits, while both public and private savings vary according to the income marginal effect.

The cumulative effects are affected to a negligible extent, since for them the working of the financial mechanism for the annual additions to PFI affects the results to a lesser extent, being compensated to a larger extent, by the indirect effects, as expressed by the last term of Equation (i') (Section 6.5).

Alternative 7 assumes that the required rate of transfer of profits is lower. The whole addition to the PFI capital stock is financed from PFI sources ($F_{Dt} = 0$). Income growth is much higher, due to the smaller rate of transfer of profits, while, again, public and private savings vary according to the income marginal effect.

As in the previous case, the cumulative effects are affected to a negligible extent, since the (negative) indirect effects through investments for the 'rest of the economy' (via the financial mechanism for the annual additions to PFI) are compensated by the (positive) indirect effects given by the last term of Equation (i') (Section 6.5).

Alternative 8 assumes a lower taxation coefficient on profits, combined with a lower taxation coefficient on wages, a higher indirect taxation coefficient, and no taxes on exports. A higher share of PFI profits is reinvested, and, consequently, more domestic resources are available for domestic investments. Growth is higher, while the relative position of the b.o.p. and private savings effects is not affected. Public savings are relatively lower, with respect to $\overline{\overline{Y}}_t$, due to the different structure of taxation. The cumulative effects vary in the opposite direction, and they become slightly less than the ones of the basic solution, being, on the whole, affected by these variations only to a negligible extent, as a consequence of the fact, as observed above for various cases, that the indirect effects, positive of negative, compensate to a larger extent.

Alternative 9 assumes more export promotion and import substitution from the PFI sector, combined with no payments to abroad for 'know-how'. This has a positive effect on the deficit, lowering it. But since the b.o.p. deficit is growth promoting, also income growth becomes less, although this is partly offset by the relative increase in taxation (on exports) and on public savings.

Something similar happens to the cumulative effects, where the deficit of the b.o.p. is almost one half of the one of the basic solution, with a subsequent effect on income.

Alternative 10 assumes more import requirements for the PFI sector, combined with no payments to abroad for 'know-how'. The deficit of the b.o.p.

becomes higher and also public savings are relatively higher. Consequently, the income growth effect is strengthened.

Again, the same happens to the cumulative effects, where both the b.o.p. deficit and public savings become larger, with a positive influence on the income effect.

Alternative 11 assumes a higher marginal propensity to save. This has a positive effect on income growth, with respect to the basic alternative, in the case of the marginal effects. It applies to a much greater extent to the cumulative effects, since the indirect effect on private savings through the increase in income 'cumulates' over the five-year period considered.

Alternative 12 assumes a lower marginal propensity to save, and this has an effect on growth contrary to the previous alternative. In both cases, also the other two marginal effects ($\bar{\bar{B}}_t$ and $\bar{\bar{S}}_{Gt}$) are slightly affected. The opposite, with respect to the previous alternative, happens to the cumulative effects, which become much less.

Alternative 13 finally, assumes that there is no current public expenditure directly related to the PFI sector, combined with payments to abroad for 'know-how' twice as much with respect to the basic solution. Both in the marginal and in the cumulative results, the first variation has a positive effect on public savings, which influence accordingly the income results, while the second assumption affects the b.o.p., with an increase in the deficit, and consequently, again, a positive influence on the income effect.

Apart from the specific comments related to each single alternative, some general considerations are possible.

Let us concentrate first on the *marginal effects*. Only in a few cases (4, 7, 8) the growth of income imputable to PFI is more than the growth of the PFI gross value added, as given by αY_t^h. This is due to the mechanism of a partial domestic financing of the additions to the PFI capital stock. When this does not hold (alternative 7), then the growth effect is much higher[3].

Private savings are directly related to income, and derive accordingly, although the marginal propensity to save plays also a certain role (alternatives 11 and 12).

Public savings depend, of course, upon the structure of taxation, given by

[3] This proves to be a rather crucial point, as it will be seen in the empirical application of the methodology, which will be presented in Part III. A discussion on this question will be given in Section 8.7.

the various τ's, and the increase in current public expenditure due to PFI (g^h). The role of the latter is pointed out by alternative 13.

The b.o.p. effect, also, varies according to the various parameters, reflecting various practical situations, connected with import requirements, export promotions, transfer of profits, and payments to abroad for 'know-how'. Its growth effect was already commented before.

Finally, it must not be forgotten that the four marginal effects are interdependent, and are given by a system of simultaneous equations. Consequently, in all cases, they are interrelated.

The crucial element is, as already pointed out, the rate of growth of the PFI capital stock, equal to the rate of growth of the PFI gross value added (α). Since all marginal effects are actually increases, their size depends directly upon it.

The situation looks somewhat different in the case of the *cumulative effects*, and in certain cases the latter react differently to some of the variations, with respect to what happens for the marginal effects.

In particular, it was noticed that the financial mechanism of the annual additions to PFI plays a minor role in the cumulative calculations, with respect to the marginal ones, due to the fact that it is compensated to a greater extent by the other indirect effects which accrue to financial availabilities, as given by the last term of Equation (i') (Section 6.5) (see alternatives 1, 6, 7).

The income effect is always much greater than the direct effect imputable to PFI in t (100 in all cases), due to the fact that the various indirect effects 'cumulate' over the period considered (five years, in this exercise).

Consequently, also the other three effects, more or less related to the income effect, are rather sizeable.

The private savings effect derives directly from the income effect, through the marginal propensity to save.

The public savings effect depends upon the direct income effect (100) and the total income effect (Y_t^*), though the structure of taxation and expenditure.

The b.o.p. effect, as was said above for the marginal calculations, depends again upon the direct and overall income effect, taking into account the underlying situation (imports, exports, 'know-how' payments, transfer of profits).

More than in the case of the marginal effects, α here plays a crucial role, since there is an inverse relation between its level and the results (alternatives 1, 4, 5).

Finally, as stated for the marginal effects, it must be kept in mind that the four cumulative effects are interdependent, and they are given by a system of simultaneous equations; consequently, in all cases, they are interrelated.

8.4. THE EFFECTS ON WAGES, PROFITS AND INCOME DISTRIBUTION

A possible solution to the problem of income distribution was outlined in Section 3.6, and there it was also said that a simpler measurement could have been given by considering the ratio

$$\frac{\text{wages}}{\text{profits}}\,.$$

Since, in deriving both the cumulative and the marginal effects, the effects on wages and profits, both for the PFI sector and for the rest of the economy, were considered in order to get the public savings effect, it is possible to use those results.

The effects on profits for the rest of the economy are:

$$\bar{\bar{P}}_t^0 = \pi^0 (\bar{\bar{Y}}_t - \alpha Y_t^h) \quad \text{and} \quad P_t^{0*} = \pi^0 (Y_t^* - Y_t^h)\,.$$

The effects on wages for the rest of the economy are:

$$\bar{\bar{W}}_t^0 = w^0 (\bar{\bar{Y}}_t - \alpha Y_t^h) \quad \text{and} \quad W_t^{0*} = w^0 (Y_t^* - Y_t^h).$$

The effects on profits in the PFI sector are:

$$\bar{\bar{P}}_t^h = \pi^h \alpha K_{t-1}^h = \pi^h \alpha Y_t^h k^h \quad \text{and} \quad P_t^{h*} = \pi^h Y_t^h k^h\,.$$

The effects on wages for the PFI sector are:

$$\bar{\bar{W}}_t^h = w^h \alpha Y_t^h \quad \text{and} \quad W_t^{h*} = w^h Y_t^h\,.$$

Consequently it is possible to compare

$$(2) \qquad \frac{\bar{\bar{W}}_t^0 + \bar{\bar{W}}_t^h}{\bar{\bar{P}}_t^0 + \bar{\bar{P}}_t^h} \quad \text{and/or} \quad \frac{W_t^{0*} + W_t^{h*}}{P_t^{0*} + P_t^{h*}}$$

with

$$(1) \qquad \frac{W_t^0 + W_t^h}{P_t^0 + P_t^h}\,.$$

(1) represents the observed ratio for the LDC's economy in t. If (2) is larger than (1), this means that the presence of PFI gives a contribution to the improvement of the income distribution situation. If the two are equal, this means that the presence of PFI is 'neutral', while if (2) is less than (1), the presence of PFI has a negative effect on income distribution.

8.5. THE EMPLOYMENT EFFECTS

In Section 2.9. it was pointed out how employment, for both sectors, could be introduced into the analysis. Since the level of employment is directly related to gross value added for both sectors, it is possible to derive also the PFI effects on employment.

The cumulative effects are given by:

$$L_t^* = \eta^0 (Y_t^* - Y_t^h) + \eta^h \check{Y}_t^h$$

while the marginal effects are given by:

$$\bar{\bar{L}}_t = \eta^0 (\bar{\bar{Y}}_t - \alpha Y_t^h) + \eta^h \alpha Y_t^h \, .$$

8.6. THE SUBSTITUTION EFFECTS

Recalling what was said in Section 3.9 about the substitution effects, it is possible to see now how the cumulative and marginal effects previously analysed should be modified if also the substitution effects are taken into account.

For simplicity, only the case of the income effect will be dealt with. But it should not be difficult to extend the analysis to all the other effects previously considered.

In Section 3.9 three cases were distinguished.

In Case (a) (no substitution) no modifications are required, apart from the necessity of re-weighing the conversion coefficients in the case of a multisectoral analysis. But in the two-sector case, nothing changes for the formulation of the cumulative and marginal effects given before.

Case (b) (full substitution) and Case (c) (intermediate situation) can be analysed as follows.

Since, both in Case(b) and (c) the substitution effect would be constant after the PFI has taken place, the cumulative income effect would be:

$$Y_t^* = \cdot \;\cdot\; \cdot - \bar{Y}_{s0}$$

then, $\overline{Y}_{s0}$ would obviously 'cumulate' through the other three main effects considered before.

The other cumulative effects (employment and income distribution) would derive accordingly.

In the case of the marginal effects, the income effect would be:

$$\overline{\overline{Y}}_t = \cdots - \overline{Y}_{s0}$$

since, in the case of the absence of PFI, the domestic firms which would be substituted in the case of its presence, would start producing again the same amount of gross value added which was originally substituted ($\overline{Y}_{s0}$). The other marginal effects would then derive accordingly.

Without too much trouble, it would also be possible to take into account the time behaviour of the substitution effect, similarly to what was outlined at the end of Section 3.9.

As it was said in Section 3.9, this way of handling the substitution effect is rather simplified, and, among other things, it requires exogenous information about the extent in which PFI substitutes existing domestic firms.

However, it might be quite relevant to take also this aspect of the problem into account; and, provided that the necessary information is given, the way of handling it depicted above and in Section 3.9 might be satisfactory enough.

Finally, it must be pointed out how the problem of substitution is considered here just to show the way it can be handled, while the analysis of this part will still be confined to the four main effects of Chapters VI and VII, without taking substitution into account.

8.7. THE IMPACT OF THE FINANCIAL MECHANISM OF THE ANNUAL ADDITIONS TO PFI

In the previous pages, it was often observed that one of the crucial features of the model underlying the methodology is given by the financial mechanism for the annual additions to PFI (see Equation (7), Section 2.2; as for the effects of F_D on the rate of growth of income for the total economy, see Section 3.2; finally, see, in general, the comments to the numerical exercises of Section 8.3). This section will analyse, to a greater extent and mainly at a theoretical level, the impact of such a mechanism on the results yielded by the methodological approach. The discussion will concentrate on the income effect, and it will be given separately for the marginal and cumulative approach, since, as it was seen in the numerical exercise of Section 8.3, they are affected by this mechanism in a different way.

The model assumes that PFI has an advantage with respect to the enterprises of the 'rest of the economy' in the utilization of the financial resources available for investments. This may, at a first sight, be considered as rather unrealistic, since one might expect that the contrary happens, i.e. enterprises of the 'rest of the economy' are preferred to PFI, thanks to policy measures which tend to this end. However, the historical experience in many LDC's shows that the opposite happens, thanks to a greater efficiency of PFI, also in getting a successful access to domestic financial resources, either through the financial market, or through the commercial banking system.

Furthermore, in the formulation of the effects of PFI on income, both in the marginal and in the cumulative case, one should look not only at the negative effects of the financial mechanism under discussion, but also at the positive indirect effect via the private savings effect, public savings effect, and b.o.p. effect, assumed to represent foreign capital inflow imputable to PFI.

If this last item proves to be in accordance with the statistical evidence, then the whole mechanism assumed by the model holds[4].

An alternative set up in the model, on this point, would have been to consider the financing of the annual additions to PFI as *exogenously* given. In this way, however, apart from the expected lack of empirical data for most cases, many of the interrelations among the various variables taken into consideration would have been lost. Consequently, it was thought preferable to give an *endogenous* solution to the problem, and the following pages will discuss its impact on the methodology obtained from the model of Chapter II.

Let us first consider the *marginal approach*.

From Equation (i) on p. 115, the effect directly imputable to the financial mechanism under discussion is:

$$\left[\alpha k^h - (\pi^k k^h - \rho\, k^h - \tau_p \pi^h k^h)\right] \frac{Y_t^h}{k^0}$$

and it is either positive (negative contribution) or negative (positive contribution) according to whether

$$\alpha \gtrless (\pi^h - \rho - \tau_p \pi^h)$$

4 In Part III, in the empirical applications of the methodology to the case of Ghana, it will be proved, at a general level, how this is fulfilled by the results of the calculations for the marginal effects on the b.o.p. This proof is made possible by the fact that detailed data are available on the share of PFI annual investments finances from foreign sources, vs the one financed from domestic sources. In most other cases, however, such a proof is not possible, due to lack of empirical evidence.

However, as it was said in the previous pages, one should take into account also the indirect effects of PFI on total financial availabilities, as given by the last term of Equation (i) (Section 7.8). In this analysis we leave out, for simplicity, the marginal effects on private and public savings. Consequently, the financial mechanism of the model (to be called *FM*) has a negative or positive contribution on the income effect ($FM \lesseqgtr 0$) according to whether

$$\alpha k^h \frac{Y_t^h}{k^0} \gtrless (\pi^h k^h - \rho k^h - \tau_p \pi^h k^h) \frac{Y_t^h}{k^0} + \frac{\overline{\overline{B}}_t}{k^0(1+\alpha)} .$$

$FM < 0$ means a negative contribution to the income effect, and $FM > 0$ means a positive contribution to the income effect.

Again, for simplicity, in $\overline{\overline{B}}_t$ the last item in the numerator which stands for the indirect marginal effect on the b.o.p. through the overall increase in income will be omitted. Working out the above expression one gets:

$$\alpha k^h \gtrless (\pi^h k^h - \rho k^h - \tau_p \pi^h k^h) +$$

$$+ \frac{\alpha \left[\varphi_m (1+m^h) - \varphi_e (1+e^h) + \rho k^h + \lambda k^h\right]}{(1+\alpha-\theta)}$$

under the assumption that $Y_t^h > 0; k^0 > 0$.

The trade gap of PFI, weighted by its capital-output ratio, in order to refer it to PFI capital stock at the beginning of the period (K_{t-1}^h) and including payments to abroad for 'know-how', will be called F_T^h:

$$\frac{\varphi_m (1+m^h) - \varphi_e (1+e^h)}{k^h} + \lambda = F_T^h .$$

Assuming that α is a close approximation for θ, there follows:

$$1 + \alpha - \theta \simeq 1 .$$

Assuming that also $k^h > 0$, the above expression becomes:

$$\alpha \gtrless \left[\pi^h(1-\tau_p) - \rho\right] + \alpha \left[F_T^h + \rho\right]$$

Assuming that also $\alpha > 0$, the following expression must hold

$$\alpha \gtreqless \frac{\pi^h(1-\tau_P)-\rho}{1-(\rho+F_T^h)} \tag{1}$$

in order to have

$$FM \lesseqgtr 0$$

That is to say, $FM \lesseqgtr 0$, according to whether the ratio between profit reinvested and the difference to one of the 'rate of b.o.p. deficit', in both cases with respect to K_{t-1}^h is greater, equal, or smaller than α. In other words, according to whether the rate of profits reinvested with respect to K_{t-1}^h, is greater, equal, or smaller than α times (where α is the rate of growth of K_{t-1}^h) the difference to one of the 'rate of b.o.p. deficit' the financial mechanism gives a positive, or negative contribution to the growth of income for the 'rest of the economy', that is to say it releases or it absorbs financial resources out of the 'investment funds' available for the 'rest of the economy'.

This is a rather strong requirement, and it is likely to be fulfilled only for smaller α (see alternative 4, Section 8.3), or for higher rate of profits reinvested (see alternative 7, Section 8.3), or for higher b.o.p. deficit (see alternative 8, Section 8.3). In all intermediate cases, when this does not happen, then the overall marginal indirect effects of PFI on income $(\bar{\bar{Y}}_t - \alpha Y_t^h)$ are likely to be negative (see all other alternatives, Section 8.3) due to the combined impact of the financial mechanism of the model for the annual additions to PFI and of the capital inflow directly imputable to PFI.

A similar reasoning can be done for the *cumulative approach*, taking into account the formulations in Section 6.5 for Equations (i') and (ii'), and using the same assumptions and new symbols considered above for the marginal approach. The effect directly imputable to the financing mechanism is given by:

$$\left[\alpha k^h - (\pi^h k^h - \rho k^h - \pi^h k^h \tau_P)\right] \frac{Y_t^h}{k^0} \frac{(1+\alpha)^t - 1}{\alpha(1+\alpha)^t}$$

and again it is either positive (negative contribution) or negative (positive contribution) according to whether

$$\alpha \gtreqless (\pi^h - \rho - \tau_P \pi^h).$$

Taking into account also the indirect contribution, in so far as the foreign capital inflow imputable to PFI, as given by the cumulative b.o.p. effect, is concerned, the following must hold

$$\alpha k^h \frac{Y_t^h}{k^0} \frac{(1+\alpha)^t - 1}{\alpha(1+\alpha)^t} \gtreqless (\pi^h k^h - \rho k^h - \tau_p \pi^h k^h) \frac{Y_t^h}{k^0} \times$$

$$\times \frac{(1+\alpha)^t - 1}{\alpha(1+\alpha)^t} + \frac{B_t^*}{k^0} \frac{(1+\alpha)^t - 1}{\alpha(1+\alpha)^t}$$

in order that

$$FM \lesseqgtr 0 .$$

Again, for implicity, in B_t^* the last item in the numerator will be left out. From the above expression one gets:

$$\alpha k^h \gtreqless (\pi^h k^h - \rho k^h - \tau_p \pi^h k^h) +$$

$$+ \frac{\left[\varphi_m (1 + m^h) - \varphi_e (1 + e^h) + \rho k^h + \lambda k^h\right]}{1 - \theta \dfrac{(1+\alpha)^t - 1}{\alpha(1+\alpha)^t}}$$

Assuming $\alpha \simeq \theta$:

$$1 - \theta \frac{(1+\alpha)^t - 1}{\alpha (1+\alpha)^t} \simeq \frac{1}{(1+\alpha)^t} .$$

Then, substituting again for F_T^h, and rearranging, the following expression must hold:

$$\left[\pi^h (1 - \tau_p) - \rho\right] \gtreqless \alpha - (1+\alpha)^t \left[F_T^h + \rho\right] \qquad (2)$$

in order that:

$$FM \gtreqless 0$$

that is to say, the financial mechanism under discussion, in the case of the cumulative effects, gives a positive contribution to the growth of income for the 'rest of the economy' provided that the rate of profit reinvested with respect to K_{t-1}^h is greater than α *less* the 'rate of b.o.p. deficit' times $(1+\alpha)^t$.

(2) is somewhat similar to (1), with the difference that now the compound

('cumulated') 'rate of b.o.p. deficit' must be taken into account, and not just its increase.

This is a much weaker requirement than in the case of the marginal approach, and, provided that

$$\pi^h (1 - \tau_P) - \rho \geqslant 0$$
$$\alpha > 0 \text{ (already assumed)}$$
$$F_T^h + \rho > 0 \text{ (deficit increasing)}$$

which is very likely to happen, then the financial mechanism assumed by the model always gives a positive contribution to the growth of income for the 'rest of the economy' (positive indirect income effect).

In order to have a negative impact ($FM < 0$) the 'rate of b.o.p. deficit' must be negative (deficit decreasing) and the following condition must be fulfilled for the 'rate of profits reinvested':

$$\left[\pi^h (1 - \tau_P) - \rho\right] < \alpha + (1 + \alpha)^t \left[F_T^h + \rho\right].$$

This, still assuming $\alpha > 0$, requires a combination of low 'rates of profit reinvested' and of high negative 'rates of b.o.p. deficit'; and in such a case a negative impact of the overall financial mechanism could be anyhow expected, being there a high absorption of financial resources from the 'rest of the economy' (little profit reinvested), and a capital outflow imputable to PFI (deficit decreasing or surplus increasing effect on the b.o.p.).

It was seen in the previous pages how the working of the financial mechanism for the annual additions to PFI affects the results of the methodology in the sense of underestimating a possible positive income effect (provided that the underlying assumptions *do* contradict the empirical evidence) much more in the case of the marginal effects than in the case of the cumulative effects, since the conditions that must be fulfilled in order to have a positive impact are much stronger for the former than for the latter. It was also seen how the deficit of the b.o.p. (standing for foreign capital inflow) plays a considerable role in both cases, but in particular in the case of the cumulative effects.

These results are quite in line with the outcomes of the numerical exercise of Section 8.3.

Alternatives 6 and 7 provided, with respect to alternative 1, two extreme cases, where either the addition to PFI was completely financed from domestic sources or completely financed from profits reinvested.

In the case of the *marginal effects* the outcomes are very sensitive to the two variations. In alternative 6 the expression (1) seen above becomes $0.05 > 0$, and consequently $FM < 0$. In alternative 7 (1) becomes

$0.05 < 0.0535$, and consequently $FM > 0$. The indirect effect $(\bar{\bar{Y}}_t - \alpha Y_t^h)$ varies accordingly.

In the case of the *cumulative effects*, the outcomes are hardly affected by the two extreme cases considered. Looking at expression (2), one finds that in alternative 6: $0 > -1.055$ and in alternative 7: $0.05 > -1.142$.

In both cases $FM > 0$, and, as a matter of fact, the indirect income effects $(Y_t^* - Y_t^h)$ are rather relevant (and positive), although the one of alternative 7 is smaller than the one of alternative 6 (contrary to what happened to the marginal effects), due to the greater b.o.p. effect in the case of alternative 6, which affects the results for the income effect much more than the working of the financial mechanism for the annual additions to PFI, as it was seen above.

To conclude, it is possible to recall what was said in Section 8.1 about cumulative vs marginal effects.

The discussion on the impact of the financial mechanism proved once more, that there is no direct correspondence between the two, and this should be kept in mind in interpreting the results which will be given in Part III for the empirical applications of the methodology.

CHAPTER IX

SECTORAL DISAGGREGATION AND INPUT-OUTPUT ANALYSIS

9.1. INTRODUCTION

The purpose of this chapter is to introduce a sectoral breakdown in the model presented in Chapter II, as often it was mentioned there. The way to introduce input-output analysis will also be discussed, although with just some few comments on the technical aspects of the problem. Some concluding remarks will also point out some other extensions, which could be possibly introduced in the methodological framework developed from the model of Chapter II.

The analysis will afterwards continue, for reasons of simplicity, on the basis of the two-sector model of Chapter II. But it should be easy to notice how more detailed sectoral information could be taken into account, with just a few modifications, in the analysis of the effects of PFI developed in this part of the research, at a macro (sectoral) level.

First two possible approaches to a sectoral or sub-sectoral analysis of the effects of PFI will be discussed. Then, as it was said, the discussion will turn to the introduction of input-output analysis.

One terminological clarification is necessary.

By *sectors*, here it is meant the major productive sectors of the economy. The empirical application of the methodology of Part III will distinguish among the following ones:

(1) Agriculture, Livestock, Forestry and Fishing	(ISIC nr 0)
(2) Mining	(ISIC nr 1, 32)
(3) Manufacturing	(ISIC nr 2, 3, except 32)
(4) Construction	(ISIC nr 4)
(5) Electricity, Gas and Water	(ISIC nr 5)
(6) Trade and Services n.e.s.	(ISIC nr 6, 8 n.e.s.)
(7) Transport and Communications	(ISIC nr 7)
(8) Government	(ISIC nr 810, 821, 822, 823).

Then, since this study refers mainly to the effects of PFI in the manufacturing sector, although still at a rather aggregate level, a number of *sub-sectors* will be distinguished. In the empirical application of the methodology of Part III, they will be the following ones:

(1) Food, Beverages and Tobacco	(ISIC nr 20, 21, 22, 312)
(2) Textiles, Footwear and Apparal	(ISIC nr 23, 24)
(3) Chemicals and Allied Products	(ISIC nr 31, except 312)
(4) Primary and Fabricated Metals	(ISIC nr 34, 35)
(5) Machinery	(ISIC nr 36, 37)
(6) Transport Equipment	(ISIC nr 38)
(7) Other Manufacturing	(ISIC nr 25, 26, 27, 28, 29, 30, 33, 39).

In the following pages, however, the various sectors and sub-sectors will still be indicated with symbols, without going into details, and without specifying whether one is talking about the former or the latter, since it makes no difference as to the theoretical treatment of the problem, but is only affects the degree and the kind of disaggregation.

9.2. THE SECTORAL USE OF THE METHODOLOGY IN GENERAL

As it was mentioned in the introduction, the methodology can be used on a sectoral basis mainly in two ways.

First of all, it is possible, in any empirical application of the methodology, to substitute 'All PFI' by any major sector or manufacturing sub-sector. Consequently the analysis concentrates in finding out what would have happened, *vis-à-vis* the 'rest of the economy', including also all the other PFI thus left out from the original 'PFI sector', in its absence.

Nothing changes with respect to the formulation of the four basic effects, given in Chapters VI and VII, and of the derived effects, given in Chapter VIII.

Otherwise, one can consider all the PFI sectors (and sub-sectors) simultaneously, with their different structural characteristics, to get their combined effect on the 'rest of the economy', which would then include no PFI, apart from what might be left out from the bunch of sectors and/or sub-sectors under consideration. The formulation of the four basic effects of Chapters VI and VII, and of the derived ones of Chapter VIII, would then have to be adapted accordingly.

This so far as concerns the PFI sectors and sub-sectors. But while the first approach suggested is still at a two-sector level, just like the one given by the model of Chapter II, in the second approach it is also possible to extend the sectoral breakdown to the 'rest of the economy', in order to get results even more realistic. This will also be discussed briefly in Section 9.4.

9.3. THE SECTORAL USE OF THE METHODOLOGY TAKING INTO ACCOUNT JUST ONE PFI SECTOR OR SUB-SECTOR

As it was said in the previous section, this first way of using the methodological framework at a sectoral level does not cause any particular problem[1].

The model of Chapter II still hold as it is, although the 'PFI sector' is replaced by the particular sector or sub-sector under consideration, while the 'rest of the economy' includes also all the rest of PFI, excluded from the one whose effects have to be obtained. Consequently, nothing changes in the basic formulations of Chapters VI and VII for the four cumulative and marginal effects, respectively, as well as for the ones derived in Chapter VIII.

9.4. THE SECTORAL USE OF THE METHODOLOGY TAKING INTO ACCOUNT VARIOUS PFI SECTORS AND/OR SUB-SECTORS

As it was said in Section 9.2, an alternative way of approaching a sectoral application of the methodology developed in the previous chapters consists in considering simultaneously a whole bunch of PFI sectors and/or sub-sectors, *vis-à-vis* the 'rest of the economy' sector of the model of Chapter II, paying attention to avoiding double countings. The basic idea consists in taking into account the different structural characteristics of the various sectors considered, and consequently most of the equations of the 'PFI sector' in the model of Chapter II should be disaggregated accordingly.

An example can be given, indicating with the superscript i the ith sector or sub-sector. The production function of Equation (1), e.g., becomes:

$$Y_t^h = \sum_i Y_t^{hi}$$

$$Y_t^{hi} = \frac{K_{t-1}^{hi}}{k^{hi}}$$

Something similar should be done will all the other equations of the 'PFI sector', with the exception of Equations (10) and (11) (exports and imports of services, respectively) which are not meant to be sectoral, as well as for the taxation equations (from (14)–(19)), for the same reason. Nothing would

[1] As it will be pointed out concluding this chapter, this approach will be the one followed in the empirical applications of the methodology, whose results will be given and commented in Part III.

change in the equations referring to the 'rest of the economy and total economy' (from (20)–(38)). But this point will be brought up again later.

Subsequently, it is possible to adapt the formulation of the four basic effects of Chapters VI and VII to this new set-up of the model.

One complication arises if α (rate of growth of PFI capital stock) varies from sector to sector. Then, the procedures followed to derive the final formulations of the four effects, both in Chapters VI and VII, should be worked out again. One simplification could come introducing $\bar{\alpha}$ as a weighted average of the various α_i, but also other simplifications might be necessary in order to achieve some simple formulations, like the ones given at the end of Chapters VI and VII, for the cumulative and marginal effects, respectively.

While handling the 'PFI sector' in the way outlined above in this section, it is possible to disaggregate also some of the equations pertaining to the 'rest of the economy and total economy'. In particular, this applies to Equation (21) (exports of goods), Equation (27) (profits), Equation (28) (wages), Equation (37) (investments) and Equation (38) (income formation), while all the other equations of the second part of the model are not meant to be sectoral.

Then one should, again, try to adapt the four basic formulations of the effects given in Chapters VI and VII, although the complications mentioned above when only the 'PFI sector' is disaggregated, would be strengthened by similar ones when introducing a breakdown for 'the rest of the economy and the total economy' in the model of Chapter II.

9.5. THE INTRODUCTION OF INPUT-OUTPUT ANALYSIS

The approach meant to get a more detailed analysis, starting from the model of Chapter II and disaggregating various equations in the way seen in the previous sections can become even more accurate introducing input-output analysis, that is to say, taking into account, in a dynamic context, the inter-industry relations between and among the various PFI and rest of the economy sectors, as well as a disaggregation of final demand, in its various items, into sectors of origin. As it was said, this should be done in a dynamic context, building a dynamic input-output (closed) model, introducing capital coefficients, income elasticities for the various items of final demand, as well as conversion matrices to get from the groups of products composing the various items of final demand their composition by sectors of origin.

From a strictly technical point of view, although what is briefly outlined above sounds complicated, it can easily be done in practice; the main problem, at a theoretical level, would be in deriving the formulation of the four effects of Chapters VI and VII as well as of the ones seen in Chapter VIII, in a way not too complicated.

The main difficulty, however, would be at the empirical level, where it will be almost impossible to get input-output tables which would distinguish between PFI and the rest of the economy in the various sectors taken into account. The only possible empirical use of this approach would be in countries where a detailed input-output table is available, and where some of the sectors taken into account can be identified as all, or mostly, PFI, while the other ones would refer to the rest of the economy.

As it was said before, this possibility of introducing input-output relations is just mentioned here, while the research will continue on the basis of the model of Chapter II, and of the methodology derived from it.

9.6. OTHER POSSIBLE EXTENSIONS

In the previous sections it was pointed out how it is possible to use the model of Chapter II and the methodology derived from it at a more detailed level, as required by the circumstances, provided that the empirical information available allows it.

Due to lack of time and data, the empirical part of this research, which will be presented in Part III, will concentrate on the approach suggested in Section 9.3, using the disaggregation outlined in Section 9.1, as well as considering, in some cases, as 'sectors' some particular groups of PFI, characterized, with respect to the rest of PFI of the economy under consideration, by a particular way of financing them. Input-output will be completely impossible, while the more detailed approach suggested in Section 9.4 would acquire little relevance as a consequence of the various assumptions necessary to fill the many gaps of the empirical evidence available. Still, it was thought useful to point out how one can, in various ways, from the simplest one (Section 9.3) to the most complicated one (Section 9.5), through two intermediate alternatives (Section 9.4), obtain a more detailed analysis, with respect to the one presented in the previous chapters.

Other refinements, with respect to the model of Chapter II and to the methodology subsequently derived, would be possible, introducing, or not, also the sectoral breakdown discussed in this chapter.

They mainly consist in a better handling of some variables, still kept at a rather aggregate level. Two examples can illustrate this point.

Gross total investments could be disaggregated, distinguishing among net fixed investments, depreciation, and stock variations.

Furthermore, 'income' could be specified in a better way. Here, as well as in the empirical exercise of Part III, one refers in general to GNP or GDP, according to the data available, and, at a sectoral level, to value added (intended to be gross value added), in all cases at market prices. It would be more accurate, but for the moment useless from the point of view of the empirical applications of the methodology, to specify between GNP and GDP at market prices, and to introduce indirect taxes net of subsidies, in order to get the corresponding concepts at factor costs. The same could apply to 'gross value added'. Taking into account depreciation allowances, one could then obtain the same concepts 'net'. Also 'disposable income', taking into account direct taxes, might prove a useful specification, especially if a more detailed analysis of final demand is required, as in the case of input-output, as outlined in Section 9.5.

VARIOUS PRACTICAL SITUATIONS AND THE USE OF THE MODEL

In Section 2.11 it was already pointed out how, with litle modifications, the model could be changed in order to take into account various practical situations not directly reflected in its structure.

There the attention was for alternative ways of financing from abroad (like loans, etc.) and for a different financing of the PFI itself (like joint ventures, etc.), in connection also with Equation (11 bis).

What was said there applies, obviously, also here. The results of these changes will be reflected in some slight modifications of some equations of the model, with the introduction of some new variables, mainly exogenous, and some new parameters. This, in turn, will bring in some modifications in the formulation of the cumulative and marginal effects, without any basic change.

Similarly, some particular situations may require the introduction of different parameters in one sector (i.e. the PFI sector), with respect to the other (i.e. the rest of the economy). An example of this case is given by the question of incentives. This was not clearly taken into account, but it can be easily introduced both in the original model and in the formulation of the effects (cumulative and marginal). Incentives, and disincentives, will be reflected in different values for the two sectors in some of the structural parameters, like the ones of taxation. And, since the two sectors are split also in the formulation of the cumulative and marginal effects, no difficulty should arise in the practical use of the methodology.

As for the financing of the annual additions to the PFI capital stock, in Section 2.10 it was also pointed out how different assumptions could be introduced, and the numerical exercise of Section 8.3 considered the two possible extreme cases.

Finally, a crucial assumption in the preceding analysis was found to be the constant rate of growth of the PFI capital stock (and gross value added). Also in this case, alternative practical situations could be considered by the methodological approach developed so far.

In the case the PFI capital stock stays constant, the marginal effects will come through PFI profits not transferred abroad, but available for the rest of the economy, while the cumulative effects will have to be re-calculated, taking into account the effects of PFI in the first year of its OP, and how it 'cumulates' through the b.o.p. deficit, private savings, and public savings, and their effects on income, from 0 to t. A simple expression could be obtained, starting from the system of Section 6.2.

In the case of an irregular time behaviour, the cumulative effects will have to be solved year by year, while the marginal effects will still be given by the same formulations, if the growth of the PFI capital stock (or gross value added) from $t-1$ to t, and from t to $t+1$ is given.

CHAPTER XI

THE USE OF THE MODEL FOR DECISION-MAKING

The methodological approach developed in the previous pages can be used both for an empirical study of the effects of PFI in LDC's, and as a basis for decision-making. The first point will be discussed in the next chapter, while the latter will be considered here.

Since the model underlying the methodological approach is meant to be a multi-sectoral model, with special reference to the various manufacturing sub-sectors, its main use for policy decisions should be at a sectoral level, that is to say to appraise the effects of allowing the entrance of PFI in certain manufacturing sub-sectors. In order to do so, it is necessary to know the structural characteristics of the LDC's economy, and the ones of the PFI manufacturing sub-sector under consideration. Then, applying the methodological approach developed in the previous pages, it will be possible to derive the cumulative effects, and, if necessary, also the marginal effects which will be caused by the introduction of PFI into the manufacturing sub-sector considered.

Once the various effects are obtained, it will be up to the decision-makers themselves to judge about the PFI under consideration, on the basis of their value judgments. It will be necessary to combine the various effects in some way, in order to reach a final judgment about the acceptability, or not, of PFI. This could be done, e.g. giving weights to the various effects, which, obviously, would be different from country to country.

But, still at a sectoral level, it is possible to use the model not merely to *analyse* the perspective effects of PFI, but to reach directly some *policy* conclusions.

Given the LDC's economy and the PFI sub-sector structural characteristics, it is possible to test what variations in the economic effects of PFI will occur if the policy-makers manipulate their policy instruments, given by some of the parameters (or variables) of the model. Or, still along this line, given all structural characteristics, except the value of the policy instruments, considered as unknown, and the desired level of the economic effects of PFI, it is possible to find the values for the instruments necessary to achieve the 'target-effects'.

The use of the model as outlined in the last paragraph is quite similar to the use of any fixed-targets econometric model, and consequently it does not need any further explanation.

Finally, the methodological approach could be used also at a project level, in the sense of analysing the perspective economic effects of a certain PFI project in a given manufacturing sub-sector. The use of the model will not differ considerably from that outlined above, and the choice between considering either cumulative or marginal effects should again be suggested, among other things, by the time behaviour of the PFI capital stock (and gross value added).

However, the analysis of the effects of PFI at a project level can be done more satisfactorily following the guidelines of 'project evaluation', in a social cost-benefit analysis framework, as it will be shown in Part IV of this study.

CHAPTER XII

THE USE OF THE MODEL FOR EMPIRICAL INVESTIGATIONS

The empirical applications of the methodology previously developed should aim at an evaluation of the effects of PFI in LDC's, considering the 'historical' situation, given by the data available.

This can be done at two levels: on a case study basis, or more generally, considering a relatively wide sample of LDC's, assumed to be representative for the purposes of the study, in order to reach some kind of international comparison among the effects of PFI on the LDC's economies both at an aggregate and at a sectoral level.

A country case study would require detailed data for a reasonably long period of time, possibly disaggregated into sectors, and particularly into manufacturing sub-sectors.

It would then be possible to evaluate the economic effects of PFI for the period considered. As pointed out above, this could be done, on one side, for the economy as a whole, and, on the other, for each manufacturing sub-sector, applying the approach developed in this study. The second part of the exercise would point out in which sub-sectors the effects of PFI are more relevant and possibly would provide some explanations for this.

A more general picture of the effects of PFI in the developing world could be obtained considering a larger sample of LDC's.

Also in the case that satisfactory data will be available only for a few years, it would be possible to calculate for each country at least the marginal effects and sometimes also the cumulative ones, and get a general picture of the impact of PFI with reference to one or two given years. These effects can then be related to the corresponding value of PFI under considerations. This way, it should be possible also to get results comparable with each other for all countries in the sample.

But, apart from the effects for the economy as a whole, also in this case it is possible, if enough data are available, to get the effects of PFI in the various manufacturing sub-sectors considered, and compare these effects for each country in the sample with the ones of the other LDC's in the same way suggested for the effects for the economy as a whole.

Part III of this Report will present the empirical application of the methodology to the data made available for India, the Philippines, Ghana, Guatemala and Argentina.

First, it will be possible to carry out five case-studies, as outlined above (from Chapters V–IX, Part III). Consequently, the various empirical results will be compared one with the other, in order to get the 'international comparison' above depicted (Chapter X, Part III).

CHAPTER XIII

EVALUATION AND CONCLUSIONS

In the previous pages a methodological framework for the study of the effects of PFI in LDC's was given. Much of it is still rather simplified, but the main elements are fully specified in a quantitative way.

This methodological framework relies upon a multi-sectoral dynamic model, whose main advantages seem to be:

– it does not require, for the purposes of the study, the introduction of price relations, although this implies some simplifications;

– it is based on data which should be available;

– with little modifications, the assumptions can be varied, to take into consideration different practical situations;

– it also allows to compare PFI with alternative ways of external financing;

– but, mainly, the consideration of the various effects of PFI in a single quantitative framework allows to establish them simultaneously, and to take into account also their interrelations.

More particularly, the model developed in Chapter II proved useful:

(a) to get more insight into what happens in a LDC's economy as a consequence of PFI;

(b) to set up the 'alternative' situation to be compared with the 'actual' situation in a historical analysis of the effects of PFI in a certain LDC, whose economy's basic characteristics correspond to the assumptions of the model;

(c) to calculate the perspective economic effects of PFI, once its structural characteristics and the ones of the LDC are given.

Moreover, the work done allows to point out some interesting methodological features, like:

(a) the need to consider a LDC's economy in a dynamic set-up, where each subsequent stage of its growth process is affected by what happens in the previous stages as a consequence of the presence of PFI;

(b) the need to consider the economic effects of PFI simultaneously and the interdependence which exists among them;

(c) what is the relevant information to be taken into account in trying to establish, on a quantitative basis, the economic effects of PFI.

Finally, one main advantage of the proposed methodological framework to appraise the economic effects of PFI is the fact that it does not need a full numerical solution of the underlying model, nor a complete reduced form. On the contrary, the model is meant to yield some general relations between variables, to appraise the various effects discussed in Chapter III, and defined as the variation between a situation with PFI and a situation without PFI. Consequently, although the model in its full structural form might look quite complicated, it was not too difficult to get some simple expressions for these effects.

LIST OF REFERENCES

. . ., *The Econometric Approach to Development Planning*, Pontificiae Academiae Scientiarum Scripta Varia No. 28, Amsterdam, North Holland Publishing Co., 1965

Alter, G. M., 'The Servicing of Foreign Capital Inflows by Underdeveloped Countries', in *Economic Development for Latin America* (ed. by H. S. Ellis), New York, MacMillan, 1961, pp. 139–160.

Chakravarty, S., *The Logic of Investment Planning*, Amsterdam, North Holland Publishing Co. 1959.

Fox, K. A., Sengupta, J. K., and Thorbecke, E., *The Theory of Quantitative Economic Policy*, Amsterdam, North Holland Publishing Co., 1968.

Ginor, F., 'The Impact of Capital Imports on the Structure of Developing Countries', *Kyklos*, 1969, pp. 104–123.

Hymer, S., 'Direct Foreign Investment and the National Interest', in *Nationalism in Canada*, (ed. by P. Russel), McGraw Hill, 1966, pp. 191–202.

Kemp, M. C., 'Foreign Investment and the National Advantage', *Economic Record*, March 1962, pp. 56–62.

MacDougall, G. D. A., 'The Benefits and Costs of Private Investment from Abroad: A Theoretical Approach', *Economic Record*, March 1960, pp. 13–35.

Meier, G. M., *The International Economics of Development*, New York, Harper & Row, 1968.

Negishi, T., 'Foreign Investment and the Long-Run National Advantage', *Economic Record*, December 1965, pp. 628–632.

Pincus, J. A., 'The Cost of Foreign Aid', *Review of Economics and Statistics,* 1963, pp. 360–367.

Tinbergen, J., *Economic Policy: Principles and Design*, Amsterdam, North Holland Publishing Co., 1956.

Tinbergen, J. and Bos. H. C., *Mathematical Models of Economic Growth*, New York, McGraw Hill, 1962.

PART III

EMPIRICAL APPLICATION OF THE MACRO-ECONOMIC METHODOLOGY

TABLE OF CONTENTS

LIST OF ABBREVIATIONS

PFI	Private Foreign Investments
LDC	Less Developed Countries
NEI (BIG)	Netherlands Economic Institute (Division of Balanced International Growth), Rotterdam
NCAER	National Council of Applied Economic Research, New Delhi
SEUP	School of Economics, University of the Philippines, Manila
SSP	Social Studies Project, University College of Cape Coast, Ghana
ICAITI	Instituto Centro Americano de Investigacion y Tecnologia Industrial, Guatemala
UCA	Instituto de Estudios Economicos, Facultad de Ciencias Sociales y Economicas, Universidad Catolica Argentina, Buenos Aires
NGOIE	Mr. J. Ngoie, IRES, Université Lovanium (for Zaire Republic, former Congo K.)
BFC	Branches of Foreign Companies (Ghana)
FB	Foreign Branches (India)
FCRC	Foreign Controlled Rupee Companies (India)
FY	Fiscal Year
r (rs)	rupee(s) (India)
₱	peso (the Philippines)
N₵	New Cedi (Ghana)
Q	Quetzal (Guatemala)
P m/n	Peso (Argentina)
Z	Zaïre (Zaire Republic)
US$	dollars (United States)
b.o.p.	balance of payments current account deficit (a positive result in the calculation of the effects means an increase in the deficit, and a negative result a decrease in the deficit).

LIST OF REFERENCES

(a) *Country Reports*

'NCAER Report' NCAER, *PFI in Developing Countries: India*, New Delhi, May 1971.

'SEUP Report' SEUP, *PFI in the Philippines*, Manila, August 1971.

'SSP Report' SSP, *PFI in Ghana*, University College of Cape Coast, July 1971.

'ICAITI Report' ICAITI, *Collection of Data on PFI in Guatemala*, Guatemala, August 1971.

'UCA Report' UCA, *PFI in Argentina*, Buenos Aires, November 1971–January 1972.

'NGOIE Report' NGOIE, J., *Quelques matériaux pour l'étude de l'importance économique du capital privé étranger au Congo*, Université Lovanium, July 1971.

(b) *Other References*

International Monetary Fund (IMF), *Financial Statistics* (monthly Bulletin), various issues.

United Nations (UN), *Yearbook of National Accounts Statistics*, various issues.

UN *Yearbook of International Trade Statistics*, various issues.

Organization for Economic Cooperation and Development (OECD), *National Accounts of Less Developed Countries*, various issues.

CHAPTER I

GENERAL INTRODUCTION

This part of the research will present some empirical applications of the methodology developed in Part II.

In applying the quantitative formulations for the effects of PFI some simplifications will be necessary with respect to the framework developed in Part II. First of all, the analysis will be kept at the two-sector level, and, although concentrating on PFI in the manufacturing sector and in the seven manufacturing sub-sectors listed in Part II, Section 9.1, the model will be used on a sectoral basis only, in the sense outlined in Section 9.3 of Part II, that is to say that 'ALL PFI' will be substituted by any major sector or manufacturing sub-sector, while the model is still kept at a two-sector level. The approach outlined in Section 9.4, viz. considering all the PFI sectors (and sub-sectors) simultaneously, with their different structural characteristics, is not feasible here, basically because one would get rather irrelevant results owing to the lack of some important data.

Lack of data will also necessitate some modifications in the formulation of the effects of PFI as given in Part II, while the empirical evidence available for the countries considered will influence the estimation of the numerical value of the parameters that are needed to obtain the effects of PFI. Both these points will be discussed before considering the results country by country; only such extra modifications as are pertinent to every practical situation will be taken into account then.

In all cases the analysis will concentrate on the four main effects derived in Part II: income, b.o.p., private savings, public savings. The 'marginal' approach will always be applied to certain selected years, while, where possible, the 'cumulative' approach will be carried out as well.

Apart from the four basic effects, it will in some cases be possible to calculate the employment effect discussed in Part II, Section 8.5. Lack of reliable data, in most cases, on wages and profits for the 'rest of the economy' will prevent the calculation of the approximate measurement for the income distribution effect given in Part II, Section 8.4. Furthermore the lack of any quantitative evidence on substitution and utilization of capacity will prevent any attempt to calculate the substitution effect in the way seen in Part II, Section 8.6.

The results of the various empirical calculations should be interpreted with great care, taking into account:

(i) the whole rationale of the methodology of Part II and the meaning of 'cumulative' and 'marginal' effects;

(ii) the general assumptions underlying the methodological approach;

(iii) the specific assumptions introduced case by case in order to adapt the methodology to the empirical evidence available;

(iv) the method used to fill the various gaps occuring in the data required for estimating the parameters which serve to quantify the effects of PFI.

As a consequence of all this, the outcomes of the empirical exercises can be considered in most cases as an application of the methodology of Part II and not as a real 'case study'. However, if one keeps in mind what was said above, the results will at least allow some insight into the effects of PFI in the countries considered.

After this introductory chapter, Chapter II will show the procedure followed to arrive at the choice of the countries to which the methodology will be empirically applied. Chapter III will discuss the main modifications introduced into the model of Part II in order to adapt the resulting methodology to the data available for the various empirical applications. Chapter IV will then outline briefly the procedure followed to estimate the various parameters necessary for the quantitative solution of the effects of PFI.

Five country case-studies will then be presented in Chapters V through IX; they include two Asian countries (India and the Philippines), one African country (Ghana) and two Latin American countries (Guatemala and Argentina).

Finally, Chapter X will give a general comparison of the results obtained for the five countries considered, while Chapter XI will show and discuss some alternative assumptions about import substitution. In the end, Chapter XII will give some conclusions on this Part of the research, concerned with the empirical application of the methodology developed in Part II.

CHAPTER II

THE CHOICE OF COUNTRIES

Since it is obviously impossible to collect detailed information on PFI for all the developing countries it was suggested at the beginning of the research that an effort be made to obtain data on a sample basis, for a limited number of developing countries.

The following selection procedure was followed. All developing countries were considered for a provisional list of possibilities. Excluded from the list were countries:

(1) dominated by the oil sector;
(2) of a lilliput size;
(3) without PFI in manufacturing;
(4) for which there were evidently no data available.

This screening procedure led to a provisional list of 28 countries, out of which a further choice had to be made.

In order to reduce the list further a number of characteristics had to be considered. For this purpose some further information was collected on an *ad-hoc* basis; population size, income per capita, average growth rates for the economy as well as for manufacturing, indications as to data availability, attitude towards PFI, the quantitative importance of PFI in the manufacturing sector and data related to the stock of PFI, total as well as in manufacturing. In addition an effort was made to obtain some sort of regional balance in the final sample.

The sample which emerged consisted of 19 countries, 1 in Europe, 6 in Africa, 6 in Asia and 6 in Latin America.

Various research institutes in the countries chosen were asked to fill out a questionnaire, giving the data and the other empirical information required for the empirical application of the methodology presented in Part II.

These research institutes were afterwards visited by some staff members of NEI (Division of Balanced International Growth) and of OECD Development Centre.

The 'NEI Questionnaire' was properly filled out for the following countries: India, the Philippines, Ghana, Guatemala, Argentina, Congo-K. (Zaire Republic)[1].

1 The replies are available on a cost basis from the Netherlands Economic Institute, Rotterdam.

For only five out of these six countries empirical applications of the methodology developed in Part II could be carried out. They will be presented in this part of the research, and a general comparison of the results obtained will be given in Chapter X. It was decided not to carry out any empirical analysis for the Congo (K.) because of the lack of some crucial data and the fact that, according to the classification procedure used to identify PFI in the 'NGOIE Report', it would have accounted for too great a share of GNP, yielding results without any relevant meaning.

CHAPTER III

THE MAIN MODIFICATIONS INTRODUCED

3.1. INTRODUCTION

As it was said in Chapter I in the empirical application of the methodology to the data for the countries listed in Chapter II, it was often necessary to introduce some slight modifications in the formulation of the four effects given in Part II, for the cumulative and marginal effects, respectively. They consist mainly in the aggregation of some parameters, which anyway would have been multiplied one by the other, so that nothing changes in the basic formation discussed in Part II.

This chapter will briefly consider such modifications, giving also a list of the countries to which they apply in the empirical exercises to be shown later.

These modifications apply both to cumulative and marginal effects, with respect to the formulations given in Part II.

3.2. THE INCOME EFFECT

The rate of profit of PFI (π^h) is estimated with reference to PFI value added (instead of capital stock, most of the times not available). So, with respect to the model, this means that K^h_{t-1} is replaced by $k^h\ Y^h_t$, and consequently π^h by:

$$\pi^h\ k^h.$$

The same applies for the rate of transfer of PFI profits to abroad, also estimated with respects to PFI value added:

$$\rho\ k^h.$$

Finally, this is also done to get the PFI profits taxation parameter, estimated with reference to PFI value added:

$$\tau_p \pi^h\ k^h.$$

As it can easily be seen in the formulation of the four basic effects given in Part II, this does not cause any real modification.

These modifications were introduced for all country case-studies.

3.3. THE B.O.P. EFFECT

Most of the times no distinction is possible between imports and exports of goods, and services, respectively. This leads to the estimation of

$$\varphi_e (1 + e^h)$$
$$\varphi_m (1 + m^h)$$
$$\mu (1 + m^0)$$

Apart from the 'transfer of profits' parameter, already given with the PFI capital-output ratio (ρk^h), also the transfer of know-how, related to PFI capital stock at the beginning of the period considered, is estimated with reference to PFI value added:

$$\lambda k^h.$$

These modifications were introduced for all country case-studies.

3.4. THE PRIVATE SAVINGS EFFECT

No particular problem arises on this point, since in both marginal and cumulative effects it derives directly from the income effect. Consequently no modification was necessary in any of the cases.

3.5. THE PUBLIC SAVINGS EFFECT

The modifications discussed for the income and the b.o.p. effects are, when necessary, included in the public savings effect, too. Moreover, the following changes have been introduced.

Since it is not always possible to calculate the direct (τ_P, τ_W) and the indirect (τ_{IND}, τ_M, τ_E) taxation coefficients one by one, they have been grouped accordingly, always with the exception of direct taxes on PFI profits, which were calculated in the way seen for the income effect. The modifications were introduced in the cases of India, the Philippines, Argentina,

Ghana, while they were not necessary in the case of Guatemala. Moreover, the expression between square brackets:

$$\left[\tau_{\text{IND}} + \tau_P \pi^0 + \tau_W w^0\right]$$

has sometimes been calculated as one parameter (Π), for lack of more detailed data. This modification was introduced in the cases of India, Argentina, the Philippines, Ghana, while it was not necessary in the case of Guatemala.

Finally, the public expenditure coefficient, imputable to PFI (g^h), is estimated with reference to PFI value added, instead of PFI capital stock:

$$g^h k^h$$

in all cases.

CHAPTER IV

ESTIMATION OF THE PARAMETERS AND SOLVING PROCEDURE

This chapter will briefly review the estimation of the parameters needed to quantify the four basic effects and the derived ones[1]. In each country study this will be considered in greater detail, but it seemed useful to give a general review of the main problems encountered and of the way followed to solve them.

As said in the previous chapter, some difficulties are overcome by grouping together parameters which would have been multiplied, anyhow, one by the other (like $\pi^h k^h$, ρk^h, $\pi_P \pi^h k^h$, λk^h, $\varphi_e (1 + e^h)$, $\varphi_m (1 + m^h)$, $\mu (1 + m^0) g^h k^h$), or by estimating a sum of parameters (like $\tau_{\text{IND}} + \tau_P \pi^0 + \tau_W w^0$), or by assuming that in some cases certain parameters are the same (like τ_P and τ_W, and $\tau_{\text{IND}}, \tau_M, \tau_E$).

Another major problem concerns the fact that almost all data available are in current prices. This is taken into account by estimating, most of the times, the parameters year by year, but it remains there when a longer time period must be considered (as in the case of $\alpha, k^0, k^h, \mu, \sigma$), especially as a consequence of time lags.

Finally, some crucial data are missing from the Reports on the various countries. In the case of national accounting data (like the ones needed for σ and $\mu(1 + m^0)$) other official sources can be used[2], which may serve as well to fill other information gaps (like in the case of θ), while, when PFI data are missing, it will be necessary to introduce some extra assumptions, like the hypothesis that the 'PFI sector' behaves like the 'rest of the economy', so that national accounting data may be used (e.g. for $\varphi_m (1 + m^h)$ and $\varphi_e (1 + e^h)$); or that a particular PFI sector or sub-sector behaves just like 'ALL PFI' in the country under consideration[3].

Of the various parameters necessary to arrive at the quantitative formulation of the four basic effects of PFI, it is interesting to spend a few words on some of them.

1 For the list of parameters, see Part II p. 76.

2 See the List of references on p. 16.

3 These are also the main reasons, as it was said in Chapter I, for the kind of sectoral use of the methodology applied here.

α since in most cases capital stock figures are not available, it is calculated from value added data (at current prices). In the case of the cumulative effects it is the average annual rate of growth over the whole period considered, while in the case of the marginal effects it is obtained as the average annual rate of growth from the year previous to the year following the one considered, according to the formula:

$$\alpha_t = \left(\frac{Y^h_{t+1}}{Y^h_{t-1}} \right)^{1/2} - 1 .$$

k^h, k^0 in most cases are calculated as ICOR's over the period covered by the analysis, considering gross investments and gross value added, with a one year lag.

ρk^h, λk^h often they are arrived at from b.o.p. data, applied, especially in the case of the former, to the sector or sub-sector under consideration.

Having estimated the parameters required, the systems of equations giving the marginal and the cumulative effects were solved with the help of a computer IBM 1130.

CHAPTER V

INDIA

5.1. INTRODUCTION

As will be seen in the next section, the data supplied by NCAER include Foreign Branches (FB) and Foreign Controlled Rupee Companies (FCRC). A further disaggregation includes the following sectors:

1. FB
   - 1.1. manufacturing
   - 1.2. trading
   - 1.3. tea plantations
   - 1.4. others
2. FCRC
   - 2.1. manufacturing
   - 2.2. trading
   - 2.3. others

Section 5.2 will discuss the source of data, their coverage and limitations.

Section 5.3 will then give a general picture of the relevance of FB and FCRC in the case of India.

Section 5.4 will discuss the methodological approach followed.

Section 5.5 will show, one by one, how the various parameters have been estimated.

Subsequently, various empirical cases will be considered. First of all, the cumulative and marginal effects for the total economy (FB + FCRC) will be calculated and analysed. Then the attention will be focused on the cumulative and marginal effects of FB and FCRC, respectively.

The analysis will then proceed to the manufacturing sector. Similarly to what was done for the general case, the cumulative and marginal effects will be calculated first for both FCRC and FB; then for FB and for FCRC separately.

This way, both for the total economy and for the manufacturing sector, it will be possible to give some general remarks, and also to compare different ways to finance an investment project from abroad, as is the case in considering FB *vis-à-vis* FCRC.

The data available do not allow an appraisal of the effects of PFI at a more detailed sectoral level, according to the list of manufacturing sub-sectors presented in Part II, Section 9.1.

The analysis will concentrate on the period from fiscal year (FY) 1962/63 to FY 1966/67. This choice was made on the basis of the data availability. Most time series go from 1961/62 to 1967/68. However, the occurrence of time lags, and the fact that the data for the last FY (when available) are mostly based on estimates, suggested leaving out the first and the last FY.

Although each FY begins April 1st, not all data given by NCAER cover a similar period, as will be pointed out again later.

This, together with the fact that the various surveys on which the NCAER Report is based have a different coverage, should be kept in mind in interpreting the results which will be given later.

5.2. SOURCE OF DATA, COVERAGE AND LIMITATIONS

As was already pointed out, the report supplied by NCAER, which provided most of the data necessary for the analysis done in the following pages, does not cover the whole of PFI in India, but only some selected data. Therefore, certain specifications are necessary[1], and they should be kept in mind interpreting the results which will be given later.

(a) The analysis of finances of foreign branches (FB) and foreign controlled rupee companies (FCRC) excludes from its purview banking, financial, investment, shipping and airline companies as well as non-profit organizations. The accounting period is July–June till 1965–66 and April–March from 1966–67. The extent of coverage in the various surveys is as follows:

	1958 –60	1961	1962 –63	1963 –64	1964 –65	1965 –66	1966 –67	1967 –68
FB								
Number of companies	201	251	251	225	209	208	219	219
% of assets [a]	63	70	78	87	89	91	93	96
FCRC								
Number of companies	108	160	169	303	291	320	365	366
% of paid-up capital [b]	75	73	75	82	72	71	86	83

[a] Book value of assets held in India by FB (excluding banking, financial, investment, shipping and airline companies).
[b] Paid-up capital of all non-financial FCRC in India.

1 These are taken from the NCAER Report.

(b) Data presented from the analysis of India's international investment position relate only to private industrial and commercial undertakings and state owned enterprises excluding banking and insurance companies.

(c) The survey of foreign collaborations excludes branches of foreign companies and individuals and partnerships and covers only joint stock companies. Information given here pertains to 224 subsidiaries and 267 companies with minority capital participation. A subsidiary is defined as a company of which a single foreign company holds more than 50% of the equity share capital, while companies where such holdings are 50% or less are grouped under minority participation category. The survey also covers companies with no foreign company equity capital participation but only technical collaboration agreements, but these have been excluded from the data presented in the NCAER Report.

5.3. PFI IN INDIA: THE GENERAL PICTURE

Before considering the empirical applications of the methodology of Part II to the case of India, on the basis of the data supplied by the NCAER, it is useful to spend a few words in analysing the general situation, such as it appears from the data referring to FB and FCRC.

The table on pp. 174–175 was obtained from the NCAER report, and the source is given at the bottom of each column. Attention was given to the sectors provided by NCAER for FB and FCRC, and to the FY at the beginning and at the end of the period which will be considered for the empirical analysis. More information can be obtained directly from the NCAER report, and from the tables giving the effects, considering those parameters whose values can better clarify the PFI situation in India as far as FB and FCRC are concerned.

The first column of the table gives the composition of FB and FCRC value added, respectively. One can see how, in the case of FB, tea plantations form the most relevant item, while manufacturing is by far predominant in the case of FCRC, and its importance is growing during the period considered.

Column (2) gives the percentage in GDP for the whole of India of the FB and FCRC sectors considered. The importance of FCRC grows with respect to the importance of FB from almost twice as much in FY 1962/63 to almost three times as much in 1966/67. Together, they account for less than 2% of GDP, and this fact should be kept in mind in analysing later their effects on the Indian economy.

Column (3) gives the percentage share of the sectors' value added in relation to the corresponding sector for the total economy. It is possible to give data only for manufacturing, and again one can notice how the importance of FCRC is much greater than the relative importance of FB.

The other FB or FCRC sectors are excluded from this comparison, since there is no straightforward correspondence between the PFI data and the value added sectoral composition for the whole of India.

Column (4) gives the total import requirements as a percentage of value added. Data are available only for all FCRC and for FCRC in the manufacturing sector. One can notice how high these items are, and this is going to affect to a substantial degree the PFI effects on the b.o.p.

This pattern is strengthened by the data given in column (5) about the export promotion of PFI with respect to value added. Again data are available only for all FCRC and FCRC in the manufacturing sector, and they are, in both cases, considerably lower than the import requirements considered before. It is also possible to notice how all FCRC, in relation to FCRC in manufacturing, have higher import requirements, and also a higher export coefficient. One can conclude that FCRC in sectors other than manufacturing (plantations, mining and petroleum, and services) are much more export-oriented and require relatively more imported inputs.

Column (6) gives the percentage of profits before taxes with respect to value added, sector by sector in all cases considered, and this should be considered in connection with column (7), which gives the same ratio for wages and salaries. In each case, the two ratios should add up approximately to one, but in certain instances this is not true. In the case of FCRC it does not happen for the trading sector in 1966/67, while all other data are satisfactory. In the case of FB, manufacturing wages in 1966/67 seem too high, while profit and wage ratios for trading, in all cases, are clearly not satisfactory. This might be simply due to errors or omissions, or it might point to cases where wages plus profits are much more than value added due to some form of subsidies (Indian or foreign) not taken into account in the value added calculations.

One notices how, at the general level, profitability is higher in the case of FCRC, and consequently the share of wages is higher in the case of FB. This might be an evidence of the fact that FB do not rely upon profits only to contribute to the total profitability of the mother company, but also on other mechanisms, well-known in the cases of multinational corporations, such as price policies and other forms of transfers.

Column (8) gives gross investments, for each year and each sector, considered as a percentage of PFI value added in that year. On the whole, gross investments are at a very high level, and this is obviously due to plans for a rapid expansion of the sectors considered.

PFI in India: The general picture

	(1)		(2)		(3)		(4)	
	v.a. composition		% of v.a. in GDP		% of v.a. of corresponding sector		import requirements/v.a. (%)	
	1962/63	1966/67	1962/63	1966/67	1962/63	1966/67	1962/63	1966/67
(1) Foreign Branches								
1.1. All companies	100.0	100.0	0.69	0.42	–	–	–	–
1.2. Manufacturing	21.4	17.9	0.15	0.08	0.94	0.52	–	–
1.3. Trading	16.2	14.5	0.11	0.06	–	–	–	–
1.4. Tea plantations	50.8	52.4	0.35	0.22	–	–	–	–
1.5. Others	11.6	15.2	0.08	0.06	–	–	–	–
(2) FCRC								
2.1. All companies	100.0	100.0	1.11	1.24	–	–	92.36	75.85
2.2. Manufacturing	85.2	89.5	0.94	1.11	6.05	7.62	75.72	63.09
2.3. Trading	8.7	3.7	0.10	0.05	–	–	–	–
2.4. Others	6.1	6.8	0.07	0.08	–	–	–	–
Source:	Table 5		Table 1,5		Table 2,5		Table 23,5	

Notes:
(a) Source: NCAER Report various tables
(b) See the text (Section 5.3) for comments
(c) – = not available
(d) More data can be found in the NCAER Report, as well as considering the parameters given for the various marginal and cumulative effects.

These data, however, should be handled with care, since they just might refer to exceptional years, followed or preceded by very low investment activity, even at a negative level[2].

2 As is the case for all FB which have very low investments in 1965/66 and negative investments in 1967/68 (see Table 27 of the NCAER Report). This fact will also affect the calculation of the ICOR, as will be seen later (see in particular Section 5.7).

(5)		(6)		(7)		(8)		(9)	
export promotion/v.a.		profits before taxes/v.a. (%)		wages/v.a. (%)		gross investments/v.a. (%)		know-how payments/v.a. (%)	
1962/63	1966/67	1962/63	1966 67	1962/63	1966/67	1962/63	1966/67	1962/63	1966/67
–	–	36.89	35.65	65.59	69.08	36.98	92.57	–	–
–	–	46.78	40.41	60.09	86.01	32.62	32.12	–	–
–	–	64.20	51.92	97.73	117.95	51.14	178.21	–	–
–	–	23.73	25.40	59.42	59.86	13.77	84.37	–	–
–	–	37.01	49.69	58.27	34.97	29.92	49.08	–	–
26.00	22.46	48.92	46.78	50.74	50.80	32.73	62.54	5.76	4.53
11.37	12.70	51.10	47.90	48.03	50.50	36.79	57.53	–	–
–	–	32.89	41.38	42.02	79.31	11.31	225.86	–	–
–	–	33.33	35.54	59.26	40.28	–	40.28	–	–
Table 21,5		Table 5,10 to 18		Table 5,6		Table 5,27,28		Table 5,7,8,9,	

Column (9), the last one, gives the percentage, in relation to value added, of payments to abroad for 'know-how'. Data are available, for the period and the sectoral breakdown considered, only for all FCRC, and they include royalty remittances, remittances of technical fees, and payments to foreign technicians. Since, for the last item, data from 1964/65 on were missing, they were assumed to be the same as in 1963/64.

5.4. THE METHODOLOGICAL APPROACH

Given the kind of data available, and the irregular behaviour of the PFI sector, it seems possible to begin by applying the 'marginal' approach. This allows to overcome at least partly the complication that almost all data are in current prices. Since most parameters will be calculated year by year, they will not be affected by the complication that almost all data are in current prices.

However, some other parameters will have to be calculated over a longer period, with the justifications which will be discussed in the next section. Although price indices are available, no attempt will be made to correct the data in current prices into data in constant prices as one seems liable to make more mistakes than improvements.

The calculation of the marginal effects for a five-year period will allow a discussion of their variation caused by varying values of the parameters as a consequence of different practical situations.

The data available will allow us to calculate only the four basic marginal effects. The lack of employment data prevents the calculation of the employment effect, while the lack of data on domestic wages and profits does not allow calculation of the income distribution effect.

Afterwards, an attempt will also be made to calculate the 'cumulative effects'. This will be done over the same period 1962/63 to 1966/67 considered for the 'marginal' effects, taking as base year 1966/67. The parameters will be calculated by taking the arithmetic average of the ones calculated for the marginal effects, including the rate of growth α. Especially this last procedure will affect the results.

Some general comparison will be possible between cumulative and marginal effects. However, one must be very careful, since the cumulative effects are expressed in 1966/67 prices, and refer to that FY, while the marginal effects are expressed in each FY's prices, and refer to just that FY. The coverage of the sample differs from year to year, and also the way the problem of current prices was handled is going to affect the results.

Finally, one must also remember that there is no direct correspondence between cumulative and marginal effects, as was proved in Part II.

5.5. ESTIMATION OF THE PARAMETERS

In the following pages, a brief description will be given of the way the various parameters were estimated, together with the various assumptions introduced.

The discussion refers first to the estimation of the parameters for the marginal effects. The ones for the cumulative effects will be discussed later.

Y_t^h, Y_t are given (at current prices) from Table 1 and 5 of the NCAER Report

α since capital stock figures are not available, and since PFI investments show an irregular behaviour, it is calculated year by year from the value added data at current prices of Table 5, taking the year previous and the year following the one considered, according to the formula:

$$\alpha_t = \left(\frac{Y_{t+1}^h}{Y_{t-1}^h} \right)^{1/2} - 1 .$$

This was calculated year by year, separately for all six cases considered.

k^h the ICOR for PFI sector was obtained by considering gross investments (Tables 27 and 28) and the increase in value added (from Table 5) over the whole period, with a one-year lag, with data at current prices:

$$k^h = \frac{\sum_{61/62}^{66/67} I}{Y_{67/68}^h - Y_{62/63}^h}$$

It was calculated separately for all six cases.

$\pi^h k^h$ was obtained by considering profits before taxes (Table 10 (FB) and Table 15 (FCRC) with respect to value added (Table 5), year by year separately for the six cases considered.

ρk^h Table 4 refers to all PFI, and not simply to FB and/or FCRC. So it is not possible to use the data provided there. Since no other information is available, it was assumed that FB profits net of taxes are all transferred, and that a share of FCRC profits net of taxes (and less profits retained) equivalent to the foreign share in the equity capital composition is transferred abroad.

Table 25 provides the equity capital composition for all FCRC and for FCRC in the manufacturing sector from 1960/61 to 1963/64. For the calculation of ρk^h an average value was taken. For FCRC in the manufacturing sector it is 46.58%, while for all FCRC it is 49.83%.

In the various cases, this parameter was calculated year by year relating the total transfer of profits thus obtained to the value added item of the corresponding case. (Data from tables 5, 10, 15 and 28). From the point of view of the financing mechanism of the annual addition to PFI this implies that no profits on FB are reinvested, while in the case of FCRC all profits going to foreign shareholders are transferred (and thus not reinvested) apart trom profits retained. In the case of domestic shareholders of FCRC, the implicit assumption is that all their profits will be reinvested. This implies that their marginal propensity to save out of profit income is one. This set of assumptions is quite crucial, because, as will be shown, the mechanism of financing the annual additions to the PFI capital stock plays quite a crucial role in the calculation of the various effects.

λk^h this parameter, giving the share of know-how payments yearly made with respect to v.a., refers only to FCRC, and it is obtained year by year and case by case from Table 7 (royalty remittances), Table 8 (remittances of technical fees), and Table 9 (payments to foreign technicians) with reference to the value added item (Table 5). In the case of only FB it is zero.

$\tau_p \pi^h k^h$ was calculated year by year from Tables 10 and 15 (FB, FCRC) and Table 5 (value added) for each case considered.

k^0 the ICOR for the 'rest of the economy' sector was calculated using (for homogeneity with the rest of the calculations) current data, similarly to what was done for k^h over the period 1961/62 to 1964/65 for gross investments, and 1962/63 to 1965/66 for GDP. Value added data were taken from Table 1 (GDP), and investment data were obtained considering the NCAER estimates given in the OECD *National Accounts of Less Developed Countries* (1970) (Table 21, Footnote (6), net investments, plus depreciation given in Table 21 and 22 under 'capital consumption'). It is assumed to be constant for all cases and all years.

$\varphi_m(1+m^h)$, $\varphi_e(1+e^h)$ since the data available (Tables 20 and 22) refer only to FCRC, the import and export coefficients (including goods and services) of the PFI sector were calculated with respect to FCRC value added (Table 5), assuming that they would be the same also for FB, for which foreign trade data are not available. As has been said, the reference is with value added, and not with gross output, as given on Table 20; they were calculated year by year. In the various cases, the situation is as follows. ALL PFI (FCRC+FB; FB; FCRC): the import requirements and the export coefficients were calculated from the information about all FCRC (Table 5, 20, 22). Manufacturing PFI (FB+FCRC; FB; FCRC): the import requirements and the export coefficients were calculated from the information about FCRC manufacturing (Tables 5, 21, 23). No information is available about the import substitution caused by PFI. For the time being it was assumed to be incorporated in the coefficients thus estimated; however, this might bias the analysis. This point will be considered in more detail later.

$\mu(1+m^0)$ the marginal propensity to import was calculated from Table 22 (inclusive of goods and services) and from Table 1, at current prices, according to the formula

$$\mu(1+m^0) = \frac{M_t - M_0}{Y_t - Y_0}$$

for the period 1960/61 to 1966/67. This parameter is assumed to be constant for all cases and for all years.

θ due to lack of data, the rate of interest on the foreign debt was assumed to be equal to the official bank rate, as given by the *Reserve Bank of India Bulletin.*

When changes occurred within one fiscal year, an approximate weighted average was taken. It is the same in all cases.

σ the marginal propensity to save is assumed to be zero, since the only savings data available do not show any significant variation in private savings with respect to variations in GDP. The data available have been taken from OECD, *National Accounts. . . op. cit.*,pp. 164–165. Of the various estimates given there, the following have been provided by NCAER:

Concept	1961	1962	1963	1964
Total savings net (i)	13.3	13.1	12.8	13.3
Total savings net (ii)	15.3	17.0	16.2	15.7
Public savings	3.69	4.12	5.15	6.04
Difference (i)	9.61	8.98	7.65	7.26
Difference (ii)	11.61	12.88	11.05	9.66

Public savings are taken from the same source, Table 22. The differences give the amount of private savings. All data are in thousand millions rupees at current prices.

Evidently, private savings are, except in one case, declining, and, anyhow, do not show any correlation with the variations in GDP from year to year.

τ_W, τ_P were assumed to be the same, for lack of more detailed data, and were calculated by relating total direct tax receipts to GDP, and taking the average value over the period considered. This is assumed to be the same in all cases. Only PFI profits direct tax rates were calculated in more accurate way, as seen above.

w^h was calculated from Table 6 (wages) and Table 5 (value added), year by year, and case by case.

$\tau_{IND}, \tau_E, \tau_M$ for lack of more detailed data were assumed to be the same and were calculated from Table 30 (indirect taxes receipts) and table 1 (GDP), year by year, since the taxation coefficient is increasing, but is the same for all cases.

$g^h\ k^h$ for lack of data the assumption was introduced that the same expenditure ratio between GDP and government current expenditure holds both for the total economy and for the PFI sector. Data were calculated for the period 1962/63 to 1966/67, and since there is no great variation, a constant value was introduced for all years and all cases.

Π as has been said in the previous section, this parameter relates indirect taxes plus direct taxes (Table 30, excluding other current revenue, included in the current account total receipts) to GDP (Table 1) at current prices. An average value was taken for the period considered for all years and all cases. This parameter, which is an average taxation coefficient, allows solving the four marginal effects, but excludes the possibility to study the PFI effects on domestic wages and profits, and thus on income distribution.

For the cumulative effects, the parameters necessary for the calculations are the same, apart from t, which is 4 in these exercises. As was said earlier, the assumption was introduced that the parameters for the cumulative effects would be the arithmetic average of the ones calculated for the marginal effects. This partly overcomes the obstacle presented by the parameters for the marginal effects being calculated from data at current prices. Consequently, this should not affect the parameters for the cumulative effects (for which constant prices would be required) except in a few cases, such as the ICOR's (due to the presence of lags), and especially in the case of α.

α is in the case of the cumulative effects an average of the rates of growth of PFI calculated in the way seen above for the marginal effects. The influence of prices is consequently still there, and also one should notice that α for the cumulative effects does not give the average annual rate of growth from 1962/63 to 1966/67, but the one from 1961/62 to 1967/68, due to the way α was calculated for the marginal effects.

Before proceeding to the analysis of the empirical results, some general comments are possible, and they will help clarifying some of the results which will be obtained later.

One first point to be discussed concerns the *import and export coefficients*. Although the import and export coefficients decrease in the case of manufacturing, with respect to what happens in the case of all PFI, there still remains quite a gap between the two, that will to a considerable degree affect the b.o.p. effect in all cases considered. A certain bias, as was said above, is given by the fact that import substitution is not taken into account, or, better, it is assumed to be included in the import and export coefficients themselves.

As a matter of fact, one might think that if the PFI under consideration had not been established (the 'alternative situation' from which the measure for the effects of PFI is obtained), then some of the goods that it produces for the domestic market would be imported. So this import-substitution effect must be taken into account in the b.o.p. effect. However, no evidence is available of the degree up to which PFI substitutes imports. On the other hand, one can easily assume that, had the PFI not been established, its exports would not have taken place at all, there being no domestic production to satisfy world demand. One could think about competition (the 'substitution effect') between PFI and domestic firms for the domestic market, but it is unrealistic to think about competition on the world markets in the case of LDC's exports.

Given these difficulties, the solution accepted for the time being is to consider these coefficients as obtained from the data provided by NCAER, under the assumption that in the absence of PFI no imports would have taken place, as far as the production of PFI is concerned (see however Chapter XI of this Part for alternative assumptions).

Another crucial point concerns the *mechanism of financing annual additions to PFI*[3]. As will be seen, the mechanism assumed by the model is

3 See a theoretical discussion on this point in Part II, Section 8.7.

quite crucial in determining the income effect, through the absorption of a share of financial resources otherwise available for domestic investments. One could think that a greater role should be played by foreign capital inflow directly related to the PFI under consideration, and meant to finance its expansion. However, this is already to some extent taken into account by the model, through the assumption by which the deficit of the b.o.p. corresponds to total capital inflow. It follows that the b.o.p. effect of PFI can also be taken as the foreign capital inflow directly imputable to PFI. And since this plays a positive role in the income effect offsetting partly the negative role played by the financing mechanism discussed above, it is possible to assume that this kind of capital inflow too is taken into account by the model.

5.6. MARGINAL AND CUMULATIVE EFFECTS FOR ALL PFI (FB + FCRC)

This first case considers the effects of all PFI, that is to say of both FB and FCRC. First the marginal effects will be calculated and discussed. Subsequently, attention will be given to the cumulative effects.

One first thing to be noticed is that the private savings effect is zero, since it was assumed that the marginal propensity to save is zero. Consequently, it does not play any role in the calculation of the other three marginal effects.

In the five FY's considered, the most significant effect is the positive b.o.p. effect. This is due mainly to the high level of import requirements of PFI, and to the comparatively low level of export promotion. Moreover, the rate of growth of PFI (α) plays also a considerable role in the b.o.p. effect.

Another interesting result is given by the fact that the income effect is generally small, almost negligible if compared year by year to GDP increases, and even negative in two cases. Here the crucial role is played by the rate of growth of PFI (α), especially as a consequence of the financing mechanism for the annual additions to the PFI capital stock. A greater α, with a fixed ICOR, requires a greater amount of (PFI) investments, and thus of financial resources. The portion of the latter that is not covered by PFI profits reinvested has to come from other domestic sources. Consequently, the increase in income caused by PFI might be less than the decrease caused by the absorption of financial resources otherwise available for domestic investments (also taking into account PFI indirect effects on financial resources via S_{Pt}, S_{Gt} and B_t). So, the whole mechanism might well end up in a negative contribution to the increase in income from one FY to another. Moreover, in

India: All PFI (FB + FCRC)
(Marginal effects of PFI for the period 1962–63 to 1966–67)

Parameters	1962–63	1963–64	1964–65	1965–66	1966–67
α	0.18	0.13	0.07	0.07	0.11
$\pi^h k^h$	0.44	0.38	0.41	0.40	0.44
ρk^h	0.10	0.07	0.07	0.07	0.08
λk^h	0.04	0.03	0.03	0.03	0.03
$\tau_P \pi^h k^h$	0.27	0.24	0.23	0.23	0.24
k^h	3.5				
k^0	2.0				
$\varphi_m (1+m^h)$	0.92	0.79	0.76	0.73	0.76
$\varphi_e (1+e^h)$	0.26	0.23	0.24	0.21	0.22
$\mu (1+m^0)$	0.08				
θ	0.04	0.045	0.05	0.06	0.06
σ	0				
τ_W, τ_P	0.03				
$\tau_{IND}, \tau_M, \tau_E$	0.08	0.09	0.09	0.10	0.10
w^h	0.56	0.50	0.53	0.52	0.55
$g^h k^h$	0.15				
Π	0.13				
Income data (mln rupees)					
Y_t^h	2 841	3 673	3 644	4 260	4 211
Y_t	159 110	182 020	213 240	220 040	252 650
Marginal effects (mln rupees)					
$\underline{Y}_t$	–72.96	–56.82	115.89	115.73	93.81
$\underline{\underline{B}}_t$	415.91	323.72	176.20	207.11	324.82
$\bar{\bar{S}}_{Pt}$	0	0	0	0	0
$\bar{\bar{S}}_{Gt}$	81.84	67.02	53.00	62.72	93.63

the case of India, this is somewhat accentuated by the difference between the domestic and the PFI ICOR.

After the general comments, it is possible to make some remarks about the results for the various FY's considered.

FY 1962/63 – The income effect is negative, due to the high value of α. Its magnitude, compared with the other income effects, is even higher, since in this starting FY PFI v.a. is the lowest. Nevertheless, the b.o.p. effect[4] is the highest, due to the reasons given above: a high rate of growth of PFI and high import requirements of PFI.

The relatively high public savings effect is mainly due to the high tax receipts on PFI profits (high profit ratio and high rate of increase of PFI v.a.).

FY 1963/64 – The income effect is still negative, due to the high level of α and to the relatively low level of PFI profits available for financing PFI additions. The b.o.p. effect is still rather high, in relation both to the high import requirements and to the high rate of growth of PFI, as seen above.

FY 1964/65 – The income effect becomes now positive, due to the lower value of α. The b.o.p. effect is still relevant, and the public savings effect is again kept up mainly by PFI profit taxes. It is interesting, as in the other cases, to point out how the income effect is rather low, and hardly significant if compared with the increase of GDP from FY 1964/65 to FY 1965/66 (6800;1.70%). It is even a small amount if compared with the increase of PFI v.a. (616;18.81%). Taking into account the various mechanism described by

4 The b.o.p. effect data can be appreciated better if compared with the b.o.p. deficit (B_t) of each year, and with the variation from year to year. The following data are calculated from OECD *Latest Information on National Accounts of Less Developed Countries*, February 1971, p. 18.

Year	B_t	$B_{t+1} - B_t$	$\overline{\overline{B}}_t$
1962/63	4 870	70	415.91
1963/64	4 940	1650	323.72
1964/65	6 590	10	176.20
1965/66	66 600	3440	207.11
1966/67	10 040		324.82

Import data for the last FY are taken from Table 22 of the NCAER report. They are, anyhow, not very significant, being expressed in post-devaluation rupees. All data are in mln. rupees at current prices.

the model, the increase in GDP imputable to PFI is less than 20% of the increase in PFI v.a. And this rather important result on the effects of PFI is strengthened by the highly negative effect it has on the b.o.p., as pointed out in Footnote (4).

FY 1965/66 – Much of the reasoning of the previous case applies also to this one. One should note, however, that although there is a small decrease in PFI v.a., the income effect (like all the others), is still positive, as a consequence of the way the rate of growth α was estimated.

FY 1966/67 – The income effect stays positive, although α is higher than in the two previous cases. This is imputable to the high level of profits, while the high level of α brings up again the b.o.p. effect.

It is also interesting to compare the results for 1965/66 with those for 1966/67, since in both cases Y_t^h is almost the same. The results come out quite different, however, due mainly to the different values of α and some other parameters. Where α is higher, the income effect is lower, and where α is lower, the b.o.p. effect is much higher. A role is played also by some other parameters, such as those of the foreign sector, which show some variations. The public savings effect, too, gets a positive contribution from a higher α.

The *cumulative* effects, as is known, point out the effects of PFI over a certain period, under the assumption that the alternative situation is that of absence of PFI, and that the effects are measured by difference between a situation with PFI and a situation without PFI the whole period. In the case of India the cumulative effects will be calculated over the same period chosen for the marginal effects, from 1962/63 to 1966/67, i.e. covering a four-year period. The parameters are calculated by taking the average of those obtained for the marginal effects, and this is crucial since, as is known, all data are given in current prices, and consequently this way of doing things affects at least the value of α.

The parameters and the results are given in the next table. Again the b.o.p. effect comes out quite high, and also the income effect is rather relevant. For the b.o.p. this happens mainly for the same reasons as discussed for the marginal effects, although there is no straightforward correspondence between the two, as pointed out before. The income effect is affected to a much lesser extent by the financing mechanisms for the annual additions to PFI, while the indirect effect on total financial resources available (through B_t^* and S_{Gt}^*) plays a more relevant role.

In order to appraise better the cumulative effects, it is possible to compare them with value of the corresponding variable for the total economy for

India: All PFI (FB + FCRC)
(Cumulative effects of PFI for the period
1962–63 to 1966–67)

Parameters	1962/63–1966/67
α	0.11
$\pi^h k^h$	0.41
ρk^h	0.08
λk^h	0.03
$\tau_P \pi^h k^h$	0.24
k^h	3.5
k^0	2.0
$\varphi_m (1+m^h)$	0.79
$\varphi_e (1+e^h)$	0.23
$\mu(1+m^0)$	0.08
θ	0.05
σ	0
τ_W, τ_P	0.03
$\tau_{IND}, \tau_M, \tau_E$	0.09
w^h	0.53
$g^h k^h$	0.15
Π	0.13
t	4
Income data (mln rupees)	
Y_t^h	4 211
Y_t	252 650
Cumulative effects (mln rupees)	
Y_t^*	13 517.84
B_t^*	4 710.55
S_{Pt}^*	0
S_{Gt}^*	2 557.84

1966/67, and with the increase in the value of these variables over the period 1962/63 to 1966/67. GDP data are taken from Table 1; b.o.p. data are taken from Footnote (4) p. 184, and public savings data are calculated from Tables 30 and 31 of the NCAER report.

Y_t^*:	as a % of $Y_{66/67}$	5.35; as a % of $(Y_{66/67} - Y_{62/63})$	14.45
B_t^*:	as a % of $B_{66/67}$	46.92; as a % of $(B_{66/67} - B_{62/63})$	91.11
S_{Gt}^*:	as a % of $S_{G66/67}$	150.46.	

As noticed above, the b.o.p. effect is quite relevant, and it is 'responsible' to quite a high degree for the total b.o.p. deficit; the income effect is also relevant if compared with total income; and the public savings effect is relatively important, due mainly to PFI taxes paid on profits and on other items. For the latter, no comparison is given with the increase in public savings for the total economy, in view of the relatively negligible increase of this item for the period considered (330 million rupees).

5.7. MARGINAL AND CUMULATIVE EFFECTS FOR ALL PFI (FB)

The parameters calculated for this case posed two problems: one is presented by the fact that in two instances α is negative, and the other by the high capital-output ratio[5].

The negative value of α for 1964/65 and 1965/66 does not pose any particular problem for the cumulative effects, for which α, being an average rate of growth between 1961/62 and 1967/68, is still positive, but it does affect the results obtained in the case of the marginal effects for those two years. Still it was thought reasonable to keep α negative in those two cases, because the underlying reality was by no means an extreme situation in the context of the analysis of the effects of PFI in LDC's.

The value originally obtained for k^h (see (5)) is affected by the extremely high investment level in 1966/67, while in that same year value added was less than in 1962/63, so in order to get a more realistic value it was thought preferable to drop two years in the formula given in Section 5.5 and to calculate k^h in the following way:

5 The original value obtained was 7.7. This also explains the relatively high value of k^h in the general case, since the ICOR for PFI (FB + FCRC) is a weighted average of the ICOR's of the various sub-cases (in this instance of FB and of FCRC – all PFI). The high level of investments in 1966/67 can be noticed from the table in Section 5.3.

India: All FB
(Marginal effects of PFI for the period 1962–63 to 1966–67)

Parameters	1962–63	1963–64	1964–65	1965–66	1966–67
α	0.15	0.03	–0.05	–0.03	0.02
$\pi^h k^h$	0.37	0.24	0.25	0.23	0.36
ρk^h	0.14	0.09	0.10	0.07	0.10
λk^h	0				
$\tau_P \pi^h k^h$	0.23	0.15	0.15	0.16	0.26
k^h	4.9				
k^0	2.0				
$\varphi_m (1+m^h)$	0.92	0.79	0.76	0.73	0.76
$\varphi_e (1+e^h)$	0.26	0.23	0.24	0.21	0.22
$\mu(1+m^0)$	0.08				
θ	0.04	0.045	0.05	0.06	0.06
σ	0				
τ_W, τ_P	0.03				
$\tau_{IND}, \tau_M, \tau_E$	0.08	0.09	0.09	0.10	0.10
w^h	0.66	0.51	0.60	0.57	0.69
$g^h k^h$	0.15				
Π	0.13				
Income data (mln rupees)					
Y_t^h	1 087	1 429	1 163	1 277	1 077
Y_t	159 110	182 020	213 240	220 040	252 650
Marginal effects (mln rupees)					
$\bar{\bar{Y}}_t$	–186.70	–51.13	71.82	46.92	–24.64
$\bar{\bar{B}}_t$	119.53	24.94	–30.30	–19.55	12.58
$\bar{\bar{S}}_{Pt}$	0	0	0	0	0
$\bar{\bar{S}}_{Gt}$	– 3.32	– 1.89	5.98	3.12	0.91

India: All FB
(Cumulative effects of PFI for the period
1962–63 to 1966–67)

Parameters	1962/63–1966–67
α	0.02
$\pi^h k^h$	0.29
ρk^h	0.10
λk^h	0
$\tau_p \pi^h k^h$	0.19
k^h	4.9
k^0	2.0
$\varphi_m (1+m^h)$	0.79
$\varphi_e (1+e^h)$	0.23
$\mu(1+m^0)$	0.08
θ	0.05
σ	0
τ_W, τ_P	0.03
$\tau_{IND}, \tau_M, \tau_E$	0.09
w^h	0.61
$g^h k^h$	0.15
Π	0.13
t	4
Income data (mln rupees)	
Y_t^h	1 077
Y_t	252 650
Cumulative effects (mln rupees)	
Y_t^*	5 127.15
B_t^*	1 390.28
S_{Pt}^*	0
S_{Gt}^*	836.27

$$k^h = \frac{\sum_{61/62}^{64/65} I}{Y^h_{65/66} - Y^h_{62/63}}$$

Finally, in some cases the sum of the profit and of the wage rates is more than 1. But since the difference is not very relevant, no modification was introduced. The situation is similar to one in the case of the cumulative effects, meaning that the rates on the average fulfil this requirement.

In the case of the marginal effects, one can notice how the negative contribution of PFI to income is strengthened with respect to the general case of Section 5.6. This is due to the assumption that all PFI profits net of taxes are transferred, and this reinforces the mechanism by which the financing of the annual additions to PFI affects adversely the growth of income. When the rate of growth of PFI is negative (FY 1964/65 and FY 1965/66), then the income effect comes out positive, underlying, again, this fact.

These two years with a negative rate of growth of PFI have been kept with no modification, in order to see how the model works in such a case. And the results are not surprising at all: the income effect becomes positive, for the reasons already given; the b.o.p. effect is negative (deficit decreasing) and the public savings effect stays positive.

As it was said, no further modification was introduced, apart from the way the ICOR for the PFI sector was calculated, seen in the previous page. And this is the only modification for the whole exercise in the case of India.

The cumulative effects become now quite relevant, and this is due to the fact that there is an inverse relation between the size of the cumulative effects and the rate of growth of PFI[6]. The general set up of the cumulative effects, apart from this fact, is not very much different from the results obtained for the general case.

5.8. MARGINAL AND CUMULATIVE EFFECTS FOR ALL PFI (FCRC)

The parameters estimated do not show any particular problem, apart from the rather high value of α which is going to affect the size of the effects.

6 The following exercises in the other cases considered, with various levels for α, will provide a good example of this, if the cumulative effects are related to the PFI value added of each case. This is due to the fact that the cumulative effects are expressed in terms of PFI value added of the year they refer to. The smaller the rate of growth, the greater the value of PFI value added in the previous years which 'cumulates' in the cumulative effects, with respect, obviously, to PFI value added in the year considered. Consequently, this fact should not surprise very much.

Another important feature is the low share of profit remitted abroad, due to the way this parameter was calculated. There remains quite a share of profits available for reinvestment, and this offsets partly the financing mechanism of the annual additions to PFI, with the result of a higher income effect than it would otherwise have been.

Contrary to the previous case, and, to a lesser extent, to the general case of Section 5.6, there is a good share of profits reinvested here to finance the annual additions to PFI (see the way ρk^h was calculated). Consequently, the mechanism by which PFI additions are financed affects the income effect to a lesser extent. All income effects are positive (contrary to the general case and to the previous one), and quite sizeable.

Moreover, although α is much higher, the ICOR for the PFI sector is smaller than in the previous cases, and this also partly offsets the financing mechanism considered above.

The b.o.p. effect is still rather high. This, again, is due to the high import requirements of PFI and to the relatively low level of export promotion. Moreover, a high income effect affects also the b.o.p. effect through the marginal propensity to import.

Finally, contrary to the previous case, also the 'know-how' payments to abroad affect in this case the b.o.p. effect.

Also the public savings effects are rather high, relatively much more than the others. It is related to the income effect, and this provides one first explanation of this fact. Moreover, it is affected by PFI profit taxation, etc.

This exercise, and the one of the previous section, provide a useful opportunity of comparing different ways of financing PFI. The main differences consist in the way profit remittances are calculated, and in the presence (in this case) or the absence (in the previous one) of transfers to abroad for 'know-how'. The latter affects only, and to a relatively small extent, the b.o.p. effect, while the former plays a very relevant role through the mechanism by which PFI are financed.

These results, as it was often stressed, should be considered with care, since further specifications should be necessary on this 'financing mechanism'; however, in both cases of Sections 5.7 and 5.8, the rate of transfer of profits was calculated in a similar way, and consequently, it should be possible to draw some conclusions about these two different ways of financing PFI, i.e. FB vs FCRC.

By all standards FCRC seem more desirable, as far as the consequences on the host country are concerned. Such a conclusion, anyhow, should have been expected also on other grounds; these quantitative results provide, furthermore, a more precise basis on which to discuss such alternatives.

India: All FCRC
(Marginal effects of PFI for the period 1962–63 to 1966–67)

Parameters	1962–63	1963–64	1964–65	1965–66	1966–67
α	0.21	0.19	0.15	0.12	0.15
$\pi^h k^h$	0.49	0.47	0.49	0.48	0.47
ρk^h	0.07	0.06	0.06	0.07	0.07
λk^h	0.06	0.05	0.05	0.05	0.05
$\tau_P \pi^h k^h$	0.29	0.30	0.27	0.26	0.23
k^h	2.6				
k^0	2.0				
$\varphi_m (1+m^h)$	0.92	0.79	0.76	0.73	0.76
$\varphi_e (1+e^h)$	0.26	0.23	0.24	0.21	0.22
$\mu(1+m^0)$	0.08				
θ	0.04	0.045	0.05	0.06	0.06
σ	0				
τ_W, τ_P	0.03				
$\tau_{IND}, \tau_M, \tau_E$	0.08	0.09	0.09	0.10	0.10
w^h	0.51	0.49	0.50	0.49	0.51
$g^h k^h$	0.15				
Π	0.13				
Income data (mln rupees)					
Y_t^h	1 754	2 244	2 481	2 983	3 134
Y_t	159 110	182 020	213 240	220 040	252 650
Marginal effects (mln rupees)					
$\bar{\bar{\bar{Y}}}_t$	175.21	175.24	248.63	282.62	335.61
$\bar{\bar{\bar{B}}}_t$	314.01	312.41	264.11	263.76	353.45
$\bar{\bar{\bar{S}}}_{Pt}$	0	0	0	0	0
$\bar{\bar{\bar{S}}}_{Gt}$	101.90	119.79	105.52	107.59	126.78

India: All FCRC
(Cumulative effects of PFI for the period
1962–63 to 1966–67)

Parameters	1962/63–1966/67
α	0.16
$\pi^h k^h$	0.48
ρk^h	0.07
λk^h	0.05
$\tau_P \pi^h k^h$	0.27
k^h	2.6
k^0	2.0
$\varphi_m (1+m^h)$	0.79
$\varphi_e (1+e^h)$	0.23
$\mu (1+m^0)$	0.08
θ	0.05
σ	0
τ_W, τ_P	0.03
$\tau_{IND}, \tau_M, \tau_E$	0.09
w^h	0.50
$g^h k^h$	0.15
Π	0.13
t	4
Income data (mln rupees)	
Y_t^h	3 134
Y_t	252 650
Cumulative effects (mln rupees)	
Y_t^*	9 134.68
B_t^*	3 300.17
S_{Pt}^*	0
S_{Gt}^*	1 874.32

The calculations of the cumulative effects do not provide any striking result. They are relatively lower than in the case of the FB, due to a higher level of α. The income effect is rather sizeable, but the b.o.p. effect comes out again very high, specially if compared with the absolute level of the corresponding variable for the total economy (see footnote (4), p. 184).

5.9 MARGINAL AND CUMULATIVE EFFECTS FOR MANUFACTURING PFI (FB + FCRC)

There is no particular problem in the parameters estimates, although there is a rather high value of α. With respect to the three preceding cases, the imports and exports coefficients are lower. However, this should not affect too much the b.o.p. effect, since the gap between the two does not vary too much.

In the marginal effects, one notices how there is no negative result in the income effects, contrary to what happened in the corresponding general case. Although α is generally higher than it was there, this does not happen mainly because of a lower ICOR for the PFI sector, and of the higher rate of profit reinvested, due to the lower foreign capital share in manufacturing PFI, with respect to all PFI. Both these features offset partly the financing mechanism of the annual additions to PFI, which was responsible for the results in the general case.

So, although α is still high, there is no negative income effect, because such financial mechanism affects it to a lesser extent.

The b.o.p. effect is still high. As it was said above, although the import requirements are lower, this happens also for the export promotion coefficients, with a similar balance as before.

The public savings effect is relatively higher than in the case of Section 5.6, due mainly to higher taxes on PFI profits.

Although α is rather high, the cumulative effects come out also rather relevant. One explanation, in the case of the income effect, which affects all the others, is provided by the smaller influence of the financial mechanism of the annual additions to PFI considered above. The other two effects are influenced, apart from this latter fact, also by the same facts already seen above for the marginal calculations.

It is possible to compare the results of this section (all manufacturing PFI) with the ones of Section 5.6 (all PFI).

In the case of the marginal effects, as seen above, the financial mechanism works to a lesser extent, because more profits are reinvested and the ICOR is lower. As it was noticed, the income effect comes out higher, and this affects the other two consequently.

India: Manufacturing (FB + FCRC)
(Marginal effects of PFI for the period 1962–63 to 1966–67)

Parameters	1962–63	1963–64	1964–65	1965–66	1966–67
α	0.18	0.17	0.13	0.13	0.19
$\pi^h k^h$	0.50	0.50	0.48	0.48	0.47
ρk^h	0.09	0.07	0.06	0.06	0.07
λk^h	0.04	0.03	0.03	0.03	0.03
$\tau_P \pi^h k^h$	0.30	0.31	0.27	0.26	0.24
k^h	2.5				
k^0	2.0				
$\varphi_m (1+m^h)$	0.76	0.64	0.63	0.65	0.63
$\varphi_e (1+e^h)$	0.11	0.12	0.13	0.12	0.13
$\mu(1+m^0)$	0.08				
θ	0.04	0.045	0.05	0.06	0.06
σ	0				
τ_W, τ_P	0.03				
$\tau_{IND}, \tau_M, \tau_E$	0.08	0.09	0.09	0.10	0.10
w^h	0.50	0.48	0.48	0.50	0.53
$g^h k^h$	0.15				
Π	0.13				
Income data (mln rupees)					
Y_t^h	1 728	2 122	2 357	2 719	2 997
Y_t	159 110	182 020	213 240	220 040	252 650
Marginal effects (mln rupees)					
$\bar{\bar{Y}}_t$	163.18	185.22	228.20	286.61	314.24
$\bar{\bar{B}}_t$	264.64	247.95	208.15	255.52	386.22
$\bar{\bar{S}}_{Pt}$	0	0	0	0	0
$\bar{\bar{S}}_{Gt}$	79.67	98.57	81.19	100.35	129.86

India: Manufacturing (FB + FCRC)
(Cumulative effects of PFI for the period
1962–63 to 1966–67)

Parameters	1962/63–1966/67
α	0.16
$\pi^h k^h$	0.49
ρk^h	0.07
λk^h	0.03
$\tau_P \pi^h k^h$	0.28
k^h	2.5
k^0	2.0
$\varphi_m (1+m^h)$	0.66
$\varphi_e (1+e^h)$	0.12
$\mu(1+m^0)$	0.08
θ	0.05
σ	0
τ_W, τ_P	0.03
$\tau_{IND}, \tau_M, \tau_E$	0.09
w^h	0.50
$g^h k^h$	0.15
Π	0.13
t	4
Income data (mln rupees)	
Y_t^h	2 997
Y_t	252 650
Cumulative effects (mln rupees)	
Y_t^*	8 519.34
B_t^*	2 997.07
S_{Pt}^*	0
S_{Gt}^*	1 732.17

The cumulative effects are, with respect to the PFI value added they refer to, not much different, although there are some variations in the parameters, which in some case compensate each other, at least up to a certain degree. In the case of manufacturing PFI α is higher, and consequently, the income effect should be lower; however, the financial mechanism, for the reasons seen above, works less, and these two somewhat compensate in the overall result.

5.10 MARGINAL AND CUMULATIVE EFFECTS FOR MANUFACTURING PFI (FB)

Similarly to what was noted in Section 5.7, α is negative in two cases (1963/64 and 1964/65) for the marginal effects, while no problem arises for the cumulative effects. For the same reason given there, no modification was introduced, although these negative values will affect the marginal results for these two years.

Again, as in Section 5.7, profit and wage rates in some cases do not add up to one. No modification was introduced, for various reasons, like the ones given commenting the table in Section 5.3. No problem arises for the cumulative effects, while in interpreting the results for the marginal effects this fact must be kept in mind. Anyhow, a high wage rate affects only the public savings effects (and the others, consequently), and it is multiplied by the direct taxation coefficient. The total impact is relatively small[7].

In the marginal effects, similarly to what happened in Section 5.7, the income effect is generally negative, when PFI value added has a positive rate of growth, due mainly to the way the financial mechanism works (no profits reinvested by assumption), and it becomes positive when α is negative.

Something similar happens to the b.o.p. effect, which is rather high, if compared with PFI value added, and becomes negative (deficit decreasing) when α is negative.

In the case of the cumulative effects, the results are relatively high, due to the low level of α, although the financial mechanism of the annual additions to PFI plays a negative role, partly offsetting the previous fact.

In general, the structure of the cumulative effects for manufacturing FB is similar to the one of Section 5.7, also because some of the variations in the parameters compensate a little, similarly to what was seen at the end of the previous section.

7 In this, like in all cases where the sum of the two rates is more than one, this justification for introducing no variation on the basis of the relatively small impact of the wage rate on the various effects, assumes implicitly that the profit rates are correct, while if there is any distorsion, this is in the wage rates.

India: FB Manufacturing
(Marginal effects of PFI for the period 1962–63 to 1966–67)

Parameters	1962–63	1963–64	1964–65	1965–66	1966–67
α	0.15	–0.09	–0.09	0.01	0.18
$\pi^h k^h$	0.47	0.33	0.25	0.21	0.40
ρk^h	0.21	0.12	0.11	0.06	0.17
λk^h	0				
$\tau_P \pi^h k^h$	0.26	0.21	0.14	0.15	0.23
k^h	3.2				
k^0	2.0				
$\varphi_m (1+m^h)$	0.76	0.64	0.63	0.65	0.63
$\varphi_e (1+e^h)$	0.11	0.12	0.13	0.12	0.13
$\mu(1+m^0)$	0.08				
θ	0.04	0.045	0.05	0.06	0.06
σ	0				
τ_W, τ_P	0.03				
$\tau_{IND}, \tau_M, \tau_E$	0.08	0.09	0.09	0.10	0.10
w^h	0.60	0.54	0.68	0.72	0.86
$g^h k^h$	0.15				
Π	0.13				
Income data (mln rupees)					
Y_t^h	233	265	197	223	193
Y_t	159 110	182 020	213 240	220 040	252 650
Marginal effects (mln rupees)					
$\overline{\overline{Y}}_t$	– 5.73	4.69	4.52	–0.64	– 9.07
$\overline{\overline{B}}_t$	30.67	–15.65	–11.06	1.34	23.76
$\overline{\overline{S}}_{Pt}$	0	0	0	0	0
$\overline{\overline{S}}_{Gt}$	4.37	– 1.85	– 0.06	0.06	4.02

India: Manufacturing (FB)
(Cumulative effects of PFI for the period
1962–63 to 1966–67)

Parameters	1962/63–1966/67
α	0.03
$\pi^h k^h$	0.33
ρk^h	0.13
λk^h	0
$\tau_P \pi^h k^h$	0.20
k^h	3.2
k^0	2.0
$\varphi_m (1+m^h)$	0.66
$\varphi_e (1+e^h)$	0.12
$\mu(1+m^0)$	0.08
θ	0.05
σ	0
τ_W, τ_P	0.03
$\tau_{IND}, \tau_M, \tau_E$	0.09
w^h	0.68
$g^h k^h$	0.15
Π	0.13
t	4
Income Data (mln rupees)	
Y_t^h	193
Y_t	252 650
Cumulative effects (mln rupees)	
Y_t^*	888.91
B_t^*	248.53
S_{Pt}^*	0
S_{Gt}^*	143.75

The same reasoning applies, *mutatis mutandis*, also to the marginal effects of FB manufacturing compared with the marginal effects for all FB.

5.11 MARGINAL AND CUMULATIVE EFFECTS FOR PFI MANUFACTURING (FCRC)

There is no particular problem in the parameters estimates, apart from the high rate of growth α. Its impact, particularly on the income effect, should be partly offset by the low rate of transfer of profits to abroad, which will provide more financial resources for the annual additions to the PFI capital stock, and partly counterbalance the consequences of the financing mechanism of the model. Similar considerations as the ones given in Section 5.9 about the import and export coefficients apply also here, and, as a matter of fact, they were calculated with reference to this particular case.

Apart from the considerations given above, one can notice how the marginal effects are rather similar to the ones obtained for all FCRC, and this is mainly due to the fact that in 1966/67 manufacturing FCRC accounted for 89.5 per cent of total FCRC value added. The same applies to the cumulative effects, and especially to these, since they are calculated with reference to 1966/67. There are no big differences also with respect to all manufacturing PFI, since most parameters are similar, and PFI value added is not much different. As a matter of fact, FCRC accounted in 1966/67 for 93.5% of PFI manufacturing, while FB accounted only for 6.5%.

So, similar considerations as the ones given in the previous sections, apply also in explaining the results obtained for the present case.

It is also possible, as it was done for all PFI, to compare the results for manufacturing FB with the ones for manufacturing FCRC. In doing so, one comes more or less to the same conclusions given there. FCRC seem to affect negatively the economy to a lesser extent (see e.g. the marginal effects on the b.o.p. deficit), while, when the effects are positive, they are stronger than in the case of FB (see e.g., the income effect).

5.12. CONCLUSIONS

The exercise carried out on the previous pages may be considered a 'case study of India', but most of all it represents an empirical application of the methodology of Part II with reference to the data supplied by NCAER for India. Consequently, the results should be interpreted mainly in this light, and they should serve to provide a better insight into the methodology, as

5.11. India: FCRC manufacturing
(Marginal effects of PFI for the period 1962–63 to 1966–67)

Parameters	1962–63	1963–64	1964–65	1965–66	1966–67
α	0.19	0.20	0.16	0.14	0.19
$\pi^h k^h$ ..	0.51	0.52	0.51	0.50	0.48
ρk^h	0.07	0.06	0.06	0.06	0.06
λk^h	0.06	0.05	0.05	0.05	0.05
$\tau_P \pi^h k^h$	0.31	0.33	0.30	0.28	0.24
k^h	2.5				
k^0	2.0				
$\varphi_m (1+m^h)$	0.76	0.64	0.63	0.65	0.63
$\varphi_e (1+e^h)$	0.11	0.12	0.13	0.12	0.13
$\mu(1+m^0)$	0.08				
θ	0.04	0.045	0.05	0.06	0.06
σ	0				
τ_W, τ_P	0.03				
$\tau_{IND}, \tau_M, \tau_E$	0.08	0.09	0.09	0.10	0.10
w^h	0.48	0.47	0.46	0.48	0.50
$g^h k^h$	0.15				
Π	0.13				
Income data (mln rupees)					
Y_t^h	1 495	1 857	2 160	2 496	2 804
Y_t	159 110	182 020	213 240	220 040	252 650
Marginal effects (mln rupees)					
$\bar{Y}_t$	160.40	180.08	220.10	271.63	327.31
$\bar{B}_t$	242.50	258.01	238.62	258.86	369.76
$\bar{S}_{Pt}$	0	0	0	0	0
$\bar{S}_{Gt}$	76.98	107.34	96.62	104.37	125.62

India: manufacturing (FCRC)
(Cumulative effects of PFI for the period
1962–63 to 1966–67)

Parameters	1962/63–1966/67
α	0.17
$\pi^h k^h$	0.50
ρk^h	0.06
λk^h	0.05
$\tau_P \pi^h k^h$	0.29
k^h	2.5
k^0	2.0
$\varphi_m (1+m^h)$	0.66
$\varphi_e (1+e^h)$	0.12
$\mu(1+m^0)$	0.08
θ	0.05
σ	0
τ_W, τ_P	0.03
$\tau_{IND}, \tau_M, \tau_E$	0.09
w^h	0.48
$g^h k^h$	0.15
Π	0.13
t	4
Income data (mln rupees)	
Y_t^h	2 804
Y_t	252 650
Cumulative effects (mln rupees)	
Y_t^*	7 905.37
B_t^*	2 830.78
S_{Pt}^*	0
S_{Gt}^*	1 639.51

well as to point out various possible improvements in order to make it more realistic.

The results allow us anyhow to get some preliminary ideas about the effects of PFI in India. It was possible to distinguish various cases, and to compare various situations: mainly all PFI vs manufacturing PFI, and FB vs FCRC, that is to say, for the second case, alternative PFI situations.

Although the exercise has various limitations, and is based on some rather radical simplifying assumptions, it is possible to reach some general conclusions:

– PFI in general affects to a minor extent the increase of income;
– PFI in general poses a heavy burden on the b.o.p.;
– totally foreign controlled PFI (i.e. FB) tends to strengthen the negative effects of PFI and to reduce the positive ones as compared with partially domestically controlled PFI (i.e. FCRC).

During the various phases of the exercise, it was also found how heavily certain assumptions affect the results. This is particularly true of :

– the financing mechanism of the annual additions to PFI;
– the calculation of the transfer of profits to abroad;
– the assumptions about import substitution.

The first point was found to be rather important in explaining most of the results.

The second point connected with the first one most probably underestimates the contribution of PFI profits to the financing of the annual additions to PFI, especially in the case of FB, where all profits net of taxes are assumed to be transferred abroad.

Finally, the third point tends to affect the b.o.p. effect by increasing it, being most probably an underestimation of the real situation.

One should keep in mind also the major limitations of the results obtained from an 'empirical' point of view, apart from the more 'theoretical' ones discussed above. They consist mainly of the fact that the exercise was carried out in current prices, instead of constant prices; that the various concepts of FY's were varying, and that the surveys for the various FY's had a different coverage, as pointed out in Section 5.2.

CHAPTER VI

THE PHILIPPINES

6.1. INTRODUCTION

This chapter will present some results with reference to the case of the Philippines and on the basis of data made available by SEUP.

The next section will describe the coverage of the data, their source and limitations, according to what was stated by SEUP.

Section 6.3 will then give a general picture of the relevance of PFI in 1964 in the case of the Philippines.

Section 6.4 will discuss the methodological approach followed.

Section 6.5 will show how, one by one, the various parameters have been estimated.

In the following sections, various empirical cases will be considered. The data supplied by SEUP can be aggregated according to Section 9.1 of Part II. Analysis is then possible for All PFI in manufacturing and for All PFI in the seven manufacturing sub-sectors.

As data on PFI are available only for 1964 and in some cases 1965, only the marginal effects of PFI can be calculated.

Some parameters for the whole economy were estimated over the period 1958–1969, as the data for the whole economy cover this period.

6.2. SOURCE OF DATA, COVERAGE, AND LIMITATIONS

The exercise carried out in this paper is based on data supplied by the School of Economics of the University of the Philippines (SEUP). The main criteria followed by SEUP are the following:

. . . The study covers private non-financial entities (and cooperatives) with adjusted net assets of ₱ 1 million or more in 1964 and 1965. This sector accounts for practically all foreign corporate investments in the country. Out of this list of entities firms belonging to the PFI sector were classified according to the criteria set in the questionnaire. No study was possible for the years 1959 to 1963 due to insufficiency of records. Furthermore, it should be noted that there is no single agency in the country that collects economic data on the effects of foreign firms in the country nor are the criteria provided for in the 'questionnaire' compatible with any method of classifying information on foreign business enterprises operating here. At most, the classification being utilized, if any, is by nationality percentage share. For the particular years 1966 to 1969 no further research was undertaken due to lack of financial resources and time. Even the way the economy is divided by sectors does not conform with the methods used in the Philippines. Instead, the following subclassifications are being used:

(1) manufacturing
(2) mining, ore processing, quarrying and mineral exploration
(3) agriculture, fishing and forestry
(4) commerce, warehousing, customs brokerage, etc.
(5) utilities
(6) construction
(7) services and
(8) real estate.

The government sector is not treated separetely in the breakdown of the economy into sectors. . . .

The time series supplied on the country's overall aggregates go from 1958 to 1969.

Because of the differences in classification, the analysis focuses on the manufacturing sectors and the manufacturing sub-sectors as mentioned in the previous section.

In Section 6.3, sectors (4), (5), (7) and (8) will be aggregated in 'Trade and services'.

Some crucial data on PFI are missing, as may be concluded from the text quoted above (imports and exports, profits, public expenditure on PFI, etc.). This will call for some additional assumptions in order to estimate them (see Section 6.5).

As most of the data available are in current prices, the exercise will be based on such current data. This influences the parameters and hence the results as do additional assumptions necessary to bridge the incompleteness of data. This must be kept in mind in interpreting the results.

6.3. PFI IN THE PHILIPPINES: THE GENERAL PICTURE

The table on pp. 206-207 gives an illustration of the relative importance of PFI in the Philippines. It is calculated mainly from various tables of the 'SEUP Report'. It is split up into PFI in the whole economy and PFI in the manufacturing subsectors.

Let us first consider PFI in the major sectors of the economy. Columns (1) and (2) show that the relative importance of PFI for the economy is rather limited in terms of GNP. PFI is completely absent – according to the underlying data – in 'Agriculture', 'Construction', 'Electricity, gas and water' and 'Transportation'. Most of PFI in 1964 was in manufacturing, where the bulk of PFI share in GNP stems from PFI in 'Mining and quarrying'. 'Trade and

PFI in the Philippines: The general picture

	(1)	(2)	(3)	(4)
	v.a. composition	% of v.a. in GNP	% of v.a. in corresponding sector	import requirement % of v.a.
All PFI	100	9.1	9.1	–
PFI agriculture and fishing	–	–	–	–
PFI mining and quarrying	7.7	0.7	75.0	–
PFI manufacturing	72.8	6.6	34.9	–
PFI construction	–	–	–	–
PFI electricity, gas, water	–	–	–	–
PFI trade and services	6.1	0.6	1.9	–
PFI transport and communication	–	–	–	–
PFI petroleum	13.3	1.2	2.3	–
PFI other services	–	–	–	–
PFI Manufacturing				
Food, beverages and tobacco	34.0	3.1	40.6	–
Textiles, footwear, apparel	2.9	0.3	0.8	–
Chemicals and allied products	9.1	0.9	64.3	–
Primary and fabricated metals	3.6	0.3	1.7	–
Machinery	1.4	0.1	1.6	–
Transport equipment	0.7	0.1	2.3	–
Other manufacturing	20.9	1.9	38.1	–
Source:	Table 1.1	Tables 1.1 1.2	Tables 1.1 (e) 1.3	

Notes:
(a) Source: 'SEUP Report', various tables.
(b) See the text (Section 6.3) for Comments–All figures refer to 1964.
(c) – = not available.
(d) Sectoral value added taken from ECAFE, *Statistical Yearbook for Asia and the Far East,* 1969.

services'. and 'Petroleum' have a rather modest share in GNP. Manufacturing PFI alone accounts for 6.6% of GNP. The rather limited contribution of the 'Mining' PFI to GNP accounts for three fourths of that sector's total value added, while PFI in manufacturing is relatively less important compared to the whole manufacturing value added (column (3)). The share of the other PFI sectors in the total value added of the corresponding sector for the whole economy is very modest.

Column (6) gives the percentage of profits with respect to value added. Value added is defined as the contribution of PFI to GNP with some modi-

(5)	(6)	(7)	(8)	(9)	(10)	(11)
exp. promotion %v.a.	profits as % of v.a.	wages %v.a.	employment/ v.a.	gross inv./ v.a.	capital stock/ v.a.	average sectoral foreign share of PFI assets in %
–	15.9	–	–	–	1.54	–
–	–	–	–	–	–	100
–	–	–	–	–	2.71	37
–	18.32	–	–	–	1.52	66
–	–	–	–	–	–	24
–	–	–	–	–	–	41
–	48.54	–	–	–	4.73	76
–	–	–	–	–	–	41
–	–	–	–	–	2.33	83
–	–	–	–	–	–	34
–	4.89	–	–	–	0.86	54
–	71.51	–	–	–	2.87	34
–	3.79	–	–	–	0.74	90
–	5.67	–	–	–	1.13	63
–	4.98	–	–	–	1.19	88
–	18.32	–	–	–	2.18	100
–	15.94	–	–	–	1.35	73
	Tables 1.1 2.1, 4.2				Tables 1.1, 2.1	Table 2.1

fication (see 'SEUP Report', comments on Table 1.1.). Profits were calculated from the 'SEUP Report' Tables 1.1, 2.1 and 4.2. The percentages of profits are not, in general, very high, but one must be cautious with any generalization, owing to the additional assumptions involved.

The data on export, import, wages, employment and investment are missing, as pointed out in Section 6.2. An assumption about a similar behaviour of PFI sectors *vis-à-vis* the 'rest of economy' was applied.

Column (10) gives the average capital-output ratios for the major PFI sectors. Only 'Trade and services' shows rather a high capital-output ratio compared to the others, which are lower.

The average sectoral foreign share of assets of PFI is based on the 'SEUP Report', Table 2.1. There is some PFI given by the 'SEUP Report', even in the sectors where no PFI value added is reported. The explanation may lie in the difference in coverage of the two tables.

Let us turn the attention to PFI in manufacturing sub-sectors. The first three columns indicate that 'Food, beverages and tobacco', 'Other manufacturing' and 'Chemicals and allied products' are the most important sub-sectors within the manufacturing sector and obviously also for their share in GNP. Their share in the corresponding overall sub-sectoral value added in also substantial, although the ranking changes in favour of 'Chemicals and allied products', followed by 'Food, beverages and tobacco' and 'Other manufacturing'.

The percentage of profits is rather low except for 'Textile, footwear and apparel' and 'Transport equipment'. The doubts expressed on the data in the higher part of this column (major PFI sectors) apply also to the various PFI manufacturing sub-sectors.

The capital-output ratios (column (10)) are generally rather low. The highest share of foreign assets (column (11)) can be observed in 'Transport equipment', 'Chemicals and allied products' and 'Machinery'.

In the case of PFI manufacturing sub-sectors data on import, export, wages, employment and investment are not available either.

In the descriptive part of 'SEUP Report', some interesting remarks can be read on the impact of employment, wages and foreign trade of PFI on the economy of the Philippines.

As these remarks are without statistical evidence, they can only be considered as an interesting side information and cannot be used as a base for calculations.

6.4. THE METHODOLOGICAL APPROACH

Given the kind of data (only for 1964 and 1965 as far as the PFI sectors are concerned), it is only possible to apply the 'marginal' approach, and to calculate the marginal effects.

This allows to overcome partly the complication given by the fact that almost all data are in current prices. Most parameters will be calculated year by year, and consequently will not be affected. However, some other parameters will have to be calculated over a longer period, with the adjustments to be discussed in Section 6.5. No attempt will be made to correct the data in current prices into data in constant prices. Although price indices are available, there is a risk of making more mistakes than improvements.

The calculation of the marginal effects over a two-year period for the manufacturing sector and sub-sectors, will allow discussion of their variation, caused by varying values of some of the parameters, as a consequence of different structural characteristics.

The data available will allow calculation of only the four basic marginal effects. The lack of employment data prevents the calculation of the employment effect, while it is not possible to calculate the income distribution effect, due to the procedure followed to get wage and profit rates.

An attempt was made to leave 'petroleum' out of the analysis, although, due to the classification procedures followed in the 'SEUP Report', some errors might be left in the data used.

6.5. ESTIMATION OF THE PARAMETERS

In the following pages, a brief description will be given of the way the various parameters were estimated, together with the various assumptions introduced.

Y_t^h, Y_t are taken in current prices from Tables 1.1 and 1.2.

α some capital stock figures (PFI assets in 1964 and 1965) are available, but α was calculated from value added data at current prices from Table 1.1, due to the fact that these figures do not stand for capital stock in real terms. As only data for 1964 and 1965 are presented in that table, α was calculated according to the formula:

$$\alpha = \frac{Y_{1965}^h - Y_{1964}^h}{Y_{1964}^h} .$$

α was calculated for all eight cases separately.

k^h The absent data on capital stock or gross investment of PFI were replaced by figures on their total value of assets (from Table 2.1) over the years 1964 and 1965. First the ICOR was calculated using data from Table 2.1 and value added data from Table 1.2 according to the formula (A^h = total assets):

$$\frac{A^h_{1965} - A^h_{1964}}{Y^h_{1965} - Y^h_{1964}} .$$

Because of the decrease in value added in the PFI sectors 'Textiles, footwear and apparel' and 'Primary and fabricated metals' in 1965, the ICOR of these two sectors comes out negative. Moreover, basing the calculations of the ICOR on only two years might be misleading, owing to the irregular behaviour of PFI over short periods. Therefore, the average capital-output ratio was calculated for 1964 according to the formula:

$$\frac{A^h_{1964}}{Y^h_{1964}} .$$

It was calculated separately for all eight cases.

$\pi^h k^h$ There is no indication on profits of PFI in the 'SEUP Report'. The only information is given in Table 4.2 on taxes paid as a percentage of net profit after taxes.

Data on direct taxes paid by private companies[a] (in pesos)

	1964		1965	
	taxes paid	% of profit	taxes paid	% of profit
(a) companies 100% foreign owned	12 728 408	48.1 %	10 308 803	47.7%
(b) 50–99 % foreign owned	36 802 589	42.5 %	30 953 293	39.6%
(c) 25–49 % foreign owned	31 961 624	36.4 %	87 729 691	32.2%
(d) 0–24 % owned		no study taken		

a (1) Direct taxes comprise only income taxes and excludes other types of direct taxes like residence tax.
(2) Profit is net profit after taxes.
(3) Source: 'SEUP Report', Table 4.2.

From this table the total profits of each group, (a), (b), and (c), were calculated. To get profits before taxes, the amount of taxes paid was added. From Table 2.1 information on the average sectoral foreign share was obtained. The sectors were then grouped in three groups according to the foreign share, and to the (a), (b) and (c) groups of Table 4.2. The total assets of these three groups were calculated as well as the relative share of the sectors in each group owing to sectoral total assets. The profits of each group were then imputed to the sectors proportionally to their assets and related to value added figures of Table 1.1.

As the results seem to be underestimated – among others due to the neglecting of some taxes – the results were rounded up to the next multiple of ten.

It is obvious that the whole procedure is rather rough and that many simplifying assumptions are involved (handling sector as one company, etc.). Still it is based on 'SEUP Report' figures and it may give some more detailed sectoral information.

ρk^h Table 2.4 gives information on profits, earnings and dividends outflow of all PFI for the period 1959–1968, in US \$. Using the exchange rate 3.90 pesos for 1 US \$ (IMF *International Financial Statistics,* July 1971), the figures for 1964 and 1965 were related to total PFI contribution to GNP of Table 1.1. Then, the average value of these two years was taken for all PFI. To take into account the sectoral profit ratios, profit transferred was related to total profits of 1964 and the sectoral profit ratios were multiplied by this latter percentage.

λk^h In this case, no data available about payments for 'know-how' to abroad. The same table mentioned above gives 'other outward investment remittances' of all PFI for the period 1959–1968, in US \$. This may be a rough approximation of the data needed. Using the same exchange rate as in the above case, the figures for 1964 and 1965 were related to 1964 and 1965 PFI total contribution to GNP. The average of the two years was used for all the cases, as any sectoral differentiation in relation to profits did not seem justified as long as more detailed data are lacking.

$\tau_p \pi^h k^h$ was calculated from Table 4.2 relating direct taxes paid by private companies to total profits before taxes (calculated, again, from Table 4.2). The percentage obtained was applied to the profit ratios obtained above.

k^0 was calculated from the data of Table 2.1 (gross investments for the economy as a whole) and Table 1.2 (GNP at current market prices). Both time series cover the period 1958–1969.

The following formula was used:

$$k^0 = \frac{\sum_{1958}^{1969} I}{Y_{1969} - Y_{1958}}.$$

In contrast to k^h, k^0 is an ICOR, as the underlying data make this possible, but no lag was introduced, for reasons of homogeneity with k^h.

$\varphi_m(1+m^h)$ was the result of relating the total value of imports for the whole economy (from Table 1.6 of the 'SEUP Report') to GNP data (from Table 1.2). Both series were in current prices for the period 1958–1969.
As data on import of PFI were absent, an assumption was introduced about a similar behaviour of PFI and the whole economy with respect to imports. An attempt was made to find some different sectoral import requirements, but the data available (Tables 1.6 and 1.2) led to unrealistic results, due to the fact that it considers imports by type of goods and not by sector of destination.

$\varphi_e(1+e^h)$ could not be calculated for PFI for lack of data. Similarly to $\varphi_m(1+m^h)$, the uniformity of export behaviour was assumed for domestic branches and PFI. Here a sectoral breakdown was possible and, based on Tables 1.4 and 1.2, the sectoral export parameters were calculated. Although within the sectors, uniformity of export performance is assumed for domestic and foreign private firms, this parameter is different in all eight cases.

$\mu(1+m^0)$ the marginal propensity to import was calculated from Tables 1.6 (inclusive of goods and services) and from Table 1.2 at current prices, according to the formula:

$$\mu(1+m^0) = \frac{M_t - M_0}{Y_t - Y_0}$$

for the period 1958 to 1969. This parameter is assumed to be constant for all cases and for all years.

θ due to lack of data the rate of interest in the foreign debt was assumed to be equal to the official bank rate, as given by the IMF, *International Financial Statistics*, July 1971.

It is the same in all cases, and it refers to 1964.

σ — the marginal propensity to save was calculated according to the formula:

$$\sigma = \frac{S_{1967} - S_{1959}}{Y_{1967} - Y_{1959}} \cdot$$

S stands for net saving, taken from OECD, *National Accounts of Less Developed Countries (1969)*, Y is GNP from Table 1.2, 'SEUP Report'.

τ_W, τ_P — were assumed to be the same, for lack of more detailed data, and were calculated by relating total direct tax receipts (Table 4.1) to GNP (Table 1.2), and taking the average value over the period considered (1958–1969). This quantity is assumed to be the same in all cases. Only PFI profits' direct tax rates were calculated in a more accurate way, as seen above.

w^h — as no information was available in the 'SEUP Report', the assumption was introduced that $\pi^h\ k^h$ and w^h add up to one. Taking into account taxes, in practice they add up to .95. This is not very accurate but, anyhow, this parameter plays a minor role in the calculation of the effects.

$\tau_{\text{IND}}, \tau_E, \tau_M$ — for lack of more detailed data were assumed to be the same and were calculated from Table 1.2 (indirect taxes receipts and GNP), as an average value over the period considered, and the same for all cases.

$g^h k^h$ — for lack of data the assumption that the same expenditure ratio between GNP and government current expenditure holds both for the total economy and for the PFI sector was introduced. Data were calculated for the period 1962–1969, and since there is no great variation, an average value was introduced for all cases.

Π — this parameter relates indirect taxes plus direct taxes (Table 4.1) to GNP (Table 1.2) at current prices. An average value was taken for the period considered for all cases.

Before proceeding to the analysis of the empirical results, some general comments are possible, and they will help clarifying some of the results which will be obtained later.

As in the previous chapter one first point to be discussed refers to the *import and export coefficients*. One first bias might be caused by the way the two parameters were estimated, as seen in the previous pages. Moreover, as has been observed before, one must remember the fact that import substitution is not taken into account, or, rather, is assumed to be included in the coefficients themselves.

There is no evidence of the extent to which import substitution is promoted by PFI. For this one would need at least an idea of how much of the value added of PFI would have been imported in its absence, and of the import requirements of PFI industries. Both are lacking, and so the analysis had to be made while no solution to this problem was available. This should be kept in mind when interpreting the results.

As in the case of India, another crucial point concerns the *mechanism of financing the annual additions to PFI*. As was seen there, the mechanism assumed by the model is crucial in determining the income effect, through the absorption of a share of financial resources otherwise available for domestic investments.

It was also observed that it was possible to presume that a greater role should be played by foreign capital inflow directly related to the PFI under consideration, and meant to finance its expansion.

It was, however, also noticed that this aspect had already, to some extent, be taken into account by the model, through the assumption by which the deficit of the b.o.p. corresponds to total capital inflow. In this *endogenous* way of handling the problem it follows that the b.o.p. effect of PFI can also be taken as the foreign capital inflow directly imputable to PFI. And since this plays a positive role in the income effect, offsetting partly the negative role of the financing mechanism under discussion, the conclusion was that it was possible to assume that also this kind of capital inflow is taken into account by the model, in an endogenous way[1].

6.6. MARGINAL EFFECTS FOR ALL PFI MANUFACTURING SECTOR

In the following pages the results of the empirical exercise are given first for the manufacturing sector as a whole, and then for PFI in the various subsectors considered.

1 The 'SEUP Report' gives, under 2, 'Foreign Private Investment inflow and outflow', distinguishing, in the 'inflow', 'Capital for investment in the Philippines' and 'Other inward investment remittances'. These data, however, refer to All PFI, and do not allow any sectoral nor subsectoral reasoning. For a theoretical discussion of this point see Part II, Section 8.7.

Some considerations are possible before analysing the results case by case.

First, one should remember what was said in the previous pages about import substitution and export promotion. Then, the reasoning about the working of the model's financial mechanism should be kept in mind. When α is high, it will influence the income effect, and consequently all the others. Both these features will be discussed in more detail when the numerical results of the various cases are commented upon.

Finally, the assumptions introduced to fill the gaps where empirical data directly pertaining to PFI were lacking should also be kept in mind in analysing the outcomes of the empirical exercise, as they influence them to a considerable extent.

Generally speaking, the income effect is surprisingly higher than the increase directly imputable of PFI (αY_t^h) in all cases but one. A possible explanation is that the working of the mechanism of financing the annual additions to PFI is favourable, since a certain share of PFI profits is available for reinvestment. Only with an extremely high α, the financial mechanism lowers the income effect of PFI.

The relative impact of the income effect on the economy of the Philippines can be appreciated by confronting the various results for the marginal effects with the increase of GNP between 1964 and 1965.

Year	Y_t	$Y_{t+1} - Y_t$
1964	19 459	1 611

Data calculated from Table 1.2 of the 'SEUP Report' in millions ₱ at current prices.

The b.o.p. effect is not so high as in the previous exercises, but still quite significant. This result may be caused by a comparatively low rate of transfer of profits to abroad, rather low payments for know-how, and low average and marginal propensities to import (0.16 and 0.21 respectively). Moreover, some of the PFI subsectors show a rather high export performance.

The relative importance of the b.o.p. effect can be guessed by considering the absolute level of the deficit of the b.o.p., and its change in the period considered similarly to the above illustration of the income effect. (See p. 216).

The private savings effect derives directly from the income effect, so there is nothing special to be said about it.

The public savings effects come out most of the times rather small. The taxation coefficients are particularly low and in some cases do not succeed in

Year	B_t	$B_{t+1} - B_t$
1964	264	−296

Data calculated from: UN *Yearbook of National Accounts Statistics 1969*, Volume 1, p. 577, in millions ₱ at current prices.

offsetting the public expenses imputable to PFI. This brings down the overall result, and even makes it negative in some cases.

In order to get an idea of the importance of the public savings effect, it is possible, similarly to what was done above, to show the absolute value and the increase in the corresponding variable in the period considered for the marginal effects:

Year	S_{Gt}	$S_{Gt+1} - S_{Gt}$
1964	265	−50

Data calculated from: UN *Yearbook of National Accounts Statistics 1969,* Volume 1, p. 576, in millions ₱ at current prices.

It is possible now to turn the attention to the analysis of the results regarding the first case, concerning All PFI in the manufacturing sector. As this is an aggregate of all manufacturing sub-sectors, the irregularities in PFI behaviour, quite considerable in the individual sub-sectors, compensate each other to some extent.

The income effect is about 9% of Y_t^h, while the direct income effect accounts for 6.5% of Y_t^h (αY_t^h). This means that the indirect effects stand for approximately one third of the whole contribution of the PFI to income. As the indirect effects consist of two parts – financial mechanism effect and the combined influence of savings and b.o.p. effects – the favourable result stems from both parts: low capital-output ratio of PFI and low profit transfers to abroad on one side, rather high exports and low imports on the other side. The private savings effect is directly proportional to income effect through the rather high marginal propensity to save.

The b.o.p. effect is comparatively modest. Owing to high exports, low imports and low profit transfers, PFI in manufacturing does not seem a very heavy burden on the b.o.p. Larger b.o.p. deficits would, on the other hand, supply resources for larger income effects.

The contribution to public savings is relatively important, due to α, the export parameter and the rather low public expenditure. The taxation parameters themselves are relatively low and also help to explain the result.

Philippines: All PFI: Manufacturing
(Marginal effects of PFI for 1964)

Parameters	1964
α	0.065
$\pi^h k^h$	0.20
ρk^h	0.026
λk^h	0.06
$\tau_P \pi^h k^h$	0.06
k^h	1.52
k^0	2.3
$\varphi_m (1+m^h)$	0.16
$\varphi_e (1+e^h)$	0.42
$\mu(1+m^0)$	0.21
θ	0.06
σ	0.14
τ_W, τ_P	0.02
$\tau_{IND}, \tau_M, \tau_E$	0.08
w^h	0.75
$g^h k^h$	0.09
Π	0.10
Income data (mln pesos)	
Y_t^h	1 293
Y_t	19459
Marginal effects (mln pesos)	
$\bar{\bar{Y}}_t$	107.75
$\bar{\bar{B}}_t$	8.51
$\bar{\bar{S}}_{Pt}$	15.09
$\bar{\bar{S}}_{Gt}$	13.54

6.7. MARGINAL EFFECTS FOR ALL PFI MANUFACTURING SUB-SECTOR 'FOOD, BEVERAGES, AND TOBACCO'

The income effect is relatively lower here than in the previous case. The reason is given by the external trade behaviour of this sector, together with a rather modest α.

The average export coefficient of this sector is the highest among the manufacturing sub-sectors. With the overall constant import parameter, this results in a b.o.p. surplus (negative $\bar{\bar{B}}_t$). This, although advantageous from a b.o.p. point of view, reduces the availability of resources for investments and hence indirectly diminishes the income effect. Moreover, α is lower than in the previous case. The influence of $\bar{\bar{B}}_t$ and α on the income effect seems to be neutralized by the low capital-output ratio of PFI in this sub-sector, which lowers the absorption of domestic financial availabilities in favour of PFI.

As for the savings effects – both private and public – the same reasoning applies as in the previous case.

6.8. MARGINAL EFFECTS FOR ALL PFI MANUFACTURING SUB-SECTOR 'TEXTILE, FOOTWEAR AND APPAREL'

In this special case, the irregular behaviour of PFI is shown by the absolute decrease in value added, with α negative. Other peculiar features are a high profit rate and a high PFI capital-output ratio. Characterised furthermore by a low export performance, this PFI sector does not seem at a first sight, to be economically very attractive from the national economy's point of view.

This intuitive judgement is confirmed by the results. Even with a negative α, this sector has positive marginal income effect. The negative direct effect (αY_t^h) is overcompensated by the positive indirect influence. Due to its financial characteristics, this sub-sector absorbs obviously a great part of domestic resources, which could efficiently be used elsewhere; consequently, it pays to reduce its value added.

The resulting deficit of the b.o.p. is partly caused by positive income effect. This latter, combined with the marginal propensity to import, overcompensates the rather neutral trade behaviour of PFI.

Nothing special can be said about the savings effects. They keep approximately the ratio to the income effect, observed in the two earlier cases.

Philippines: All PFI: Food, beverages and tobacco (Marginal effects of PFI for 1964)

Parameters	1964
α	0.044
$\pi^h k^h$	0.10
ρk^h	0.013
λk^h	0.06
$\tau_P \pi^h k^h$	0.03
k^h	0.86
k^0	2.3
$\varphi_m (1+m^h)$	0.16
$\varphi_e (1+e^h)$	0.68
$\mu(1+m^0)$	0.21
θ	0.06
σ	0.14
τ_W, τ_P	0.02
$\tau_{\text{IND}}, \tau_M, \tau_E$	0.08
w^h	0.85
$g^h k^h$	0.09
Π	0.10
Income data (mln pesos)	
Y_t^h	605.2
Y_t	19 459
Marginal effects (mln pesos)	
$\bar{\bar{Y}}_t$	33.06
$\bar{\bar{B}}_t$	– 5.26
$\bar{\bar{S}}_{Pt}$	4.63
$\bar{\bar{S}}_{Gt}$	3.97

Philippines: All PFI: Textile, footwear and apparel (Marginal effects of PFI for 1964)

Parameters	1964
α	–0.075
$\pi^h k^h$	0.70
ρk^h	0.091
λk^h	0.06
$\tau_p \pi^h k^h$	0.21
k^h	2.87
k^0	2.3
$\varphi_m (1+m^h)$	0.16
$\varphi_e (1+e^h)$	0.12
$\mu(1+m^0)$	0.21
θ	0.06
σ	0.14
τ_W, τ_P	0.02
$\tau_{IND}, \tau_M, \tau_E$	0.08
w^h	0.25
$g^h k^h$	0.09
Π	0.10
Income data (mln pesos)	
Y_t^h	51.9
Y_t	19459
Marginal effects (mln pesos)	
$\bar{\bar{Y}}_t$	12.07
$\bar{\bar{B}}_t$	1.87
$\bar{\bar{S}}_{Pt}$	1.69
$\bar{\bar{S}}_{Gt}$	0.91

6.9. MARGINAL EFFECTS FOR ALL PFI MANUFACTURING SUB-SECTOR 'CHEMICALS AND ALLIED PRODUCTS'

The marginal income effect is some 15% of the corresponding PFI value added, more than for the All PFI sector 'Manufacturing'. This result can be explained by the high α, although the low capital-output ratio and the low profit transfers play an important role.

As for the b.o.p., a sizeable surplus results from the high export parameters, and, as a consequence, the income effect is smaller than it would be with less export activity.

The savings effects, both public and private, do not behave in a different way than in previous cases.

6.10. MARGINAL EFFECTS FOR ALL PFI MANUFACTURING SUB-SECTOR 'PRIMARY AND FABRICATED METALS'

The first thing to be noticed is a very minor share of this PFI sub-sector in the whole economy. The second remarkable feature is a negative α, with a high absolute value.

The latter leads to all four marginal effects being negative. The reasoning of Section 6.8, where the income effect was positive in spite of a negative α, for several reasons does not apply here. First, the capital-output ratio of this PFI sub-sector is even lower than the overall ICOR and the transfer of profits to abroad is also low; consequently, the absorption of domestic financial resources is relatively lower.

Moreover, due to the absence of exports and the presence of some imports of PFI, the b.o.p. improves, due to the negative α and the negative income effect. Simultaneously, the b.o.p. surplus (negative $\overline{\overline{B}}_t$) lowers the income effect.

As a consequence of what was analysed above, the public savings effect also comes out negative.

6.11. MARGINAL EFFECTS FOR ALL PFI MANUFACTURING SUB-SECTOR 'MACHINERY'

The structure of PFI in 'Machinery' does not differ much from the major sector All PFI 'Manufacturing'. Accordingly the results are not very much different.

With a high positive α, a rather low capital intensity and a low transfer ratio, a relatively high income effect results. A b.o.p. deficit should also be

Philippines: All PFI: Chemicals and allied products (Marginal effects of PFI for 1964)

Parameters	1964
α	0.192
$\pi^h k^h$	0.10
ρk^h	0.013
λk^h	0.06
$\tau_P \pi^h k^h$	0.03
k^h	0.74
k^0	2.3
$\varphi_m (1+m^h)$	0.16
$\varphi_e (1+e^h)$	0.63
$\mu(1+m^0)$	0.21
θ	0.06
σ	0.14
τ_W, τ_P	0.02
$\tau_{IND}, \tau_M, \tau_E$	0.08
w^h	0.85
$g^h k^h$	0.09
Π	0.10
Income data (mln pesos)	
Y_t^h	162.3
Y_t	19 459
Marginal effects (mln pesos)	
$\overline{\overline{Y}}_t$	24.74
$\overline{\overline{B}}_t$	−7.51
$\overline{\overline{S}}_{Pt}$	3.46
$\overline{\overline{S}}_{Gt}$	2.90

Philippines: All PFI: Primary and fabricated metals (Marginal effects of PFI for 1964)

Parameters	1964
α	−0.14
$\pi^h k^h$	0.10
ρk^h	0.013
λk^h	0.06
$\tau_P, \pi^h k^h$	0.03
k^h	1.13
k^0	2.3
$\varphi_m (1+m^h)$	0.16
$\varphi_e (1+e^h)$	0
$\mu(1+m^0)$	0.21
θ	0.06
σ	0.14
τ_W, τ_P	0.02
$\tau_{IND}, \tau_M, \tau_E$	0.08
w^h	0.85
$g^h k^h$	0.09
Π	0.10
Income data (mln pesos)	
Y_t^h	65.3
Y_t	19 459
Marginal effects (mln pesos)	
$\bar{\bar{Y}}_t$	−5.23
$\bar{\bar{B}}_t$	−3.46
$\bar{\bar{S}}_{Pt}$	−0.73
$\bar{\bar{S}}_{Gt}$	−0.15

expected owing to a low PFI export performance and to the indirect impact of the income effect via marginal propensity to import.

The absolute importance of this PFI sub-sector is still extremely modest.

6.12. MARGINAL EFFECTS FOR ALL PFI MANUFACTURING SUB-SECTOR 'TRANSPORT EQUIPMENT'

This PFI sub-sector is a noticeable one, owing to the fact that its value added will more than double within the next year.

One would expect a corresponding high income effect. Although the income effect is 17.2% of corresponding PFI value added (Y_t^h), which is nearly twice as much as in other cases, owing to α a much higher figure should come out.

The surprisingly low income effect is once more imputable to the way PFI is assumed to be financed. Absorbing part of the domestic financial resources, according to α, to the capital-output ratio and to the transfer of profits, it prevents domestic investments from taking place. Due to direct relation with α, the claim on domestic resources is very high in this case, while the advantage in efficiency – illustrated by capital intensities – is quite small. The indirect effects, therefore, lower the initial direct income yield substantially.

The negative indirect effects amount to quite a high absolute figure, through the combined taxation parameter Π and the share of public expenses imputable to PFI make the public savings effect also negative.

The b.o.p. effect is only in this case larger than the income effect. Export performance is half of the import requirement per one unit of PFI value added. The rapid expansion of PFI calls for high imports without similarly high exports.

6.13. MARGINAL EFFECTS FOR ALL PFI MANUFACTURING SUB-SECTOR 'OTHER MANUFACTURING'

Nothing particular can be said about this sector. The results are similar to All PFI in Manufacturing.

The income effect is the most substantial in absolute terms among the marginal effects calculated. Its direct component (αY_t^h) accounts for some three fourths of the total effect, leaving one fourth to be imputed to indirect effects.

The positive b.o.p. effect is imputable in this case to the demand for imports of the whole economy, stemming from additional income generated by PFI. The PFI sector by itself would create a b.o.p. surplus.

Philippines: All PFI: Machinery
(Marginal effects of PFI for 1964)

Parameters	1964
$\alpha^{\cdot\cdot}$	0.12
$\pi^h k^h$	0.10
ρk^h	0.013
λk^h	0.06
$\tau_P \pi^h k^h$	0.03
k^h	1.19
k^0	2.3
$\varphi_m (1+m^h)$	0.16
$\varphi_e (1+e^h)$	0.08
$\mu(1+m^0)$	0.21
θ	0.06
σ	0.14
τ_W, τ_P	0.02
$\tau_{IND}, \tau_M, \tau_E$	0.08
w^h	0.85
$g^h k^h$	0.09
Π	0.10
Income data (mln pesos)	
Y_t^h	24.7
Y_t	19 459
Marginal effects (mln pesos)	
$\bar{\bar{Y}}_t$	2.68
$\bar{\bar{B}}_t$	1.08
$\bar{\bar{S}}_{Pt}$	0.37
$\bar{\bar{S}}_{Gt}$	0.18

Philippines: All PFI: Transport equipment
(Marginal effects of PFI for 1964)

Parameters	1964
α	1.33
$\pi^h k^h$	0.20
ρk^h	0.026
λk^h	0.06
$\tau_P \pi^h k^h$	0.06
k^h	2.18
k^0	2.3
$\varphi_m (1+m^h)$	0.16
$\varphi_e (1+e^h)$	0.08
$\mu(1+m^0)$	0.21
θ	0.06
σ	0.14
τ_W, τ_P	0.02
$\tau_{IND}, \tau_M, \tau_E$	0.08
w^h	0.75
$g^h k^h$	0.09
Π	0.10
Income data (mln pesos)	
Y_t^h	12.4
Y_t	19 459
Marginal effects (mln pesos)	
$\bar{\bar{Y}}_t$	2.14
$\bar{\bar{B}}_t$	3.29
$\bar{\bar{S}}_{Pt}$	0.30
$\bar{\bar{S}}_{Gt}$	−0.10

Philippines: All PFI: Other manufacturing
(Marginal effects of PFI for 1964)

Parameters	1964
α	0.054
$\pi^h k^h$	0.15
ρk^h	0.019
λk^h	0.06
$\tau_P \pi^h k^h$	0.04
k^h	1.35
k^0	2.3
$\varphi_m (1+m^h)$	0.16
$\varphi_e (1+e^h)$	0.32
$\mu(1+m^0)$	0.21
θ	0.06
σ	0.14
τ_W, τ_P	0.02
$\tau_{IND}, \tau_M, \tau_E$	0.08
w^h	0.80
$g^h k^h$	0.09
Π	0.10
Income data (mln pesos)	
Y_t^h	371.4
Y_t	19 459
Marginal effects (mln pesos)	
$\bar{\bar{Y}}_t$	27.60
$\bar{\bar{B}}_t$	4.43
$\bar{\bar{S}}_{Pt}$	3.86
$\bar{\bar{S}}_{Gt}$	2.91

By estimating the export parameters of this sector, 'products of petroleum' were included both in exports and value added, as it was not possible to isolate them from the underlying statistical data. In all other cases, the sector 'Petroleum' was kept out of the empirical analysis.

6.14. CONCLUSIONS

As in the case of India, the exercise carried out in the previous pages can be considered a 'case study of the Philippines', but, most of all, it represents an empirical application of the methodology of Part II with reference to the data supplied by the 'SEUP Report' for this country. Consequently, in this case as in the previous one the results should be interpreted mainly in this light, and they should serve to provide a better insight into the methodology, as well as to point out various possible improvements in order to make it more realistic. Anyhow the results allow also to get some ideas about the effects of PFI in the Philippines. It was possible, moreover, to distinguish various cases, viz. total PFI manufacturing and PFI in the various sub-sectors of manufacturing.

Before analysing in more detail the empirical results for the Philippines, it is useful to point out the most interesting features of this exercise *vis-à-vis* the previous ones for India.

In the case of India it was possible to distinguish between Foreign Branches (FB) and Foreign Controlled Rupee Companies (FCRC) both for the whole economy and for the manufacturing sector, and thus to use the methodology to appraise the effects of different ways of financing a PFI project (i.e. FB vs FCRC). This was not possible with respect to the Philippines, where, in most cases, only All PFI figures were reported in the 'SEUP' statistical material. However, in the case of the Philippines it was possible to use the methodological approach to appraise the effects of All PFI in the various sub-sectors of the manufacturing sector.

Although this sectoral application of the methodology proved an interesting exercise, yet there are some drawbacks, due to the fact that in the various sub-sectors many parameters are the same through lack of better empirical evidence; so it was not possible to appraise fully the effects in the various cases of all possible differences; still, the analysis pointed out what happened as a result of varying values for some of the key-parameters.

As shown above and in the previous pages, the exercise has various limitations, and it is based on some rather radical simplifying assumptions; nevertheless it is possible to reach some general conclusions, similarly to what was done before:

– in the case of the Philippines, PFI, although it is rather a minor part of the country's GNP, still contributes favourably to the growth of income;

– the b.o.p. deficit imputable to PFI is generally limited in the Philippines. In 3 of the eight cases, PFI even leads to a b.o.p. surplus. In the other cases, PFI deteriorates the b.o.p.;

– in the Philippines, public savings generated directly and indirectly by PFI are a very minor portion of GNP; still in absolute terms they are of a magnitude comparable to that of the b.o.p. effect. They are 8–13% of the corresponding income effect.

The objections raised before about import substitution are still there in the case of the Philippines and it was also necessary to introduce certain assumptions rather crucial especially in the case of imports, to estimate the PFI foreign trade coefficients. This applies also to the question of the financial mechanism of the model of Part II.

Finally, as in the previous case, one should remember the limitations of the data used to estimate the parameters, and the way the various gaps were filled, together with the fact that it was necessary to use data in current prices.

CHAPTER VII

GHANA

7.1. INTRODUCTION

This chapter will present some results with reference to the case of Ghana on the basis of data made available by the Social Studies Project (SSP), University College of Cape Coast, Ghana. The source of data, their coverage and their limitations will be discussed in the next section.

Section 7.3 will then give a general picture of the relevance of PFI in Ghana, distinguishing between Branches of Foreign Companies (BFC) in the major sectors of the economy, and all PFI in the manufacturing sector and sub-sectors.

Section 7.4 will discuss the methodological framework.

Section 7.5 will show, one by one, how various parameters have been estimated.

Subsequently, various empirical cases will be discussed. First, the attention will be for all PFI in manufacturing, and in seven manufacturing sub-sectors.

Then, BFC will be considered, both at the level of the total economy and for the manufacturing sector. This way, it will be possible to compare different PFI (BFC vs all PFI), and to make some general remarks about the various manufacturing sub-sectors.

The analysis will concentrate on 1963 (for all cases) and on 1968 (both years for all PFI). This choice was made on the basis of data availability. Most time series run from 1962 to 1969. However, the presence of time lags, and the fact that data for 1969 are sometimes not available, suggested leaving out the first and last years. Years intermediate will also be left out, since the results, for various reasons which will be discussed later, would not be of too much interest.

7.2 SOURCE OF DATA, COVERAGE, AND LIMITATIONS

As was said in the previous section, the analysis of the effects of PFI in Ghana will be based on data supplied by the Social Studies Projects at the University

College of Cape Coast, in Ghana. Most of the data are based on a survey carried out at the end of 1963[1], while some others refer to a longer period. Some crucial data are missing (such as PFI exports, or PFI transfer of profits) and this will lead to the introduction of some additional assumptions so that they can be estimated.

The data of the 1963 survey distinguish between four kinds of PFI, and the situation in the *manufacturing sector 1963* is the following:

Type	Amount '000 N₵	Percent
Controlled partnerships	248	1.65
Branches of foreign companies (BFC)	2 960	19.66
Subsidiaries of foreign companies	9 146	60.75
Companies with 40% or more of shares held abroad	2 702	17.94
Total 1963 manufacturing sector	15 056	100.00

Source: 'SSP Report' - see also table on pp. 232-233.

Some of the tables of the 'SSP Report' refer simply to BFC for 1963, while some others (manufacturing sector and sub-sectors) refer to all PFI, that is to say to the four types together.

On pp. 232–233, a table gives the various types of PFI considered above, subdivided into major productive sectors, for 1963. The table is based on the survey quoted above, and does not include financial investments.

As said above, the empirical exercises of this chapter will concentrate mainly on all PFI in manufacturing (sector and sub-sectors). However, an attempt will be made to set up an exercise with reference to BFC, in order to provide a basis to judge the effects of different ways of financing PFI projects.

Most time series are in current prices, and consequently the exercise will be based on such current data, which will affect the calculation of some of the parameters. Moreover, one should remember that some crucial data are missing, and keep well in mind the assumptions that will be needed to fill this gap.

1 See Ramanujam, K. N. R., *Report on the Survey of Ghana's Foreign Liabilities and Assets* – December 1963.

1963 Analysis of total non-financial direct investment in Ghana: business-wise (N₵ '000)

Nature of business	Total		Controlled partnerships		Branches of foreign companies	
	Number	Amount	Number	Amount	Number	Amount
Trading	82	44 074	11	438	19	13 494
Manufacturing	36	15 056	4	248	8	2 960
Other serivices (including elect.)	42	2 606	11	98	6	492
Construction	7	290	–	–	4	28
Transport, storage and communication	10	1 090	–	–	8	820
Petroleum and refining	8	20 554	–	–	4	11 752
Mining and quarrying	6	44 552	–	–	6	44 552
Agriculture and fishing	3	566	–	–	3	566
Total	194	128 788	26	784	58	74 664

Source: 'SSP Report'.

7.3. PFI IN GHANA: THE GENERAL PICTURE

The tables in the previous section already provide an idea of the relative importance of the various types of the PFI in the various productive sectors of Ghana in 1963. The table on pp. 234–235 gives some more information on the general relevance of PFI in Ghana. It has been calculated from various tables of the 'SSP Report', and it is divided between BFC and all PFI. The former gives an idea of the various major sectors in 1963 but refers to BFC only (because more or less complete information is available only for BFC), while the latter gives a more precise idea of the relevance of the various manufacturing sub-sectors for all PFI (based, again, on data availability).

Let us consider first *Branches of Foreign Companies* (BFC). Columns (1) and (2) show that the general relevance of the manufacturing sector is rather limited, while most of PFI in BFC in 1963 was in 'trading', in 'petroleum, including refinery', and in 'mining and quarrying'[2]. The total of BFC accounted for a little more than 10% of GNP, while the manufacturing sector alone accounted for 51%. This may be compared with the relative share of all

2 In the case of BFC, value added refers to total production or sales, while in the case of all PFI, it is more similar to the correct national accounting concept.

Subsidiaries of foreign companies			Companies with 40% or more of shares held abroad		
Number	Total equity values	Paid up value	Number	Total equity value	Paid up value
30	28 820	16 182	22	1 322	660
11	9 146	6 416	13	2 702	544
18	1 934	1 116	7	82	44
2	234	500	1	28	4
–	–	–	2	270	64
4	8 802	7 650	–	–	–
–	–	–	–	–	–
–		–	–	–	–
65	48 936	31 864	45	4 404	1 316

PFI manufacturing in GNP, which was almost 2%. BFC is about one fourth of total PFI in manufacturing, and this is more or less confirmed by the figures given in Section 7.2, although there is a certain difference (one fourth vs one fifth), due to the different way the various data were obtained.

Column (4) gives the import requirements as a percentage of value added. They are in general rather high, and this is true also of the manufacturing sector.

No data are available to appraise the export promotion of PFI (column 5).

Column (6) gives the percentage of profits with respect to value added. With a few exceptions, the figure is not very high, and the same applies to the percentage of wages in value added (column (7)). This might also be due to the concept of value added used for BFC.

Column (8) gives employment of BFC with respect to value added (number of man-years for 1000 N₵ v.a.). Some sectors are rather more capital-intensive than others, in particular 'mining and quarrying' and 'transport and communications', and these are also the ones with a higher wage rate, although 'agriculture and fishing' has a high wage rate and relatively low employment.

No data are available about gross investments in 1963 for BFC (column (9)), although the capital stock for 1963 in the various sectors is avail-

PFI in Ghana: The general picture

	(1)		(2)		(3)		(4)
	v.a. composition		% of v.a. in GNP		% of v.a. in corresponding sector		Import requirement % v.a.
	1963		1963		1963		1963
Branches of foreign companies	100.00		10.83		10.83		35.13
BFC agriculture and fishing	0.85		0.09		–		3.64
BFC mining and quarrying	23.20		2.51		–		7.58
BFC manufacturing	4.65		0.51		–		43.09
BFC construction	1.01		0.11		–		16.06
BFC trading	46.24		5.01		–		48.68
BFC transport, storage and communications	2.79		0.30		–		3.12
BFC petroleum, including refining	20.79		2.25		–		36.48
BFC other services	0.47		0.05		–		27.62
	1963	1968	1963	1968	1963	1968	
All PFI manufacturing	100.00	100.00	1.99	2.34	–	35.40	–
All PFI food, beverages and tobacco	65.40	50.93	1.25	1.19	–	52.42	–
All PFI textile, footwear and apparel	2.44	13.65	0.09	0.32	–	13.67	–
All PFI chemicals and allied products	0.57	0.61	0.02	0.01	–	3.55	–
All PFI primary and fabricated metals	2.97	3.57	0.06	0.08	–	36.27	–
All PFI machinery	–	0.37	–	0.01	–	15.26	–
All PFI transport equipment	0.67	1.17	0.03	0.03	–	17.51	–
All PFI other manufacturing	27.95	29.70	0.54	0.70	–	60.12	–
Source:	Tables 1.2, 1.3		Tables 1.1 1.2, 1.3		Tables 1.1, 1.2, 1.3		Tables 1.1 1.6

Notes:
(a) Source: 'SSP Report', various tables.
(b) See the text (Section 7.3) for comments.
(c) – = not available.

(5)	(6)		(7)		(8)	(9)		(10)
Export promotion %v.a.	Profits as % of v.a.		Wages %v.a.		Employment % v.a.	Gross investments % of v.a.		Capital stock/v.a.
	1963		1963		1963			1963
–	20.94		9.95		0.17	–		0.58
–	4.37		34.97		0.07	–		0.52
–	66.49		19.68		0.44	–		1.49
–	11.06		10.99		0.21	–		0.49
–	11.65		11.50		0.09	–		0.02
–	7.42		5.65		0.07	–		0.23
–	15.25		38.17		0.47	–		0.15
–	4.66		3.58		0.03	–		0.44
–	14.60		8.89		0.03	–		0.78
	1963	1968	1963	1968		1963	1968	
–	33.74	37.86	18.97	15.19		6.77	7.95	–
–	28.32	21.94	5.49	8.66	–	1.77	3.21	–
–	–186.27	41.98	280.22	23.98	–	7.43	11.90	–
–	58.55	–1.32	38.99	33.95	–	2.82	171.19	–
–	52.91	10.97	34.49	34.56	–	2.24	10.62	–
–	–	51.82	–	15.91	–	–	9.15	–
–	56.84	14.05	29.08	27.49	–	2.07	18.26	–
–	36.14	68.03	45.82	21.96	–	5.20	3.03	–
	Table 1.3 and p.10		Table 1.3 and p.10		Table p.10	Table 1.3 and 2.3		Table p.10

(d) More data can be found in the 'SSP Report' as well as considering the parameters given in the various tables with the effects.

(e) Column 8 - employment - gives the number of man-years for 1000 N₵ of v.a.

able. Column (10) then gives the average capital-output ratio for each BFC sector in 1963, showing, in most cases, not a very high ratio. This is true both in the various 'all PFI cases' and in the whole economy.

It is possible now to turn the attention to *all PFI*, which includes the four types considered for the manufacturing sector and its sub-sectors in Section 7.2.

Value added data are available, in general, from 1962 to 1969 (see Table 1.3 of the 'SSP Report'), as follows:

- value added (without any better specification)
- wages
- depreciation
- indirect taxes.

It was assumed that 'value added' is 'gross value added at market prices'[3], and consequently profits before taxes were derived by difference. The results obtained exclude depreciation[4].

Column (1) gives the relative importance of the various manufacturing sub-sectors. Traditional industries ('food, beverages and tobacco' and 'textile, footwear and apparel') are by far predominant. Although the former slightly declines from 1963 to 1968, the latter partly compensates this. The more 'modern' sectors show some increase from 1963 to 1968, although not very relevant.

The importance of all PFI manufacturing in GNP has already been discussed when BFC was dealt with (see column (2)).

Column (3) gives the relative shares of the various sub-sectors in the corresponding ones for the total economy. PFI accounted for more than one third of total manufacturing in Ghana in 1968, and in some sectors this ratio is higher ('food, beverages and tobacco', and 'other manufacturing'). However, one can notice a high predominance of domestic enterprises in some crucial sub-sectors, like 'chemical and allied products' and 'machinery'.

No data are available for the import requirements (column (4)) and the export promotion (column (5)) of all PFI manufacturing.

The ratio of profits to value added (column (6)) is higher for all PFI than for the corresponding BFC, and the same applies to the one for wages (column (7)). However, it should be remembered what was said above about the

3 Considering all PFI manufacturing in 1963, and relating the concept to GNP (column (2)), the results, compared to the similar one for manufacturing BFC, tally (approximately) with the data supplied in Section 7.2, and this might be a proof of a correct guess.

4 Something similar was done for India, where profits were available, but these were considered without depreciation allowances.

concept of value added used. There are some considerable variations from 1963 to 1968, and some figures clearly reflect exceptional situations. In general, however, it is possible to notice a general decrease in wage rates, and a general increase in profit rates, stemming, most probably, from an overall increase in capital-intensity.

No data are available for employment (column (8)).

Column (9) gives new gross investments as a percentage of value added. Also in this case, some data reflect exceptional cases, although, in general, these items are not very high. No data are available about the real capital-stock (column (10)), as distinguished from the financial capital stock (see tables Section 7.2 and following page). The two tables below provide some more data on BFC, which will be used to derive most of the parameters for the empirical exercise.

Rates of return for BFC vs other PFI

Branches of foreign companies				Subsidiaries and other controlled companies		
Nature of business	Net investment in N₵'000[a]	Total gross profits in N₵'000	Rate of return	Paid-up capital in N₵ '000	Dividends	Rate of return
Trading	13 494	4 422	65.4	16 842	430	5.0
Manufacturing	2 960	664	44.8	6 960	824	23.6
Petroleum	11 752	1 250	21.2	7 650	202	5.2
Mining and quarring	44 552	19 870	89.2	–	–	–
Transport	820	548	1.4	64	14	42.0
Construction	28	148	1 057.2	504	–	–
Agriculture	566	48	17.0	–	–	–
Other services	492	92	37.4	1 160	168	29.0
Total	74 664	26 988	72.2	33 180	1 638	9.8

[a] Refers to cumulated net investments, that is to say the capital stock in real terms.

The first one compares the rate of return of BFC with that of subsidiaries and other PFI companies, showing quite some difference, although the rate of return of BFC is calculated with respect to cumulated net investments (equal to the real capital stock), while the rate of return for the rest of PFI is calculated with respect to the paid-up capital (financial capital stock). The latter may not include all the items included by the former, due to other forms of financing their capital formation, such as loans, etc.

The second table gives the contribution of BFC to production (used as

Contribution of branches of foreign companies to production, employment and taxes (business-wise) 1963
(Amount = N₵'000; number = in thousands)

Nature of business	No. of companies	Value of total production or sales	Imports	Employment				Income tax liability
				Ghanaians		Non-Ghanians		
				No.	Amount	No.	Amount	
Mining and quarrying	6	29 884	3 366	12.1	3 974	0.9	1 908	7 264
Trading	19	59 580	29 006	3.1	1 874	1.0	1 492	1 266
Petroleum including refining	4	26 836	9 790	0.6	568	0.1	392	532
Manufacturing	8	6 006	2 588	1.2	428	0.06	232	252
Transport, storage and communications	8	3 594	112	1.5	952	0.2	420	240
Construction	4	1 270	204	0.1	46	0.02	100	494
Agriculture and fishing	3	1 098	40	0.8	322	0.01	62	10
Other services	6	630	174	0.02	32		24	50
Total	58	128 898	45 280	19.42	8 196	2.3	4 630	10 108

Source: Ramanujan, K.N.R., *Survey of Ghana's Foreign Liabilities and Assets, op. cit.*, quoted by the 'SSP Report' value added in the exercise), employment and taxes, giving also the import requirements.

7.4. THE METHODOLOGICAL APPROACH

As discussed in the previous pages, the exercise may be subdivided into two parts: All PFI manufacturing sector and sub-sectors, and BFC (total economy and manufacturing sector).

In the case of BFC, data are available for 1963 only. Consequently, introducing some assumptions about the data which are missing, and about the rate of growth of PFI (which is not available either), one can calculate the marginal effects for BFC in two cases (total economy and manufacturing sector). No calculation of the cumulative effects is possible.

In the case of All PFI data are available for the manufacturing sector as a whole, and for 7 sub-sectors, mostly from 1962 to 1969. Consequently, it is possible to calculate the 'marginal effects' for 1963 (in order to be able to compare the results with those for BFC) and for 1968, dropping the last year, for which data are not always available, while there is the time lag to be considered, too. It is then possible to calculate the 'cumulative' effects over the period 1963–1968.

It does not seem useful to calculate also the marginal effects for the years between 1963 and 1968 (from 1964 to 1967) in view of the many simplifications required for the exercise. The results for 1963 and 1968 will already require some crucial assumptions, and consequently no benefit is to be expected from having the figures for intermediate years.

The use of the marginal approach allows one to overcome partly the complication that almost all data are in current prices. Most parameters will be calculated year by year, and consequently they will not be affected. There are, however, some parameters which have to be calculated over a longer period, with the justifications which will be discussed in Section 7.5. No attempt will be made to correct data in current prices into data in constant prices. Although price indices are available, there seems to be a risk of making more mistakes than improvements.

The calculation of the marginal effects in the case of all PFI for 1963 and 1968 will make it possible to discuss their variation, caused by varying values of the parameters as a consequence of different practical situations.

In the case of all PFI, the data available will allow calculation of only the four basic marginal and cumulative effects. Lack of employment data prevents the calculation of the employment effect, while the lack of data on domestic profits makes it impossible to calculate the income distribution effect, although some data on domestic wages are available (Table 1.2).[5]

However, in the case of BFC, where employment data are available, it will be possible also to calculate the employment effect associated with the marginal effects for 1963. For the income distribution effect no such possibility exists, no more than for All PFI.

Some general comparison will be possible in the case of All PFI between cumulative and marginal effects, and between the results for manufacturing all PFI and BFC in 1963 (marginal effects). One must be very careful, however, since the cumulative effects will be expressed in 1968 prices and will refer to that year, while the marginal effects will be expressed in the prices of the year they refer to. Moreover, in the case of all PFI *vis-à-vis* BFC, one should also remember that they are calculated with reference to different concepts of value added, and that consequently the results might not be quite comparable.

7.5. ESTIMATION OF THE PARAMETERS

In the following pages a brief description will be given of the way the various parameters have been estimated, together with the various assumptions introduced. A distinction will be made, when necessary, between the way the parameters for the marginal effects and the way in which those for the cumulative effects were estimated, as well as a distinction between the cases of *all PFI* and of *BFC*. In some of the cases considered later, a few slight variations will be necessary, with respect to the general procedures discussed below. They will be pointed out there, when the various empirical calculations are considered.

Y_t^h, Y_t — value added data are taken from Tables 1.1, 1.2, 1.3 in current prices.

α — In the case of all PFI, since capital stock figures are not available, and since PFI investments have an irregular behaviour, it is calculated year by year, for the marginal effects, from v.a. data at current prices (Table 1.3), taking the year preceding and the year following the one considered, according to the formula:

5 As a matter of fact some profit data, also for domestic enterprises, are available, not from national accounting figures, but from the *Annual Report of the Central Revenue Department 1970*, covering the period 1965/66 to 1968/69 (they will be used, e.g., to estimate the rate of transfer of profits to abroad). However, this set of data does not seem reliable enough to estimate the 'income distribution effect'.

$$\alpha_t = \left(\frac{Y^h_{t+1}}{Y^h_{t-1}}\right)^{1/2} - 1.$$

In the case of the cumulative effects for all PFI, it is calculated, with a similar procedure, by considering the average annual rate of growth over the period 1962–1969, again in current prices.

For BFC, due to lack of data, it is assumed to be the same as the average rate of growth of all PFI manufacturing value added, over the period 1962–1969, as it was calculated for the cumulative effects.

k^h the ICOR for the various cases of all PFI was obtained by considering gross investments (Table 2.1 and 2.3), and the increase in v.a. (Table 1.3) over the whole period, with a one-year lag, and with data at current prices:

$$k^h = \frac{\sum_{1962}^{1968} I^h}{Y^h_{1969} - Y^h_{1963}}.$$

It was calculated separately for all cases. For the two cases of BFC, it was obtained considering capital stock data and value added data according to the formula:

$$k^h = \frac{K^h_t}{Y^h_t}$$

this is not an ICOR, but an average capital-output ratio; the lack of data prevented the inclusion of any lag.

$\pi^h\ k^h$ was obtained in all cases considering profits before taxes (see table in Section 7.3, and comments on the derivation of profits for all PFI), and v.a., separately for all cases. In the case of the cumulative effects, it was obtained considering the average ratio over the period 1963–1968.

ρk^h no data are available to estimate directly the share of PFI profits remitted abroad for the various cases considered. Consequently, it was necessary to look for an indirect measurement. This was done by taking from IMF *International Finan-*

cial Statistics (various issues) 'investment income transfers', and relating them to total PFI profits[6] as given in the 'SSP Report' in the table 'Analysis of assessable income of companies by industrial group and country of incorporation 1965/66–1968/69' (obtained from the *Annual Report of the Central Revenue Department of Ghana – 1970)*. Data on investment income transfers were converted from US $ into N¢, at the rate of 0.98 US $ to 1 N¢. Then, the average rate over the period 1965–1969 was taken.

Year	Investment income transfers (1)	Total PFI profits before taxes (2)	(1)/(2)
1965	27.6	89.0	0.31
1966	20.5	45.8	0.45
1967	24.7	51.3	0.48
1968	32.8	68.4	0.48
1965–1968	105.6	254.5	0.41

(1) and (2) in million N¢.

Consequently, it was assumed that 40% of PFI profits before taxes, in all cases, are transferred abroad, and the parameter was estimated accordingly. It also came out equivalent to the taxation ratio for PFI profits ($\tau_p \pi^h k^h$), and this is why the two parameters are the same in all cases.

λk^h No data being available, it was necessary to put it equal to zero; the implicit assumption is that 'know-how' payments to abroad are included in profit remittances to abroad.

$\tau_p \pi^h k^h$ in the case of the BFC it was calculated from profit data and total tax liabilities, as given in the table at the end of Section 7.3. In the case of all PFI it was not possible to use the same ratio of taxes on profits to v.a., profits being higher (due also to the way v.a. is obtained). The 'SSP Report' gives the taxation coefficients (Table 4.2) which in the case of manufacturing go from 40% (1962/63) to 50% (1968/69) for income retained in Ghana, and are higher (up to 65%) for income not retained in the country. In the case of BFC, these tax rates are 36% for BFC manufacturing, and 38% for all BFC. All this taken into account, and any possible cases of

6 Total PFI profits were needed, and not just the items calculated for the various 'All PFI' cases.

exemption considered, the tax rate on all PFI profits was assumed to be 40% for all cases, and this parameter was calculated accordingly.

k^0 the ICOR for the rest of the economy was calculated in a way similar to the various PFI cases, relating gross investments over the period 1964–1968 to the increase in GNP over the same period, with a one-year lag (1965–1969):

$$k^0 = \frac{\sum_{1964}^{1968} I}{Y_{1969} - Y_{1965}}$$

Data are taken from IMF *International Financial Statistics* (various issues) and from Table 1.1 at current prices. No reliable data for the previous years are available.

$\varphi_m(1+m^h)$ data are available only for BFC. The import ratio for manufacturing BFC (inclusive of goods and services), with respect to v.a., was supposed to hold for the various all PFI manufacturing sector and sub-sectors.

$\varphi_e(1+e^h)$ No data are available for PFI exports. Consequently, in the case of manufacturing (both BFC, and all PFI, including the sub-sectors) it was assumed that the ratio of exports to v.a. is the same as for the whole manufacturing sector's total exports of goods and services (Table 1.4) to its v.a. (Table 1.2). This is reasonable, considering that in 1968 all PFI manufacturing accounted for 35.4% of the sector's v.a. (see table Section 7.3). The average value for the period 1966–1968 was taken for all cases. Similarly, this ratio for all BFC was assumed to be the same as the one of all exports of goods and services (Table 1.4) to GNP (Table 1.1).

$\mu\ (1+m^0)$ the marginal propensity to import was calculated from Table 1.6 (imports of goods and services) and from Table 1.1 (GNP), in current prices, according to the formula:

$$\mu(1+m^0) = \frac{M_t - M_0}{Y_t - Y_0}$$

for the period 1962–1969. It is the same in all cases.

θ due to lack of better information, the rate of interest on the foreign debt was assumed to be equal to the official discount rate, as given by the IMF *International Financial Statistics* (various issues) of the year considered. In the case of the cumulative effects for all PFI, the average value of the period 1963 to 1968 was taken.

σ the marginal propensity to save was calculated over the period 1964–1968, according to the formula:

$$\sigma = \frac{S_{Pt} - S_{P0}}{Y_t - Y_0}.$$

GNP data were taken from Table 1.1, while no private savings data are available. Consequently, for the period considered, private savings were estimated as a difference between gross total capital formation, and b.o.p. current account deficit plus public savings (current account surplus). The first two items were obtained from IMF *International Financial Statistics* (various issues), while public savings were calculated from Table 4.1 of the 'SSP Report'.

τ_W, τ_P were assumed to be the same, for lack of more detailed data, and were calculated by relating total direct tax receipts (Table 4.1) to GNP (Table 1.1), and taking the average value over the period considered for all cases. Only direct taxes on PFI profits were calculated in a more accurate way, as indicated above.

w^h was calculated case by case, for all PFI by relating wages to v.a. (Table 1.3) of the year considered in the case of marginal effects; over the whole period in the case of the cumulative effects (1963 to 1958); for BFC from the table in Section 7.3, relating again wages to v.a.

$\tau_{IND}, \tau_M, \tau_E$ for lack of more detailed data were assumed to be the same. In the case of all PFI, Table 1.3 gives indirect taxes sector by sector; in general they are very high and vary to quite a degree from case to case, and from year to year, from zero to over 75% of v.a. For all PFI manufacturing, the average indirect tax rate over the period 1963–1968 amounts to 42% of v.a.

However, by considering total indirect taxes, as given by Table 4.1, and relating them to GNP (Table 1.1), over the period 1963–1968, the average indirect taxation coefficient emerges as 3% only. Because of these great variations it was thought better to look for just one average taxation coefficient, rejecting in general the data supplied in Table 1.3 which might include all kinds of double counting. An example of this appears when taxes on imports and exports are considered, which are assumed to be equal to this average coefficient and which one might expect to account for a large share of indirect taxes in the PFI sector(s). Relating total imports (from Table 1.6) to all indirect taxes (Table 4.1) – under the assumption that all indirect taxes are just import duties – over the period 1963–1968, one would get 18%; doing the same for exports (Table 1.4), one would get 20%. Consequently, the average tax rate on imports and exports cannot be more than 10%, and this upper limit would be reached when all indirect taxes were just import and export duties. All these calculations suggested choosing an indirect taxation coefficient between 3% and 10%. Since manufacturing PFI, being better organized than the rest of the economy, is probably taxed heavier, 8% was 'guessed' to be the average indirect taxation coefficient for all cases and all years, both for all PFI and for BFC.

$g^h k^h$ for lack of data, the assumption was introduced that the same expenditure ratio between government current expenditure and GNP holds for the total economy and for the various PFI sectors (for all PFI as well as for BFC). Data were taken from Table 4.1 and Table 1.1, and an average value was introduced with reference to the period 1963–1968 for all years and all cases.

Π As said in the previous section, this parameter relates to GNP at current prices (Table 1.1) all indirect taxes plus direct taxes (Table 4.1), other current revenue included in the current account total receipts being excluded. An average value (1963–1968) was taken for all years and all cases, both BFC and PFI. This parameter, which is an average taxation coefficient, allows one to solve the four marginal effects, but not to study the PFI effects on domestic wages and profits, and thus on income distribution. This is also prevented, as seen earlier, by the lack of data on domestic profits, although some data on domestic wages in manufacturing are available (see Table 1.2).

η^h, η^0 the labour-output ratio, necessary to get the employment effect in the case of BFC (there are no data for all PFI), is calculated by relating employment to v.a. for the two BFC cases. It is calculated in man-year per 1000 N¢ of v.a. with reference to 1963. For lack of data the same parameters had to be calculated for the rest of the economy with reference to 1964 (from Tables 1.1 (GNP), 1.4 (manufacturing output), 3.1 (sectoral and total employment), no better data being available for manufacturing v.a. in 1964).

The above discussion covers the parameters of both marginal and cumulative effects. Further modifications for particular cases will be discussed later.

Whereas under the above assumptions no problem arises for BFC, for all PFI *some cases will have to be omitted*, for the following reasons:

(a) 'Textile, footwear, and apparel' (see Section 7.8): the marginal effects for 1963 are omitted because of the negative profit ratio and the very high wage rate (see table Section 7.3);

(b) 'Chemicals and allied products' (see Section 7.9): the marginal effects for 1968 are omitted, because of the negative profit ratio (see table Section 7.3);

(c) 'Machinery' (see Section 7.11): the marginal effects for 1963 as well as the cumulative effects are omitted because before 1968 there was no PFI (see Table 1.3 and table Section 7.3).

Before embarking upon the analysis of the empirical results, some general comments and specifications are possible which will help clarify some of the results to be obtained later.

One first point to be discussed refers to the *import and export coefficients*. There is a sizeable gap between the two, which will obviously affect the b.o.p. effect in all cases considered. A first bias might lie in the way the two parameters were estimated, as indicated on the previous pages. Moreover, as observed before, one should remember that import substitution is not taken into account, or rather, is assumed to be included in the import and export coefficients themselves. In the case of India it was also remarked that one might suppose that, if the PFI under consideration had not taken place (the 'alternative' situation by which the effects of PFI are measured), then some of the goods it produces for the domestic market would have to be imported. So, this import-substitution effect must be taken into account in the b.o.p. effect. However, no evidence is available of the degree to which PFI substitutes imports. On the other hand one may well assume that, had this PFI not been established, its exports would not have taken place at all, there being no domestic production to satisfy world demand.

As indicated above, a further point in the case of Ghana refers to the way import and export coefficients have been estimated. The latter especially might well be an underestimation of the real situation, if PFI promotes more exports than the rest of manufacturing. All these difficulties should be kept in mind while interpreting the results which will be obtained for Ghana.

Another crucial point – also discussed before – concerns *the mechanism of financing the annual additions to PFI*. The mechanism assumed by the model very much determines the income effect through the absorption of a portion of financial resources otherwise available for domestic investments.[7] It was also observed before that one might imagine a greater role to be played by foreign capital inflow directly related to the PFI under consideration, intended to finance its expansion. It was added then, however, that the model already takes account of this to some extent, through the assumption that the deficit of the b.o.p. corresponds to total capital inflow. When the problem is thus handled *endogenously*, it follows that the b.o.p. effect of PFI can be taken to be the foreign capital inflow directly or indirectly imputable to PFI, and, by playing a positive role in the income effect, partly to offset the negative role of the financing mechanism under discussion. The conclusion was that one could assume that this kind of capital inflow is endogenously taken account of by the model.

As regards Ghana, information is available for All PFI about the financing of annual PFI investments (that is to say, additions to the capital stock for the expansion of v.a., in the terminology of the model). The foreign share, vs the domestic one, varies considerably from case to case, and consequently it seems more desirable to concentrate on the manufacturing sector for all PFI, without going into sub-sectors.

The situation in the period considered is as follows (data have been calculated from Table 2.1):

Financing of annual investments–All PFI: Manufacturing

Year	Share financed from foreign sourced (percentage)	Share financed from domestic sources (percentage)
1963	0.97	0.03
1964	0.87	0.13
1965	0.62	0.38
1966	0.36	0.64
1967	0.77	0.23
1968	0.81	0.19
1963–1968	0.71	0.29

7 This point is discussed, at a more theoretical level, in Part II, Section 8.7.

Although the foreign share shows a declining trend, it evidently still constitutes a sizeable portion of total investments as compared to the portion financed domestically.

On the basis of this empirical evidence, it is possible to analyse how the model's financial mechanism would affect the income effect, and consequently how realistic it would be to leave it as it is.

For the sake of simplicity, the income effect will be considered from the point of view of the marginal effects only, although the parameters for the numerical example will be taken from the cumulative ones calculated for all PFI manufacturing. In this way we have average parameters, not reflecting the particular situation of one year. The income effect is:

$$\overline{\overline{Y}}_t = \alpha\, Y_t^h - [\alpha - (\pi^h - \rho - \tau_P\, \pi^h)]\, Y_t^h\, \frac{k^h}{k^0} + \frac{\overline{\overline{S}}_{Pt} + \overline{\overline{B}}_t + \overline{\overline{S}}_{Gt}}{k^0\,(1+\alpha)},$$

where:

– the first addendum gives the increase in income directly imputable to PFI;

– the second addendum gives the decrease in income caused by the financing mechanism under discussion;

– the third addendum gives the indirect effect on income through the increase in total financial availabilities for investments.

Concentrating the attention on the financial mechanism of the annual additions to PFI, and introducing the modifications shown in Section 3.2, one gets:

$$[\alpha\, k^h - (\pi^h\, k^h - \rho k^h - \tau_P\, \pi^h\, k^h)]\, \frac{Y_t^h}{k^0}\,.$$

In the case of total manufacturing, the various parameters have the following value:

$$\begin{aligned} k^h &= 0.95 \\ \alpha &= 0.10 \\ \pi^h\, k^h &= 0.30 \\ \rho\, k^h &= 0.12 \\ \tau_P\, \pi^h\, k^h &= 0.12. \end{aligned}$$

By subtraction, one finds that profits reinvested amount to 0.06 (20% of total PFI profits), under the assumption that profits going to domestic shareholders (if any) are also all reinvested.

The total impact of this mechanism comes out as:

$$- 0.04 \frac{Y_t^h}{k^0} \cdot$$

Since the increase in Y_t^h is 0.10 Y_t^h, this means that (as far as the financial mechanism is concerned) 60% of it is financed from PFI sources, and 40% from domestic sources. As for the total income effect, k^0 being = 1.7, this means that out of 0.10 Y_t^h increase in Y_t^h, 0.024 Y_t^h is the decrease in income imputable to PFI due to the financial mechanism under discussion.

The above calculations show results slightly different from those in the table on p. 247, where 71% of PFI investments were shown to be, on the average, financed from PFI sources, and 29% from domestic sources.

However, there is still the third term of the income effect to be considered, which gives the increase in investment funds imputable to PFI, and its effect on income, via domestic investments. This partly offsets the financial mechanism under discussion, and special attention should be given to $\bar{\bar{B}}_t$, the b.o.p. effect, which is assumed to represent also capital inflow directly imputable to PFI. The other two terms ($\bar{\bar{S}}_{Pt}$ and $\bar{\bar{S}}_{Gt}$) will not be considered, since they are only indirectly imputable to PFI. If $\bar{\bar{B}}_t$ covers the 11% difference left, then one may conclude that for Ghana, on the basis of the data considered, the endogenous approach to the problem fully and realistically takes account of the financial mechanism.

Working out the calculations, one finds that $\bar{\bar{B}}_t$ must be at least 1.21% of Y_t^h, as will, indeed, be true in most cases.[8]

So the choice was between using again in the model the financial mechan-

8 The situation in the various cases will come out as follows:

Marginal effects of PFI ($\bar{\bar{B}}_t$ as a percentage of Y_t^h)

Section	Year	Percentage	Section	Year	Percentage
7.6	1963	11.97	7.11	1968	25.00
	1968	1.11			
			7.12	1963	29.42
7.7	1963	5.70		1968	14.20
	1968	4.89			
7.8	1968	13.08	7.13	1963	16.79
7.9	1963	1.47		1968	−14.44
7.10	1963	5.77	7.14	All BFC	
	1968	0.36		1963	3.96
				Man. BFC 1963	4.09

ism and its endogenous way of working, or to introduce, case by case, some variations on the basis of the available evidence.

The findings presented above seemed to suggest sticking to the mechanism of the model, which appeared realistic enough, while the 'case by case' approach would have caused difficulties and confusion, without, in general, offering any real improvement.

7.6. MARGINAL AND CUMULATIVE EFFECTS FOR ALL PFI MANUFACTURING SECTOR

In the previous pages, the way the various parameters for the empirical exercise were derived was analysed to some extent. Now it seems sufficient to add a few remarks about each of the empirical cases to be considered.

One of the things to be noticed, recalling also what was said on the previous pages about the financing mechanism of PFI, is the relatively low level of both k^h and k^0; the former reaching a high level in two manufacturing sub-sectors only (Section 7.9 and 7.10), and there it will affect adversely the income effect. On the other hand, the relatively low level of k^h requires less investments to finance the annual additions to PFI, although the relatively low level of k^0 raises the income effect which would derive. Anyhow, the two combined do not affect the results so much as, for example, in India.

The marginal and cumulative effects are given in the table on p. 251. For 1963, for the reasons already discussed at length, the income effect is not adversely affected by the financing mechanism, although the level of it is very high. Consequently, the income effect turns out to be almost one fourth of v.a. of PFI in 1963, that is to say that it almost corresponds to the direct effect of PFI on income (i.e. αY_t^h).

In order to appraise the income effect, the table on p. 252 will give GNP for the years considered, and its increase to the next year, and over the whole period.

Apart from one case (Section 7.6,1968) where it is almost at the required level, and apart from the results obtained where α is negative (Section 7.10,1968; Section 7.13,1968), foreign capital inflow imputable to PFI is in all cases above the level required, according to the general and simplified calculations given in the text, to offset the negative impact of the financial mechanism of the annual addition to PFI on the income effect. The results depend, of course, on the characteristics of each case, and on the level of α in particular. This could mean that in all cases capital inflow imputable to PFI is more than sufficient to complete the financing of its annual expansion, so that indirectly it benefits the rest of the economy too. Each single case should, however, be studied in depth before any more specific conclusion is drawn, so that various possible particular situations can be taken into account.

Ghana: All PFI – Manufacturing
(Marginal and cumulative effects of PFI)

Parameters	1963	1968	1963–1968
α	0.25	0.01	0.10
$\pi^k k^h$	0.34	0.38	0.30
ρk^h	0.14	0.15	0.12
λk^h	0	0	0
$\tau_P \pi^h k^h$	0.14	0.15	0.12
k^h	0.95	0.95	0.95
k^0	1.7	1.7	1.7
$\varphi_m (1+m^h)$	0.43	0.43	0.43
$\varphi_e (1+e^h)$	0.20	0.20	0.20
$\mu(1+m^0)$	0.10	0.10	0.10
θ	0.045	0.055	0.053
σ	0.10	0.10	0.10
τ_W, τ_P	0.10	0.10	0.10
$\tau_{\text{IND}}, \tau_M, \tau_E$	0.08	0.08	0.08
w^h	0.19	0.16	0.22
$g^h k^h$	0.14	0.14	0.14
Π	0.13	0.13	0.13
t	–	–	5
Income data (mln N₵)			
Y_t^h	23.73	47.56	47.56
Y_t	1190	2028	2028

	Marginal effects (mln N₵)		Cumulative effects (mln N₵)	
$\overline{\overline{Y}}_t$	5.46	3.21	Y_t^*	476.00
$\overline{\overline{B}}_t$	2.85	0.53	B_t^*	80.40
$\overline{\overline{S}}_{Pt}$	0.55	0.32	S_{Pt}^*	47.60
$\overline{\overline{S}}_{Gt}$	0.87	0.46	S_{Gt}^*	65.80

Year	Y_t	$Y_{t+1} - Y_t$	$Y_{1968} - Y_{1963}$
1963	1190	155	
1968	2028	257	838

Source: data calculated from Table 1.1 at current prices (mln N₵).

The private savings effect will in all cases adapt itself to the income effect, being 10% of it. The b.o.p. effect is rather high, and to appraise it better, the following table gives the b.o.p. deficit for the years considered, similarly to what was done for GNP:

Year	B_t	$B_{t+1} - B_t$	$B_{1968} - B_{1964}$
1964	76.4	140.0	
1965	216.4	– 96.5	
1966	119.9	– 49.2	
1967	70.7	– 29.9	
1968	40.8	–	–35.6

Source: IMF *International Financial Statistics* (various issues); data converted into mln N₵; no other data available.

The public savings effect also turns out relatively high, and in order to appraise it, it is again possible to give the situation in the years considered:

Year	S_{Gt}	$S_{Gt+1} - S_{Gt}$	$S_{G1968} - S_{G1963}$
1963	8.1	43.6	
1968	–2.3	19.4	–10.4

Source: 'SSP Report' Table 4.1 (mln N₵); obtained from total revenue less current expenditure.

The marginal effects for 1968 are relatively higher, if the new level of α and of Y_t^h is taken into account; this is true in particular of the income effect. This is mainly due to the lower level of α and the higher level of PFI profits available for reinvestments, leaving extra financial resources for domestic investments and hence positively affecting the level of income. The same happens with public savings, while as said previously, private savings adapt themselves to the income effect.

The b.o.p. effect, too, is relatively higher, due to the higher indirect effect through the increase in income. Its importance, in the case of Ghana, is strengthened by the fact that the b.o.p. deficit shows a decreasing trend in the period considered (see table above).

The first conclusion one may derive from these results is that in Ghana, PFI affects income to a considerable degree, due mainly to more PFI profits available for investments, and also, obviously, the other differences in the various parameters. Still, the b.o.p. effect comes out as rather high, both in absolute terms and as compared with the actual situation.

With the cumulative effects one should remember first of all that the level of the cumulative effects is, *ceteris paribus*, inversely proportionate to the level of α, due to the fact that a higher α means lower effects in the previous years which 'cumulate', and vice versa.

Moreover, what was said previously about the working of the financial mechanism for the annual additions to PFI applies also here, in the sense that its consequences for the income effect are to a substantial degree offset by profits reinvested and by the effect of PFI on capital inflow.

Taking this into account, and remembering that the analysis concentrates on a five-year period, one still finds that the cumulative effects turn out quite relevant. The income effect in particular is rather high, and its relevance can be compared with the increase in income which actually took place between 1963 and 1968 (see table p. 252; mln N₵ 838), considering the relative share of All PFI manufacturing in GNP (see table Section 7.3).

A similar appraisal can be carried out for the other effects and for all the other cases, considering their relative share in GNP, as given by the table in Section 7.3, and the absolute value over the period 1963–1968, as given earlier in this section.

The private and public savings effects derive accordingly, while the b.o.p. is relatively lower as compared to what happened with the marginal effects.

Its relevance in the various cases will vary mainly as a consequence of the rate of profit transfer to abroad (with respect to v.a.), the import and export coefficients being always the same.

In general, the picture appears more favourable for the cumulative effects than for the marginal effects, and this will apply also the cases to be discussed next, although, as has been often stressed, the results should be interpreted in the light of all the underlying assumptions and of the procedure followed to estimate the parameters.

7.7. MARGINAL AND CUMULATIVE EFFECTS FOR ALL PFI MANUFACTURING SUB-SECTOR 'FOOD, BEVERAGES AND TOBACCO'

There is nothing particularly remarkable to notice. As regards marginal effects, the comments of the previous section apply also here, especially in view of the rather steady behaviour of the sub-sector. The income effect in both cases is rather high, relatively higher than before, and higher than the actual increase of PFI v.a. in the two years considered (represented, as usual, by αY_t^h) apart from the causes already mentioned, the very low level of k^h plays a role here. The b.o.p. effect is relatively higher, as a consequence, among other things, of the indirect effect of income on it.

As regards cumulative effects, there is no particular variation from the case of 'All PFI manufacturing' considered in the previous section. Again, the income effect is sizeable, although relatively less than in the previous case because there are less profits available for reinvestment in PFI additions, and hence financial resources for domestic investments amount to less, too. The b.o.p. effect is also relatively smaller, owing to a smaller rate of transfer of profits to abroad. Private and public savings effects are in accordance with what was to be expected.

7.8. MARGINAL AND CUMULATIVE EFFECTS FOR ALL PFI MANUFACTURING SUB-SECTOR 'TEXTILE, FOOTWEAR, AND APPAREL'

As has been said before, the marginal effects for 1963 have been omitted because of the negative profit ratio and the very high wage rate (see the table in Section 7.3).

The marginal effects for 1968 still turn out rather high; the income effect is only slightly lower than the increase in income directly imputable to PFI (αY_t^h), for the reasons shown previously, and because of the lower level of k^h together with a relatively high level of profits available for reinvestment. The b.o.p. effect is still relatively high, as is the public savings effect.

The cumulative income effect is relatively less than in the previous cases, owing to the much higher rate of growth of PFI. Although the rate of profit is still high so that the financial mechanism works positively for the income effect, the influence of α is much more relevant, since, as remarked earlier, a higher α means lower effects in the previous years, which 'accumulate' in the overall result. The b.o.p. effect is similarly affected by the high level of α, although an upward influence is exerted by the high rate of transfer of profits

Ghana: All PFI: Food, beverages, and tobacco
(Marginal and cumulative effects of PFI)

Parameters	1963	1968	1963–1968
α	0.11	0.10	0.10
$\pi^h k^h$	0.28	0.22	0.08
ρk^h	0.11	0.09	0.03
λk^h	0	0	0
$\tau_P \pi^h k^h$	0.11	0.09	0.03
k^h	0.36	0.36	0.36
k^0	1.7	1.7	1.7
$\varphi_m (1+m^h)$	0.43	0.43	0.43
$\varphi_e (1+e^h)$	0.20	0.20	0.20
$\mu(1+m^0)$	0.10	0.10	0.10
θ	0.045	0.055	0.053
σ	0.10	0.10	0.10
τ_W, τ_P	0.10	0.10	0.10
$\tau_{IND}, \tau_M, \tau_E$	0.08	0.08	0.08
w^h	0.05	0.09	0.19
$g^h k^h$	0.14	0.14	0.14
Π	0.13	0.13	0.13
t	–	–	5
Income data (mln N₵)			
Y_t^h	14.95	24.22	24.22
Y_t	1190	2028	2028

	Marginal effects (mln N₵)		Cumulative effects (mln N₵)	
$\overline{\overline{Y}}_t$	2.58	3.51	Y_t^*	190.39
$\overline{\overline{B}}_t$	0.85	1.19	B_t^*	31.79
$\overline{\overline{S}}_{Pt}$	0.26	0.35	S_{Pt}^*	19.04
$\overline{\overline{S}}_{Gt}$	0.32	0.39	S_{Gt}^*	24.08

Ghana: All PFI: Textile, footwear, and apparel
(Marginal and cumulative effects of PFI)

Parameters	1963	1968	1963–1968
α		0.23	0.35
$\pi^h k^h$		0.42	0.33
ρk^h		0.17	0.13
λk^h		0	0
$\tau_P \pi^h k^h$		0.17	0.13
k^h		0.40	0.40
k^0		1.7	1.7
$\varphi_m (1+m^h)$		0.43	0.43
$\varphi_e(1+e^h)$		0.20	0.20
$\mu(1+m^0)$		0.10	0.10
θ		0.055	0.053
σ		0.10	0.10
τ_W, τ_P		0.10	0.10
$\tau_{IND}, \tau_M, \tau_P$		0.08	0.08
w^h		0.24	0.37
$g^h k^h$		0.14	0.14
Π		0.13	0.13
t		–	5
Income data (mln N₵)			
Y_t^h		6.49	6.49
Y_t	2028		2028

Marginal effects (mln N₵)		Cumulative effects (mln N₵)	
$\overline{\overline{Y}}_t$	2.13	Y_t^*	17.75
$\overline{\overline{B}}_t$	0.85	B_t^*	4.68
$\overline{\overline{S}}_{Pt}$	0.21	S_{Pt}^*	1.78
$\overline{\overline{S}}_{Gt}$	0.38	S_{Gt}^*	2.63

to abroad in relation to PFI v.a. The private and public savings effects adapt themselves as usual to the income effects.

7.9. MARGINAL AND CUMULATIVE EFFECTS FOR ALL PFI MANUFACTURING SUB-SECTOR 'CHEMICAL AND ALLIED PRODUCTS'

As stated previously, the marginal effects for 1968 have been omitted because of the negative profit ratio (see also the table in Section 7.3)..

Moreover it was necessary, for the marginal effects in 1963, to introduce certain modifications in the estimation of some parameters as compared with what was outlined in Section 7.5. The rate of growth of PFI, α, if calculated according to the formula given there, would be extremely high owing to one exceptional year (1962: $Y_t^h = 115.1$; 1964: $Y_t^h = 1{,}581.9$; 1969: $Y_t^h = 200.1$). α would be over 500%, so it was decided to use the average rate of growth calculated for the cumulative effects also for the marginal ones in 1963.

In the calculation of k^h the last year was dropped from the formula given in Section 7.5 because of the low value of v.a. in that year, while 1961 was added to the calculation, thus:

$$k^h = \frac{\sum_{1961}^{1967} I^h}{Y_{1968}^h - Y_{1962}^h}$$

This modification was necessary to get a positive and reasonable k^h, although it is still biased by the fact that investments in 1961, for lack of data, were assumed to be zero.

Even so, k^h emerges very high, contrary to all other cases (except the one that will be considered in the next section). With the marginal effects this affects the income effect: it turns out negative, owing to the financial mechanism of the model for the annual additions to PFI working stronger. The limited absolute value of the income effect and the other two negative effects are due simply to the low level of $\dot{Y}_t^h$.

The b.o.p. effect still comes up positive, with a low absolute value, for the same reason. The indirect effect on it related to income, offsets partly, but not totally, the direct PFI effect on it.

As for the cumulative effects: the very high level of k^h may be expected to affect the income effect in a negative sense, through the working of the financial mechanism for the annual additions to PFI. However, it turns out

Ghana: All PFI: Chemicals and allied products
(Marginal and cumulative effects of PFI)

Parameters	1963	1968	1963–1968
α	0.08		0.08
$\pi^h k^h$	0.59		0.61
ρk^h	0.24		0.24
λk^h	0		0
$\tau_P \pi^h k^h$	0.24		0.24
k^h	7.72		7.72
k^0	1.7		1.7
$\varphi_m (1+m^h)$	0.43		0.43
$\varphi_e (1+e^h)$	0.20		0.20
$\mu(1+m^0)$	0.10		0.10
θ	0.045		0.053
σ	0.10		0.10
τ_W, τ_p	0.10		0.10
$\tau_{IND}, \tau_M, \tau_E$	0.08		0.08
w^h	0.39		0.25
$g^h k^h$	0.14		0.14
Π	0.13		0.13
t	–		5
Income data (mln N₵)			
Y_t^h	0.30		0.29
Y_t	1190		2028

Marginal effects (mln N₵)		Cumulative effects (mln N₵)	
$\overline{\overline{Y}}_t$	– 0.07	Y_t^*	3.10
$\overline{\overline{B}}_t$	0.00	B_t^*	0.56
$\overline{\overline{S}}_{Pt}$	– 0.01	S_{Pt}^*	0.31
$\overline{\overline{S}}_{Gt}$	– 0.01	S_{Gt}^*	0.46

relevant, owing to the high rate of profit (and consequently of profit reinvested) and to the relatively low level of α, which affects it positively. We shall see a similar case in the next section.

The private and public savings effects adapt themselves, as usual, to the income effect, while the b.o.p. effect appears of the same order as in most of the previous cases.

7.10. MARGINAL AND CUMULATIVE EFFECTS FOR ALL PFI MANUFACTURING SUB-SECTOR 'PRIMARY AND FABRICATED METALS'

In this case one notices at once the high value of k^h, which is going to affect negatively the results (according to the sign of α), in the same way as seen in the previous case. This case and the one treated in Section 7.9 are the only ones out of the whole exercise showing a very high ICOR for the PFI sector.

Moreover, in the case of the marginal effects, one notices a negative sign for α in 1968, though with a very low absolute value. It was left negative without any correction, to see the working of the model in this, not at all extraordinary, case as well.

As was to be expected, the income and the two savings effects come up with a sign opposite to that of α, for the same reasons as explained in the previous section, the principal one being the high level of k^h in the financial mechanism of the model. The b.o.p. effect proves exceptional in 1968, for in this case the indirect effect through the increase in income succeeds in offsetting the direct effect of PFI, as a consequence, among other things, of the very low level of α, which determines it.

Similarly to the previous case, the overall result with the cumulative effects is, in spite of a not too high value of α, kept down by the very high level of k^h, through the financial mechanism of the annual additions to PFI. The private and public savings effects are derived accordingly, while the b.o.p. effect, owing to the indirect impact on it of PFI through the income effect, is also relatively low.

7.11. MARGINAL EFFECTS FOR ALL PFI MANUFACTURING SUB-SECTOR 'MACHINERY'

As in the previous sectors, the marginal effects as well as the cumulative effects have been omitted, because of the absence of PFI before 1968 (see Table 1.3 in the 'SSP Report').

The high level of α, together with the high level of PFI profits available for

Ghana: All PFI: Primary and fabricated metals
(Marginal and cumulative effects of PFI)

Parameters	1963	1968	1963–1968
α	0.55	–0.01	0.09
$\pi^h k^h$	0.53	0.11	0.45
ρk^h	0.21	0.04	0.18
λk^h	0	0	0
$\tau_P\ \pi^h k^h$	0.21	0.04	0.18
k^h	7.22	7.22	7.22
k^0	1.7	1.7	1.7
$\varphi_m (1+m^h)$	0.43	0.43	0.43
$\varphi_e (1+e^h)$	0.20	0.20	0.20
$\mu(1+m^0)$	0.10	0.10	0.10
θ	0.045	0.055	0.053
σ	0.10	0.10	0.10
τ_W, τ_P	0.10	0.10	0.10
$\tau_{IND}, \tau_M, \tau_E$	0.08	0.08	0.08
w^h	0.34	0.35	0.30
$g^h k^h$	0.14	0.14	0.14
Π	0.13	0.13	0.13
t	–	–	5
Income data (mln N₵)			
Y_t^h	0.74	1.70	1.70
Y_t	1190	2028	2028

	Marginal effects (mln N₵)		Cumulative effects (mln N₵)	
$\bar{\bar{Y}}_t$	–1.36	0.10	Y_t^*	10.72
$\bar{\bar{B}}_t$	0.04	0.01	B_t^*	2.22
$\bar{\bar{S}}_{Pt}$	–0.14	0.01	S_{Pt}^*	1.07
$\bar{\bar{S}}_{Gt}$	–0.15	0.02	S_{Gt}^*	1.60

Ghana: All PFI: Machinery
(Marginal effects of PFI)

Parameters	1968
α	0.41
$\pi^h k^h$	0.52
ρk^h	0.21
λk^h	0
$\tau_P \pi^h k^h$	0.21
k^h	0.22
k^0	1.7
$\varphi_m (1+m^h)$	0.43
$\varphi_e (1+e^h)$	0.20
$\mu(1+m^0)$	0.10
θ	0.055
σ	0.10
τ_W, τ_P	0.10
$\tau_{IND}, \tau_M, \tau_E$	0.08
w^h	0.16
$g^h k^h$	0.14
Π	0.13
t	–
Income data (mln N₵)	
Y_t^h	0.18
Y_t	2028
Marginal effects (mln N₵)	
$\bar{\bar{Y}}_t$	0.11
$\bar{\bar{B}}_t$	0.05
$\bar{\bar{S}}_{Pt}$	0.01
$\bar{\bar{S}}_{Gt}$	0.02

investments and the low level of k^h (in the working of the financial mechanism for the annual additions to PFI) cause the income effect to be relatively high, higher than the increase in income directly imputable to PFI (i.e. $\alpha\ Y_t^h$); needless to say that the absolute value of the effects is low, simply as a consequence of the low value of Y_t^h. The private and public savings effects are derived accordingly, while the b.o.p. effect is still sizeable, although, relatively speaking, not much higher than the one obtained in other cases. This is just another illustration of the fact that, since the parameters for the foreign sector are almost all the same for all cases, no great variation can be expected, apart from the direct and indirect influence of the increase in income.

7.12. MARGINAL AND CUMULATIVE EFFECTS FOR ALL PFI MANUFACTURING SUB-SECTOR 'TRANSPORT EQUIPMENT'

1967 being an exceptional year, the value of α for the marginal effects for 1968, instead of being calculated with the formula given in Section 7.5, was substituted by the one obtained over the whole period for the cumulative effects (1966: $Y_t^h = 250.5$; 1967: $Y_t^h = 3038.4$; 1968: $Y_t^h = 555.9$).

The high level of α in both cases for the marginal effects causes a high level of the income effect, relatively speaking. The private and public savings effects are accordingly high. The b.o.p. effect is relatively high, too, for the same reasons as discussed before.

As regards the cumulative effects the high level of α keeps the general results down, and in particular the income effect, although the rate of transfer of profits to abroad is very high, and the value of k^h is the lowest of all cases.

The private and public savings effects are then derived accordingly, while the b.o.p. effect is also heavily affected by the indirect impact of income, though relatively less than in the previous cases, where α was lower and the income effect (always in relative terms) higher.

7.13. MARGINAL AND CUMULATIVE EFFECTS FOR ALL PFI MANUFACTURING SUB-SECTOR 'OTHER MANUFACTURING'

In the calculation of the ICOR for PFI, the last year of the formula given in Section 7.5 was dropped, since in 1969 Y_t^h was exceptionally low (and less than in 1963). k^h was then calculated in the following way:

Ghana: All PFI: Transport equipment
(Marginal and cumulative effects of PFI)

Parameters	1963	1968	1963–1968
α	0.47	0.33	0.33
$\pi^h k^h$	0.57	0.14	0.70
ρk^h	0.23	0.06	0.28
λk^h	0	0	0
$\tau_P \pi^h k^h$	0.23	0.06	0.28
k^h	0.20	0.20	0.20
k^0	1.7	1.7	1.7
$\varphi_m (1+m^h)$	0.43	0.43	0.43
$\varphi_e (1+e^h)$	0.20	0.20	0.20
$\mu(1+m^0)$	0.10	0.10	0.10
θ	0.045	0.055	0.053
σ	0.10	0.10	0.10
τ_W, τ_P	0.10	0.10	0.10
$\tau_{IND}, \tau_M, \tau_E$	0.08	0.08	0.08
w^h	0.29	0.27	0.20
$g^h k^h$	0.14	0.14	0.14
Π	0.13	0.13	0.13
t	–	–	5
Income data (mln N₵)			
Y_t^h	0.31	0.56	0.56
Y_t	1190	2028	2028

	Marginal effects (mln N₵)		Cumulative effects (mln N₵)	
$\bar{\bar{Y}}_t$	0.21	0.22	Y_t^*	2.25
$\bar{\bar{B}}_t$	0.09	0.08	B_t^*	0.58
$\bar{\bar{S}}_{Pt}$	0.02	0.02	S_{Pt}^*	0.23
$\bar{\bar{S}}_{Gt}$	0.05	0.02	S_{Gt}^*	0.40

$$k^h = \frac{\sum_{1962}^{1967} I^h}{Y^h_{1968} - Y^h_{1963}}$$

As regards the marginal effects for 1968, α, was left negative so as to test the model for this case. The same was done in Section 7.10, but in the present case the absolute value of α is much higher.

The marginal effects are affected accordingly. When α is positive, all effects are positive, and sizeable, for the reasons shown before; when α is negative, they are also negative, but still of a relatively relevant absolute value, in particular for the b.o.p. effect, owing, among other things, to the high level of profits, and thus of profit remittances to abroad (especially in 1968).

As to the cumulative effects, the low level of α, in the context of this exercise, combined with a high rate of profits reinvested and a low k^h, affects the income effect positively; this effect is the highest, in relative terms in relation to Y^h_t, of all cases. As a consequence, the cumulative effects on private and public savings are rather high, too. The latter are also positively affected by the high taxes on PFI profits.

The b.o.p. effect is also relevant, although relatively less than with the marginal effects. It is affected by a relatively high rate of transfer of profits to abroad in relation to v.a., and by the indirect impact of the income effect, through the marginal propensity to import.

Before turning to the two cases with BFC data, it is possible to make some general remarks about the results obtained for the various cases of All PFI, both at the level of total manufacturing, and at the level of each sub-sector.

A drawback of the whole exercise is that – as observed before – some of the parameters are the same for all sub-sectors, so that for lack of better information the various possible empirical situations cannot be fully taken into account.

However, it was still possible to appraise certain particular cases, as given by varying values for α, for k^h, for the rate of profit reinvested and remitted abroad, etc. More information would be necessary to be able to draw detailed conclusions about the various sub-sectors; anyhow, the exercise has provided a better insight into the working of the model at a 'sub-sectoral' level, as well as some evidence of the effects of PFI in the various sub-sectors, at least as far as the available evidence allowed to carry out the analysis.

Ghana: All PFI: Other manufacturing
(Marginal and cumulative effects of PFI)

Parameters	1963	1968	1963–1968
α	0.33	–0.22	0.11
$\pi^h k^h$	0.36	0.68	0.62
ρk^h	0.14	0.27	0.25
λk^h	0	0	0
$\tau_P \pi^h k^h$	0.14	0.27	0.25
k^h	0.52	0.52	0.52
k^0	1.7	1.7	1.7
$\varphi_m (1+m^h)$.	0.43	0.43	0.43
$\varphi_e (1+e^h)$	0.20	0.20	0.20
$\mu(1+m^0)$	0.10	0.10	0.10
θ	0.045	0.055	0.053
σ	0.10	0.10	0.10
τ_W, τ_P	0.10	0.10	0.10
$\tau_{IND}, \tau_M, \tau_E$	0.08	0.08	0.08
w^h	0.46	0.22	0.22
$g^h k^h$	0.14	0.14	0.14
Π	0.13	0.13	0.13
t	–	–	5
Income data (mln N₵)			
Y_t^h	6.41	14.13	14.13
Y_t	1190	2028	2028

	Marginal effects (mln N₵)		Cumulative effects (mln N₵)	
$\overline{\overline{Y}}_t$	2.56	–3.52	Y_t^*	179.97
$\overline{\overline{B}}_t$	1.08	–2.04	B_t^*	30.69
$\overline{\overline{S}}_{Pt}$	0.26	–0.35	S_{Pt}^*	18.00
$\overline{\overline{S}}_{Gt}$	0.45	–0.96	S_{Gt}^*	26.71

7.14. MARGINAL EFFECTS FOR ALL BFC AND MANUFACTURING BFC

The relative relevance of BFC was discussed at length previously, especially in Sections 7.2 and 7.3 (see the tables given there). The data available allowed only the calculation of the marginal effects for 1963 for All BFC and for Manufacturing BFC.

Still, some assumptions were necessary for the calculations to be possible, as discussed in Section 7.5. While interpreting the results, one should keep them in mind, and remember in particular that α was taken from All PFI manufacturing, and that the value of k^h is not the ICOR, but an average capital-output ratio.

However, it was also possible to calculate some of the parameters with more accuracy than in the cases of All PFI (such as import coefficients, profit ratios, profit tax rates), and this should make the exercise more interesting. Finally, the availablility of employment data made it possible to calculate the employment effect as well, which was not possible in the case of All PFI.

In this case too, the reasoning about the working of the financial mechanism for the annual additions to PFI is valid, and it is strengthened by the low levels of k^h. In both cases the income effect turns out quite relevant, more than the direct increase in income imputable to PFI ($\alpha\, Y^h_t$, i.e. 10% of Y^h_t).

As in previous cases, the b.o.p. effect is still sizeable, for the same reasons as given before, since some of the parameters, also those taken directly from BFC, are still the same.

The private savings effect has been obtained automatically from the income effect, while the public savings effect appears, in both cases, a little lower, a result which, especially in the second case, is due to a generally lower level of PFI profits, and thus of PFI profit taxation, in relation to Y^h_t.

Because η is expressed in man-years per thousand units of v.a., and Y^h_t is given in millions (and consequently the effects are in millions of N₵), the employment effect is given in thousands of man-years, in both cases.

As said above, this case of BFC proves quite interesting, both for the more direct way of deriving some of the parameters, and for the comparison which can now be established with All PFI, at any rate at the level of the manufacturing sector.

Comparing the results for Manufacturing BFC, with the marginal effects for 1963 for All PFI manufacturing one notices that the former are relatively smaller than the latter, owing to, mainly, the lower level of α in the case of BFC.

Of course, one should be careful in such a comparison, with a view to,

Ghana: BFC
(Marginal effects of PFI – 1963)

Parameters	All BFC	Manufacturing BFC
α	0.10	0.10
$\pi^h k^h$	0.21	0.11
ρk^h	0.08	0.04
λk^h	0	0
$\tau_P \pi^h k^h$	0.08	0.04
k^h	0.58	0.49
k^0	1.7	1.7
$\varphi_m (1+m^h)$	0.35	0.43
$\varphi_e (1+e^h)$	0.18	0.20
$\mu(1+m^\text{U})$	0.10	0.10
θ	0.045	0.045
σ	0.10	0.10
τ_W, τ_P	0.10	0.10
$\tau_{\text{IND}}, \tau_M, \tau_E$	0.08	0.08
w^h	0.10	0.11
$g^h k^h$	0.14	0.14
Π	0.13	0.13
η^h	0.17	0.21
η^o	0.29	0.32
Income data (mln N₵)		
Y_t^h	128.90	6.01
Y_t	1190	1190

Marginal effects (mln N₵)

	All BFC		Manufacturing BFC
$\bar{\bar{Y}}_t$	16.75	$\bar{\bar{Y}}_t$	0.73
$\bar{\bar{B}}_t$	5.11	$\bar{\bar{B}}_t$	0.25
$\bar{\bar{S}}_{Pt}$	1.67	$\bar{\bar{S}}_{Pt}$	0.07
$\bar{\bar{S}}_{Gt}$	1.57	$\bar{\bar{S}}_{Gt}$	0.05
$\bar{\bar{L}}_t$	3.31	$\bar{\bar{L}}_t$	0.17

Note: $\bar{\bar{L}}_t$ in '000 man-year

among other things, the different concepts of v.a. used for the two cases, as pointed out in Section 7.3.

7.15. CONCLUSIONS

Like before, the exercise carried out in the previous pages may be considered a 'case study of Ghana', but most of all, it represents an empirical application of the methodology of Part II with reference to the data supplied by the 'SSP Report' for this country. Consequently, in this case too the results should be interpreted mainly in this light, and they should serve to provide a better insight into the methodology, as well as to point out various possible improvements to make it more realistic. And anyhow, the results give some idea about the effects of PFI in Ghana. It was possible also to distinguish various cases, and to compare various situations, both at the level of the manufacturing sector and of the various manufacturing sub-sectors.

Before analysing the empirical results in more detail, it is interesting to point out the most interesting features of the exercise for Ghana, *vis-à-vis* those for India and the Philippines.

With India, it was possible to distinguish between Foreign Branches (FB) and Foreign Controlled Rupee Companies (FCRC) both for the whole economy and for the manufacturing sector, and thus to use the model to appraise the effects of different ways of financing a PFI project (FB vs FCRC).

In the case of Ghana such a distinction was possible only between All PFI and BFC, where a comparison is difficult though, as a consequence of the way various parameters have been estimated, and of the different concepts of v.a. used. However, it was possible to use the methodological approach to appraise the effects of PFI in the various sub-sectors of the manufacturing sector, just as it was done for the Philippines.

Interesting as this sectoral application of the methodology proved to be, there are some drawbacks, due to the fact that in the various sub-sectors many parameters are the same owing to lack of better empirical evidence. Even if it was not possible to appraise fully the effects in the various cases of all conceivable differences, still the analysis pointed out what happened as a result of varying values for some of the key parameters (α, k^h, rate of profits, etc.).

Moreover, it was necessary to put the 'know-how' parameter at zero, and hence the b.o.p. effect, and consequently all other effects, might be somewhat underestimated.

In spite of the limitations of this exercise, and although it is based on some radical simplifying assumptions, it is possible to reach some general conclusions, as in the case of India:

– in Ghana, PFI affects positively the growth of income, and sometimes to a considerable extent;

– PFI, in general, poses quite a heavy burden on the b.o.p., especially if compared with the actual situation;

– totally foreign controled PFI (i.e. BFC) tend to affect the growth of income less than All PFI, but this might simply be due to their smaller rate of growth, and to the smaller rate of profit (and hence of reinvested profit), owing to the method of estimating the parameters.

Another interesting feature of the Ghana exercise is that it was possible, at least in a simplified way, to show how the methodology, on the basis of the empirical evidence available, takes into account in an endogenous way, through the mechanism of financing the annual additions to PFI, what actually happens in practice. Consequently, some of the objections to this mechanism, raised before, may be considered as taken into account by the model, at any rate as far as Ghana is concerned.

The objections to the assumptions about import substitution still stand, however, and moreover it was not possible to estimate the import and export coefficient in a way at least as satisfactory as with India.

Finally, one should remember the limitations of the data used to set up the exercise, and the way various gaps were filled, as well as the necessity to use data in current prices.

CHAPTER VIII

GUATEMALA

8.1. INTRODUCTION

This chapter will present some results with reference to the case of Guatemala, on the basis of data made available by ICAITI. The source of data, their coverage, and limitations will be discussed in the next section. As will be seen there, the data supplied include all PFI and are disaggregated among the major sectors of the economy, and the manufacturing sub-sectors listed in Section 9.1, Part II. It will be possible to set up the empirical analysis accordingly.

Section 8.3 will then give a general picture of the relevance of PFI in the case of Guatemala, distinguishing among the major sectors of the economy, and the various manufacturing sub-sectors.

Section 8.4 will discuss the methodological approach followed.

Section 8.5 will show, one by one, how the various parameters have been estimated.

Subsequently, various empirical cases will be considered, first by the marginal approach for 1963 and 1968, and then by the cumulative approach over the period 1963–1968, for All PFI in the manufacturing sector, and in the various manufacturing sub-sectors. In this way it will be possible to make some general remarks about the effects of PFI from the two points of view, i.e. marginal and cumulative, as well as in the various sectors and sub-sectors considered, according to their structural characteristics.

The period was chosen on the basis of the data availability. Most time series run from 1962 to 1969. However, the occurence of time lags and the lack of data for the last year in some cases, led to dropping the first and last years.

8.2. SOURCE OF DATA, COVERAGE AND LIMITATIONS

The empirical application of the methodology was carried out in the case of Guatemala with data supplied by the 'Instituto Centroamericano de Investigacion y Tecnologia Industrial'.

In order to fill out the NEI questionnaire, ICAITI used various sources available in the country, such as: Banco de Guatemala, Secretaria Permanente de Integración Económica Centroamericano (SIECA), Consejo Nacional de Planificación Económica, Dirección General de Estadística, Oficina de Estadísticas de Trabajo, as well as direct consultation with high level officers directly concerned with PFI in Guatemala. Data are supplied in current prices, with a few exceptions explicitly mentioned in the 'ICAITI Report'. All data are in the national currency, the Quetzal (Q), equivalent to one U.S. Dollar.

Before the separate sections of the questionnaire are considered, a note is necessary on the criteria used to define PFI. Guatemala does not have a general and specific regulation about PFI. This means that there are no controls, apart from some statistical ones, on the composition of PFI capital and on the share it has in the enterprises of the country. As for the remittance of profits, the control established by the 'Departamento de Cambios' of the Banco de Guatemala has the purpose of not allowing a disinvestment greater than what actually came into the country. The Register established by this institution for this purpose was one of the main sources for the 'ICAITI Report'. According to it, the foreign capital, along with some domestic shares, was in 1969 Q 83 940 800 in the whole of Guatemala, scattered in 226 enterprises. Moreover, a sample of 51 enterprises revealed that on the average the share of PFI in total investments was 30.8%, the rest being imputable to national capital.

In supplying the v.a. data, a disaggregation greater than the one asked for was followed for the manufacturing sub-sectors, while the major sectors of the economy were given as requested. Consequently, it was necessary to aggregate the various industrial data according to the seven basic subsectors given in the questionnaire. In order to get v.a. data, ICAITI started from gross production data, and then applied for each sector and sub-sector a coefficient giving the share of value added in the various cases. In order to get the contribution of PFI, the level of PFI v.a. within its gross production was estimated first. Then the percentage of v.a. in gross production of each industrial branch and of each sector of the economy was applied to PFI gross production obtained for the corresponding years (1962–1969).

As for the data on capital formation, the Banco de Guatemala has some basic data which allow of estimating capital formation in the PFI sectors, but they are neither processed nor published, and consequently it was necessary to investigate separately all the information corresponding to the PFI enterprises registered in its 'Departamento de Cambio'. For the total economy it was possible at all levels to use official data published by the Banco de Guatemala.

Consequently, in the empirical analysis it is possible to distinguish between sectors and manufacturing sub-sectors, but no information is available for the various kinds of PFI.

Moreover, some basic data are missing, and it was necessary to fill these gaps using other sources and certain assumptions. The next section, in considering the general picture of PFI in Guatemala, will already give an idea of the data missing, while in Section 8.5 it will be shown how the various gaps were filled.

8.3. PFI IN GUATEMALA: THE GENERAL PICTURE

The table on pp. 274–275, obtained from the data supplied by the 'ICAITI Report', gives a general picture of PFI in Guatemala. The first half refers to the major sectors of the economy, while the second half refers to the various manufacturing sub-sectors. As can be noticed, out of the sub-sectors distinguished by the NEI questionnaire (whose data have been obtained by grouping accordingly the information given by the 'ICAITI Report' in more detail) the sixth, 'Transport equipment' is missing, PFI v.a. there being zero, consequently it will be excluded from the analysis of this chapter.

Column (1) gives the composition of PFI v.a. The largest sector, as can be seen, is manufacturing, although a certain role is played also by 'Commerce', and by 'Agriculture, forestry and fishing'. Within the manufacturing sector, the most important one, apart from 'Other manufacturing', is 'Food, beverages, and tobacco', although, from 1963 to 1968, 'Chemicals and allied products' and 'Machinery' acquired greater importance.

Column (2) derives accordingly, giving the relative importance of each sector and manufacturing sub-sector in GNP. The total of PFI does not play a predominant role in GNP, being, in 1968, less than 5%, and this should be kept in mind in interpreting the results of the empirical analysis.

Column (3) gives the importance of each sector and sub-sector in the corresponding one for the total economy. Some PFI sectors are relatively more important than other, such as 'Mining' and 'Electricity, gas, and water', apart, of course, from 'Manufacturing'. Within the latter, 'Chemicals and allied products', 'Primary and fabricated metals', 'Machinery', and 'Other manufacturing' have a heavy share of PFI. As the 'ICAITI Report' shows, some industries, in particular among those belonging to the category 'Other manufacturing', are based almost completely on PFI, e.g. 'Rubber industry' and 'Non-metallic mineral products'.

As stated earlier, no data are available on PFI imports or exports, and this will necessitate certain assumptions in order to be able to carry out the empirical analysis. The 'ICAITI Report', however, gives sectoral export data for the whole economy, and from them one can see that, within the manufacturing sector, the only exporting sub-sectors are 'Food, beverages, and tobacco', which accounts for almost all exports of manufactured products, and 'Other manufacturing', with a much smaller share.

Data on PFI profits before taxes (column (6)) are not available either, and this gap will have to be filled by introducing certain assumptions which will be presented in Section 8.5.

Column (7) then gives the share of wages in each sector's and sub-sector's v.a. As for employment, use was made of social security data from the Instituto Guatemalteco de Seguridad Social, and in some cases there are some obvious inconsistencies, due also to the way v.a. was obtained, as seen in the previous section. The most obvious cases are 'Mining', 'Transportation', and 'Other services'; within the manufacturing sector the situation looks much more reasonable. However, no data are available for 'Machinery', and the same is true of employment, probably due to classification inconsistencies.

Column (8) gives employment as a percentage of v.a. for each sector and sub-sector. One can see that within the manufacturing sector there are some sub-sectors more labour-intensive than others, such as 'Textile, footwear, and apparel'.

Next, column (9) gives employment in the various PFI cases as a percentage of employment in the corresponding sector of the total economy, and these data can be checked with PFI share in sectoral v.a. (column (3)). It is not possible to give any information about the manufacturing sub-sectors, since the employment data available at the level of the total economy are not comparable with the PFI ones, being obtained, contrary to all other cases, not from the Social Security Institute, but from the Dirección General de Estadística. The same applies to PFI wages as a percentage of total wages in the corresponding sector of the total economy (column (10)). Data are available for the major sectors of the economy only, and an idea of wage differentials between PFI and the rest of the economy can be obtained by checking the data given in column (10) with the ones of column (9), as well as with the share of each PFI sector in the corresponding one for the total economy (column 3).

It was possible to give the last four columns (7)–(10) only for 1968, due to lack of data for any other year.

Finally, column (11) gives gross investments, in 1963 and in 1968 over value added (v.a.) of the corresponding PFI sector or sub-sector. Due to some

PFI in Guatemala: The general picture

	(1)		(2)		(3)		(4)
	v.a. composition		% of v.a. in GNP		% of v.a. in corresponding sector		Import requirement % v.a.
	1963	1968	1963	1968	1963	1968	
All PFI	100.00	100.00	2.84	4.92	2.84	4.92	–
Agriculture, forestry, fishing	12.65	17.05	0.36	0.84	1.28	2.99	–
Mining	0.35	0.25	0.01	0.01	8.12	14.24	–
Electricity, gas, water	5.28	3.58	0.15	0.18	18.67	14.75	–
Commerce	35.48	25.07	1.01	1.23	3.14	4.22	–
Transportation	1.20	0.53	0.03	0.03	0.91	0.49	–
Others	0.02	0.43	0.00	0.02	0.00	0.09	–
Manufacturing PFI	45.02	53.09	1.28	2.61	9.67	16.09	–
	100.00	100.00					
Food, beverages, tobacco	24.38	24.58	0.31	0.64	4.64	9.40	–
Textile and apparel	7.06	6.47	0.09	0.17	2.60	4.12	–
Chemicals and allied products	6.88	14.29	0.09	0.37	18.30	54.52	–
Primary and fabricated metals	3.34	8.03	0.04	0.21	16.19	15.22	–
Machinery	4.83	10.96	0.06	0.29	71.66	61.34	–
Transport equipment	–	–	–	–	–	–	–
Others	53.51	35.67	0.69	0.93	33.33	35.58	–
Source:	Table 1.2, 1.3		Table 1.2 1.3		Table 1.2 1.3		

Notes:

(a) Source: ICAITI Report various tables.
(b) See text (Section 8.3) for comments.
(c) – = not available or not existing.
(d) column (8) – employment – gives the number of man-years per 1000 Q of v.a.

differences in classification in the 'ICAITI Report' in Table 2.2 (gross investments) and in Table 1.2 (v.a.) it was not possible to give the ratio for some sectors.

As was said earlier, there is no evidence about the relative relevance of alternative kinds of PFI, apart from the sectoral classification depicted above.

(5)	(6)	(7)	(8)	(9)	(10)	(11)	
Exp. promotion % v.a.	Profits before taxes % v.a.	Wages / v.a.	Employment/ v.a.	Employment % of corresponding sector	Wages % of corresponding sector	Gross investments / v.a.	
		1968	1968	1968	1968	1963	1968
–	–	0.41	0.35	6.65	12.72	0.51	0.28
–	–	0.63	1.01	5.70	11.29	0.25	0.03
–	–	2.31	1.21	16.09	39.08	–	–
–	–	0.96	0.31	23.25	54.95	–	–
–	–	0.37	0.15	13.76	25.05	–	–
–	–	2.29	2.08	7.22	6.51	0.62	0.05
–	–	1.27	1.35	0.54	0.51	–	–
–	–	0.29	0.20	20.71	31.92	0.34	0.30
–	–	0.41	0.27	–	–	0.47	0.75
–	–	0.41	0.47	–	–	1.20	0.15
–	–	0.26	0.16	–	–	0.39	0.08
–	–	0.14	0.12	–	–	0.90	0.06
–	–	–	–	–	–	0.18	0.11
–	–	–	–	–	–	–	–
–	–	0.20	0.20	–	–	0.14	0.21
		Table 1.2, 1.3 and		Instituto Guatemalteco De Seguridad Social		Table 1.2, 1.3, 2.2, 2.3	

8.4. THE METHODOLOGICAL APPROACH

The data available, in general for the period 1962–1969, would allow both the use of the marginal approach and that of the cumulative approach.

The irregular behaviour of the PFI sectors and sub-sectors, as some of the parameters in the various tables giving the effects will point out, justifies the application of the marginal approach for the four main effects. This also allows to overcome partly the difficulty that almost all data are in current prices. Most parameters will be calculated year by year, and consequently will not be affected. However, some other parameters will have to be calculated over a longer period, with the justifications which will be discussed in Section 8.5. No attempt will be made to correct the data in current prices into data in constant prices. Although price indices are available, there seems to be danger of making more mistakes than improvements. The empirical application of the methodology, in the case of the marginal effects, will be limited to two years, 1963 and 1968. The intermediate years were skipped, since the assumptions necessary to estimate some of the parameters would make yearly results less meaningful.

The data available allow also to apply the cumulative approach. This will be done over the period 1963–1968, for the same reason as given for the marginal effects. Certain assumptions will be necessary in order to estimate the parameters. However, as for the marginal effects, the estimation will be done year by year in most cases, and consequently the fact that most data are in current prices should not considerably affect the results.

Owing to the lack of employment data, apart from 1968, the 'employment effect' can be calculated only for the marginal effects for 1968. Moreover, the lack of data on wages both PFI and domestic, apart from 1968, and the lack of profits data, apart from the figure for the total economy, will prevent the calculation of the 'income distribution effect'.

The analysis will be carried out with reference to the All PFI manufacturing sector, and to the sub-sectors outlined in Section 9.1, Part II, apart from the sub-sector 'Transport equipment', whose PFI v.a. is zero in all years, as already noticed while deriving the table in Section 8.3.

At the end, some general comparisons will be possible between the results for the various cases. One should be careful, however, and keep in mind the various simplifying assumptions which were necessary to get the parameters, as well as the fact that the marginal effects are expressed, respectively, in 1963 and in 1968 prices, the cumulative ones in 1968 prices. Finally, one must also remember that there is no direct correspondence between cumulative and marginal effects.

8.5. ESTIMATION OF THE PARAMETERS

In the following pages a brief description will be given of the way the various parameters were estimated, together with the various assumptions introduced. The discussion will refer to both cumulative and marginal effects.

Y_t^h, Y_t — are taken in current prices from Tables 1.1, 1.2 and 1.3.

α — since capital stock figures are not available, and since PFI investments have an irregular behaviour, it is calculated from value added data at current prices from Table 1.2 and 1.3, taking, in the case of the marginal effects, the year preceding and the year following the one considered, according to the formula;

$$\alpha_t = \left(\frac{Y_{t+1}^h}{Y_{t-1}^h}\right)^{½} - 1.$$

It was calculated separately for all cases, year by year. In the case of the cumulative effects, the average annual rate of growth was calculated over the period 1963–1968 case by case, by applying a similar formula.

k^h — the ICOR for the various PFI sectors considered was calculated case by case by considering gross investments (from Tables 2.2 and 2.3) over the period 1963–1968, and the increase in value added (from Tables 1.2 and 1.3) over the period 1964–1969, with a one-year lag, and using data at current prices according to the formula:

$$k^h - \frac{\sum_{1963}^{1968} I^h}{Y_{1969}^h - Y_{1964}^h}.$$

The lack of investment data previous to 1963 prevented the use of a longer period. Moreover, in the case of all manufacturing PFI, products of petroleum were excluded, since they are not included in the v.a. of any other sub-sector. Transport equipment data were included in 'Other manufacturing', since, as seen before, there is no separate v.a. data for this sector. Finally, in the case of 'Textile, footwear, and apparel' the last year was omitted, because of irregular data, as will be seen better later (Section 8.8).

k^0 — the ICOR for the rest of the economy was calculated by using gross investments data over the period 1962–1968, and the increase in GNP over the period 1963–1969, at current prices, from Tables 2.1 and 1.1 respectively, using a formula similar to the one given for k^h above.

$\pi^h k^h$ — no profit data are available for the various PFI sectors and sub-sectors, as was seen in Section 8.3. Consequently, the assumption that the same profit rate as for the rest of the economy holds also for the various PFI cases was introduced. An average coefficient over the period 1962–1966 (there being no information for later years) was calculated from the data at current prices given in the U.N. *Yearbook of National Accounts Statistics* 1968, Vol. 1, p. 281.

π^0 — similarly, the rate of profits for the rest of the economy, was calculated, with respect to the national income; it is obviously the same as the one seen above for PFI.

$\tau_p \pi^h k^h$ — from the same source it was possible to calculate the taxation coefficient, relating 'direct taxes on corporation' to 'national income'; the same value was obtained as the general direct taxation coefficient which will be seen later.

w^0 — using the same source (U.N. *Yearbook of National Accounts Statistics 1969*, Vol. 1, p. 281), it was possible to calculate the general wage rate with respect to 'national income' for the rest of the economy similarly to what was done for profits.

w^h — in this case, in view of the lack of better information, one could have used either the result obtained for w^0, similarly to what was done in the case of the profit rates, or, for the various PFI cases, the results for 1968 obtained (see the table in Section 8.3) by using data with reference to 1968 which the ICAITI report had taken from the 'Instituto Guatemalteco de Seguridad Social'. This second solution was adopted, and for the two marginal and the cumulative calculations the results were used that had been obtained for 1968 from these social security data, case by case.

ρk^h — No data are available in the 'ICAITI Report' about the transfer of profits to abroad. The U.N. *Yearbook of National Accounts Statistics 1969*, Vol. 1, p. 286, gives 'factor income payments to the rest of the world'. This was related to the total PFI contribution to GNP (Table 1.1) over the period 1963–1968 and an average value was obtained, the possibility of other factor income payments to abroad than profit remittances (0.40 instead of 0.43 was used) being taken into account. All calculations are from data at current prices.

λk^h — In this case, no data are available either about payments for 'know-how' to abroad. The same source mentioned above gives, still on p. 286, 'current transfers to the rest of the world'. It was assumed that they consist of royalties, technical fees, etc., and the rate of transfer was calculated in the period 1963–1968 by relating such payments to PFI value added (Table 1.1) using, as usual, data in current prices. Since there are some variations, in the case of the marginal effects the separate ratios for 1963 and 1968 were used, while for the cumulative effects an average value over 1963–1968 was calculated.

σ in order to calculate the marginal propensity to save, private savings data were obtained from the U.N. *Yearbook of National Accounts Statistics 1969*, Vol. 1, p. 282, at current prices, using GNP data from Table 1.1. The parameter was calculated over the period 1963–1967 (no data available for later years) with the formula:

$$\sigma = \frac{S_{P\,1967} - S_{P\,1963}}{Y_{1967} - Y_{1963}} .$$

$\mu(1+m^0)$ the marginal propensity to import goods and services was calculated according to the formula:

$$\mu\,(1+m^0) = \frac{M_{1968} - M_{1963}}{Y_{1968} - Y_{1963}} ;$$

imports of goods and services were taken from the U.N. *Yearbook of National Accounts Statistics 1969*, Vol. 1, p. 286, and GNP data were taken from Table 1.1, in all cases at current prices.

$\varphi_m(1+m^h)$ no data on PFI imports are available. Consequently, it was assumed that the same import coefficients hold both for the total economy and for the various PFI sectors considered.
The same source as for the marginal propensity to import was used to calculate this parameter, inclusive of goods and services, for 1963 and 1968 for the marginal effects, and as an average value over the period 1963–1968, for the cumulative effects, with data at current prices related to GNP (Table 1.1).

$\varphi_e(1+e^h)$ no data for PFI exports are available, but only sectoral and sub-sectoral exports of goods and services for the whole economy (Tables 1.4 and 1.5). Consequently, it was assumed that the same export coefficients for goods and services hold for total economy and for the PFI sectors and sub-sectors. By relating this to v.a. data in current prices from Table 1.2 and 1.3, this parameter was calculated for 1963 and 1968 for the marginal effects, and as an average over 1963–1968 for the cumulative effects. As said in Section 8.3, the only export sectors, within the manufacturing sector, are 'Food, beverages and tobacco', and 'Other manufacturing'.

θ On the basis of the information given under 5, in the 'ICAITI Report' (Characteristics of the external public debt contracted by the public sector at September 30, 1970), an arithmetic average was taken over the various yearly interest rates, in order to get the rate of interest on the foreign debt.

τ_P, τ_W were assumed to be the same, for lack of more detailed data, and were calculated by relating total direct tax receipts to GNP (Tables 4.1 and 1.1, respectively), at current prices: Every year shows the same value, assumed constant for all cases. As was said above, it comes out the same as the rate of taxation on PFI profits (with respect to PFI v.a.).

τ_M the average import duty was calculated by relating imports of goods and services (from U.N., op.cit.) to total import duty receipts, given under 4 in the 'ICAITI Report' (Movimiento de Caja del Gobierno Central). In the case of the marginal effects, separate values for 1963 and 1968 were calculated, while for the cumulative effects the average over the period was taken.

τ_E similarly, from the same sources of information, the average export duty (for all cases) was calculated for 1963 and 1968 for the marginal effects, and as an average value over the period 1963–1968 for the cumulative effects.

τ_{IND} from the same sources as given above for import and export duties it was possible to get, by difference with Table 4.1, indirect taxation net of these two items. Then, it was related to GNP (Table 1.1), to get the indirect taxation coefficient, for 1963 and 1968, in the case of the marginal effects, and as an average over the period for the cumulative effects. As stated, these taxation coefficients are assumed to hold for all cases.

$g^h k^h$ for lack of better information, the assumption that the same expenditure ratio between GNP (Table 1.1) and public current expenditure (Table 4.1) holds both for the total economy and for the PFI sector was introduced. Separate values were calculated for 1963 and 1968 for the marginal effects, and as an average over 1963–1968 for the cumulative effects; in all cases data in current prices were used.

t in the case of the cumulative effects, is five.

$\eta^h; \eta^0$ data for PFI are available only for 1968, and consequently the study of the employment effect is limited to the case of the marginal effects in 1968.
For the various PFI cases, data are taken from the 'ICAITI Report' (which uses information supplied by the 'Instituto Guatemalteco de Seguridad Social') and related to PFI v.a. (Tables 1.2 and 1.3); a result is obtained in terms of man-years per '000 Q.
For the parameter pertaining to the rest of the economy, the labour-output ratio was obtained from the 'ICAITI Report' which uses, for homogeneity with the PFI cases, data supplied by the Social Security Institute, and the figure for 1968 related to GNP (Table 1.1) in the same year.

Before proceeding to the analysis of the empirical results, some general comments are possible; they will help clarifying some of the results which will be obtained later.

One first point to be discussed, as in the previous chapters, refers to the *import and export coefficients*. There is, especially in some cases, a sizeable gap between the two, and this will have an influence on the b.o.p. effect. As seen in the previous pages, one bias might be given by the way the two parameters were estimated. Moreover, as observed earlier, one must also remember that import substitution is not taken into account, or rather, is assumed to be included in the coefficients themselves.

One extra thing to be noticed in the case of Guatemala is that there can be no export promotion by PFI in any sub-sector, except 'Food, beverages, and tobacco' and 'Other manufacturing', since all other manufacturing sub-sectors, even at the level of the whole economy, do not export at all. Consequently, the export promotion of PFI, if any, is limited essentially to the food processing industry. As to import substitution, there is no evidence of the degree to which it is promoted. The breakdown of manufacturing v.a. (see Table 1.3 'ICAITI Report') shows that in some industries almost all v.a. is imputable to PFI (e.g. rubber industry, manufacture of non-metallic mineral products, electrical machinery, etc.). Consequently, had PFI not been established there, some of these products would have had to be imported. Moreover, lack of information prevented taking this into account. One would have needed at least some idea of how much of the v.a. of these industries would have been imported in the absence of PFI, and of the import requirements of these industries. Both things are lacking, and so the analysis was left without any better handling of the problem; this should be kept in mind in interpreting the results.

Another crucial point, as was seen before, concerns the *mechanism of financing the annual additions to PFI*[1]. As shown, the mechanism assumed by the model is crucial in determining the income effect, through the absorption of a share of financial resources otherwise available for domestic investments.

It was observed there that one might imagine a greater role to be played by foreign capital inflow directly related to the PFI under consideration, and intended to finance its expansion. However, as was pointed out, the model already takes this idea into account to some degree, through the assumption that the deficit of the b.o.p. corresponds to total capital inflow. In this *endogenous* way of handling the problem, it was logical to conceive of the b.o.p. effects of PFI as the foreign capital inflow directly or indirectly imputable to PFI. Now, since this inflow plays a positive part in the income effect, offsetting in part the negative role of the financing mechanism, the conclusion was that one could assume that this kind of capital inflow, too, is endogenously taken into account by the model. Moreover, in the case of Ghana (Section 7.5), it was possible to prove with the information available that this endogenous mechanism does not cause an under-estimation, but in some cases even an over-estimation of the income effect, and, consequently, of the other effects.

A similar reasoning would be valid here, but the information available does not seem enough to carry out a test similar to the one given for Ghana[2]. One may, however, consider that some of the parameters involved in the financial mechanism for the annual additions to PFI are the same in all cases, in particular:

$$\begin{aligned} \pi^h k^h &= 0.50 \\ \rho k^h &= 0.40 \\ \tau_p \pi^h k^h &= 0.01. \end{aligned}$$

1 For a theoretical discussion on this point, see Part II, Section 8.7.

2 The ICAITI Report gives on Table 2.1 total PFI investments, and in Table 2.4 'Financing of net investment, for the economy as a whole', distinguishing in the latter, among (1) Net investments; (2) share financed through reinvested profits; (3) share financed from domestic sources; (4) share financed by parent company. The data supplied, however, are not complete, and it is impossible to draw any conclusion from them, similarly to what was done in the case of Ghana, about the impact of the financing mechanism of the model.

This means that 0.09 of Y_t^h is left to finance directly the annual additions to PFI, apart from the 'foreign capital inflow effect' via the b.o.p. deficit.

Let us consider first the case of the *marginal effects*. Looking at the working of the financial mechanism one can see that it affects the results according to whether $\alpha k^h \gtrless 0.09$. If $\alpha k^h > 0.09$, then the financial mechanism makes a negative contribution to the growth of income, absorbing some financial resources otherwise available for domestic investments. In the opposite case ($\alpha k^h < 0.09$), it makes a positive contribution to the increase of income, accruing to financial resources available for domestic investments. After this, in order to get a complete picture, one should in both cases also check the indirect effect through the capital inflow imputable to PFI, and then look at the empirical information (which is missing here) to see the impact of all this on the results, similarly to what was done for Ghana.

As can be seen in the next sections, αk^h is < 0.09 only for the two negative cases (1968 marginal effects for 'Textile, footwear and apparel', and 1968 marginal effects for 'Machinery') and in the 1968 marginal effects for 'Other manufacturing'.

In the case of the *cumulative effects*, a similar reasoning applies, with the difference that, apart from taking into account the indirect effect through the capital inflow as given by the b.o.p. effect, one has to see how the financial
marginal effects for 'Machinery') and in the 1968 marginal effects for 'Other

In the empirical exercise, αk^h, as can be seen in the next sections, is never less than 0.09. This whole matter must well be kept in mind, then, in interpreting the results which will be given in the next pages.

8.6. MARGINAL AND CUMULATIVE EEFECTS FOR ALL PFI MANUFACTURING SECTOR

In the following pages the results of the empirical exercise are given first for the manufacturing sector as a whole, and then for PFI in the various sub-sectors considered.

Various considerations are possible before analysing the results case by case.

First of all one should remember what was said in the previous pages about import substitution and export promotion. The argument will be strengthened by the fact that, as observed earlier, most sub-sectors, apart from the first and the last do not export at all.

Then, the reasoning about the working of the financial mechanism of the model should be kept in mind. Due to the high value of α, most of the time it will influence the income effect, and consequently all the others.

Guatemala: All PFI: Manufacturing (Marginal and cumulative effects of PFI)

Parameters	1963	1968	1963–1968
α	0.55	0.06	0.20
$\pi^h k^h$	0.50	0.50	0.50
ρk^h	0.40	0.40	0.40
λk^h	0.09	0.03	0.05
$\tau_P \pi^h k^h$	0.01	0.01	0.01
k^h	2.31	2.31	2.31
k^0	2.78	2.78	2.78
$\varphi_m (1+m^h)$	0.16	0.19	0.18
$\varphi_e (1+e^h)$	0.09	0.10	0.10
$\mu (1+m^0)$	0.34	0.34	0.34
θ	0.04	0.04	0.04
σ	0.10	0.10	0.10
τ_W, τ_P	0.01	0.01	0.01
τ_{IND}	0.02	0.04	0.03
τ_M	0.14	0.09	0.11
τ_E	0.03	0.02	0.03
w^h	0.29	0.29	0.29
w^0	0.49	0.49	0.49
π^0	0.50	0.50	0.50
$g^h k^h$	0.06	0.08	0.07
η^0	–	0.26	–
η^h	–	0.20	–
Y_t^h (1000 Q)	16 001	40 086	40 086
Y_t (1000 Q)	1 248 600	1 532 875	1 532 875

	Marginal effects (1000 Q)			Cumulative effects (1000 Q)
$\overline{\overline{Y}}_t$	3550	2570	Y_t^*	119 319
$\overline{\overline{B}}_t$	313	2210	B_t^*	70 240
$\overline{\overline{S}}_{Pt}$	356	257	S_{Pt}^*	11 932
$\overline{\overline{S}}_{Gt}$	14	84	S_{Gt}^*	6 393
$\overline{\overline{L}}_t$	–	524 (man-years)		

Finally, the assumptions introduced to fill the gaps when empirical data directly pertaining to PFI were missing should also be kept in mind in analysing the outcomes of the empirical exercise.

Generally speaking, one can notice how the income effect is lower than what would be expected, in the case of the marginal effects, and in particular lower than the increase in income directly imputable to PFI ($\alpha\ Y_t^h$) due to the quoted mechanism of financing the annual additions to PFI. In the case of the cumulative effects, this mechanism still plays a role, as was shown earlier. Moreover, one should remember that the higher α, the lower the results of the cumulative effects, due to smaller effects 'accumulating' over the previous years. This can be noticed in particular with the income cumulative effects, but it obviously affects all the others, too.

The relative impact of the income effect on the economy of Guatemala can be appreciated by confronting the various results for the marginal effects with the increase in GNP between 1963 and 1964, and between 1968 and 1969, respectively, and for the cumulative effects with the increase over the period 1963–1968.

Year	Y_t	$Y_{t+1} - Y_t$	$Y_{t+5} - Y_t$
1963	1 248 600	28 394	284 275
1968	1 532 875	132 950	

Data calculated from Table 1.1 in thousand Q at current prices.

In both sets of calculations, but particularly for the marginal cases, the b.o.p. effect comes out extremely high, due, in general, to the low level of export promotion, to the payments to abroad for know-how, and in particular to the very high rate of transfer of profits to abroad (0.40 in all cases) as well as to the high marginal propensity to import (0.34). Its relative importance can be guessed considering the absolute level of the deficit and its increase in the period considered, similarly to what was done for the income effect:

Year	B_t	$B_{t+1} - B_t$	$B_{t+5} - B_t$
1963	30 600	19 400	18 300
1968	48 900	not available	

Data calculated from U.N. *Yearbook of National Accounts Statistics 1969*, Vol. 1, p. 286 in thousand Q at current prices.

The private savings effects derives directly from the income effect, so there is nothing special to be said about it.

The public savings effects, contrary to the results of the previous cases, come out negligible most times, and in some cases even negative (apart from the ones where a negative effect was to be expected, due to the negative sign of α).

One first explanation is given by the fact that the taxation coefficients are particularly low, and in some cases do not succeed in offsetting the public expenses imputable to PFI. Moreover, in the second term of the public savings effect in order to avoid double-counting, one has to subtract from the income effect the share pertaining to PFI already taken into account, for the taxation effect, in the first term of the formulations. This brings down the overall result, and even it makes it negative in some cases.

To get an idea of the importance of the public savings effect, it is possible, similarly to what was done above, to show the absolute value and the increase in the corresponding variable in the periods considered for the marginal and the cumulative effects:

Year	S_{Gt}	$S_{Gt+1} - S_{Gt}$	$S_{Gt+5} - S_{Gt}$
1963	27 629	16 632	5 599
1968	32 868	3 855	

Data calculated from Table 4.1 in thousand Q at current prices, taking total revenue less current expenditure.

Some final words should be spent on the employment effect. Its size depends directly upon that of the income effect, and varies also according to PFI value added and to the rate of growth of PFI α apart from the PFI and 'rest of the economy' labour-output ratio:

$$\bar{\bar{L}}_t = \eta^0 \left(\bar{\bar{Y}}_t - \alpha Y_t^h\right) + \eta^h \alpha Y_t^h ;$$

that is to say it is composed of the indirect effect made via the income effect on the rest of the economy, and the effect directly imputable to the growth of PFI in the period considered.

As was said previously, it was possible to calculate it for 1968 only, and in the various cases it varies according to the income effect, and to the gap between the labour-output ratios of the PFI under consideration and for the whole economy, respectively.

The following table gives PFI employment in 1968 in the various sub-sectors, so as to allow a certain appraisal of the results for the various cases which will be considered later:

Sector or sub-sector	Employment in 1968	$\bar{\bar{L}}_{1968}$
All PFI Manufacturing	8 177	524
All PFI 'Food, beverages and tobacco'	2 692	336
All PFI 'Textile, footwear and apparel'	1 228	44
All PFI 'Chemicals and allied products'	923	46
All PFI 'Primary and fabricated metals'	376	19
All PFI 'Machinery'	38	–
All PFI 'Other manufacturing'	2 920	200
All PFI 'Transport equipment'	–	–
All Economy	395 818	–

Data from heading 3 of the 'ICAITI Report', obtained from 'Instituto Gualtemalteco de Seguridad Social'; the marginal employment effects are taken from the tables in Sections 8.6 to 8.12.

What was said above clarifies to some extent the results obtained for the various cases, and in particular those under consideration in this section 'All PFI in Manufacturing'.

The high level of α is responsible for the generally high level of the marginal results for 1963, relatively and absolutely more so than those for 1968. It is also responsible for the negative value of the public savings effect in 1963.

The cumulative effects are sizeable, and even the public savings effect comes out positive, though relatively less than all the others.

8.7. MARGINAL AND CUMULATIVE EFFECTS FOR ALL PFI MANUFACTURING SUB-SECTOR 'FOOD, BEVERAGES AND TOBACCO'

As was remarked earlier in Section 8.3, most manufacturing exports come from this sub-sector, and in the empirical calculations the PFI import and export coefficients cancel each other out. Consequently, the b.o.p. effect comes out a little lower than in all other cases, relatively speaking, although it is still kept up by the high rate of transfer of profits and, among other things, by the high marginal propensity to import.

Moreover, in the case of the marginal effects as in the previous case, the level of α determines the relative magnitude of the income effect, while the

Guatemala: All PFI: Food, beverages and tobacco
(Marginal and cumulative effects of PFI)

Parameters	1963	1968	1963-1968
α	0.37	0.16	0.18
$\pi^h k^h$	0.50	0.50	0.50
ρk^h	0.40	0.40	0.40
λk^h	0.09	0.03	0.05
$\tau_P \pi^h k^h$	0.01	0.01	0.01
k^h	1.88	1.88	1.88
k^0	2.78	2.78	2.78
$\varphi_m (1+m^h)$	0.16	0.19	0.18
$\varphi_e (1+e^h)$	0.16	0.19	0.18
$\mu (1+m^0)$	0.34	0.34	0.34
θ	0.04	0.04	0.04
σ	0.10	0.10	0.10
τ_W, τ_P	0.01	0.01	0.01
τ_{IND}	0.02	0.04	0.03
τ_M	0.14	0.09	0.11
τ_E	0.03	0.02	0.03
w^h	0.41	0.41	0.41
w^0	0.49	0.49	0.49
π^0	0.50	0.50	0.50
$g^h k^h$	0.06	0.08	0.07
η^0	—	0.26	—
η^h	—	0.27	—
Income data (1000 Q)			
Y_t^h	3 900	9 852	9 852
Y_t	1 248 600	1 532 875	1 532 875

	Marginal effects (1000 Q)			Cumulative effects (1000Q)
$\bar{\bar{Y}}_t$	898	1232	Y_t^*	33 280
$\bar{\bar{B}}_t$	1046	1138	B_t^*	18 077
$\bar{\bar{S}}_{Pt}$	90	123	S_{Pt}^*	3 329
$\bar{\bar{S}}_{Gt}$	22	38	S_{Gt}^*	1 869
$\bar{\bar{L}}_t$	—	336 (man-years)		

private savings effect adapts itself to it. The public savings effect is in both marginal cases almost negligible, for the reasons given in the previous section.

In the case of the cumulative effects, nothing special happens with respect to the general considerations given in the previous section, apart, again, from the beneficial effect on the b.o.p. of the relatively high export coefficient.

As in the previous section, the employment marginal effect for 1968 depends upon the results for the income marginal effect, and upon the levels of α and of the two labour-output ratios.

8.8. MARGINAL AND CUMULATIVE EFFECTS FOR ALL PFI MANUFACTURING SUB-SECTOR 'TEXTILE, FOOTWEAR AND APPAREL'

Because of the extremely high value of α obtained for 1963, in the case of the marginal effects, owing to an abnormal situation, this particular parameter was substituted by the one obtained for the cumulative effects ($Y^h_{1962} = 278$; $Y^h_{1963} = 1129$; $Y^h_{1964} = 1867$). In 1968, α comes out negative, but it was left this way in order to see the results in such a case, which is by no means exceptional.

As was said in Section 8.5, the ICOR for the PFI sub-sector was calculated in a way differing slightly from what was done for all PFI cases, that is to say the last year was left out, both for gross investments and v.a., in order to avoid too large a value for k^h (it would have been 15.48 instead of the one now obtained: 8.14). Even so, k^h is very high, and this is going to affect the results for both the marginal and cumulative effects, mainly by raising financial requirements for the annual additions to PFI, and thus making negative contributions to the growth of income (i.e. to the income effect).

Finally, one notices that there are no exports at all from PFI in this sub-sector, and this is going to influence the b.o.p. effect.

The marginal effects for 1963 come out negative, with the exception of the b.o.p. effect (where the direct effect imputable to PFI offsets the indirect PFI effect through income, which is in this case negative). This is due, as said before, to a rather high level of α, combined with the very high ICOR. The opposite happens for the marginal effects in 1968. Although α is negative, through the financial mechanism of the annual additions to PFI the very high level of k^h leaves financial resources available for investments in the rest of the economy, with a positive balance for the income effect and for all the other effects.

The cumulative effects are relatively much smaller than in all other cases, due to a relatively high level of α, and even more to the high level of k^h and,

Guatemala: All PFI: Textile, footwear and apparel
(Marginal and cumulative effects of PFI)

Parameters	1963	1968	1963-1968
α	0.18	−0.02	0.18
$\pi^h k^h$	0.50	0.50	0.50
ρk^h	0.40	0.40	0.40
λk^h	0.09	0.03	0.05
$\tau_P \pi^h k^h$	0.01	0.01	0.01
k^h	8.14	8.14	8.14
k^0	2.78	2.78	2.78
$\varphi_m (1+m^h)$	0.16	0.19	0.18
$\varphi_e (1+e^h)$	0	0	0
$\mu (1+m^0)$	0.34	0.34	0.34
θ	0.04	0.04	0.04
σ	0.10	0.10	0.10
τ_W, τ_P	0.01	0.01	0.01
τ_{IND}	0.02	0.04	0.03
τ_M	0.14	0.09	0.11
τ_E	0.03	0.02	0.03
w^h	0.41	0.41	0.41
w^0	0.49	0.49	0.49
π^0	0.50	0.50	0.50
$g^h k^h$	0.06	0.08	0.07
η^0	–	0.26	–
η^h	–	0.47	–
Income data (1000 Q)			
Y_t^h	1 129	2 592	2 592
Y_t	1 248 600	1 532 875	1 532 875

	Marginal effects (1000 Q)		Cumulative effects (1000 Q)	
$\overline{\overline{Y}}_t$	−374	212	Y_t^*	1602
$\overline{\overline{B}}_t$	5	42	B_t^*	2493
$\overline{\overline{S}}_{Pt}$	– 37	21	S_{Pt}^*	160
$\overline{\overline{S}}_{Gt}$	– 27	15	S_{Gt}^*	32
$\overline{\overline{L}}_t$	–	44 (man-years)		

as usual, to its effect on the results via the financial mechanism of the model. The b.o.p. effect still comes out sizeable, as a consequence of the absence of exports, of the high rate of transfer of profits, and, among other things, of the high marginal propensity to import.

The public savings effect is in accordance with the general considerations given in Section 8.6, while the private savings effect derives directly from the income effect, and the employment effect in the marginal calculations for 1968 is determined, as shown in Section 8.6, by the income effect, via the increase in PFI and the two labour-output ratios.

8.9. MARGINAL AND CUMULATIVE EFFECTS FOR ALL PFI MANUFACTURING SUB-SECTOR 'CHEMICALS AND ALLIED PRODUCTS'

The only particular thing to be noticed here is, as in the previous case, the absence of exports, which will affect the b.o.p. effect.

The marginal effects in 1963 are influenced by the high rate of growth of PFI, but still come out relatively higher than those for 1968, where α is much smaller. In 1963, the high level of α has an influence also on the b.o.p. effect, which is much higher, both in relative and in absolute terms, than that of 1968. The marginal public savings effect of 1963 is negative, that of 1968 very small, for the reasons seen in Section 8.6.

The high level of α in the case of the cumulative effects keeps the results rather low, due to the inverse proportion which holds between α and the income effect, and thus all the others. In this case, too, the b.o.p. effect is sizeable, while the public savings effect is again rather small.

The marginal employment effect for 1968 depends, as usual, upon the results for the marginal income effect, together with the value of α and that of the two labour-output ratios.

8.10. MARGINAL AND CUMULATIVE EFFECTS FOR ALL PFI MANUFACTURING SUB-SECTOR 'PRIMARY AND FABRICATED METALS'

As in the previous case, the only specific feature of this case is the absence of exports, with its consequences on the b.o.p. effect.

α is rather high, and its effect on the marginal result both for 1963 and 1968 is straightforward. Again, in 1963, the public savings effect comes out negative, whereas in 1968 it is positive, though very limited.

The cumulative effects are influenced, as in the previous case, by the high

Guatemala: All PFI: Chemicals and allied products
(Marginal and cumulative effects of PFI)

Parameters	1963	1968	1963-1968
α	0.53	0.06	0.39
$\pi^h k^h$	0.50	0.50	0.50
ρk^h	0.40	0.40	0.40
λk^h	0.09	0.03	0.05
$\tau_P \pi^h k^h$	0.01	0.01	0.01
k^h	2.79	2.79	2.79
k^0	2.78	2.78	2.78
$\varphi_m (1+m^h)$	0.16	0.19	0.18
$\varphi_e (1+e^h)$	0	0	0
$\mu(1+m^0)$	0.34	0.34	0.34
θ	0.04	0.04	0.04
σ	0.10	0.10	0.10
τ_W, τ_P	0.01	0.01	0.01
τ_{IND}	0.02	0.04	0.03
τ_M	0.14	0.09	0.11
τ_E	0.03	0.02	0.03
w^h	0.26	0.26	0.26
w^0	0.49	0.49	0.49
π^0	0.50	0.50	0.50
$g^h k^h$	0.06	0.08	0.07
η^0	–	0.26	–
η^h	–	0.16	–
Income data (1000 Q)			
Y_t^h	1 101	5 729	5 729
Y_t	1 248 600	1 532 875	1 532 875

	Marginal effects (1000 Q)		Cumulative effects (1000 Q)	
$\bar{\bar{Y}}_t$	138	309	Y_t^*	7129
$\bar{\bar{B}}_t$	438	331	B_t^*	6608
$\bar{\bar{S}}_{Pt}$	14	31	S_{Pt}^*	713
$\bar{\bar{S}}_{Gt}$	– 9	6	S_{Gt}^*	278
$\bar{\bar{L}}_t$	–	46 (man-years)		

Guatemala: All PFI: Primary and fabricated metals
(Marginal and cumulative effects of PFI)

Parameters	1963	1968	1963-1968
α	0.31	0.16	0.43
$\pi^h k^h$	0.50	0.50	0.50
ρk^h	0.40	0.40	0.40
λk^h	0.09	0.03	0.05
$\tau_P \pi^h k^h$	0.01	0.01	0.01
k^h	2.28	2.28	2.28
k^0	2.78	2.78	2.78
$\varphi_m (1+m^h)$	0.16	0.19	0.18
$\varphi_e (1+e^h)$	0	0	0
$\mu(1+m^0)$	0.34	0.34	0.34
θ	0.04	0.04	0.04
σ	0.10	0.10	0.10
τ_W, τ_P	0.01	0.01	0.01
τ_{IND}	0.02	0.04	0.03
τ_M	0.14	0.09	0.11
τ_E	0.03	0.02	0.03
w^h	0.14	0.14	0.14
w^o	0.49	0.49	0.49
π^0	0.50	0.50	0.50
$g^h k^h$	.06	0.08	0.07
η^0	–	0.26	–
η^h	–	0.12	–
Income data (1000 Q)			
Y_t^h	535	3 218	3 218
Y_t	1 248 600	1 532 875	1 532 875

Marginal effects (1000 Q)			Cumulative effects (1000 Q)	
$\overline{\overline{Y}}_t$	89	349	Y_t^*	4282
$\bar{\bar{B}}_t$	143	454	B_t^*	3795
$\bar{\bar{S}}_{Pt}$	9	35	S_{Pt}^*	428
$\bar{\bar{S}}_{Gt}$	– 0.02	2	S_{Gt}^*	169
$\bar{\bar{L}}_t$	–	19 (man-years)		

level of α, which keeps them down. The b.o.p. effect is again sizeable, while the public savings effect is, as usual, limited.

The marginal employment effect for 1968 depends, as was seen in Section 8.6 upon the results for the marginal income effect, together with the value of α, and of the two labour-output ratios.

8.11. MARGINAL AND CUMULATIVE EFFECTS FOR ALL PFI MANUFACTURING SUB-SECTOR 'MACHINERY'

There are various features to be noticed in this case. First of all, as said in Section 8.3, there are no reliable employment data for this sector for 1968, and consequently it was not possible to calculate the employment marginal effect for that year, as was done in all the other cases.

Also PFI wages data are not reliable, as was observed again in Section 8.3, and consequently it was necessary to use the same wage rate with respect to PFI value added as in the case of All PFI Manufacturing (Section 8.6).

As in the three previous cases, there are no exports from this sector, and this will affect the b.o.p. effect in all cases.

Finally, it must be pointed out that α in 1968 is negative. It was left this way, just as in the case of 'Textile, footwear, and apparel' for the marginal effects in 1968, in order to see what happens in such a situation.

The high level of α is responsible for the marginal results for 1963. The b.o.p. effect is relatively quite high, while the public savings effect although very small, is still positive.

As could be expected, the marginal results for 1968 come out negative, due to the negative sign of α, with, again, a sizeable, although in this particular case negative, b.o.p. effect and hence decreasing deficit. The public savings effect is positive, basically for the same reasons as discussed in Section 8.6.

The cumulative effects are also influenced by the high level of α, with a sizeable b.o.p. effect, and a rather limited public savings effect.

8.12. MARGINAL AND CUMULATIVE EFFECTS FOR ALL PFI MANUFACTURING SUB-SECTOR 'OTHER MANUFACTURING'

Contrary to the previous four cases, there is some export, although very limited, with still a sizeable gap between the import and export coefficients, and a corresponding influence on the b.o.p. effect; this and the other factors

Guatemala: All PFI: Machinery
(Marginal and cumulative effects of PFI)

Parameters	1963	1968	1963-1968
α	0.45	0.17	0.42
$\pi^h k^h$	0.50	0.50	0.50
ρk^h	0.40	0.40	0.40
λk^h	0.09	0.03	0.05
$\tau_P \pi^h k^h$	0.01	0.01	0.01
k^h	2.09	2.09	2.09
k^0	2.78	2.78	2.78
$\varphi_m (1+m^h)$	0.16	0.19	0.18
$\varphi_e (1+e^h)$	0	0	0
$\mu(1+m^0)$	0.34	0.34	0.34
θ	0.04	0.04	0.04
σ	0.10	0.10	0.10
τ_W, τ_P	0.01	0.01	0.01
τ_{IND}	0.02	0.04	0.03
τ_M	0.14	0.09	0.11
τ_E	0.03	0.02	0.03
w^h	0.29	0.29	0.29
w^0	0.49	0.49	0.49
π^0	0.50	0.50	0.50
$g^h k^h$	0.06	0.08	0.07
η^0	–	–	–
Income data (1000 Q)			
Y_t^h	773	4 396	4 396
Y_t	1 284 600	1 532 875	1 532 875

	Marginal effects (1000 Q)		Cumulative effects (1000 Q)	
$\bar{\bar{Y}}_t$	191	–312	Y_t^*	6416
$\bar{\bar{B}}_t$	300	–597	B_t^*	5402
$\bar{\bar{S}}_{Pt}$	19	– 31	S_{Pt}^*	642
$\bar{\bar{S}}_{Gt}$	1	8	S_{Gt}^*	272
$\bar{\bar{L}}_t$	–			

affecting it, have already been discussed at some length.

The high level of α is responsible for the marginal results for 1963, with also sizeable b.o.p. effect, and an almost negligible public savings effect, especially in relative terms.

α is much lower in 1968, and this affects the marginal results, which show also a sizeable b.o.p. effect, and an almost negligible public savings effect, b.o.p. effect.

The results for the cumulative effects are positively influenced by the relatively small level of α, compared with the previous cases. The income effect comes out extremely high, the more so because the influence of the financing mechanism is reduced by the low α, and the b.o.p. is affected by such a result. Also, the public savings effect is relatively higher than in the previous cases.

The employment marginal effect for 1968 depends, as usual, upon the marginal income effect for 1968, together with α and the two labour-output ratios.

Some general considerations are now possible on the various results obtained in the empirical calculations.

Using information provided by ICAITI, and after filling the various gaps, especially about profitability of PFI, and in the foreign trade sector, it was possible to carry out a sectoral and sub-sectoral analysis for Guatemala in 1963, in 1968 and over the period 1963–1968. Moreover, in most cases, it was also possible to calculate the marginal employment effect for 1968.

The results are rather interesting; apart from an income effect in general below the direct increase in income imputable to PFI, given by $\alpha\ Y_t^h$ in the case of the marginal effects, they indicate a very heavy burden on the b.o.p., together with a negligible contribution to public savings, for which the tax structure in Guatemala is partly responsible.

It is possible also to appraise variations from sector to sector, although lack of data prevented a more detailed analysis, some of the crucial parameters being the same in all cases (e.g. profit rates, transfer of profits, know-how payments, import coefficient), apart from the ones necessarily constant (e.g. marginal propensity to save and to import).

Moreover, it was not possible to appraise the effects of alternative ways of financing PFI, due to the way PFI is defined in Guatemala (see Section 8.2).

Finally, it was often noticed how crucial is the effect of the mechanism of financing the annual additions to PFI on the results. Still, looking at the b.o.p. effect, which is supposed to represent foreign capital inflow imputable to PFI, one gets the idea that except when α is very high, it offsets to quite an extent such absorption of financial resources as would be otherwise avail-

Guatemala: All PFI: Other manufacturing
(Marginal and cumulative effects of PFI)

Parameters	1963	1968	1963-1968
α	0.60	0.04	0.10
$\pi^h k^h$	0.50	0.50	0.50
ρk^h	0.40	0.40	0.40
λk^h	0.09	0.03	0.05
$\tau_P \pi^h k^h$	0.01	0.01	0.01
k^h	2.00	2.00	2.00
k^0	2.78	2.78	2.78
$\varphi_m (1+m^h)$	0.16	0.19	0.18
$\varphi_e (1+e^h)$	0.01	0.01	0.01
$\mu(1+m^0)$	0.34	0.34	0.34
θ	0.04	0.04	0.04
σ	0.10	0.10	0.10
τ_W, τ_P	0.01	0.01	0.01
τ_{IND}	0.02	0.04	0.03
τ_M	0.14	0.09	0.11
τ_E	0.03	0.02	0.03
w^h	0.20	0.20	0.20
w^0	0.49	0.49	0.49
π^0	0.50	0.50	0.50
$g^h k^h$	0.06	0.08	0.07
η^0	–	0.26	–
η^h	–	0.20	–
Income data (1000 Q)			
Y_t^h	8 562	14 300	14 300
Y_t	1 248 600	1 532 875	1 532 875

	Marginal effects (1000 Q)		Cumulative effects (1000 Q)	
$\bar{\bar{Y}}_t$	2760	902	Y_t^*	111 126
$\bar{\bar{B}}_t$	4349	682	B_t^*	55 137
$\bar{\bar{S}}_{Pt}$	276	90	S_{Pt}^*	11 113
$\bar{\bar{S}}_{Gt}$	6	34	S_{Gt}^*	6 332

able for domestic investments, apart from a certain portion which may reasonably be assumed to be absorbed by PFI anyhow.

8.13. CONCLUSIONS

Like before, the exercise carried out in the previous pages may be considered a 'case study of Guatemala', but, most of all, it represents an empirical application of the methodology of Part II with reference to the data supplied by the 'ICIATI Report' for this country. Consequently, in this case, as well as in the previous ones, the results should be interpreted mainly in this light, and they should serve to provide a better insight into the methodology, as well as to point out various possible improvements in order to make it more realistic. Anyhow, the results will also give some idea about the effects of PFI on Guatemala. It was possible to distinguish various cases, that is to say total PFI manufacturing and PFI in the various sub-sectors of manufacturing.

Before analysing in more detail the empirical results for Guatemala, it is interesting to point out the more striking features of this exercise, *vis-à-vis* the three previous ones.

In the case of India it was possible to distinguish between Foreign Branches (FB) and Foreign Controlled Rupee Companies (FCRC) both for the whole economy and for the manufacturing sector, and thus to use the methodology to appraise the effects of different ways of financing a PFI project (i.e. FB vs FCRC). In the case of Ghana such a distinction was possible only between All PFI and Branches of Foreign Companies (BFC); comparison was difficult, however, mainly as a consequence of the way various parameters were estimated, and of different concepts of v.a. used. No such appraisal was possible in the case of Guatemala where, as pointed out in Section 8.2, the data available include all PFI without any distinction. But for Guatemala, as for Ghana and the Philippines, it was possible to use the methodological approach to appraise the effects of All PFI in the various sub-sectors of the manufacturing sector.

Although this sectoral application of the methodology proved to be an interesting exercise, there are some drawbacks, due to the fact that in the various sub-sectors many parameters are the same, through lack of better empirical evidence; so it was not possible to appraise fully the effects, in the various cases, of all possible differences; still the analysis did point out what happened as a result of varying values for some of the key-parameters.

In spite of the exercise's various limitations indicated above and in the previous pages and though it is based on some radical simplifying assumptions, it is possible to reach some general conclusions, similarly to what was done before:

– in the case of Guatemala, PFI affects the growth of income more than was the case in India, although less than in Ghana and the Philippines, in most cases;

– similarly to what happened for India and Ghana, and even more so, PFI poses a very heavy burden on the b.o.p.; this is the opposite of what happened for the Philippines;

– in general, in Guatemala PFI has a negligible effect on public savings, due to the country's tax structure.

An interesting feature in the case of Ghana was that it was possible, at least in a simplified way (see Section 7.5), to show how the methodology, on the basis of the empirical evidence available and through the mechanism of financing the annual additions to PFI, can endogenously take account of what actually happens in practice. Consequently, some of the objections to this mechanism could be considered as dealt with by the model. No such proof was possible in the case of Guatemala, where it was simply possible to show how in most cases it was necessary to see the explicit effect of the b.o.p. effect, which stands for capital inflow directly imputable to PFI, on income, and on financial resources for domestic investments. But, the lack of data on the share of PFI financed from abroad, *vis-à-vis* the share financed from domestic sources, prevented the analysis from being carried any further.

Moreover, the objections about import substitution raised before are still valid in the case of Guatemala, while it was also necessary to introduce certain crude assumptions especially in the case of imports, to estimate the PFI foreign trade coefficients.

Finally, as in the two previous cases, one should remember the limitations of the data used to estimate the parameters, and the way the various gaps were filled, together with the fact that is was necessary to use data in current prices.

CHAPTER IX

ARGENTINA

9.1. INTRODUCTION

This chapter will present some results with reference to Argentina on the basis of data made available by UCA.

Though the 'UCA Report' gives a great quantity of data on PFI in Argentina, most of these are not useful for an exercise such as carried out for India, Ghana, Guatemala and the Philippines. Some crucial data are missing and the ones given are often at an enterprise level. Still it was considered useful to take advantage of the data collected and to undertake the empirical exercise. The additional assumptions, necessary to bridge the various gaps, are discussed at length later.

The next section will describe the coverage of the data, their source and limitations, according to what is given in the 'UCA Report'.

Section 9.3 will then give a general picture of the relevance of PFI in 1965 in the case of Argentina.

Section 9.4 will discuss the methodological approach followed.

Section 9.5 will show how, one by one, the various parameters have been estimated. In the following sections, various empirical cases will be considered.

The data applied by UCA can be aggregated according to Section 9.1 of Part II. The analysis is then possible for All PFI in manufacturing and for All PFI in six manufacturing sub-sectors.

The data allow the calculation of the marginal effects for 1962 and 1965 and the cumulative effects for the period 1962-1965.

Some parameters for the whole economy were estimated over the period 1956–1968, as the data for the whole economy cover this period.

9.2. SOURCE OF DATA, COVERAGE AND LIMITATIONS

The exercise carried out in this paper is based on data supplied by 'Instituto de Estudios Economicos, Facultad de Ciencias Sociales y Economicas, Universidad Catolica Argentina' in Buenos Aires (UCA). The data collected reached the NEI in September 1971 and two supplements to the first data were obtained in December 1971 and January 1972, respectively.

UCA gathered the information mainly from the 'Banco Central de la Republica Argentina'. In some cases, where empirical evidence was not available, UCA provided its own estimates.

To get PFI value added (sales) and profits, UCA made use of a list of the 100 largest companies according to sales. This publication appeared in various issues of *Panorama de la Economia Argentina* for the period 1958–1969. UCA enclosed a list of 82 enterprises coinciding more or less with the sample of 100 largest companies and classified as foreign or as Argentine according to the majority ownership of the assets.

In the two supplements to the original report, data on sub-sectoral sales and profits were given for the largest 131 domestic and foreign companies. The sample of 100 was thus enlarged to 131. No further information was available on capital, investment, foreign trade and wages of PFI.

Moreover, the sub-sectoral totals of sales were the only approximation of the value added generated in the 131 most important enterprises, a large portion of them being PFI. It is obvious that data on sales are not at all a precise approximation of v.a. and comparing them with GDP one can make serious mistakes. However, there was no better information available.

The data in the 'UCA Report' pertain to the sub-sectors of Section 9.1, Part II, although the sub-sector 'Machinery' is not included in the sample. Obviously, the sales of this sub-sector were incorporated partly with 'Primary and fabricated metals', and partly with 'Transport equipment'.

As was stated above, the empirical exercise of this paper will concentrate on all PFI in manufacturing, as the data on PFI in the other major sectors of the economy are not available. In estimating one coefficient (PFI capital-output ratio) it was necessary to stick to data on US manufacturing PFI only, as no data on all manufacturing PFI capital stock had been supplied.

Most time series are in current prices, and consequently, the exercise will be based on such current data. This will affect the calculation of some parameters owing to the data missing and the additional assumption involved, and it should be kept in mind in interpreting the results.

9.3. PFI IN ARGENTINA: THE GENERAL PICTURE

The table on pp. 302-303 gives an idea of the relative weight of manufacturing PFI in the economy of Argentina. It was calculated from various tables of the 'UCA Report' and of its supplements (Tables 12–16 bis, 12–16ter).

PFI in Argentina: The general picture, in 1965

	(1)	(2)	(3)	(4)
	v.a. composition	% of v.a. in GDP	% of v.a. in corresponding sector	Import requirement % of v.a.
PFI Manufacturing				
Total manufacturing	100	12.0	62.3	–
Food, beverages and tobacco	20.8	2.5	44.9	–
Textiles, footwear and apparel	1.1	0.1	13.0	–
Chemicals and allied products	25.5	3.1	80.1	–
Primary and fabricated metals	12.6	1.5	50.6	–
Transport equipment	32.2	3.9	93.9	–
Other manufacturing	7.7	0.9	53.2	–
Source	Tables 12-16 bis	Tables 12-16 bis	Tables 12-16 bis	

Notes:

(a) Source 'UCA Report', various tables.
(b) See the text (Section 9.3) for comments. All figures refer to 1965.
(c) See the text (Section 9.2) for the concept of value added.
(d) See the text (Section 9.3) for the concept of profit ratio's.
(f) The above data are an extract only from 'UCA Report' where more data can be found. For more ratios and parameters, see the various tables of the numerical exercises.
(g) – = not available.
[a] US PFI only, which, however, represent 68% of total PFI Manufacturing considered in this table.

For a good understanding of the table, the following features of the underlying data must be kept in mind.

The shares have been calculated from data on 131 major industrial enterprises, ranked according to their sales, such as they were supplied by the 'UCA Report'. The sales of these enterprises represented 68.4% of the GDP at current factor costs originating in manufacturing in 1965. The table, consequently, stands for about two thirds of the performance of the sector.

Moreover, as was mentioned in Section 9.2, 'value added' stands for sales in the 'UCA Report'. It is just an approximation to the GDP data, but, as better data are missing, the figures on sales were used for calculations.

Data on profits were taken from Table 12–16ter. Though these figures seem too low, even if the concept of v.a. (sales) is taken into account, they were used in the calculation to be consistent with rest of the data.

Neither in the 'UCA Report' nor in supplements, data on capital stock or assets of PFI were available, no more than realized new investments in foreign enterprises. The average capital-output ratio of PFI in manufacturing was

(5)	(6)	(7)	(8)	(9)	(10)
Export promotion %v.a.	Profits % of v.a.	Wages % of v.a.	Employment/ v.a.	Gross inv./v.a.	Capital stock/v.a.
–	0.04	–	–	–	0.34[a]
–	0.01	–	–	–	–
–	0.17	–	–	–	–
–	0.05	–	–	–	–
–	0.06	–	–	–	–
–	0.04	–	–	–	–
–	0.10	–	–	–	–
	Tables 12-16 ter				

calculated from data on US manufacturing only. For a more detailed description of this, see Section 9.5.

While being aware of the above limitations, the following general remarks suggest themselves:

The most important concentration of manufacturing PFI is in the sub-sector 'Transport equipment'. The sub-sectors 'Chemicals and allied products' and 'Food, beverages and tobacco' also seem to have been rather attractive to foreign enterprises.

From column (2) one notices that manufacturing PFI generates a share of GDP that is not to be neglected.

In the first two of those sub-sectors PFI is quite dominant over domestic enterprises ('Transport equipment' v.a. stems for 93.9% from foreign enterprises). There is a prevailing domestic participation in 'Textile, footwear and apparel', and also in 'Food, beverages and tobacco'. Not much can be said about the profit ratios, taking into account what was said above. Still, the profitability of PFI in 'Food, beverages and tobacco' seems to be underestimated. To a lesser degree, this underestimation seems to hold for the other sub-sectors too (except 'Textile, footwear and apparel').

Nothing can be concluded on PFI with respect to export and import behaviour, wages, employment, gross investment and capital stock. These data were not available in the 'UCA Report'.

Owing to the approximative character of many data of the 'UCA Report', no attempt was made to include more than one year in the table.

9.4. THE METHODOLOGICAL APPROACH

Given the kind of data available, it is possible to apply the 'marginal' and 'cumulative' approach, and to calculate the cumulative and the marginal effects. The marginal effects have been calculated for 1962 and 1965, and the cumulative ones over this three-year period.

Most parameters will be calculated year by year and this allows to overcome partly the complication that almost all data are given in current prices.

However, some other parameters will have to be calculated over a longer period, with the justifications which will be discussed in Section 9.5. No attempt will be made to correct the data in current prices into data in constant prices. Although price indices are available, there seems to be a danger of making more mistakes than improvements.

The calculation of the marginal effects in two different years for the manufacturing sector and sub-sectors, and of the cumulative effects over a period of three years will allow us to discuss their variation, caused by varying values of some of the parameters as a consequence of different structural characteristics. This variation will be limited somewhat by the many assumptions introduced to fill the gaps in the data.

The lack of employment data prevents the calculation of the employment effect, nor is it possible to calculate the income distribution effect, owing to the procedure followed to get wage and profit rates.

9.5. ESTIMATION OF THE PARAMETERS

In the following pages a brief description will be given of the way the various parameters were estimated, together with the various assumptions introduced. A distinction will be made, when necessary, between the way the parameters for the marginal effects and those for the cumulative effects were estimated.

Y_t GDP in current prices from Table 1 of the 'UCA Report'.

Y_t^h sales in current prices (Tables 12–16bis), assumed to stand for v.a.

α Since capital stock figures are not available α was calculated year by year, for the marginal effects, from sales data at current prices (Tables 1 up to 6 of the 'UCA Report'), according to the formula:

$$\alpha_t = \frac{Y^h_{t+1} - Y^h_t}{Y^h_t} .$$

In the case of the cumulative effects for manufacturing PFI it is calculated by a similar procedure, considering the average annual rate of growth over the period 1962–1965, again in current prices.

k^h Any information on PFI capital stock investment is missing. There is empirical evidence of financial flows of long and short term capital into Argentina and of yearly approbations of new PFI for various sectors of the economy. This is not enough to estimate capital-output ratios. The only useful data are the ones about the value of US manufacturing investments in Argentina, taken from 'Survey of current business' (various issues). The sales of US manufacturing investments were also published by 'Survey of current business' 1966, and they represented 63% of the sales of the 131 enterprises examined by UCA. Consequently, it seemed reasonable to calculate the average capital-output ratio of US manufacturing PFI as an approximation for all manufacturing PFI in Argentina. It was calculated according to the formula:

$$k^h = \frac{K^h_{t-1}}{Y^h_t} .$$

For the marginal effects it was calculated separately for 1962 and 1965, and for the cumulative effects as the yearly average over the period 1962–1965.

No distinction was possible for the various PFI manufacturing sub-sectors.

$\pi^h\ k^h$ for 1962 and 1965 were obtained from Tables 12–16ter, relating profits of PFI to the corresponding sales figures of Tables 12–16bis.

For the cumulative approach the average profit ratio was taken for the period 1962–1965.

ρk^h Table 33 gives royalty and know-how payments, profit transfers and interest payments with respect to all PFI in Argentina in the years 1965–1968. Since there are no figures on value added or sales of *all* PFI in Argentina, these figures could not be used. However, data are given about US undistributed profits (from 'Survey of current business', No. 9, 1966), indicating that they account for about 50% of total profits. Consequently, it was assumed that the other 50% was distributed and transferred, and this share was applied to each case, taking into account the profit ratio, to get this parameter.

λk^h Table 33 could not be used for the same reasons as given above. Still, the know-how payments amount to 91% of profits and dividends transferred in the period 1965–1968. Assuming that this relation holds for the total economy, this parameter was calculated at 90% of the profit transfer ratio.

$\tau_p \pi^h k^h$ was found by applying the taxation coefficient (see later) to the profit ratio.

k^0 was calculated from data of Table 41 (gross investment for the domestic economy in current prices) and Table 1 (GDP at current market prices). The following formula was used:

$$k^0 = \frac{\sum_{1958}^{1968} I}{Y_{1969} - Y_{1959}}.$$

As is evident a one-year lag was introduced. k^0 stands for an ICOR, as against k^h, which is an average capital-output ratio.

$\varphi_m(1+m^h)$ was calculated by relating the total value of imports for the whole economy (from Table 35 of the 'UCA Report') to GDP data (from Table 1). Both series were in current prices for the period 1958–1969.

As data on import of PFI were absent, the assumption was introduced about a similar behaviour of PFI and the whole economy with respect to imports.

$\varphi_e(1+e^h)$ could not be calculated for the various PFI manufacturing sub-sectors for lack of data. Similarly to $\varphi_m(1+m^h)$, the uniformity of export behaviour was assumed for domestic branches and PFI. The same parameter for all cases had to be used for lack of sub-sectoral data homogeneous with respect to Y_t^h.

$\mu(1+m^0)$ the marginal propensity to import was calculated from Table 35 (inclusive of goods and services) and from table 1 at current prices, according to the formula:

$$\mu(1+m^0) = \frac{M_t - M_0}{Y_t - Y_0}$$

for the period 1958–1969. This parameter is assumed to be constant for all cases and for all years.

θ Any information on the rate of interest on the foreign debt is missing. Other sources of information (IMF *International Financial Statistics*) proved unsufficient, too. Therefore, a very crude assumption was introduced, namely, that the rate of interest on foreign debt equals 6%, that rate being rather common on the capital markets in the period considered.

σ The marginal propensity to save was calculated according to the formula:

$$\frac{S_{1968} - S_{1959}}{Y_{1968} - Y_{1959}}.$$

S stands for net saving, taken from OECD *National Accounts of Less Developed Countries (1969)*, Y is GDP from Table 1, 'UCA Report'.

τ_W, τ_P were assumed to be the same, for lack of more detailed data, and were calculated by relating receipts from income and property taxes (Table 60) to GDP (Table 1), and taking the average value over the period considered (1956–1968). This is assumed to be the same in all cases.

w^h was calculated by relating wages and salaries to GDP for the period 1959–1966. The former was taken from OECD *National Accounts of Less Developed Countries (1969),* the latter from Table 1 of the 'UCA Report'. Both time series were in current prices. However, w^h was obtained from value added data and *not* from sales. Accordingly, it is higher than it would be in the latter case. Moreover, the same wage share in v.a. is assumed for PFI and for the whole economy.

τ_{IND} was obtained from Tables 60 and 1 of the 'UCA Report', as the average share of receipts from taxes on production, consumption and transport in GDP for the period 1956–1968.

τ_M, τ_E Similarly to τ_{IND}, this parameter was found by relating tax receipts from foreign trade to GDP. The underlying tables were the same as in the preceding paragraph.

$g^h\, k^h$ for lack of data the assumption that the same expenditure ratio between GDP and government current expenditure holds both for the total economy and for the PFI sector was introduced. These ratios (Table 60, 'UCA Report') were calculated for the period 1956–1968, and since there is no great variation, an average value was introduced for all cases.

Π As said in the previous section, this parameter relates indirect taxes plus direct taxes (Table 60) to GDP (Table 1) at current prices. An average value was taken for the period considered for all years and all cases.

Before proceeding to the analysis of the empirical results, some general comments are possible, and they will help to clarify some of the results which will be obtained later.

As in the previous case studies the first point to be discussed refers to the *import and export coefficients*. One bias might be caused by the way the two parameters were estimated, as seen in the previous pages. Moreover, one must also remember the fact that import substitution is not taken into account, or rather, is assumed to be included in the coefficients themselves.

There is no evidence of the degree up to which import substitution is promoted by PFI. One would have needed, at least, an idea of how much of the v.a. of PFI would have been imported in its absence, and of the import requirements of PFI industries. Both things are lacking, and so the analysis had to be carried out without any better handling of the problem. This should be kept in mind in interpreting the results.

As in the previous case studies, another crucial point concerns the *mechanism of financing the annual additions to PFI*[1]. As was seen there, the mechanism assumed by the model very much determines the income effect, through the absorption of a promotion of financial resources otherwise available for domestic investments. It was also observed before, that one might suppose that a greater role should be played by foreign capital inflow directly related to the PFI under consideration, and intended to finance its expansion. But

1 For a theoretical discussion on this point, see Part II, Section 8.7.

then, as noticed before, this is already to some extent taken into account by the model, through the assumption that the deficit of the b.o.p. is equal to the total capital inflow. It follows in this *endogenous* way of handling the problem that the b.o.p. effect of PFI can also be taken as the foreign capital inflow directly or indirectly imputable to PFI. And since this plays a positive role in the income effect and partly offsets the negative role of the financing mechanism under discussion, the conclusion was that it was possible to assume that this kind of capital inflow, too, is endogenously taken account of by the model. Moreover, in the case of Ghana (Section 7.5) using the information available, it was possible to prove that this endogenous mechanism does not cause an underestimation of the income effect, but, on the contrary, in some cases an over-estimation of it, and consequently, of the other effects.

A similar reasoning would be valid here, but the information available does not seem enough to carry out a test similar to the one given for Ghana. As a matter of fact, some data are given on financing of investments in the latest supplement received to the 'UCA Report', but, as it was said, they are not sufficient for any generalization on this matter.

9.6. MARGINAL AND CUMULATIVE EFFECTS FOR ALL PFI MANUFACTURING SECTOR

In the following pages the results of the empirical exercise are given first for the manufacturing sector as a whole, and then for PFI in the various subsectors considered.

Some considerations are possible before analysing the results case by case.

First, one should remember what was said in the previous pages about import substitution and export promotion. Then, the reasoning about the working of the financial mechanism of the model should be kept in mind. Finally, the assumptions introduced to fill the gaps when empirical data directly pertaining to PFI were missing should also be kept in mind in analysing the outcomes of the empirical exercise, as they influence them to a considerable extent.

Generally speaking, the income effect is rather high, also considering the level of α. A possible explanation is that the working of the mechanism of financing the annual additions to PFI is favourable, since a fixed share of PFI profits is available for reinvestment.

The relative impact of the income effect on the economy of Argentina can be appreciated by confronting the various results for the marginal effects with the increase of GDP in 1962 and 1965.

Argentina: All PFI: Manufacturing
(Marginal and cumulative effects of PFI)

Parameters	1962	1965	1962-1965
α	0.25	0.30	0.27
$\pi^h k^h$	0.04	0.04	0.04
ρk^h	0.02	0.02	0.02
λk^h	0.18	0.018	0.018
$\tau_P \pi^h k^h$	0.001	0.001	0.001
k^h	0.35	0.34	0.38
k^0	0.78	0.78	0.78
$\varphi_m (1+m^h)$	0.09	0.09	0.09
$\varphi_e (1+e^h)$	0.09	0.09	0.09
$\mu(1+m^0)$	0.08	0.08	0.08
θ	0.06	0.06	0.06
σ	0.16	0.16	0.16
τ_W, τ_P	0.03	0.03	0.03
τ_{IND}	0.05	0.05	0.05
τ_M			
τ_E	0.02	0.02	0.02
w^h	0.35	0.35	0.35
$g^h k^h$	0.11	0.11	0.11
t	–	–	3
Π	0.10	0.10	0.10
Income data (1000 mln P m/n)			
Y_t^h	174.75	434.31	434.31
Y_t	1484.90	3618.30	3618.30

	Marginal effects (1000 mln P m/n)		Cumulative effects (1000 mln P m/n)	
$\overline{\overline{\overline{Y}}}_t$	37.46	107.25	Y_t^*	1643.54
$\overline{\overline{\overline{B}}}_t$	4.87	14.32	B_t^*	166.86
$\overline{\overline{\overline{S}}}_{Pt}$	6.00	17.16	S_{Pt}^*	262.97
$\overline{\overline{\overline{S}}}_{Gt}$	2.52	– 7.98	S_{Gt}^*	104.05

Year	Y_t	$Y_{t+1} - Y_t$
1962	1484.9	370
1965	3618.3	904

Data calculated from Table 1 in thousand million Pm/n at current prices.

The b.o.p. effect is rather modest. It amounts to one fifth or less of the corresponding income effects. This may be caused by the rather low, and mutually outweighing propensities to import and export, and by the even lower marginal propensity to import. There is also a certain regularity in the results owing to the assumption of a uniform percentage of profits transferred abroad, although the absolute profit levels vary among the sub-sectors. The relative importance of the b.o.p. effect can be seen by considering the absolute level of the deficit of the b.o.p. and its change in the period concerned, similarly to the above illustration of the income effect.

Year	B_t	$B_{t+1} - B_t$
1962	–543	1009
1965	446	63

Calculated from UN *Yearbook of National Accounts Statistics, 1969,* Vol. 1, p. 577, in mln Pm/n.

The private savings effect derives directly from the income effect, so there is nothing special to be said about it.

The public savings effect comes out rather small most of the times, and in the marginal calculations is often negative.

The explanation is that the taxation coefficients are very low and in most cases of the marginal effects do not succeed in offsetting public expenses imputable to PFI. Moreover, in the second term of the public savings effect, in order to avoid double-counting one has to subtract from the income effect the share pertaining to PFI, already taken into account, for the taxation effect, in the first term of the formulations. And this brings down the overall result, and even makes it negative in most cases.

In order to get an idea of the importance of the public savings effect, it is possible, similarly to what was done above, to show the absolute value and the increase in the corresponding variable in the period considered.

Year	S_{Gt}	$S_{Gt+1} - S_{Gt}$
1962	−13.5	15.1
1965	38.2	20.7

Data calculated from OECD, *National Accounts of Less Developed Countries, 1970.* Data in current prices and in thousand million Pm/n.

There is not much to be added to these general remarks with respect to the numerical results of All PFI in the manufacturing sector. The numerical outcomes give an average view of what happens in the various sub-sectors. The indirect income effect in the case of the marginal effects is negative ($\overline{\overline{Y}}_t < \alpha\ Y_t^h$). Relatively low profit percentages imply also rather low profit transfers and know-how payments. These in turn affect the b.o.p. effect. The public savings effect is negative, and grows from 1962 to 1965 according to $\overline{\overline{Y}}_t$.

As for the cumulative effects, the b.o.p. effect is still rather small. Private savings, as usual, adapt themselves to the income effect. Public savings are still very small, although not negative. The income effect, finally, is relatively less than in some of the previous case studies, as a consequence of the high level of α, and of the inverse relation which holds between α and Y_t^*.

9.7. MARGINAL AND CUMULATIVE EFFECTS FOR ALL PFI MANUFACTURING SUB-SECTOR 'FOOD, BEVERAGES, AND TOBACCO'

As regards the marginal effects, in both 1962 and 1965 the direct income effect (αY_t^h) is higher than the total income effect; the indirect effect is negative. The reason why this happens is clear if one looks at the parameters. High rates of growth of PFI mean a considerable amount of additional finance required for the expansion of PFI. Profit rates are not high, and consequently reinvested profits are not high either. Financial resources must

Argentina: All PFI: Food, beverages and tobacco
(Marginal and cumulative effects of PFI)

Parameters	1962	1965	1962-1965
α	0.42	0.35	0.29
$\pi^h k^h$	0.04	0.01	0.02
ρk^h	0.02	0.005	0.01
λk^h	0.18	0.005	0.009
$\tau_P\ \pi^h k^h$	0.001	0.0	0.001
k^h	0.34	0.34	0.38
k^0	0.78	0.78	0.78
$\varphi_m(1+m^h)$	0.09	0.09	0.09
$\varphi_e(1+e^h)$	0.09	0.09	0.09
$\mu(1+m^0)$	0.08	0.08	0.08
θ	0.06	0.06	0.06
σ	0.16	0.16	0.16
τ_W, τ_P	0.03	0.03	0.03
τ_{IND}	0.05	0.05	0.05
$\left.\begin{matrix}\tau_M\\ \tau_E\end{matrix}\right\}$	0.02	0.02	0.02
w^h	0.35	0.35	0.35
$g^h k^h$	0.11	0.11	0.11
t	–	--	3
Π	0.10	0.10	0.10
Income data (1000 mln P m/n)			
Y_t^h	47.85	90.49	90.492
Y_t	1484.90	3618.30	3618.30

	Marginal effects (1000 mln P m/n)			Cumulative effects (1000 mln P m/n)
$\overline{\overline{\overline{Y}}}_t$	15.42	23.54	Y_t^*	254.58
$\overline{\overline{B}}_t$	2.91	3.83	B_t^*	25.16
$\overline{\overline{S}}_{Pt}$	2.47	3.77	S_{Pt}^*	40.73
$\overline{\overline{\overline{S}}}_{Gt}$	–1.35	–2.23	S_{Gt}^*	12.75

therefore be acquired on the domestic financial market, at the expense of domestic enterprises, which are, moreover, less efficient than PFI (see the difference between k^h and k^0), requiring consequently more financial resources for a unitary increase in production.

The b.o.p. effect is rather low and it affects to a lesser extent the income effect, since it stands for capital inflow from abroad.

The same applies to public savings, which are negative due to low tax receipts from PFI, if compared with the public expenditure imputable to it.

The results for the cumulative approach show some interesting variations with respect to the outcomes for the marginal approach. The b.o.p. effect is a smaller share of the income effect than in the previous set of calculations.

The income effect is in a more direct way influenced by the growth rate of PFI. As was said earlier, its level varies inversely to the level of α. However, the other three effects tend to give a positive influence on the overall result for the income effect.

9.8. MARGINAL AND CUMULATIVE EFFECTS FOR ALL PFI MANUFACTURING SUB-SECTOR 'TEXTILE, FOOTWEAR, AND APPAREL'

The minor role of this PFI sub-sector in the whole economy of Argentina is also reflected in the results. They are very low in absolute terms, if compared with the performance of the whole economy.

In the marginal effects, contrary to the previous case, $\alpha Y_t^h < \overline{\overline{Y}}_t$; this means that the indirect influence of PFI is positive. Relatively high profit ratios lead to a relatively higher share of PFI financial resources coming available to finance its growth (i.e. profit reinvested), with a smaller claim on domestic financial resources.

The b.o.p. shows higher profits than were yielded in the cases previously described; these, in their turn, have a corresponding impact on the transfer of profits to abroad. That is why, relatively, the b.o.p. effect is more important than the income effect. Public savings, as was to be expected, were negative in 1962 and zero in 1965, showing a positive trend.

Nothing special can be said about the cumulative effects. The general remarks given before apply also to this case.

Argentina: All PFI: Textile, footwear and apparel
(Marginal and cumulative effects of PFI)

Parameters	1962	1965	1962–1965
α	0.24	0.32	0.46
$\pi^h k^h$	0.07	0.17	0.06
ρk^h	0.35	0.085	0.03
λk^h	0.32	0.077	0.027
$\tau_P \pi^h k^h$	0.002	0.005	0.002
k^h	0.34	0.34	0.34
k^0	0.78	0.78	0.78
$\varphi_m (1+m^h)$	0.09	0.09	0.09
$\varphi_e (1+e^h)$	0.09	0.09	0.09
$\mu (1+m^0)$	0.08	0.08	0.08
θ	0.06	0.06	0.06
σ	0.16	0.16	0.16
τ_W, τ_P	0.03	0.03	0.03
τ_{IND}	0.05	0.05	0.05
$\left.\begin{matrix}\tau_M \\ \tau_E\end{matrix}\right\}$	0.02	0.02	0.02
w^h	0.35	0.35	0.35
$g^h k^h$	0.11	0.11	0.11
Π	0.10	0.10	0.10
Income data (1000 mln P m/n)			
Y_t^h	1.49	4.94	4.94
Y_t	1484.90	3618.30	3618.30

Marginal effects (1000 mln P m/n)			Cumulative effects (1000 mln P m/n)	
$\overline{\overline{Y}}_t$	0.37	2.18	Y_t^*	8.36
$\overline{\overline{B}}_t$	0.06	0.45	B_t^*	1.06
$\overline{\overline{S}}_{Pt}$	0.06	0.35	S_{Pt}^*	1.34
$\overline{\overline{S}}_{Gt}$	−0.01	0.00	S_{Gt}^*	0.14

9.9. MARGINAL AND CUMULATIVE EFFECTS FOR ALL PFI MANUFACTURING SUB-SECTOR 'CHEMICALS AND ALLIED PRODUCTS'

This sector is an important one for the share of PFI in comparison with the domestic companies operating within the sector (see the table in Section 9.3).

With respect to the marginal effects, the rather high growth rates of PFI lead to a correspondingly unfavourable indirect effect on income, through the financial mechanism for the annual additions to PFI. This fact is strengthened by the rather low profit rates which do not allow for any sizeable financing of these additions to the PFI capital stock.

As for the cumulative effects, both the b.o.p. effect and the public savings effect become more favourable than they were in the marginal approach. Although they influence the income effect positively, the overall result is still rather low, as a consequence of the high rate of growth of PFI.

9.10. MARGINAL AND CUMULATIVE EFFECTS FOR ALL PFI MANUFACTURING SUB-SECTOR 'PRIMARY AND FABRICATED METALS'

Nothing special can be said about this particular sub-sector. As for the marginal effects, in 1965 the rate of growth of PFI is much higher, but the rate of profit is lower than in 1962, and this affects the income effect, as well as the other ones. While in 1962 the total income effect is more than the direct effect (given by αY_t^h), in 1965 it becomes less than the corresponding direct income effect.

The high rate of growth of PFI is also in part responsible for the worsening of the b.o.p. effect in 1965, with respect to 1962. The public savings effect, in turn, becomes negative. The cumulative effects are kept down, in their absolute values, by the high rate of growth of PFI. Their structure does not deviate from the general remarks given in the previous pages.

Argentina: All PFI: Chemicals and allied products
(Marginal and cumulative effects of PFI)

Parameters	1962	1965	1962–1965
α	0.30	0.31	0.35
$\pi^h k^h$	0.03	0.05	0.04
ρk^h	0.015	0.025	0.02
λk^h	0.014	0.023	0.018
$\tau_P \pi^h k^h$	0.001	0.002	0.001
k^h	0.34	0.34	0.38
k^0	0.78	0.78	0.78
$\varphi_m (1+m^h)$	0.09	0.09	0.09
$\varphi_e (1+e^h)$	0.09	0.09	0.09
$\mu (1+m^0)$	0.08	0.08	0.08
θ	0.06	0.06	0.06
σ	0.16	0.16	0.16
τ_W, τ_P	0.03	0.03	0.03
τ_{IND}	0.05	0.05	0.05
τ_M, τ_E	0.02	0.02	0.02
w^h	0.35	0.35	0.35
$g^h k^h$	0.11	0.11	0.11
t	–	–	3
Π	0.10	0.10	0.10
Income data (1000 mln P m/n)			
Y_t^h	43.49	110.97	110.97
Y_t	1484.90	3618.30	3618.30

Marginal effects (1000 mln P m/n)			Cumulative effects (1000 mln P m/n)	
$\bar{\bar{Y}}_t$	10.13	29.55	Y_t^*	250.48
$\bar{\bar{B}}_t$	1.26	4.25	B_t^*	27.37
$\bar{\bar{S}}_{Pt}$	1.62	4.73	S_{Pt}^*	40.08
$\bar{\bar{S}}_{Gt}$	–0.86	–1.95	S_{Gt}^*	9.37

Argentina: All PFI: Primary and fabr. metals
(Marginal and cumulative effects of PFI)

Parameters	1962	1965	1962–1965
α	0.10	0.43	0.43
$\pi^h k^h$	0.07	0.06	0.05
ρk^h	0.035	0.03	0.025
λk^h	0.032	0.027	0.023
$\tau_P \pi^h k^h$	0.002	0.002	0.002
k^h	0.34	0.34	0.38
k^0	0.78	0.78	0.78
$\varphi_m (1+m^h)$	0.09	0.09	0.09
$\varphi_e (1+e^h)$	0.09	0.09	0.09
$\mu (1+m^0)$	0.08	0.08	0.08
θ	0.06	0.06	0.06
σ	0.16	0.16	0.16
τ_W, τ_P	0.03	0.03	0.03
τ_{IND}	0.05	0.05	0.05
τ_M, τ_E	0.02	0.02	0.02
w^h	0.35	0.35	0.35
$g^h k^h$	0.11	0.11	0.11
t	–	–	3
Π	0.10	0.10	0.10
Income data (1000 mln P m/n)			
Y_t^h	19.57	54.79	54.79
Y_t	1484.90	3618.30	3618.30

Marginal effects (1000 mln P m/n)			Cumulative effects (1000 mln P m/n)	
$\bar{\bar{Y}}_t$	2.96	19.55	Y_t^*	96.28
$\bar{\bar{B}}_t$	0.39	3.07	B_t^*	11.54
$\bar{\bar{S}}_{Pt}$	0.47	3.13	S_{Pt}^*	15.40
$\bar{\bar{S}}_{Gt}$	0.02	–1.40	S_{Gt}^*	1.90

9.11. MARGINAL AND CUMULATIVE EFFECTS FOR ALL PFI MANUFACTURING SUB-SECTOR 'TRANSPORT EQUIPMENT'

This sub-sector is a relevant one, owing to the fact that its v.a. is a relevant share of GDP for the whole economy, and its share grows between 1962 and 1965. The importance of this sub-sector can also be appreciated by considering the table in Section 9.3.

Out of the marginal effects the one on income is both in 1962 and in 1965 lower than the direct effect imputable to PFI. This, again, can be explained considering the way PFI is assumed to be financed. Absorbing a share of domestic financial resources, according to the capital-output ratio 10 α and to the transfer of profits, it prevents a certain amount of domestic investments from taking place. The indirect effects therefore lower the initial direct income contribution.

The negative indirect effects on income, together with the taxation parameters and with the share of public expenditure imputable to PFI, explain also the negative public savings effect.

The b.o.p. effect is, as in most cases, rather low.

The cumulative effects are in general also rather low, as a consequence, again, of the high level of the rate of growth of PFI. Their structure falls within the general remarks given in the previous pages.

9.12. MARGINAL AND CUMULATIVE EFFECTS FOR ALL PFI MANUFACTURING SUB-SECTOR 'OTHER MANUFACTURING'

Both for the marginal and for the cumulative effects, the results in this case are in line with what was said about the other PFI sub-sectors.

Again it can be shown that the combination of not very high growth rates for PFI, relatively high profit rates and hence high reinvested profits leads to a marginal income effect higher than the direct effect imputable to PFI (αY_t^h). As a consequence of higher tax receipts out of PFI profits, as compared with the other sub-sectors, even the public savings effect becomes positive.

In the case of the cumulative approach, the income effect is relatively high due to the same reasons as given above for the marginal calculations, although still partly hampered by the high level of the rate of growth of PFI. The other cumulative effects do not show any particular feature.

Argentina: All PFI: Transport equipment
(Marginal and cumulative effects of PFI)

Parameters	1962	1965	1962–1965
α	0.16	0.31	0.43
$\pi^h k^h$	0.03	0.04	0.03
ρk^h	0.015	0.02	0.015
λk^h	0.014	0.018	0.014
$\tau_P \pi^h k^h$	0.001	0.001	0.001
k^h	0.34	0.34	0.38
k^0	0.78	0.78	0.78
$\varphi_m (1+m^h)$	0.09	0.09	0.09
$\varphi_e (1+e^h)$	0.09	0.09	0.09
$\mu (1+m^0)$	0.08	0.08	0.08
θ	0.06	0.06	0.06
σ	0.16	0.16	0.16
τ_W, τ_P	0.03	0.03	0.03
τ_{IND}	0.05	0.05	0.05
τ_M, τ_E	0.02	0.02	0.02
w^h	0.35	0.35	0.35
$g^h k^h$	0.11	0.11	0.11
t	–	–	3
Π	0.10	0.10	0.10
Income data (1000 mln P m/n)			
Y_t^h	46.14	139.88	139.88
Y_t	1484.90	3618.30	3618.30

Marginal effects (1000 mln P m/n)			Cumulative effects (1000 mln P m/n)	
$\bar{\bar{Y}}_t$	6.58	35.43	Y_t^*	218.50
$\bar{\bar{B}}_t$	0.79	4.74	B_t^*	24.08
$\bar{\bar{S}}_{Pt}$	1.05	5.67	S_{Pt}^*	34.96
$\bar{\bar{S}}_{Gt}$	–0.40	–2.68	S_{Gt}^*	1.93

Argentina: All PFI: Other manufacturing
(Marginal and cumulative effects of PFI)

Parameters	1962	1965	1962–1965
α	0.12	0.16	0.25
$\pi^h k^h$	0.11	0.10	0.11
ρk^h	0.055	0.05	0.055
λk^h	0.05	0.045	0.05
$\tau_P \pi^h k^h$	0.003	0.03	0.003
k^h	0.34	0.34	0.34
k^0	0.78	0.78	0.78
$\varphi_m (1+m^h)$	0.09	0.09	0.09
$\varphi_e (1+e^h)$	0.09	0.09	0.09
$\mu (1+m^0)$	0.08	0.08	0.08
θ	0.06	0.06	0.06
σ	0.16	0.16	0.16
τ_W, τ_P	0.03	0.03	0.03
τ_{IND}	0.05	0.05	0.05
$\left.\begin{matrix}\tau_M \\ \tau_E\end{matrix}\right\}$	0.02	0.02	0.02
w^h	0.35	0.35	0.35
$g^h k^h$	0.11	0.11	0.11
t	–	–	3
Π	0.10	0.10	0.10
Income data (1000 mln P m/n)			
Y_t^h	16.21	33.25	33.25
Y_t	1484.90	3618.30	3618.30

Marginal effects (1000 mln P m/n)			Cumulative effects (1000 mln P m/n)	
$\overline{\overline{Y}}_t$	3.49	7.71	Y_t^*	239.16
$\overline{\overline{B}}_t$	0.51	1.19	B_t^*	25.90
$\overline{\overline{S}}_{Pt}$	0.56	1.26	S_{Pt}^*	38.27
$\overline{\overline{S}}_{Gt}$	0.08	0.02	S_{Gt}^*	19.55

9.13. CONCLUSIONS

As in the previous cases, the exercise carried out in this chapter can be considered a 'case-study on the effects of PFI in Argentina', but, most of all, it represents an empirical application of the methodology of Part II with reference to the data supplied by the 'UCA Report' for this country. Consequently, in this case as in the previous ones, the results should be interpreted mainly in this light, and they should serve to provide a better insight into the methodology, as well as to point out various possible improvements in order to make it more realistic. Anyhow, the results should allow forming some ideas about the effects of PFI in Argentina. It was also possible to distinguish various cases, viz. total PFI manufacturing and PFI in the various sub-sectors of manufacturing.

Before analysing in more detail the empirical results for Argentina, it is useful to point out the most interesting features of the exercise, *vis-à-vis* the previous ones.

In the case of India it was possible to distinguish between Foreign Branches (FB) and Foreign Controlled Rupee Companies (FCRC) both for the whole economy and for the manufacturing sector, and consequently to use the methodology to appraise the effects of different ways of financing a PFI project (i.e. FB vs FCRC). In the case of Ghana such a distinction was possible only between All PFI and Branches of Foreign Companies (BFC), where, however, a comparison was difficult mainly as a consequence of the way various parameters were estimated, and of the different concepts of v.a. used. No such appraisal was possible in the case of the Philippines, of Guatemala and of Argentina, where the data available include All PFI without any distinction for various kinds.

However, in the case of Argentina, as in all other cases except India, it was possible to use the methodological approach to appraise the effect of All PFI in the various sub-sectors of the manufacturing sector, as distinguished in Section 9.1 of Part II.

But, as in the previous cases, although this sectoral application of the methodology proved to be an interesting exercise, there are quite a few drawbacks, because in the various sub-sectors many parameters are the same, owing to the lack of better empirical evidence; consequently, it was not possible to appraise fully the effects of PFI, in the various cases, of all possible differences, but the analysis did point out what happened as a result of varying values for some of the key-parameters. Moreover, the concept of v.a. used (i.e. sales) also influenced the various parameter estimates, and hence the results.

Although the exercise has various limitations, and is based on some rather radical simplifying assumptions, it is possible to reach some general conclusions, similarly to what was done in the other cases.

In Argentina PFI is a rather important part of the country's GDP, and in general it contributes favourably to the growth of income, although often with adverse indirect effects. The behaviour of PFI in the various sub-sectors is rather uniform, and this is due among other reasons to the way the parameters were estimated.

The b.o.p. effect of PFI is generally limited, although in no case it is negative (deficit decreasing), as in the Philippines.

The public savings effect is in general negligible, and in the marginal approach is even mostly negative.

An interesting feature in the case of Ghana was the fact that it was possible, at least in a simplified way (see Section 7.5), to show how the methodology, on the basis of the empirical evidence available, takes into account in an endogenous way, through the mechanism of financing the annual additions to PFI, what actually happens in practice. Consequently, some of the objections to this mechanism raised elsewhere could be considered as taken into account by the model. No such test was possible in the case of Argentina, for lack of sufficient data.

Moreover, the objections raised in the previous cases about import substitution still stand in the case of Argentina, and it was also necessary to introduce rather radical assumptions as regards imports and exports, to estimate the PFI foreign trade coefficients.

Finally, even more than in the four previous cases, one should remember the limitations of the data to estimate the parameters, discussed at length in Section 9.5 to show the way the various gaps were filled, together with the fact that it was necessary to use data in current prices.

CHAPTER X

A GENERAL COMPARISON OF THE EMPIRICAL OUTCOMES

This chapter will try to give a general view of the empirical results obtained for the five countries considered before, in order to reach some general conclusions on the effect of PFI on their economy.

As became evident in the previous chapters, apart from the four basic effects (income, b.o.p.[1], private savings, public savings), the data available allowed calculation of the employment effect only in two cases (BFC in Ghana: marginal effect for 1963; All PFI in Guatemala: marginal effect for 1968). Lack of data prevented any other calculation of the employment effect, while, for similar reasons, it was not possible to calculate the income distribution and the substitution effects.

When the results of the calculations in current prices of the year they refer to, in the national currency, had become available, these were related to the PFI value added of the sector or sub-sector concerned for some selected years. The outcomes are given in percentages in the tables in the next pages in order to allow a comparison.

Not all calculations refer to the same years. There are some differences in the case of India, because lack of data for FY 1967/68 prevented the calculation of the marginal effects for that year, and left a four-year period for the cumulative effects. For similar reasons, the marginal effects for the Philippines had to be calculated with reference to 1964. Finally, the data available for Argentina suggested concentration on a slightly different period, as explained in Chapter IX.

As a consequence of the different definitions, a comparison between the two approaches is not possible. They should simply be considered separately, according to their definitions.

The *marginal effects* are the changes in the endogenous variables of the model underlying the methodological approach; they correspond to the four effects (Y_t, B_t, S_{Pt}, S_{Gt}), which occur from t to $t+1$ as a consequence of PFI, under the assumption that it was there up to time t, and that one is

1 It may be useful to remember that b.o.p. refers to the *deficit* of the balance of payments, consequently, a positive result in the effects, means an increase in the deficit (and vice-versa).

simply interested in finding out the changes which occur in those variables as a consequence of the presence of PFI from t to $t+1$.

The *cumulative effects* point out the effects of PFI over a certain period (from $t-n$ to t), with respect to the endogenous variables corresponding to the effects, again under the assumption that the alternative situation is the one of absence of PFI, and that the effects are measured in time t by the difference between the development from $t-n$ to t of those variables in the presence of PFI, and the development over the same period of those variables, when PFI is assumed absent.

Let us consider first the outcomes of the *marginal approach calculations.*

In the case of India, the income effect is always smaller than the b.o.p. effect, and sometimes even negative[2]. A favourable impact of the presence of PFI would be given by the opposite situation, while here, basically as a consequence of the difference between PFI imports and exports, of the high rate of transfer of profits to abroad and of a partial absorption of financial resources otherwise available for investments in the 'rest of the economy', the contribution to income growth is negligible, if not negative, while the burden on the b.o.p. is sizeable with respect to PFI value added. In the case of alternative ways of financing a PFI project, FCRC seem to have a more positive impact on the economy, in proportion to FB, and this is pointed out in the public savings effect as well.

The situation looks more favourable to PFI *in the case of the Philippines,* where the income effect is rather relevant, and the b.o.p. effect small, and sometimes even negative (i.e., deficit decreasing)[3], due, basically, to the different structure of the foreign trade sector for PFI. The private savings effect derives from the income effect through the marginal propensity to save, while the public savings effect is rather limited (and sometimes negative) as a consequence of the structure, of taxation and public expenditure.

In the case of Ghana, some marginal calculations have been omitted, because of lack of data or of other difficulties. In the case of All PFI, a negative rate of growth of the PFI capital stock is responsible for the negative results

2 In certain cases the marginal effects are negative due to the negative rate of growth of PFI capital stock. A negative rate of growth occurs in the following cases:
the Philippines: 'Textile, footwear and apparel'; 'Primary and fabricated metals';
Ghana: 'Primary and fabricated metals'; 'Other manufacturing' (both in 1968);
Guatemala: 'Textile, footwear, apparel'; 'Machinery' (both in 1968).

3 However, the rate of growth of PFI in 'Textile, footwear and apparel' is negative, and consequently a positive b.o.p. effect still means a deficit-decreasing pattern. It is still negative in the case of 'Primary and fabricated metals', which can then be considered deficit increasing. *Mutatis mutandis*, similar considerations apply to the other three effects.

A general comparison of the marginal effects

Country	India										
Concept	All PFI							FCRC			
$\frac{\text{Effects}}{Y_t^h} \times 100$	$\bar{Y}_t$		$\bar{B}_t$		$\bar{S}_{Pt}$	$\bar{S}_{Gt}$		$\bar{Y}_t$		$\bar{B}_t$	
Year	1962/63	1966/67	1962/63	1966/67	–	1962/63	1966/67	1962/63	1966/67	1962/63	1966/(
All economy	−2.57	2.23	14.64	7.71	0	2.88	2.22	9.99	10.71	17.90	11.28
Manufacturing	9.44	10.49	15.31	12.89	0	4.61	4.33	10.73	11.67	16.22	13.19
Food, beverages and tobacco											
Textile, footwear and apparel											
Chemicals and allied products											
Primary and fabricated metals											
Machinery											
Transport equipment											
Other manufacturing											

Country	Ghana												
Concept	All PFI								BFC				
$\frac{\text{Effects}}{Y_t^h} \times 100$	$\bar{Y}_t$		$\bar{B}_t$		$\bar{S}_{Pt}$		$\bar{S}_{Gt}$		$\bar{Y}_t$	$\bar{B}_t$	$\bar{S}_{Pt}$	$\bar{S}_{Gt}$	$\bar{L}_t$
Year	1963	1968	1963	1968	1963	1968	1963	1968	1963	1963	1963	1963	19(
All economy									12.99	3.96	1.30	1.22	2.5
Manufacturing	23.01	6.74	12.00	1.11	2.30	0.67	3.66	0.96	12.14	4.08	1.21	0.79	2.7
Food, beverages and tobacco	17.25	14.48	5.70	4.89	1.73	1.45	2.11	1.59					
Textile, footwear and apparel	–	32.89	–	13.08	–	3.30	–	5.79					
Chemicals and allied products	−23.47	–	1.47	–	−2.35	–	−2.13	–					
Primary and fabricated metals	−184.41	6.13	5.77	0.36	−18.44	0.61	−19.70	0.91					
Machinery	–	59.39	–	25.00	–	5.94	–	11.72					
Transport equipment	68.16	40.02	29.42	14.20	6.82	4.00	15.06	3.79					
Other manufacturing	39.92	−24.93	16.79	−14.44	3.99	−2.49	7.04	−6.79					

only in 'Primary and fabricated metals' (1968) and in 'Other manufacturing' (1968). The results look more satisfactory than in the case of India, although not so favourable to the presence of PFI as in the case of the Philippines, with some exceptions, in the sub-sectors, due to varying empirical situations.

A comparison between alternative PFI, confronting the outcomes of the marginal approach for 1963, for All PFI *vis-à-vis* BFC in the manufacturing sector, shows that the former, as in India, have in general a more positive impact, apart from the b.o.p. effect.

In the case of Guatemala, there is a negative rate of growth for the PFI capital stock only for 'Textile, footwear and apparel' and for 'Machinery', in

											Philippines			
			FB								All PFI			
…$_{Pt}$	$\bar{\bar{S}}_{Gt}$		$\bar{Y}_t$		$\bar{B}_t$		$\bar{\bar{S}}_{Pt}$	$\bar{\bar{S}}_{Gt}$			$\bar{Y}_t$	$\bar{B}_t$	$\bar{\bar{S}}_{Pt}$	$\bar{\bar{S}}_{Gt}$
	1962/63	1966/67	1962/63	1966/67	1962/63	1966/67	–	1962/63	1966/67		1964	1964	1964	1964
	5.81	4.05	−17.18	−2.29	11.00	1.17	0	−0.31	0.08					
	5.15	4.48	−12.46	−4.70	13.16	12.31	0	1.88	2.08		8.33	0.66	1.17	1.05
											5.46	−0.87	0.77	0.66
											23.21	3.60	3.25	1.75
											15.27	−4.64	2.14	1.79
											−8.01	−5.30	−1.12	−0.23
											10.85	4.37	1.50	0.73
											17.26	26.53	2.42	−.81
											7.43	1.19	1.04	0.78

uatemala									Argentina							
l PFI									All PFI							
		$\bar{\bar{B}}_t$		$\bar{\bar{S}}_{Pt}$		$\bar{\bar{S}}_{Gt}$		$\bar{L}_t$	$\bar{Y}_t$		$\bar{\bar{B}}_t$		$\bar{\bar{S}}_{Pt}$		$\bar{\bar{S}}_{Gt}$	
63	1968	1963	1968	1963	1968	1963	1968	1968	1962	1965	1962	1965	1962	1965	1962	1965
22.19	6.41	39.46	5.51	2.22	0.64	−0.09	0.21	1.31	21.44	24.69	2.79	3.30	3.43	3.95	−1.44	−1.84
23.01	12.51	26.82	11.55	2.30	1.25	0.58	0.39	3.41	32.23	26.10	6.08	4.25	5.16	4.18	−2.82	−2.47
33.08	8.19	0.40	1.61	−3.31	0.82	−2.39	0.56	1.71	24.83	44.13	4.03	9.11	4.03	7.08	−0.67	0
12.50	5.40	39.80	5.78	1.25	0.54	−0.85	0.11	0.80	23.29	26.63	2.90	3.83	3.72	4.25	−1.98	−1.76
16.59	10.85	26.66	14.11	1.66	1.08	−0.01	0.06	0.58	15.13	35.68	1.99	5.60	2.40	5.71	0.10	−2.56
24.67	– 7.10	38.81	−13.59	2.47	−0.71	0.10	0.18	–	–	–	–	–	–	–	–	–
–	–	–	–	–	–	–	–	–	14.26	25.33	1.71	3.39	2.28	4.05	−0.87	−1.92
32.23	6.31	50.80	4.77	3.22	0.63	0.07	0.24	1.40	21.53	23.19	3.15	3.58	3.45	3.79	0.49	0.06

both cases in 1968. For the former, the results are affected in a way contrary to what would be expected, owing to the very high ICOR of this PFI sub-sector, and to its impact via the mechanism of the model.

The results for 1963 are quite a bit larger, at the level of the manufacturing sector, than the ones for 1968, due to a difference in the rate of growth of PFI.

In general the b.o.p. effect is still sizeable, and only in 1968 smaller than the income effect.

The public savings effect is negligible, and sometimes even negative, due to the structure of taxation and of public expenditure.

A general comparison of the cumulative effects

Country	India												Philippines
Concept	All PFI				FCRC				FB				–
Period	1962/63–1966/67				1962/63–1966/67				1962/63–1966/67				–
$\frac{\text{Effects}}{Y_t^h}$ x 100	Y_t^*	B_t^*	S_{Pt}^*	S_{Gt}^*	Y_t^*	B_t^*	S_{Pt}^*	S_{Gt}^*	Y_t^*	B_t^*	S_{Pt}^*	S_{Gt}^*	–
All economy	321.01	111.86	0	60.74	291.47	105.20	0	59.81	476.06	129.09	0	77.65	–
Manufacturing	284.26	100.00	0	57.80	281.93	100.96	0	58.47	460.58	128.77	0	74.48	–
Food, beverages and tobacco													
Textile, footwear and apparel													
Chemicals and allied products													
Primary and fabricated metals													
Machinery													
Transport equipment													
Other manufacturing													

Country	Ghana				Guatemala				Argentina			
Concept	All PFI				All PFI				All PFI			
Period	1963–1968				1963–1968				1962–1965			
$\frac{\text{Effects}}{Y_t^h}$ x 100	Y_t^*	B_t^*	S_{Pt}^*	S_{Gt}^*	Y_t^*	B_t^*	S_{Pt}^*	S_{Gt}^*	Y_t^*	B_t^*	S_{Pt}^*	S_{Gt}^*
All economy												
Manufacturing	1000.85	169.05	100.08	138.36	297.66	175.22	29.77	15.95	378.43	38.42	60.55	23.
Food, beverages and tobacco	786.07	131.25	78.61	99.42	377.80	183.48	37.78	18.97	281.33	27.80	45.01	14.
Textile, footwear and apparel	273.54	72.05	27.35	40.49	61.82	96.17	6.18	1.22	169.23	21.46	27.13	2.
Chemicals and allied products	1067.97	194.17	106.80	159.93	124.44	115.34	12.44	4.86	225.72	24.66	36.12	8.
Primary and fabricated metals	630.80	130.80	63.08	94.08	133.05	117.92	13.30	5.26	175.73	21.06	28.11	3.
Machinery	–	–	–	–	145.95	122.89	14.60	6.19	–	–	–	
Transport equipment	402.15	103.96	40.21	71.54	–	–	–	–	156.21	17.21	24.99	1.
Other manufacturing	1273.70	217.21	127.37	189.01	777.10	385.57	77.71	44.28	719.28	77.89	115.10	58.

In the case of Argentina, the results of the marginal calculations are sizeable for the income effect, mainly as a result of the very high rate of growth of PFI, which is in turn affected by the fact that the underlying data are in current prices. Still the b.o.p. effect is rather limited, especially if compared with the income effect. The private savings effect derives from the income effect, while the public savings effect is mostly negative, as a consequence of the structure of taxation and of public expenditure.

Let us now turn our attention to the results of the *cumulative approach*.

It was observed earlier that they are much more important than the marginal outcomes, and that there is no straightforward correspondence between the two.

In the case of India, FB appear preferable to FCRC, and also to All PFI in general. This is basically due to the small average rate of growth of PFI in the case of FB, *vis-à-vis* the other two cases, since the outcomes of the cumulative approach vary inversely to the rate of growth of PFI (i.e., a higher rate of growth means lower effects which cumulate over the previous years, as was noticed earlier).

The same is true of the b.o.p. effect, while the public savings effect depends upon the income effect, through the structure of taxation and of public expenditure.

In the case of Ghana, the results are much more sizeable than in the case of India, although a comparison is prevented by the fact that the two sets of calculations cover two different periods (5 years for Ghana, 4 years for India). Here, the b.o.p. effect, as compared with respect to the income effect, is less sizeable, though larger in absolute figures.

In the case of Guatemala the size of the income effect becomes much smaller (due, e.g. in the case of the manufacturing sector, to a rate of growth of PFI twice as much with respect to Ghana), although the b.o.p. effect still remains quite sizeable.

In the case of Argentina, the size of the income effect is relatively less than in the other cases (especially Ghana), as a consequence of the high rate of growth of PFI. Comparison, however, is hampered by the different time period covered by the calculations for Argentina.

The b.o.p. effect is again quite limited, similarly to what was shown by the outcomes of the marginal calculations. Also the public savings effect is in general small, for the same reasons as with the marginal effects.

In the three cases considered with the cumulative approach, it was possible to appraise what happens at a sub-sectoral level, although one should be careful in drawing conclusions about the relative impact of PFI in the various sub-sectors, in view of the many assumptions which had to be introduced in order to fill various gaps in the data.

As was stressed earlier, the exercise could be considered as a set of 'case studies' for those countries on the effects of PFI, but, it is better, to see them as a set of empirical applications of the methodological approach developed by the NEI, with reference to the data supplied for the five countries. Consequently the results should be interpreted mainly in this light, and they should serve to provide a better insight into the methodological framework, as well as to point out various possible improvements in order to make it more realistic, taking into account the problems and limitations discussed in Part II.

Anyhow, the empirical results should also give some preliminary ideas about the effects of PFI in the five countries considered, on the basis of the more interesting features of the various country-exercises, and it is possible to point out some conclusions.

With respect to the *increase of income*, the results of the marginal calculations point out that in general PFI plays a minor role: in most cases, the overall PFI effect on income was found to be less than the direct effect imputable to it, mainly as a consequence of the absorption of financial resources otherwise available for investments in the 'rest of the economy'. The situation varies from country to country, but this seems to be the general picture. In the case of the cumulative effects, the overall impact on income looks much more favourable, although, again, it should be considered in the general context of the definition of these effects.

As for the *b.o.p.*, both marginal and cumulative results point out that in general PFI tends to pose a heavy burden on the deficit. Again, the situation varies from country to country, and in some cases (e.g. the Philippines) PFI even has a deficit-decreasing effect.

The effect on *private savings* derives directly from the income effect, and nothing particular need to be said on this point.

Finally, PFI seems to have a positive effect on *public savings*, although with some exceptions (e.g. Argentina) and to varying degrees, as a consequence of the structure of taxation and of public expenditure in the countries considered.

Before concluding this chapter, it seems useful to stress once again that the results should be interpreted not only in the context of the methodological approach, but also keeping in mind the set of assumptions underlying the results. These assumptions often introduced to fill various gaps in the data available in order to be able to apply the quantitative methodological approach, were discussed at length in the previous chapters.

CHAPTER XI

ALTERNATIVE ASSUMPTIONS ABOUT IMPORT SUBSTITUTION

The purpose of this chapter is to provide an exercise, on the basis of the empirical applications of the methodology of this study, on how the results obtained in the previous chapters would vary, if empirical evidence were available suggesting that PFI indeed does substitute imports to some extent.

As it can be remembered, in all country studies the fact that no empirical evidence on import substitution in any of the cases considered was available, was mentioned to be one of the main drawbacks of the empirical results obtained. As a matter of fact, all the estimates for the parameter standing for export promotion and/or import substitution $\varphi_e(1+e^h)$ were obtained in a rather unsatisfactory way, with just one exception concerning the export behaviour of PFI (India), but without being able, in any of the cases considered, to take into account import substitution, for lack of any quantitative information.

Only *in the case of India* (see p. 178) this parameter was estimated directly from PFI data for PFI exports. First it was calculated for FCRC, and then it was assumed to be the same also for FB, and thus for All PFI, being foreign trade data available only for PFI in FCRC. *In the case of the Philippines* (see p. 213) it was assumed that domestic firms and PFI firms have the same export behaviour, and thus this parameter, for lack of better data, was calculated from foreign trade statistics referring to the whole economy, according to the sectors or sub-sectors under consideration. Also *in the case of Ghana* (see p. 243) it was necessary to introduce a similar assumption, having no information on PFI external trade. The same applies for *the case of Guatemala* (see p. 279), where, however, it was possible to notice that the only export firms, within the manufacturing sector, belong to the subsectors 'Food, beverages and tobacco' and 'Other manufacturing'. Finally, also *in the case of Argentina* (see pp. 306–307), the same assumption of a uniform export behaviour for domestic and PFI firms had to be introduced, for lack of better data.

Consequently, not only this parameter was estimated without taking into account import substitution, but, apart from the case of India[1], it is also just

1 In the case of India, in 1966/67 (which is the FY considered in this exercise), FCRC produced 94% of total PFI value added in the manufacturing sector, while FB only 6%.

an approximation of the export behaviour of PFI. So, it is difficult to say whether the values used in the various cases are underestimations of the 'real values', or whether in some cases they may even be an overestimation. The only exception is the case of India, where any evidence on a positive contribution of PFI to import substitution would indeed raise the value of this parameter, and thus bring about lower results for the b.o.p. effects, as well as different results for the other effects considered, these being interrelated.

Given this state of affairs, in order to test how the results obtained in the previous chapters would change if there were some evidence of a positive contribution of PFI to import substitution, it was thought better to test two assumptions for all the countries considered (with reference to the manufacturing sector), without taking into account the values previously used for this parameter.

Assumption 1 considers the case where the whole of PFI value added is either exported or it replaces imports. Consequently, in this extreme case, $\varphi_e(1+e^h) = 1.00$.

Assumption 2 considers an intermediate situation, where 50% of PFI value added is either exported or it replaces imports. This is still higher than all the values considered in the previous chapters for the whole of the manufacturing sector, as it can be seen in the tables on the next pages. Only in the case of the Philippines (1964 marginal effects) it is just 8% more, while in all other cases considered here it is always at least more than twice as much, as it can be seen in the same tables. In this case $\varphi_e(1 + e^h) = 0.50$.

In both cases it is also assumed that all the other parameters required for the empirical application of the methodology are still the same as in the corresponding cases studied in Part III.

The cases to be considered here are the following ones:

India: 'All PFI manufacturing (FB + FCRC)', marginal effects for FY 1966/67 (see p. 195) and cumulative effects for the period from FY 1962/63 to 1966/67 (see p. 196);

Philippines: 'All PFI manufacturing', marginal effects for 1964 (see p. 217);

Ghana: 'All PFI manufacturing', marginal effects for 1968 and cumulative effects for the period 1963–1968 (see p. 251);

Guatemala: 'All PFI manufacturing', marginal effects for 1968 and cumulative effects for the period 1963–1968 (see p. 284);

Argentina: 'All PFI manufacturing', marginal effects for 1965 and cumulative effects for the period 1962–1965 (see p. 310),

Consequently, the value used for the parameter under consideration could indeed be assumed to hold also for the case of All PFI in the sector.

The results for the marginal effects are given in the table on p. 334, and the results for the cumulative effects in the table on p. 335. In both cases, apart from the previous value of $\varphi_e(1+e^h)$, also the results obtained earlier are given in order to allow an appraisal of their variation as a consequence of the two alternative values assumed for the export and import substitution parameter.

Before considering the results obtained in this exercise, it is necessary to stress once more that they do not rely on any empirical evidence, but are simply the outcomes of the introduction of two possible values for $\varphi_e(1+e^h)$ which may not be there at all in practice, especially in the case of assumption 1, given the level of aggregation considered (All PFI in the whole of the manufacturing sector).

Let us consider first the outcomes for the *marginal effects*[2]. In the case of *assumption 1* the b.o.p. effect, with the exception of Ghana, becomes negative, showing a deficit-decreasing pattern of PFI. However, this also means, in the context of the assumptions of this study, a capital outflow, and thus less financial resources available for investment in the 'rest of the economy', apart from the share absorbed by PFI. This causes a lower level of the income effect, with respect to the former results, and thus, lower results for the other two effects (with also a feed-back on the b.o.p. effect through the marginal propensity to import). However, all four effects should be seen simultaneously, being interrelated, as it was seen in Part II. In the case of Argentina, a very high negative result for the b.o.p. effect causes, again through the financial mechanism assumed for the additions to the PFI capital stock and for the financing of domestic investments, a negative value both for the income effect and for the other two effects. This is also strengthened by the very high value of α in the case considered (0.30; see p. 310), together with the low share of profit rèinvested (less than 2 per cent of PFI value added). Also a value of k^h less than k^0 plays a negative role in the income effect, again as a consequence of the assumptions of the methodology for the financing of PFI and of domestic investment.

In the case of *assumption 2* the b.o.p. effect remains negative (deficit decreasing) only in the case of Argentina and, to a more limited extent, in the case of the Philippines. However, the income effect is always positive, al-

2 In the case of Guatemala, also for the cumulative effects, the results are in millions Q, instead of being in thousands Q, in Chapter VIII. This is done in order to have less sizeable results, as compared with the other four countries considered. Furthermore, the (marginal) employment effect, calculated in the case of Guatemala (for All PFI in the manufacturing sector), is omitted, although it could be easily obtained from the results for assumption 1 and assumption 2 (starting from the income effect).

Alternative assumptions about import substitution
(All PFI – Manufacturing – Marginal effects)

Country	India	Philippines	Ghana	Guatemala	Argentina
Year	1966-67	1964	1968	1968	1965
Former value					
$\varphi_e\,(1+e^h)$	0.13	0.42	0.20	0.10	0.09
Y_t^h	2997	1293	47.56	40.09	434.31
Monetary unit	mln rupees	mln pesos	mln N₵	mln Q	billion P m/n
Assumption 1					
$\overline{\overline{Y}}_t$	52.23	78.87	2.88	1.60	– 79.54
$\overline{\overline{B}}_t$	–157.51	– 49.60	0.09	–0.38	–125.88
$\overline{\overline{S}}_{Pt}$	0	11.04	0.29	0.16	– 12.73
$\overline{\overline{S}}_{Gt}$	50.01	4.95	0.36	–0.08	– 27.30
Assumption 2					
$\overline{\overline{Y}}_t$	190.66	101.28	3.06	2.11	22.56
$\overline{\overline{B}}_t$	153.95	– 0.08	0.36	1.05	– 48.89
$\overline{\overline{S}}_{Pt}$	0	14.18	0.31	0.21	3.61
$\overline{\overline{S}}_{Gt}$	68.01	7.19	0.39	–0.06	– 17.09
Former results					
$\overline{\overline{Y}}_t$	314.24	107.75	3.21	2.57	107.25
$\overline{\overline{B}}_t$	386.22	8.51	0.53	2.21	14.32
$\overline{\overline{S}}_{Pt}$	0	15.09	0.32	0.26	17.16
$\overline{\overline{S}}_{Gt}$	129.86	13.54	0.46	0.08	– 7.98

though less than estimated in the previous chapters, for the same reasons discussed above for the first assumption.

The trend which can be observed shows, as one could easily expect, a negative relation between the export and import substitution parameter and the b.o.p. effect. The higher this parameter, the lower is the b.o.p. effect, to the point that it becomes negative, like in all cases but one in assumption 1. This decrease of the b.o.p. effect, however, causes also a decrease of the income effect, for the reasons mentioned above, connected with the situation assumed by the methodology for the financing both of PFI and of domestic

Alternative assumptions about import substitution
(All PFI – Manufacturing – Cumulative effects)

Country	India	Philippines	Ghana	Guatemala	Argentina
Year	1962/63–1966/67 ($t = 4$)	–	1963–1968 ($t = 5$)	1963–1968 ($t = 5$)	1962–1965 ($t = 3$)
Former value					
$\varphi_e\,(1+e^h)$	0.12	–	0.20	0.10	.09
Y_t^h	2997	–	47.56	40.09	434.31
Monetary unit	mln rupees	–	mln N₵	mln Q	billion P m/n
Assumption 1					
Y_t^*	1710.85	–	–100.64	8.02	–5824.02
B_t^*	–677.15	–	– 39.37	–13.73	– 960.13
S_{Pt}^*	0	–	– 10.06	0.80	– 931.84
S_{Gt}^*	537.10	–	– 15.37	– 1.97	– 646.90
Assumption 2					
Y_t^*	5249.74	–	217.89	64.81	–1739.97
B_t^*	1392.22	–	30.22	31.11	– 341.48
S_{Pt}^*	0	–	21.79	6.48	– 278.40
S_{Gt}^*	997.15	–	26.04	0.30	– 238.49
Former results					
Y_t^*	8519.34	–	476.00	119.32	1643.54
B_t^*	2997.07	–	80.40	70.24	166.86
S_{Pt}^*	0	–	47.60	11.93	262.97
S_{Gt}^*	1732.17	–	65.80	6.39	104.05

investment. This can be seen immediately comparing the results of assumption 1 and 2 with the ones previously obtained. The results of the other two effects adapt to this situation, although they also play a role in it, being determined simultaneously.

Something similar happens also in the case of the *cumulative effects*, although with some variations, as a consequence of the different definitions underlying the two approaches.

In the case of *assumption 1* the b.o.p. effect is always negative (deficit decreasing), although the income effect is still positive both for India and Guatemala, while it becomes negative in the cases of Ghana and of Argentina. For the last case, the same explanation given for the marginal effects still holds, while a similar reasoning would explain also the negative results for Ghana, in connection with the financial mechanism of the methodology, a low rate of profit reinvested (6% of PFI value added; see p. 248) and a value of k^h much less than the value of k^0, combined with a rate of growth of PFI somewhat sizeable ($\alpha = 0.10$ as compared to $\alpha = 0.01$ in the case of the marginal effects considered above; see p. 251). In all cases, anyhow, the income effect decreases considerably with respect to the results previously obtained, again as a consequence of the fact that a negative b.o.p. effect means a capital outflow, and thus less financial resources for investment, both domestic and PFI.

In the case of *assumption 2* a negative set of results is still obtained for Argentina, where, although the b.o.p. effect is now almost one third (in absolute value) with respect to the previous case, the low rate of profit reinvested (less than 2% of PFI value added), combined with the high rate of growth of PFI ($\alpha = 0.27$; see p. 310) through the financial mechanism of the model causes the income effect (and thus the other two effects) to be also negative. In the other three cases the b.o.p. effect is smaller than in the previous results, and consequently also the income effect becomes smaller, although still positive. The other two effects adapt to these results, although, as it was said, they also play a role in them.

The trend which it is possible to get from these results, compared with the previous ones, is similar to the one observed for the marginal effects. A higher level of the export promotion and import substitution parameter affects inversely the b.o.p. effect, but this, in turn, affects the income effect, standing for foreign capital inflow (or outflow, if negative), and thus all the other results. Consequently, a more satisfactory result in terms of the b.o.p., given the assumptions of the model about the financing of PFI and of investment in the 'rest of the economy', has the drawback of causing a lower contribution of PFI to income. These considerations should remind the discussion given in Part II about the double role played by the b.o.p. in the context of the methodological set-up of this study, and the results obtained in this chapter provide a clear numerical illustration of this question.

CHAPTER XII

GENERAL CONCLUSIONS ON THE EMPIRICAL APPLICATIONS OF THE METHODOLOGY

Apart from the general remarks made at the end of Chapter X, the limitations of the exercises of this Part III of the research on the effects of PFI in LDC's, as well as some conclusions based on the outcomes of the empirical calculations were discussed at the end of each of the chapters dedicated to the five countries considered. The limitations can be seen on two levels: theoretical and empirical.

On a *theoretical* level, the use of a quantitative methodology, although allowing considerable advantages, necessarily introduces also a certain degree of simplification of the underlying reality, and assumes a certain degree of uniform behaviour, which might not be there in many cases.

But this could, at least partly, be overcome, as was pointed out throughout Part II when discussing possible improvements of the methodology, or at least, if well kept in mind, should still allow a useful interpretation of the results.

The major problems seem to arise on the *empirical* level, where the practical application of the methodology to the various countries considered suffered from many gaps in the data availability, which had to be filled in various ways, discussed at length in the chapters dedicated to the five countries.

The suggestions for future research in this field, on the basis of the experience accumulated through this study, are mainly in the field of the empirical data. The results of the attempt sponsored by the NEI, in co-operation with the OECD Development Centre, to gather for a wide sample of countries a variety of quantitative information on PFI, points out the unsatisfactory state of affairs in this field, but it should also point out the direction into which future efforts should be channelled.

Even with the limitations discussed above, the empirical outcomes of the NEI research are still felt to provide a useful starting point for a discussion on the effects of PFI in LCD's. Chapter X pointed out certain common trends in the empirical results, which often contrast with the conclusions arrived at by the literature in this field.

The methodological set-up provides at least a first attempt to look at a problem of such great relevance in the field of development economics in a consistent and comprehensive way, while still leaving open the possibility for future refinements and extensions (as was discussed throughout Part II and at the end of each country study), once the data problem, above discussed, is at least partially solved.

PART IV

THE APPRAISAL OF PRIVATE FOREIGN INVESTMENT PROJECTS – A SOCIAL COST-BENEFIT APPROACH

TABLE OF CONTENTS

CHAPTER I

INTRODUCTION

The NEI research on private foreign investment has been mainly concerned with the development and application of a macro-economic framework for the measurement and evaluation of the effects of private foreign investment on the economies of the less developed countries. The reason for choosing such a macro-economic approach was that policy makers in formulating the broad outlines of economic policies need information of a macro-economic nature rather than detailed information on a few individual, and perhaps not representative, cases of private foreign investments.

Nevertheless, in the end outlines of economic policy have to be translated into action, which inevitably takes place at a project level. It is well known that a number of developing countries face severe difficulties in translating their strategy towards private foreign investment into an appraisal machinery for investment activities proposed by foreign firms. Indeed in a substantial number of cases decisions on whether to allow a particular foreign enterprise to operate a factory within the developing country are taken at present almost without any substantial appraisal of the proposal. In view of this the NEI has, as a somewhat independent part of the research, thought it desirable to present a rather simple manual on the appraisal of private foreign investment at the project level. A further justification of this part of the research is that it would seem that existing schemes for social cost-benefit analysis, useful as they are, do not lend themselves to straightforward application in the case of private foreign investment. The reason for this is that the financing mechanism of PFI projects not only complicates the appraisal of these projects, but also affects the outcome. Existing methods for project appraisal do not allow for this.

The paper is addressed mainly to those who are engaged, in Foreign Investment Boards etc., in decision-taking on individual foreign investment projects, and generally are not professional economists. Because of this, and since, moreover, in many developing countries no information permitting sophisticated methods is available, the paper emphasizes practical usefulness rather than theoretical rigour. The professional economist may, consequently, find little that strikes his theoretical interest.

Chapter II gives a basic exposition of social cost-benefit analysis. Starting with a discussion of the project cycle (Section 2.2), it continues with a discussion of the differences between commercial and social profitability (Section 2.3). In Section 2.4 social benefits and costs are discussed more thoroughly, whereas Section 2.5 deals with the measurement of benefits and costs, applying accounting prices. The discount rate is briefly discussed in Section 2.6, the accounting price for unskilled labour in Section 2.7.

Chapter III deals with the basic characteristics of private foreign investment projects as distinct from domestic investment projects, such as the impact of foreign financing (Section 3.2), domestic participation in the foreign-owned project (Section 3.3) and the impact of the possible availability of domestic alternatives on the appraisal of foreign investment projects (Section 3.4).

In Chapter IV the impact of these characteristics of private foreign investment on the methodology of social cost-benefit analysis is determined with the aid of four basic cases.

In Chapter V an outline of a social cost-benefit scheme for appraising foreign investment proposals is presented. Basically this chapter puts together the findings of Chapters II, III and IV in a systematic way, without adding new elements to the discussion. In a sense this chapter forms the hard core of this Part as it contains all basic elements for the appraisal of foreign investment proposals in a schematic form. The major purpose of this chapter is to provide practical guidelines for the appraisal of private foreign investment projects, which could be of use also to the non-economist responsible for project evaluation.

Chapter VI introduces a limited number of refinements and complications to be taken into account in applying the scheme presented in Chapter V.

Finally in Chapter VII some remarks are made on the role social cost-benefit-analysis can play as an aid in negotiations with foreign investors.

CHAPTER II

PRINCIPLES OF SOCIAL COST-BENEFIT ANALYSIS

2.1. INTRODUCTION

Cost-benefit analysis can best be defined as a method aiming at providing criteria for ensuring the most economic use of scarce resources in selecting investment projects. In other words, it is a method for appraising proposed investment activities in such a way that no projects are approved unless the analysis shows that the benefits of the project surpass the costs. In the case of projects which are competing, in the sense that for whatever reason they cannot all be executed, cost-benefit analysis is in addition to give criteria for ensuring that only the most profitable propositions are approved.

The problem of investment selections can be approached from a commercial point, in which case one generally speaks about private profitability, or it can be approached from a national economic point, in which case the term social cost-benefit analysis is generally used. Our concern will be with establishing rules for measuring the national economic or social profitability of intended investment activities; consequently we deal with social cost-benefit analysis. The major reason why differences between commercial and social profitability may be expected are briefly discussed in Section 2.3.

Of course, the aim of ensuring the most economic use of scarce resources is not limited to the problem of selecting individual investment projects. Indeed it is the central problem in economics, and the *raison d'être* for planning. However, whereas the broad outlines of economic policy can be formulated at a macro-economic level of analysis, in the end the outlines of economic policy have to be translated into action, which in most cases takes place at a project level. It is for this reason, and also because at a project level more detailed analysis is possible than at a macro-economic level, that project appraisal should play an important role in preparing investment decisions.

Although its origins can be traced back to the 19th century, to be precise to 1844 when Dupuit's famous article appeared[1], cost-benefit analysis as a

1 Jules Dupuit, 'On the Measurement of the Utility of Public Works', first published in *Annales des Ponts et Chaussées*, Sér. 2, No. 8, 1844; English translation in International Economic Papers, No. 2, London 1952.

subject in economics is of recent origin. Its first applications were in the U.S.A. in the 1930's, where as a consequence of the expansion of public investment activity, especially in the field of water-resources development, the need was felt to ensure that of the investment proposals 'the benefits to whomsoever they may accrue (be) in excess of the estimated costs'[2]. This requirement added an economic appraisal of investment proposals to the already existing technical studies, in other words, it required the introduction of cost-benefit analysis. After World War II, cost-benefit analysis was increasingly applied not only in the U.S.A., but also elsewhere. In particular the IBRD contributed significantly to the spread of cost-benefit analysis in developing countries through its requirement that no projects were to be financed with their assistance unless an economic appraisal of the proposed project indicated its economic soundness.

As is often the case in economics, crude practical applications of cost-benefit analysis were made in advance of the availability of a thorough theoretical framework. It is only in the late fifties and especially in the 1960's that cost-benefit analysis attracted the attention of economic theory, as can be witnessed from the literature[3]. Most of these contributions to the subject were concerned with separate aspects of project appraisal, rather than with cost-benefit analysis in a complete sense. It is only in the last few years that publications covering the complete area have appeared; foremost amongst these are the *Manual of Industrial Project Analysis* of the OECD[4], and the UNIDO *Guidelines for Project Evaluation*[5].

The remarks made in the preceding paragraph, sketchy as they are, indicate that cost-benefit analysis is not only a relatively new subject in economics, but also that the subject is still very much in a stage of development. It should not come as a surprise, therefore, that as yet there is no general

2 The quotation is from the U.S.A. Flood Control Act of 1936 as cited in Stephen A. Marglin, *Public Investment Criteria*, London 1967.

3 Surveys of the recent literature can be found in A. R. Prest and R. Turvey, 'Cost-Benefit Analysis: A Survey', in A.E.A.: *Surveys of Economic Theory, Vol. III*, New York 1966; A. C. Harberger, 'Survey of Literature on Cost-Benefit Analysis', in *Evaluation of Industrial Projects*, UNIDO Sales, No. 67IIB.23, New York 1968 and P. D. Henderson, 'Investment Criteria for Public Enterprises', in R. Turvey (ed.), *Public Enterprise*, Penguin Modern Economics Readings, 1968. Detailed references to the literature can also be found in A. K. Sen, General Criteria for Industrial Project Evaluation', in *Evaluation of Industrial Projects*, UNIDO Sales, No. 67IIB.23, New York 1968.

4 Ian M. D. Little and James A. Mirrlees, *Manual of Industrial Project-Analysis in Developing Countries, Vol. II, Social Cost Benefit Analysis*, OECD Development Centre, Paris 1968.

5 UNIDO, *Guidelines for Project Evaluation*, United Nations, New York 1972.

standard methodology for cost-benefit analysis. Indeed, it is one of the major problems in social cost-benefit analysis that views and opinions of different authors differ on various aspects of social cost-benefit analysis and that consequently, because of different approaches, different authors may easily arrive at different conclusions. One of the major aims of the present chapter is, therefore, to provide a basic framework for the application of social cost-benefit analysis in which the assumptions made are exposed explicitly, in order to ensure that the methodology is at least a consistent one. The price to be paid for this, however, is that it becomes impossible in this part of the study to do full justice to the many and often important contributions made on the topic by a large number of authors. To this extent the contents of the present chapter no doubt contains a large number of arbitrary decisions.

There is another reason for being forced to treat the subject of cost-benefit analysis, at least in this context, in an arbitrary way. This reason is that social cost-benefit analysis tends to become, if treated with theoretical thoroughness, a highly complicated affair. Indeed, theoretical rigour would lead to a methodology of such a complicated character that an application of the theory in practical situations becomes next to impossible. Work on cost-benefit analysis concentrating on practical decision rules, on the other hand, may also be unsatisfactory, as in such a procedure not sufficient attention is sometimes given to economic analysis. In the end social cost-benefit analysis remains an art, in which the quality is determined by the proper mix of theoretical rigour and practical usefulness.

The present chapter aims at giving – in a nutshell – a description of social cost-benefit analysis which compromises between theory and practice; although the treatment given to the subject is theoretically, at least so it is intended, correct, major emphasis is in practical usefulness. Of course, this can only be obtained by giving up a considerable degree of refinement. The framework for social cost-benefit analysis presented here can correctly be described as a simple and rather straightforward approach which does not contain more than the basic elements of the method. In addition project appraisal in this context refers only to those projects which generate goods and services which can be sold in the market, leaving out infrastructure, education, health and other sectors producing public goods. The reason for this limitation is that social cost-benefit analysis in the context of this paper is introduced as a means of appraising investment proposals by private foreign firms, which typically invest in projects which generate goods and services to be sold in the market, either domestically or abroad.

In addition to the reason presented in the last paragraph for not aiming at a detailed and sophisticated survey of the fine points of social cost-benefit analysis, there is another reason for giving only the main outlines of social cost-benefit analysis. This reason has to do with the fact that the special characteristics of private foreign investment lead to a number of special complications in setting up a scheme for project appraisal. If, also for the conventional social cost-benefit approach sophisticated methods were applied, the combination of the two aspects would lead to unmanageable formulations for practical application. Since it is felt that developing countries are better off with simple methods which can be applied than with refined methods which cannot be applied, a determined effort was made to restrict the subject to main lines only.

2.2. WHAT HAPPENS IF A PROJECT IS EXECUTED ?

In this section we shall briefly review what happens if a project is executed, mainly in order to illustrate the factors to be taken into account by the criterion to be applied in project appraisal. In giving this summary review we omit those aspects which have to do with the preparation of projects; it is assumed that apart from the economic evaluation the project is ready for implementation. We also disregard, as a simplification, the existence of direct as well as indirect taxes. The justification for this omission is that taxes, although relevant for a private economic analysis, are generally not relevant for a national economic appraisal of investment projects.

The life of an investment project typically starts with a period in which almost exclusive attention is given to the formation of productive capacity. Characteristic for this period, to be called the *investment or construction* period, is that major emphasis is given to the procurement of machinery and other equipment, either from domestic producers or throught imports, to construction activity and to the procurement of land as a site for the project. Towards the end of the investment period there is typically a shift in the investment pattern in that stocks of raw materials and other supplies are bought, and labour is attracted and trained for work in the *operation period*. Throughout this period investment funds are required for financing the purchases made. These investment funds may become available either in foreign savings, in the form of foreign aid, or through domestic savings, in which latter case the savings may accrue at the expense of reduced consumption or at the cost of alternative investment opportunities. During the investment period there may also be some form of return on the investments made, e.g. a particular part of the project may already be in operation and generate revenue. But apart from this possibility, what happens is that during this period the total investment activities require expenses which are made with the idea of recovering them during the period that the project produces goods and services for the market. Note that the term expenses here covers both financial costs to the firm and national economic costs in the sense that during the investment period the project puts a claim on scarce resources, savings, foreign exchange, labour and land, which in the absence of the project could have been utilized for other purposes.

In the second stage the project starts producing output to be sold on the market. Normally one would expect that at the beginning the output is well below rated capacity, but increasing rapidly to a level which is in accordance with full capacity utilization. In this period the gross benefits of the project dominate the picture. These benefits consist of the value of sales in the case of a private analysis. For a socio-economic appraisal sales may, as will be discussed in the next section, not be the appropriate yardstick. Nevertheless, also here output is to be treated as the gross benefit, as it makes available, directly or indirectly, scarce resources for additional consumption and investment.

In order to reap these benefits costs have to be incurred for the procurement of raw materials and other supplies, energy, transportation facilities and for covering labour expenditure and sales expenditure. These costs have to be deducted from the gross benefits in order to obtain the net benefits of the project in a given year. If the project is a sound one the net benefits in a given year will normally be positive. In some years they may be negative because of major repairs and renewal of equipment. There are, for viable projects, exceptions only, however.

So far we have not paid attention to the time period over which benefits accrue. There is, of course, no fixed operation period for investment projects in general. This will differ from project to project. In certain sectors capital equipment may not have a long life as it becomes obsolete due to technical progress, for other industries the life of the project will depend on the technical wear and tear, whereas for still other projects the operation period will depend on the time in which mineral resources are depleted. Not only will the operation period differ from project to project, it is also difficult to estimate for each individual project. The uncertainty in estimating the life of a project has sometimes given rise to the practice of adding depreciation allowances to the operation costs of a project, and treating the life of the project as infinite, by tactfully assuming that depreciation allowances are immediately reinvested in the project. This practice is not correct, since depreciation allowances are determined for fiscal reasons only and do not show very much of a relationship with the expected lifetime of a project. As such, giving projects an infinite life through the gimmick of deducting depreciation allowances is harmful rather than helpful in tracing the effects of a project over time. There would seem to be no alternative but to estimate the time period over which benefits accrue as carefully as possible, even if this means that uncertainty plays a significant role.

Finally a word should be said about what happens at the end of the operation period. Sometimes the answer may be that nothing happens after the end of the operations period. This is not the general case, however. In general one may expect that at the end of the operation period some equipment used in the project still can be sold, either for use elsewhere or for scrap. Buildings still have a residual value, and land can be sold. These final sales are additional benefits of the project, and consequently have to be accounted for in the appraisal. Not always, however, does the final stage of a project gives rise to benefits; in some cases the closing down of an enterprise may lead to negative benefits, e.g. in mining if pits have to be filled and closed.

Having discussed in a summary fashion what happens if a project is executed, there remains, even if we have perfect knowledge of costs and benefits in future years, the very important question of how to compare the benefits and costs at different periods in such a way that a judgment can be made as to the desirability of the proposed project. Simply adding all the benefits of the project gives rise to benefits; in some cases the closing down of an enterprise a decision, but this method is hardly defensible, since it implies that we attach an equal weight to benefits independent of whether they occur this year or in the far away future. Since such an implication is not acceptable, another criterion, not showing these shortcomings, for the appraisal of investment projects has to be developed.

A criterion often applied, especially by private enterprises, is the so-called *recoupment period* or *pay-out period*. In its simplest version this criterion estimates the number of years which are needed to earn back, in the form of net benefits, the investment outlays made for the project. Applying this criterion, the decision rule is: choose from all potential projects those which show the shortest recoupment period. Under certain very specific circumstances this decision rule may give the correct answers. In general, however, the criterion is inadequate, in particular since it gives no weight to benefits accruing after the recoupment period.

A criterion which does not have these shortcomings is the *present value* criterion, in which all future benefits and costs are converted through discounting into comparable units. In formula form the criterion is:

$$PV = \sum_{t=1}^{T} \frac{B_t - C_t}{(1 + i)^t}$$

where:

PV = present value of the future of net benefits
B_t = benefits accruing in period t
C_t = costs incurred in period t
i = the discount rate
T = the economic life of the project.

The decision rule for this criterion is: given the rate of discount i execute all projects with a positive present value. The problem with this criterion is, of course, the determination of the discount rate, which is, as will be discussed in Section 2.4, not at all an easy affair. It is for this reason that it is sometimes suggested to change the criterion into the *internal rate of return* criterion. For this criterion the essence is that that discount rate has to be determined for which PV is zero. The decision rule then becomes: from all possible projects choose those projects with the highest internal rate of return.

This criterion, although often applied, has a number of shortcomings which make it less appropriate than the PV criterion. Objections raised to the internal rate of return criterion, are the possibility of the formula having multiple roots, the fact that the criterion is not able to take into account the absolute value of the net benefits, and, less often heard but perhaps the most important shortcoming, that the criterion implicitly assumes that all benefits are immediately reinvested against a rate of return equal to the internal rate of return.

The question of internal rate of return vs present value has been discussed at considerable length in the literature on cost-benefit analysis, generally showing that the present value formula is to be preferred[6]. In what follows the present value criterion is accepted as the appropriate criterion. The question of defining and measuring benefits and costs is dealt with in Sections 2.4 and 2.5. Before turning to these subjects, the question of social vs private profitability is discussed in Section 2.3.

2.3. SOCIAL VS COMMERCIAL PROFITABILITY OF INVESTMENT PROJECTS

The aim of this section is to give, as an introduction to the discussion on

6 For a clear exposition see: Ronald N. McKean, *Efficiency in Government through Systems Analysis*, New York, no date.

national economic benefits and their measurement in Section 2.4 and 2.5, an exposition of the reasons why the commercial attractiveness of a project may be expected to be different from its national economic attractiveness. As will be seen, there are good reasons for expecting that there is a divergence between national and commercial profitability, which does not mean, however, that the two yardsticks of profitability are always incompatible. A very basic reason for expecting the social profitability of a project to be different from its commercial profitability is a difference in the concept of benefits. In commercial analysis the benefits of a project are expressed in terms of profits. For social cost-benefit analysis profits are not the ultimate aim. Here what is of relevance for the appraisal of an investment project is the contribution the project is making to the aims of economic policy, as they are expressed in, for instance, the development plan. In other words, the national economic benefits of a project have to be expressed in terms of the aims of economic policy. such as, an increase in GNP, a more equal income distribution *etc.* The question of national economic benefits is discussed in Section 2.4. At this place we shall limit our attention to only one of the aims of economic policy, an increase in GNP, and ask the question whether there is a difference in profitability measured in terms of profits and profitability measured in terms of contribution to GNP.

In classical economic theory it is assumed that there is no such difference, and consequently that by maximizing profits one also maximizes the contribution to GNP. This is a correct assumption provided a number of specific conditions are fulfilled. These conditions are:

(1) perfect competition on all markets;
(2) the absence of external effects;
(3) all goods and services can be sold in the market (no public goods).

In a real world the strict conditions necessary for making profit maximization equal to income maximization are not fulfilled.

First of all, the assumption of perfect competition in alle markets is not realistic. Both in the prices for factors of production and in the prices for goods and services distortions do occur, which make the market prices an insufficient indication of the real scarcities. Examples of these distortions are not difficult to find. In the case of structural unemployment the market price for unskilled labour does not reflect the marginal productivity of labour. The market price for capital, the interest rate, is often determined by other factors than the scarcity of capital. Countries with severe balance of payments problems may ration foreign exchange by means of government interference in the foreign exchange market, leading to foreign exchange rates different from those which would prevail in a situation of full competition. As a consequence of the price distortions for factors of production the market prices for goods and services will not reflect real scarcities. In addition there will be further price distortions because of indirect taxes and subsidies, monopolistic tendencies and restrictive practices.

In the second place external effects do play a role and also because of this reason private profitability is not an adequate yardstick for social profitability.

In the third place a number of goods and services do not have a market price, because they are public goods, meaning that the consumption by one economic subject does not affect the consumption of others. Examples are highways, traffic control and radio broadcasting. As an output these public goods are not relevant in our context, since we explicitly restrict the discussion to the evaluation of projects which produce goods and services which are to be sold in the market. They are of importance, however, in our context to the extent that these public goods are inputs for the project to be appraised as in that case the social cost of providing the public good is not reflected in the commercial costs of production and for that reason leads to differences between commercial and social profitability.

From what was said in the paragraphs above, it is rather obvious that commercial profitability is a poor indication of social profitability, even if there is just one aim of economic policy, an increase in GNP. The differences between social and commercial profitability will even become larger if more aims of economic policy, and thus more types of benefits, are taken into account. This does not mean that a commercial appraisal of investment projects is of no value. Indeed, it may be very useful to have a commercial analysis in addition to a social analysis as this enables the policy maker to see whether a project which is socially profitable is also commercially profitable, and, if not, which steps the government could take to make it commercially attractive. This latter may be essential if the project is to be undertaken in the private sector.

2.4. SOCIAL BENEFITS AND COSTS

In commercial cost-benefit analysis the question of what are benefits is a simple one. Since the basic objective of the firm is to maximize profits, net benefits of a project are to be expressed in terms of profits. In the case of national economic analysis this matter is more complex. One then has to refer to the national economic objectives as reflected in the economic policy of the country concerned. Often these objectives are stated explicitly in for instance the development plan. Benefits in a national economic sense can then be defined as contributions to the objectives of economic policy. Not all objectives need to be relevant for the purpose of social cost-benefit analysis, however. There is the possibility that one or more of the so-called objectives of economic policy, is in reality a derived aim or an instrument for realizing the more basic aims of economic policy. There is also the possibility that basic aims may not be relevant for social cost-benefit analysis as individual projects do not influence the realization of these aims. An example is the aim of price stability, which is no doubt a fundamental aim but need not be taken into account as the rate of inflation does not depend on the selection of individual projects, but on the macro-economic management of the economy.

Taking these limitations into account the following five potential benefits can be distinguished:

(1) Consumption or income benefits;
(2) Contributions to a better income distribution;
(3) Employment benefits;
(4) Merit want benefits;
(5) Contributions to the aim of a higher degree of selfsufficiency.

These five benefits need not apply in all circumstances. Whether they apply in a particular country depends on what policy makers deem important. Moreover, it can be argued that certain aims are not desired for their own sake, but because of the contribution they give to other aims. This is for instance frequently argued in the case of employment benefits, as will be discussed below.

Ad 1: Consumption or Income Benefits

The major aim of economic policy in almost all cases is framed as a maximum increase in GNP. This objective, however, is not pursued for its own sake, but in order to better satisfy the more fundamental aim of increasing consumption levels. As such the proper benefit to be taken into account in social cost-benefit analysis should be the contribution of a project to consumption. This is indeed what one finds in most of the literature[7]. The question of whether to measure benefits in terms of contributions to consumption or in

7 At first glance Little and Mirrlees would seem to deviate from this general principle, since they express benefits in terms of savings. Since savings are maximized in order to maximize consumption over time, however, also in their method the ultimate benefits are consumption benefits. What they do is to express increases in consumption in terms of savings, whereas most other authors express savings in terms of consumption. Consequently there is in this respect no fundamental difference between the OECD *Manual* and for instance the UNIDO *Guidelines*.

terms of increases in GNP arises because of the sub-optimal level of savings in developing countries. Because of this factor it is felt that savings out of additional income are more valuable than consumption out of additional income, and that consequently a higher weight is to be attached to the former. No doubt a strong case can be made for the argument that in a situation where savings are a real bottleneck for development, savings should be given a higher weight than consumption and that consequently benefits should be expressed either in savings or in consumption, meaning that GNP is not the appropriate yardstick. Nevertheless, one may have doubts as to whether this should be taken into account at a project level. These doubts may arise for theoretical as well as practical reasons. At a theoretical level one may question whether it is correct to use project appraisal as an instrument to pursue the macro-economic aim of increasing national savings, or whether it would not be better to use macro-economic instruments for this, such as tax devices. This latter alternative would seem to be more correct, and therefore is to be preferred[8]. In addition there are some other reasons for preferring contributions to GNP to contributions to consumption as a yardstick for expressing the benefits of a project. Firstly, applying consumption as a yardstick means that a weight has to be given to savings in order to express savings in terms of consumption. This giving of weights unavoidably leads to value judgments since there are no objective ways of finding the appropriate weights, and although value judgments do play an important role in social cost-benefit analysis, there is some merit in restricting the impact of subjective value judgments to minimal proportions. In the second place there is the question of measurement of savings and consumption out of the income created by a project. This is difficult enough if all market prices reflect equilibrium prices, as one has to trace which social groups, or even persons, benefit from the income generated by a project. If market prices are not a fair indication of real scarcity value, it becomes almost impossible to estimate which part of the income generated by the project is consumed and which part is saved, as the income generated will be measured at accounting prices, whereas consumption and savings decisions are determined by the income

8 Whereas there is little disagreement on this point, some authors strongly feel that macro-economic instruments to raise the level of savings have thus far not been very effective, and therefore suggest that project appraisal be used as an instrument for raising savings. See for instance S. Marglin, *Public Investment Criteria*, p. 51. Although the experience of the last 20 years undoubtedly indicates that a rapid increase in the savings ratio is difficult to achieve by means of macro-economic instruments, there is no evidence that it is impossible. Moreover, also in those countries where it was attempted to increase savings mainly by means appropriate at a project level, often in the form of maximizing profits in the private sector, the achievements were not all that evident.

accruing in the form of profits, wages and taxes at market prices. To translate the one into the other is an extremely complex affair, and may well be impossible for practical work[9].

For the above mentioned reasons we prefer to use the contribution to GNP as a yardstick for measuring the benefits of a project. This is what will be done in this paper, acknowledging, however, that the contribution to GNP has to be considered as a proxy for the contribution to consumption. From a theoretical point this procedure is correct only if,

(a) the savings rate can be influenced through macro-economic policy measures, or

(b) savings are at an optimal level.

Ad 2: Contributions to a Better Income Distribution

Under a better income distribution one has to understand a more equal income distribution, either in a personal sense, or in a regional sense. The rationale for including the aim of a more equal income distribution in the aims of economic policy is that the utility of an additional unit of income is not independent of the absolute income level. For a poor person an addition to income of, say Rs 10, has a higher value than the same increase in income for a rich person. Government objectives normally reflect this by stating that it intends to follow policies leading to a more equal income distribution. The same reasoning applies to regional income distribution, where a higher value may be given to income creation in backward regions.

It is not an easy task to find the appropriate weights to be given to the aim of a more equal income distribution. As elsewhere in socio-economic project analysis, value judgments are involved. This is not the domain of the economist; decisions involving value judgments have to be taken by policy makers. All the project analyst can do, and should do, is to make sure that policy makers take the relevant decisions explicitly, and are aware of the implications of the decision taken. Once this is done the economist can take the decision into account by attaching different weights to the incomes of different groups[10].

9 The literature is not very precise on this matter. Quite often no attention at all is given to the problems involved. An exception to this general rule is to be found in the UNIDO *Guidelines*, where an effort is made to carry out the required calculations.

10 It may, of course, also be decided to pursue the aim of a more equal income distribution by other means, e.g. transfer payments. In that case social cost-benefit analysis does not have to take income distribution aims into account.

Ad 3: Employment Benefits

In the literature no consensus exists as to whether employment benefits are to be included as a special item in the list of benefits to be taken into account in project appraisal. Those who are opposed to the inclusion of employment benefits reason that employment is not an end in itself, but an instrument for realizing the income benefits and the income distribution benefits. Others argue that employment is an aim of economic policy by itself.

No doubt, the employment issue is interrelated with the objectives of a higher income and a better income distribution. On the other hand, it can at least be argued that more employment, even apart from its effects on income and income distribution, is a good thing in itself. This may be argued by a government, it may also be argued by individuals. Assuming that the income and income distribution aims could also be realized without additional employment, the question of whether employment should be treated as a separate aim depends to a large extent on subjective matters. If to be without employment is to be translated by 'having leisure time', then employment should not be treated as a separate aim. If, on the other hand, unemployment implies that persons willing to work are not able to find employment, the picture changes. In that case, employment has to be added to the list of benefits.

It is, of course, impossible to reach an easy consensus on the social implications of unemployment, certainly among economists. Nor is this necessary. Much more important than the opinions held by the project analyst is the judgment of the policy maker, whose judgment will in the end decide whether the aim of employment is relevant for project evaluation.

Ad 4: Merit Want Benefits

Policy makers may attach specific values to particular goods and services, arguing that these items are from a social point of view more valuable than their prices indicate. This is what is generally called the merit want argument. The argument is not in all cases a correct one, and on occasion may even be put forward as a simple way to justify non-profitable projects. Merit want arguments should therefore not be too easily accepted. In a number of cases, however, the argument may be correct. Education, for instance, may be more valuable to society than is reflected in the costs of providing it, even if cost data are corrected for market imperfections.

Merit wants are often mentioned in relation with food. The typical argument here is that since malnutrition is to be removed, special value has to be attached to food production, over and above market prices, in order to stipulate the high importance of providing a better diet. In this case the argument would not seem to be correct since food items can, if necessary, be imported. Production decisions should not be based on consumption patterns alone, but should also take into account comparative advantages. If, as an illustration, it is more profitable to produce tobacco than to produce cereals, tobacco can be produced for export and cereals can be imported.

Ad 5: Contributions to the Aim of a Higher Degree of Self-Sufficiency

If this aim means autarchy, then it cannot be justified. Normally, however, what is meant is balance of payments equilibrium. Although policy objectives often include aims related to the balance of payments, these objectives should be treated as constraints rather than as separate aims. Moreover, the balance of payments does not depend on the choice of individual projects, but on macro-economic policy with regard to savings and investment. Provided benefits and costs are measured correctly, a scheme for social cost-benefit analysis leads, given the investment volume, by means of the income benefits, to the right decision with respect to the balance of payments.

The Combination of Benefits

With the given list of potential benefits to be taken into account, the question arises of how to combine these benefits in such a way that they can be brought under a single *numéraire.* For practical work, what should be done is to ask the policy makers what weight they give to one type of benefits in terms of another benefit. In other words, the question is how much income policy makers are willing to give up in order to provide e.g. one more unit of employment. For other benefits the same procedure should be applied, which then leads to a situation where all aims are expressed in terms of increases in GNP, and consequently can be added up. It should perhaps be stressed that the combination of benefits is theoretically a much more complex affair than it would appear at first sight, especially because of the problem that the subjective weights given to different benefits may differ from the possibilities for the transformation of one type of benefit into another.[11] In the present summary we shall not tackle this problem, as this would involve a theoretical discussion of considerable complexity.

National Economic Costs

Having given a rather detailed discussion of national economic benefits, the discussion on national economic costs can be very short indeed. National

11 The problems involved are presented clearly in Stephen M. Marglin, *Public Investment Criteria*, p. 23–39.

economic costs are basically negative contributions to the aims of economic policy. In other words, benefits foregone because of the project. This refers to operating as well as investment costs, the idea being that without the project the expenditure items would have been available for satisfying, for instance, consumption demand.

2.5. THE MEASUREMENT OF BENEFITS AND COSTS

As was discussed in Section 2.3 there are good reasons to expect that market prices for goods and services are not a correct indication of real scarcity, and consequently corrections have to be made in this respect.

For this correction procedure two basic alternatives are available. The first is to express all inputs and outputs in terms of domestic consumption benefits. This is the procedure proposed by Sen [12], Marglin [13] and the UNIDO *Guidelines* [14]. The method implies that benefits and costs have to be measured at those prices which consumers would be willing to pay. This willingness to pay includes the consumers' surplus, which may lead to severe problems of measurement, since for measuring 'willingness to pay' knowledge about the demand curves is required.

The second alternative expresses all inputs and outputs in international prices, the argument being that directly or indirectly the execution of a project affects foreign trade. This alternative is the one applied by Little and Mirrlees. [15] Which of these two alternatives is the appropriate one depends on the assumptions made concerning economic policy. If it is assumed that the government pursues a rational economic policy, then the Little and Mirrlees approach is appropriate. If it is assumed, as is done explicitly in the UNIDO *Guidelines*, that because of pressure groups and other reasons, the government is not able to pursue rational economic polices, then the first alternative, to measure benefits in terms of willingness to pay, is more appropriate. Even in this case, however, practical applicability of the proposed procedure is limited because of severe problems in estimating demand curves.

Here, it is assumed that the government follows a rational economic policy, which implies that benefits and costs are to be measured in international prices. How this is to be done precisely will not be discussed here, as a clear

12 A. K. Sen, 'General Criteria for Project Appraisal', in *Evaluation of Industrial Projects*,, UNIDO, New York 1968.

13 S. A. Marglin, *Public Investment Criteria*, London, 1967.

14 UNIDO, *Guidelines for Project Evaluation*, United Nations, New York 1972.

15 I. M. D. Little and J. Mirrlees, *Manual of Industrial Project Analysis, Vol. II, Social Cost Benefit Analysis*, Paris 1968.

exposition of the procedure is given in Little and Mirrlees [16]. A few remarks on the principles may be required, however.

To be able to express goods and services in international prices requires first of all that there is an international price for the goods concerned. Whereas this is the case for many products, it is not true of all goods and services. Certain commodities, e.g. dwellings, electricity etc., cannot be obtained through importing. A distinction should, therefore, be made between goods and services which can participate in international trade, to be called *international* goods and services, and goods and services for which this is not the case, such as construction, electricity, many retail services, to be called *national* goods and services [17].

For international goods and services no severe problems arise; they can be expressed in either c.i.f. prices, if the commodity concerned is imported, or is an import substitute, or at f.o.b. prices if export is relevant. In certain cases complications may arise, but also these can be solved in a relatively simple way.

More severe problems arise in the case of national goods and services, as for this category no international prices are available. However, the problem can be solved as national goods and services can be broken down in terms of inputs of international goods and services, payment for capital services and labour costs. In principle the appropriate shadow price for national goods and services can then be calculated from a present value formula, for producing the national goods concerned, in which the present value is put at zero, all inputs are known as well as the discount rate, and where the unknown is the value of the output. This type of procedure assumes, correctly if a rational economic policy is pursued, that with a given discount rate the capacity in national goods industries is expanded up to the point where the present value of a further increase in production becomes negative.

The procedure is no doubt a cumbersome one, the more so as for the production of national goods and services also inputs of other national industries may be required, which necessitates the simultaneous solution of a system of (present value) equations. On the other hand this needs only to be done for the more important national inputs, and need not be done separately for individual projects, as shadow prices for national goods can, and should

16 Little and Mirrlees, *op. cit.*, Chapter 12.

17 Little and Mirrlees use the terms 'trade' and 'non-trade' which are defined in nearly the same way as the terms 'international' and 'national', the difference being that our term 'international' all goods and services which *can* participate in international trade, whereas 'traded' refers to goods and services which *are* imported or exported or *should* be imported or exported.

be, determined by central authorities. For inputs from national industries which are of minor importance only, Little and Mirrlees suggest a shortcut in the form of a Standard Conversion Factor, based on the average ratio of world prices to domestic prices for a representative selection of commodities.

2.6. THE DISCOUNT RATE

In project appraisal few things are as important as the choice of the discount rate. As will be obvious, the present value of a project will be severely influenced by the magnitude of the discount rate. Not only will a higher rate of discount lead to a decrease in present value, but it will also give a bias against projects with long economic lives or long gestation periods. It is therefore of the utmost importance that the discount rate is selected with great care.

Unfortunately very little agreement exists on the question of the appropriate discount rate. As space does not allow a complete discussion of this aspect of project appraisal, the discussion in this paper is limited to the major proposals only.

One proposal concerning the choice of discount rate is that in social cost-benefit analysis prevailing interest rates, e.g. the bond rate, should be applied. An advantage of applying the bond rate is that it is known, but against this advantage there is the serious disadvantage that market rates of interest are not determined by real scarcity of capital, as the interest rate is at least partly determined by institutional factors. Also, the bond rate does not reflect intertemporal consumption preferences, the major reason for this being that savings do have external effects, in the sense that also persons other than those who save benefit, via the increase in GNP, from the savings. In other words, individual savings decisions do not reflect benefits for the community as a whole. For these reasons the bond rate is to be rejected as a discount rate for project appraisal.

An alternative for the bond rate is the social discount rate, reflecting in the words of *Marglin* "the intertemporal consumption preferences that the government holds as a proxy for the public" [18]. This rate is determined by two factors: pure time preference and secondly the declining marginal utility of consumption with increasing per capita income.

A problem with this yardstick for the discount rate is that it cannot be measured, and that consequently its magnitude depends on the value judgment of the policy maker. Although this is a disadvantage, this would not be a sufficient reason for rejecting the social discount rate as the discount rate to

18 S. A. Marglin, *op. cit.*, p. 53.

be applied in social cost-benefit analysis. There are, however, other reasons why the social discount rate is less relevant. This can best be seen by making explicit the assumption underlying the social discount rate. This assumption is that investments are financed through a reduction in consumption. To the extent that this assumption holds, that is to the extent that an increase in investment expenditure is financed through an equal decline in consumption expenditure, the social discount rate is the appropriate discount rate. In that case all investment projects showing a positive present value can be executed, which latter assumes that national savings are optimal.

In reality savings are suboptimal, which means that at least part of the proposed projects have to be financed at the cost of other possible projects, leading to budget constraints which cannot be properly taken into account in this approach.

This leads to a third, and in our opinion correct way of approaching the problem of fixing the discount rate. This is the 'opportunity cost approach', indicating the marginal social productivity of capital. In the literature this approach is often referred to as the 'social rate of return on private investment'. This restriction is not completely correct; what is important is the social rate of return on *alternative* investment either in the private or in the public sector. The whole distinction may even be of little relevance anyway, as one should expect, under the assumption of a rational economic policy, that the marginal social rate of return in the public sector equals the marginal social rate of return in the private sector. Where this is not the case investment funds should be reallocated between the two sectors.

This approach to the discount rate assumes that the volume of savings available for investment is fixed, which although not necessarily completely correct, is a reasonable assumption for any given period. It is also in agreement with the assumption made earlier that the government applies macroeconomic instruments for fixing the level of savings. Under those circumstances the discount rate should be such that the total amount of investment required for executing projects with a positive present value equals the total availability of savings. The discount rate, in other words, ensures that demand equals supply. [19] No special attention has to be paid to budget constraints.

The estimation of the discount rate reflecting the opportunity cost, is in principle a matter of trial and error. Starting from an arbitrary discount rate one may find that more projects are showing positive present values than is permissible from the point of available savings. This means that an upward

19 If an increase in GNP is the only aim, the discount rate also ensures that the total of the projects selected gives the best position of the balance of payments.

revision of the discount rate is required, which may again lead to inequality between savings and investment, and consequently to a further revision of the discount rate. This procedure should be continued until available savings are just sufficient for financing all projects with a positive present value.

2.7. THE SHADOW PRICE FOR UNSKILLED LABOUR

So far no attention was paid to the accounting price for unskilled labour. As is well known, in a situation of structural unemployment as is characteristic for most developing countries, market wages do not reflect the true opportunity costs of labour. It has, therefore, been widely suggested that for unskilled labour an accounting price be applied reflecting the marginal productivity of labour, which may, under conditions of severe unemployment, be approached zero. This suggestion has been criticized to a considerable extent, mainly because consumption out of wage income is higher than consumption out of non-wage income. Since savings are more valuable than consumption, so the argument goes, this should be reflected in the accounting price for labour, which should therefore be higher than its marginal productivity. As this type of argument implies that project selection is also used as an instrument for raising the level of savings we need not go into this type of argument. As we have explicitly assumed that macro-economic instruments are used for raising the level of savings, the arguments used are not relevant in our case, which brings us back to the position that the accounting price for unskilled labour should reflect the marginal productivity of labour.

CHAPTER III

BASIC CHARACTERISTICS OF PRIVATE FOREIGN INVESTMENT PROJECTS AS DISTINCT FROM DOMESTIC INVESTMENT PROJECTS

3.1. INTRODUCTION

In this chapter a summary is given of the basic characteristics of private foreign investment projects as distinct from domestic investment projects. Here a distinction is required between what happens to a project in a physical sense and the impact of the financing mechanism on the profitability of the project. This latter aspect is of crucial importance in the case of foreign investment projects. What happens in a physical sense if a project is undertaken was described in Section 2.2. In this respect private foreign investment projects show the same pattern. In the investment period almost exclusive attention is given to the creation of productive capacity, with major emphasis on the procurement of machinery and other equipment, procurement of land as a site for the project and on construction activity. In a second stage, the operation period, investment activity ceases and is replaced by utilizing the capacity created for production processes. In this sense foreign-owned investment projects do not differ from domestically-owned projects.

What is different is the way of financing the project, as in the case of private foreign investment all or part of the financial means necessary for the project execution is financed from abroad, and to the extent that this occurs does not lay a claim on scarce domestic resources. In the operation period, however, the foreign investor is entitled to all or part of profits made and to the extent that this is the case the national economic profitability of the project is reduced.

In Section 3.2 a survey is presented of the impact of foreign financing of investment projects, assuming that all investment funds are supplied by the foreign parent company. In Section 3.3 this assumption is released by allowing for domestic financial participation in the project in the form of equity capital (joint ventures) as well as domestic borrowing. Section 3.4 deals with the question of alternatives to a foreign investment project. Finally in Section 3.5 four basic cases depicting the impact of foreign financing of an investment project are presented.

3.2. THE IMPACT OF FOREIGN FINANCING

In Section 2.2 the physical aspects of the execution of an investment project were described. Making a distinction between the investment period and the operation period it was noted that in the former period expenses are incurred for procurement of land, payment for construction activity, the procurement of machinery and other equipment, and towards the end of the investment period for obtaining stocks of raw material and other supplies, as well as for attracting and training of labour. All these expenses can be treated as investment costs, either directly at market prices if these market prices reflect real scarcities of factors of production, or if this is not the case at accounting prices determined in the way described in Section 2.5.

During the operation period the picture may be expected to be different, in the sense that benefits exceed costs. Benefits can be calculated from sales of the project priced at accounting prices, and costs of production as value of inputs at accounting prices used in the production process. Deduction of costs from benefits gives the contribution to GNP in any particular year.

In case of a private foreign investment project fully financed from abroad a different picture arises. Assume that all prices reflect real scarcity, and that consequently market prices do not deviate from accounting prices. In that case the impact of financing from abroad is relatively simple to describe.

During the investment period the foreign firm supplies all the necessary investment resources needed to realize the project and consequently does not lay a claim on scarce domestic resources expressed in terms of investment outlays. Part of the investment funds of the private foreign investor will be required for obtaining equipment, machinery and other supplies from abroad, and to the extent that this is the case also no claim will be laid on scarce domestic resources in a physical sense. Another part of the investment resources will be utilized for obtaining domestic physical resources, such as land, construction materials, labour and perhaps domestic machinery, etc.

Since, however, it is assumed that market prices reflect real scarcities, payments made by the foreign investor for these scarce domestic resources will be just sufficient for covering the loss of domestic resources because of the project. Under these assumptions, therefore no national economic costs are incurred during the investment period. Also know-how and management will normally be obtained from abroad, but here the difference with domestically financed projects may be less dramatic. In the investment period private foreign investment has therefore as its main characteristic that investment can take place without laying claims on resources, that is, provided the project is fully foreign financed and the assumption of perfect market prices holds.

In the operation period, however, the situation is reverse. Whereas with a domestic investment project, under the assumption of perfect market prices, the net benefits of a project are equal to output minus cost of production, this is not the case with a foreign investment project. The foreign investor now can claim part of the benefits of the project, as payment for his investment activity in the past, which part has to be treated as national economic costs. Also depreciation allowances will accrue to the foreign investor and therefore have to be deducted from the benefits of the project.

So far it was assumed that all prices prevailing in the market reflect real scarcities. This is not a realistic assumption and therefore has to be discarded. This makes the impact of foreign financing considerably more intricate.

In the investment period it can now no longer be assumed that the investment outlay borne by the foreign investment is precisely sufficient to cover the cost of using scarce domestic resources. One now has to go into a detailed comparison of the use of scarce resources for the project and the value of the foreign exchange brought into the country by the foreign investor. To the extent that the foreign investor uses his investment funds for importing machinery, equipment and other supplies, no problems do occur, as in this case no scarce domestic resources are involved. Import duties, to be paid on these imports of foreign machinery and other supplies, have to be taken into account, however, and should be treated as national economic benefits.

Serious complications arise in the case of domestic physical resources to be used in the investment period. The price paid by the foreign investor for land, for instance, may well deviate from its real opportunity costs, for example because the host country may, in order to attract foreign investors, make land available below real costs, in which case national economic costs are incurred. Another example may be construction activities in the investment period. Here corrections are generally needed since market wages and market prices for building materials generally do not reflect the opportunity costs. For labour, market prices will normally be higher than the accounting price and this will result in a positive difference to be included in the present value formula as a benefit, or negative investment costs during the investment period.

For building materials, and other material inputs, the picture is less clear. The difference between prices paid by the foreign investor and the true scarcity prices may be either positive or negative; both situations require adjustments in the estimation of benefits and costs during the investment period. The same is true for any taxes paid and subsidies received during the investment period.

The total effects of private foreign investment during the investment period cannot be predicted; they may be either positive, or they may be negative. In order to determine this, the foreign exchange brought into the country by the foreign investor has to be compared with the total amount of physical resources used by the foreign investor during the investment period and valued at their real scarcity costs. If this difference is positive, there is a national economic benefit during the investment period, if it is negative national economic costs are incurred.[1]

During the operation period the introduction of the assumption of market prices which do not reflect real scarcity does not lead to severe complications. Here, in order to arrive at net annual benefits, one has to deduct from the gross value of production the production costs, both valued at accounting prices, as well as profits remitted and all other payments to abroad (fees, etc.) resulting from the project.

3.3. DOMESTIC PARTICIPATION IN THE FOREIGN OWNED PROJECT

Thus far it was assumed that the private foreign investment project was fully foreign financed. Although this is sometimes the case, it is by no means the general case. More often than not, foreign firms use domestic investment funds in order to finance part of the investment expenditure. This domestic financial participation can take the form of domestic equity investment, either through government participation or through a joint venture with private domestic entrepreneurs, or it can take the form of local loan capital. The second type of domestic participation would seem to be almost always present, whereas domestic participation in the form of joint ventures occurs less frequently.

From the literature one gets the impression that foreign investors do rely to a considerable extent on domestic loan capital, generally obtained through the banking system. Some evidence of this was presented in Part III of this study dealing with the macro-economic evaluation of private foreign invest-

1 Note that it is not necessary to check whether the stated costs of imported equipment reflects their real international prices. Although overinvoicing may influence commercial profitability, and therefore through the tax system, also national economic profitability, in order to estimate the national economic profitability of a proposed foreign investment project, this question is of no relevance.

ment. Whether domestic participation in the form of equity participation plays a significant role is more difficult to say. Much will depend on the attitude of the foreign firm concerned on the attitude of the host country.[2]

For questions of policy formulation of the host countries, the question of domestic participation through loan capital versus participation in the form of equity may be a very important one. For the purpose of drafting guidelines for social cost-benefit analysis for foreign investment projects there is no need to go deep into this matter. To the extent that these two varieties of domestic participation do lead to different results this will automatically come to the fore in the present value of the project appraised.

What is important at this stage is to recognize that domestic participation does play a role, and that its consequences should be taken care of both during the investment period and during the operation period.

3.4. THE QUESTION OF ALTERNATIVES

The characteristics presented so far are valid for all private foreign investment projects. However, in order to be able to determine the impact of these characteristics it is essential to distinguish between investment activities which, for reasons of know-how and management skills, could not be undertaken in the absence of private foreign investment, and investment activities for which a domestic alternative is available[3], either in the form of a perfect substitute or in the form of a close economic substitute.[4]

As will be shown in the next chapter, the existence of a domestic alternative to a particular project affects the appraisal of a private foreign investment proposal in a substantive way, as in that case a distinction has to be made between the evaluation of the project as such and the evaluation of the way of financing the project.

In this Part only one alternative to private foreign investment is considered: the possibility of a domestic investment. To this one could object that we

2 Some multinational companies refuse to operate in the form of joint ventures, whereas some governments insist on joint ventures, e.g. India.

3 This may mean that know-how and management skills have to be bought, which is not always impossible; royalties and licencing fees are a frequent phenomenon in modern manufacturing industry!

4 By close economic substitutes goods and services are meant which are technically different but serve the same purpose; as an example, cotton textiles are a close economic substitute for man-made-fibre textiles.

have neglected other possible alternatives, such as importing the commodity to be produced by the project rather than producing in the host country, financing the project with suppliers credits, to conclude a licensing and management contract with the foreign firm instead of straight foreign investment and lastly, financing the project through foreign aid.

A closer look at these suggested alternatives learns that some of these alternatives are not real alternatives, whereas others are really a particular form of domestic investment. The first suggestion, importing instead of producing, is equivalent to the decision not to accept a PFI proposal and, if available, to reject also the domestic alternative because of a negative present value.

The second alternative, suppliers credit, is basically identical to choosing for the domestic investment alternative, with as only difference that in cases where the loan would not be available for other purposes than the particular project, the relevant concept of investment costs is not the original investment outlay, but the amortization of the loan. Although this may affect the outcome of the analysis, this adjustment would in no way affect the methodology of the analysis.

The third suggested alternative, concluding a licensing and management contract, is obviously equivalent to domestic investment.

The fourth alternative, financing through foreign aid, is somewhat more complicated. Much here depends on the assumption made concerning foreign aid. If a donor country would be willing to finance a particular project, but would not be willing, in case the project was rejected, to supply this foreign aid for any other purpose, than indeed foreign aid would have to be considered as an alternative to PFI. This, however, is not generally the case. The normal procedure is that a donor country offers a specific amount of aid, to be utilized for projects and programmes of the recipient country, which are subject to negotiation between the donor and recipient country. This implies, that under these terms and at the project level foreign aid has to be treated as part of the investment resources, not different from domestic savings.

The further implication of this is that for social cost-benefit analysis it does not make a difference whether a particular project is financed through foreign aid or through domestic savings, and that consequently foreign aid is not, to be sure, at the project level, an additional alternative to PFI.

This does not mean that there is no difference between PFI and foreign aid. In all likelihood, there is such a difference, and there is at least some impression that as a *way of financing* investment activities foreign aid is superior to PFI. The appropriate level to deal with this question, however, is the macro-economic level, rather than the project level.

3.5. SUMMING UP

The discussion in this chapter leads to four basic cases, in each of which the special characteristics of private foreign investment influence the adjustments needed in the social cost-benefit scheme in a different way. These four basic cases are:

(I) no domestic alternative: 100% financed from abroad
(II) no domestic alternative: partly financed from domestic resources
(III) alternative domestic investment: 100% financed from abroad
(IV) alternative domestic investment: partly financed from abroad.

Chapter IV will indicate for each of these four basic cases how the social cost-benefit framework is affected.

CHAPTER IV

THE IMPACT OF THE SPECIAL CHARACTERISTICS OF PRIVATE FOREIGN INVESTMENT ON THE METHODOLOGY OF SOCIAL COST-BENEFIT ANALYSIS

4.1. BASIC CASE I: NO DOMESTIC ALTERNATIVE, FULLY FINANCED FROM ABROAD

This is the simplest case, and after what was said in Section 3.2 little more detail is required. What follows is partly a repetition of the remarks made in that section, and is presented here mainly for completeness' sake. A distinction is again made between the effects in the investment period and the effect in the operation period.

4.1.1. *The Investment Period*

Since the project is completely financed from abroad, and since moreover this financing is tied to the specific project[1], the host country does not give up domestic savings for the project. Consequently, in principle and under the condition that all market prices reflect real scarcity, there are no investment costs to the host country. Since, however, market prices cannot be expected to equal prices which would prevail under perfect market conditions, some complications do arise. These complications arise because the foreign investor generally realizes his investment partly through bringing in foreign exchange for buying land and for financing construction activities and perhaps also for buying some domestic equipment. This would cause no complications if all domestic prices reflected opportunity costs, a situation which is not likely to prevail. In addition the foreign investor may have to pay certain indirect taxes and may receive certain implicit or explicit subsidies. For all these reasons one may not assume that the foreign exchange brought into the country by the foreign investor equals the use of factors of production expressed in accounting prices. The price paid for land may be below its opportunity cost, market wages for construction labour may deviate from the opportunity cost of labour, etc. Therefore, in order to estimate the national economic investment costs of a foreign project proposed, a careful comparison between the use of scarce resources and the inflow of foreign exchange has to be made.

1 Were this not the case, the investment outlays had to be considered as domestic investment funds.

In a schematic way the comparison can be indicated as is done in the table below:

Table 4.1.1. A schematic presentation of investment costs in a national economic sense for private investment projects

Expenditure item	Total expenses in market prices converted into exchange	Total expenses in accounting prices expressed in foreign exchange
Domestic		
1. Land	m_1	a_1
2. Labour	m_2	a_2
3. Materials bought	m_3	a_3
4. Services bought	m_4	a_4
5. Taxes paid – subsidies received	m_5	a_5
6. Others	m_6	a_6
Total	$m = m_1+m_2+m_3+m_4+m_5+m_6$	$a = a_1+a_2+a_3+a_4+a_5+a_6$

The total use of domestic resources expressed at their opportunity costs is equal to $a - a_5$. The amount of foreign exchange brought into the country is equal to m. As will be obvious there is no reason to expect these terms to be equal. The national economic investment costs incurred because of the foreign investment project equal $m - (a - a_5)$. If this leads to a positive figure, this measures the benefits to be derived from the proposed investment project during the investment period, if the figure is negative it measures national economic costs in a specific year. In order to get the total impact during the investment period, the same procedure should be followed for each year, and the resulting benefits and costs should be discounted at an appropriate discount rate.

4.1.2. *The Operation Period*

During the operation period the methodological consequences for the appraisal of a private foreign investment project are less severe than during the investment period. In order to arrive at the annual net benefits one has to deduct from gross value of production, valued at accounting prices, the costs of labour as well as intermediate inputs, likewise measured at accounting prices. This is the normal procedure for any benefit-cost analysis. For foreign projects, however, in addition to the items mentioned, profits accruing to the foreign investor[2] as well as all other payments to abroad, royalties, fees, etc., resulting from the project have to be deducted in order to arrive at net annual benefits expressed in contribution to GNP.

4.2. BASIC CASE II: NO DOMESTIC ALTERNATIVE, PARTLY FINANCED FROM DOMESTIC RESOURCES

This case differs only slightly from the case discussed in Section 4.1, the only difference being that in the investment period part of the financial outlays are financed from domestic resources, whereas in the operation period the domestic investors obtain payment in the form of dividends or interest, both of which have to be treated as national economic benefits. Below it is indicated what the differences are in this case compared with basic Case I.

4.2.1. *The Investment Period*

The position in this case resembles the position in basic Case I, with as only difference that we now have to take into account that part of the total investment is financed from domestic savings. If the domestic participation is small in relation to the total investment no problems arise, as it then can be reasonably assumed that the domestic participation is used to pay for domestic investment outlays only. This can easily be taken into account. Referring to the schematic presentation in Table 4.1.1 it means that all domestic investment costs, measured in accounting prices expressed in foreign exchange have to be added. This gives the total value of scarce domestic resources used in the investment period. Next one has to subtract the foreign exchange brought in by the foreign investor as partial payment for the domestic investment components required. This subtraction gives the net investment costs to be borne by the host country as a result of the project execution.[3]

If the domestic participation exceeds the costs of the domestic component in the investment project, and this may well be the case, the estimation of national investment costs resulting from the domestic participation is slightly

2 It could be argued that profits have to be deducted only to the extent that they are indeed transferred. Whereas in a sense this is correct, there are practical reasons to follow the suggestion of deducting all profits of accruing to the foreign investor, if only because the transfer of profits is generally left to the discretion of the foreign investors. Reinvested earnings can then be treated as new investments, and if desirable be bubjected to a separate appraisal.

3 It should be noted that the national investment costs are a mixture of investments by domestic participants and benefits or costs resulting from a difference between market prices paid by the foreign investor and accounting prices for domestic inputs.

different. In this case domestic financial resources are also used to finance part of the import component of the project. If this is the case the national economic investment costs equal the value of imports expressed in foreign exchange prices financed through domestic savings plus the value of the domestic investment requirements valued at accounting prices.

No distinction was made in the paragraphs above between domestic participation in the form of equity capital and participation in the form of loan capital. For tracing the effects during the investment period this distinction is not required as, at least in principle, loan and equity capital should, under a rational economic policy, have the same opportunity costs. In the operation period there are some differences, but these need not be discussed at this place. There is one question, however, which merits attention at this stage, namely, that if the domestic participation is in the form of loan capital, there will be a repayment of principal in future periods, which should be taken into account in the project appraisal exercise. The simplest way to do so is to treat repayments of principal as national economic benefits in the years that they occur.

4.2.2. *The Operation Period*

Also here the procedure is basically the same as in basic Case I. As in the former case, in order to arrive at net benefits one has to deduct from the gross value of production, valued at accounting prices, the costs of labour and intermediate inputs, likewise measured at accounting prices. The financial costs of amortization of domestic loans should not be subtracted, however, as both the interest payments and repayments of principal belong to the national economic benefits. In addition, in order to arrive at the national benefits expressed in terms of GNP, that part of profits after taxes and after repayment of principal on which the foreign investor can put a claim, as well as all other payments to abroad because of the project, have to be deducted. As is evident, profits accruing to domestic equity investors should not be subtracted, as this is part of the national benefits.

4.3. BASIC CASE III: ALTERNATIVE DOMESTIC INVESTMENT; FULLY FINANCED FROM ABROAD

As soon as a particular investment proposal could, in the absence of private foreign investment, be realized through means of an alternative domestic investment, financed either from domestic savings, from suppliers credits or from foreign aid, the project appraisal procedure becomes somewhat more complicated. It then becomes relevant to make a distinction between the evaluation of tne project as such and the evaluation of the way of financing the project.

In this case a positive present value of the project proposed by the foreign investor remains a necessary condition but is no longer a sufficient condition for accepting the project, as it has to be compared with its alternative.

The analysis now consists of three parts. First one has to establish the present value of the proposed project if financed through means of private investment. This part of the analysis is identical to the procedure outlined for basic Case I. If this present value is negative the project proposal has to be rejected. If it is positive, one has to determine, as a second step in the appraisal procedure the present value of the alternative domestic project. (As will be obvious, some items will be identical with those of the foreign investment proposal; others, however, will be different due to different financing arrangements, different technology, different timing, etc.). As a third and final step in the appraisal procedure a comparison has to be made between the present value of the foreign investment proposal and the domestic alternative. If the foreign investment proposal has a higher present value than the domestic alternative, the foreign investment proposal should be approved, if the reverse is the case the domestic alternative should be chosen. The difference in present value reflects the present value, positive or negative, of the way of financing the project.

4.4. BASIC CASE IV: ALTERNATIVE DOMESTIC INVESTMENT, PARTLY FINANCED FROM DOMESTIC SOURCES

In this case the procedure is identical to the one to be followed in Case III, with as only difference that the comparison now has to consist of the one outlined for basic Case II and the domestic alternative.

CHAPTER V

OUTLINE OF A SOCIAL BENEFIT-COST SCHEME FOR APPRAISING PRIVATE FOREIGN INVESTMENT PROPOSALS

5.1. INTRODUCTION

This chapter presents an outline of a social benefit-cost analysis approach for the appraisal of projects proposed by foreign investors. In giving this outline emphasis is put on the practical applicability of the proposed scheme. Among others this means that the scheme presented is of a relatively simple nature; theoretical refinements which in most cases do not lend themselves to application in a practical situation are excluded from the framework given below.

For expository reasons the outline of the proposed appraisal procedure does not take into account other benefits than the contribution to GNP. Other benefits may, however, be introduced without changing the social benefit-cost scheme in any fundamental way.[1]

It is assumed that the government of the host country is able to pursue rational economic policies. As was shown in Section 2.5 this assumption allows us to measure benefits and costs in international prices, following the approach suggested by *Little and Mirrlees*[2].

In addition it should be mentioned that the scheme presented here can be applied both in cases with and in cases without domestic participation. It also covers those cases where there is a domestic alternative to the proposed foreign project and cases where no such alternative is, for other than financial reasons, available.

Section 5.2 deals with some general questions of project formulation and preparation. It also covers the requirements the appraising authority should insist upon before it accepts to undertake a detailed scrutiny of the proposed project.

Since the estimation of appropriate accounting prices plays a crucial role in the entire appraisal procedure, a short description of how to obtain reliable accounting prices is presented in Section 5.3. Section 5.4 then deals with the calculation of the present value of the proposed project. In cases where no

1 This question was discussed in Section 2.4.

2 Little and Mirrlees, *op. cit.*

domestic alternative is available, the present value calculated in this way determines whether the project is to be accepted. In cases where domestic alternatives are available, the analysis is slightly more complicated. This is discussed in Section 5.5. Finally Section 5.6 contains a number of concluding remarks. Throughout this chapter the discussion is limited to basic considerations only. A discussion of certain important refinements in the scheme is postponed to Chapter VI.

5.2. PROCEDURE PRIOR TO THE APPRAISAL OF THE PROJECT

A proposal put forward to the authorities in the host country for approval of a foreign investment project may have originated because the host country's government has attempted to attract foreign firms for the project concerned, or it may be the autonomous initiative of a multinational corporation. If the former situation applies, that is if the host country's government has been actively engaged in attracting certain specific foreign investments, it may be expected that it is familiar with at least some, if not most, of the technical and marketing aspects of the preparation of the project concerned. In those cases where the initiative was in the hands of the foreign firm this is less likely to be the case, and consequently a greater effort is needed for the host country to check the technical and marketing aspects of the proposed project.

It should be stressed here, that, although in the end projects are to be approved or rejected on the basis of the results obtained by submitting the proposed project to the test of the social benefit-cost analysis, it is of the greatest importance to make sure, before a project is submitted to such a test, that the project is well prepared and technically sound, and that moreover it is based on demand studies which indicate that the proposed level of production is the correct one. This applies to all projects, not only to foreign investment projects.

It is sometimes stated that in the case of foreign investment projects the need for a detailed scrutiny by the host country of the technical studies and the marketing reviews is not essential, as the foreign investor will have taken care of this before he submits his project for approval to the host country. Whereas this is true in a sense, namely that the foreign investor will have satisfied himself that the project as proposed by him is profitable in a commercial sense, it would not seem to be correct to say that the host country has no role at all to play in this respect. One can generally be assured that the proposed technology is appropriate for the foreign firm, but this does not automatically mean that it is also the most appropriate one from the point of view of the host country. If technical alternatives are available, they should at least be considered, and if the alternatives are more desirable from a national economic point, efforts should be made to have the foreign firm accept the alternative. Whether the host country will succeed in this is, of course, a different matter, and will depend upon the bargaining powers of the parties concerned. In all situations a scrutiny of the technical studies should be made. In some cases this may lead to a change in the project proposal, and in cases where these results are not obtained it gives at least a safeguard against unviable projects which should always be avoided, even in those cases where the risks involved are fully borne by foreign investors.

There is even more reason for a careful scrutiny of the demand projections used in preparing the project. If these are faulty, the project size may either be too small or too large for the project to be economical. If the project is too small this will result, particularly when economies of scale play an important role, in too high unit costs, if it is too large idle capacity will occur. In both these cases an approval of the project may lead to undesirable effects. Of course, one may reasonably expect that the foreign investor has assured himself of the commercial profitability of the project, but this may differ from its social profitability. To a large extent these differences will become obvious in the social benefit-cost analysis, and need for that reason no special care in the preparatory stages of the project scrutiny. This is not always the case, however, particularly not if indirect taxes are used for discouraging certain types of consumption expenditure. For this reason demand estimates should be checked before the evaluation proper. This is the more important as approvals based on misleading demand estimates may give rise to pressures from the investing company at a later stage to change certain aspects of a deliberate and well-conceived economic policy, in order to make the approved project perform better.

Only after the appraisal agency has reasonably assured itself of the technical soundness of the proposed project, as well as of the correctness of the demand studies, can it start its proper job, the economic appraisal of the project. For this to be possible a considerable amount of information is needed concerning the investment outlay, expected output of the project and inputs needed for the production process, timing of the project, the financing of the investment outlays, etc. This information is required, to the extent applicable, both in physical terms and in the form of prices to be attached to the different inputs and outputs. The question of prices is discussed in Section 5.3. Here we are concerned only with physical inputs and outputs, as well as with the financing of the investment outlay. In order to make the appraisal of the investment proposal feasible this information is definitely required by the agency entrusted with the appraisal of foreign investment proposals.

How does this agency obtain the necessary data ? As it is clearly not operationally feasible for the agency to collect all of it through its own efforts, other ways of obtaining the required information are called for. This should not be a difficult problem, as one may reasonably assume that the private entrepreneur has made a commercial evaluation, based on his technical studies and market surveys, of the profitability of the project before he asked the government for approval. For this commercial evaluation, even if it were a crude one, to be possible, detailed information regarding investment outlays, expected output and operating costs as well as details on the financing of the investment were needed. In addition his profitability calculations will contain other useful information for the national economic appraisal. It is, therefore, only logical that the appraisal by the host government starts from the data brought together by the potential investor, which means that, together with the request for approval, the foreign investor has to submit the data used in his commercial analysis, which, if presented in sufficient detail, should be a sufficient basis for the social benefit-cost analysis of the project.

Naturally the foreign firm may be hesitant to give a full picture of the profits it expects to make, as a result of which its information may not be completely correct. This problem can be tackled in a number of ways, the most important of which is in all likelihood the assurance that the host country is not so much interested in the expected profits of the foreign firm as in the composition, in physical terms, of inputs and outputs, including investment. In addition, and depending on rules and regulations, it can impress upon the potential investor that the requested information is required for obtaining the necessary licenses and guarantees for the repatriation of profits and principal.

5.3. THE ESTIMATION OF ACCOUNTING PRICES

5.3.1. *Material Goods and Services*

In Section 2.3 we saw that there are good reasons to expect that prices prevailing in the market are a poor indication for real scarcity value. Whenever this is the case market prices have to be corrected, in other words accounting prices have to be used. In Section 2.5 two alternatives for estimating accounting prices were discussed. The first alternative is to express prices in terms of willingness to pay, a procedure which leads to severe complications, as it requires that the shape of the demand curve for individual goods and services is known. The second alternative is to use international prices as an indication of the true scarcity prices. This latter approach requires the assumption that the government pursues a rational economic policy, as in that case international prices are a proper indication of the opportunity costs of the commodity concerned. As the assumption of rational economic policies was made explicitly in Section 5.1, in estimating the accounting prices the second alternative, the use of international prices, will be followed in the proposed scheme for the appraisal of foreign investment proposals.

A well-known problem in this respect is, of course, that international prices do not exist for all goods and services, but only for those which are traded internationally. Therefore, a distinction has to be made between goods and services which can participate in international trade, and goods and services for which this is not the case, to be called national goods and services. This latter category consists of goods and services which for physical reasons cannot be transported across international borders, examples of which are dwellings and inland transport, and goods and services where transportation costs are so high as to prohibit international trade. Retail services are a clear example of this second category.

For international goods and services the estimation of accounting prices is relatively simple. For all material inputs as well as for the output of a project in case of import substitution c.i.f. prices are the appropriate accounting prices. For material inputs which in the absence of the project would have been exported, either directly or indirectly, as well as for the output of the project in case it is exported f.o.b. prices are the appropriate yardstick for measuring opportunity costs. In some cases complications may occur, for instance because part of the output of production is exported and part of it is to be treated as import substitution. In those cases the accounting price will be below the c.i.f. price but higher than the f.o.b. price. But also in this case the accounting price can be estimated by calculating the weighted average of c.i.f. and f.o.b. price.

In social benefit-cost analysis generally border prices have to be established for all international goods and services. In the case of the appraisal of foreign investment proposals, however, an exception to this general rule should be made for all those goods and sevices which are supplied directly through the foreign parent company, such as machinery, engineering services, raw materials and intermediate inputs. For these deliveries actual prices as charged by the parent company should be used as accounting prices[3]. The

[3] If these prices are substantially higher than those prevailing in the international market, the host government should induce the foreign firm to lower the prices charged. This does not affect the statement that actual prices should be used as indication of the accounting price.

same reasoning applies, *mutatis mutandis*, for the export of the output of the project to the parent company directly.

The estimation of accounting prices for national goods and services is a much more complicated affair, as, per definition, no international prices exist for this category[4]. The problem of determining accounting prices for national goods and services, although by no means a simple affair, can be solved, however, in an indirect way. The approach towards solving the problem is the following. The accounting prices of national goods should express the real cost of producing them in the most efficient way. The costs of production can be broken down in the costs of intermediate inputs, labour costs and payment for capital. For labour costs accounting prices can be established. Also the opportunity costs of employing capital for the production of national goods can be determined through reference to the discount rate used in social benefit-cost analysis. The estimation of the accounting prices for intermediate outputs does not lead to complications either, insofar as they are international goods and services. Real problems arise if part of the intermediate inputs required for the production of the national good concerned are themselves national goods and services, as is likely to be the case. One then has to go further and decompose also this intermediate input into labour costs, payment for capital and costs of intermediate inputs used in its production. Again this may require a repetition of the procedure for some of the intermediate inputs. In the end, however, the cost of producing can be expressed in terms of international intermediate inputs, labour costs and payment for capital. If these are expressed in accounting prices, their sum is the appropriate accounting price for the national good and consideration.

The procedure sketched above is no doubt a cumbersome one, and could not be followed for each individual project separately, as the amount of calculation work to be performed would become unmanageable. Fortunately, it is not necessary to make the estimates for the accounting prices of national goods for each project separately. This can and should be done periodically by the central authorities, and may be limited to the more important national goods and services. For minor items it may be sufficient to apply a standard conversion factor, based on the average ratio of world prices to domestic prices for a representative selection of commodities.[5]

4 The following discussion is limited to national goods used as inputs. The question of an output in the form of national goods is omitted, as this is of little relevance in the case of private foreign investment.

5 Further details on the determination of accounting prices can be found in Little and Mirrlees, *op.cit.*, Ch. 12, on which our remarks lean heavily.

5.3.2. *Land*

As land is a non-reproduceable resource, special rules are required for the estimation of accounting prices for land. Also in this case market prices may not be a reliable indication of its true scarcity value. The accounting price for land, reflecting its opportunity cost, is equal to the present value of its future contribution to national income. In the case of agricultural land this means that the opportunity cost equals the present value of future agricultural production *minus* the costs of all inputs with the exception of land. Wherever applicable, the cost of making the land suitable as a building site has to be added to the opportunity cost calculated in order to arrive at the accounting price.

5.3.3. *The Discount Rate*

The question of finding the appropriate discount rate was discussed at some length in Section 2.6. There the conclusion was reached that of the different ways to approach this question, the best approach was the 'opportunity cost approach' under which the discount rate is to equal the marginal social rate of return of capital. As was discussed in 3.6, this approach assumes that the volume of savings available for investment is fixed, which although not necessarily completely correct, is a reasonable assumption for any given period, especially if, as was assumed, the government relies on macro-economic instruments for fixing the level of savings. This approach to the discount rate implies that the discount rate should be such as to equalize the total supply of savings with the investment requirements for executing all those projects which show a positive present value if discounted at the appropriate discount rate.

Whereas the principles underlying the fixation of the discount rate are simple and straightforward, its actual estimation is far from easy. Fortunately, also in this case the estimation of the discount rate to be applied in project appraisal should be left to the central planning authorities, and can be treated as given by the project evaluator. For the central planning authorities the procedure to be followed in establishing the discount rate is, if no prior experience is available, a matter of trial and error, as was explained in Section 2.3. In practice, however, the central planning authorities generally do have quite some knowledge concerning the rate of return of investment projects in the recent past. This can then be used as a starting point for the determination of the discount rate for future periods, in which process suitable adjustments can be made. Although discount rates for different countries will be different, one would expect that for most countries a figure in the neighbourhood of 10% would be a reasonable starting point.

5.3.4. *Unskilled Labour*

The question of the accounting price for unskilled labour was touched upon in section 2.7. It was there argued that the accounting price for unskilled labour should reflect its opportunity costs, in other words its contribution to GNP in the absence of the project[6]. In a situation of structural unemployment, as is characteristic of many developing countries, this will lead to an accounting price for unskilled labour which is lower, and often very much lower, than the going market rate. How low the accounting price should be in relation to market wages cannot be said with any degree of precision unless detailed knowledge of the employment situation is available. In most cases, however, the accounting price should definitely be higher than zero, as even in situations of substantial agricultural unemployment, there is normally some shortage of labour during the harvest season. A precise determination of the accounting price for unskilled labour is again the task of the central planning authorities; its findings are data for the project evaluator.

5.3.5. *Skilled Labour*

Whereas in underdeveloped countries there is generally severe underemployment for unskilled labour, this is not typical for skilled labour. There may even be a significant shortage of skilled manpower. The estimation of accounting prices for different types of skilled labour is a difficult and time-consuming affair. As skilled labour is normally only of minor importance in relation with other production costs, it is not unpractical to assume that in principle the wage rates for skilled labour reflect the opportunity costs, and are therefore equal to the accounting price. Only in cases where there is a structural unbalance between supply and demand for specific skills would it be worthwhile, from a practical point of view, to allow for accounting prices different from market prices.

5.3.6. *Foreign Exchange*

The suggestions given above cover accounting prices for all factors of production and intermediate and final products, with the exception of one factor of production: foreign exchange. This is not an omission, but is a logical consequence of the fact that we have expressed all accounting prices in international prices. This is true, not only of material inputs and outputs, but also of factors of production, where the opportunity cost is to be expressed in foreign exchange. Consequently there is in this approach no need to have a

6 Arguments for accepting a higher accounting price, based on a distinction between the value of consumption and the value of savings out of additional income were rejected. See Section 2.7.

separate accounting price for foreign exchange, as the yardstick applied is already expressed in foreign exchange.

5.4. CALCULATING THE PRESENT VALUE

In Section 5.2. it was discussed that the logical basis from which a macro-economic appraisal of a proposed foreign investment project is to be undertaken is the data collected by the foreign firm for the commercial analysis of the proposed investment. It was also mentioned that this commercial appraisal, or at least the data underlying the analysis, should be submitted to the agency in charge of the national-economic appraisal of foreign investment projects, in order to enable it to assess the social benefits and costs of the proposed project.

If this approach is followed the system of the appraisal procedure is rather simple. The actual implementation of the system may still be rather complex, however, as all private benefits and costs have to be translated, through the use of accounting prices, in social benefits and costs, before the present value of the proposed project can be determined. The system to be applied is outlined below. For explanatory reasons a distinction is again made between the investment period and the operation period.

5.4.1. *Costs and Benefits During the Investment Period*

Table 5.4.1. gives a schematic breakdown of investment expenditure and its financing in a form frequently used for a commercial profitability analysis. Normally such a table contains both quantities needed and prices applied. (In cases where the physical inputs are not mentioned in the table, it is to be found in the background material to the table.)

This type of scheme is a good starting point for the assessment of national costs involved in the investment period, as it enables the project appraisal to make, item by item, corrections in the commercial prices, and means of accounting prices, in order to derive the national economic costs. In that way an estimate for the real use of scarce resources can be made. In order to obtain net costs (or benefits) during each year of the investment period, also the effect of the financing mechanism has to be taken into account.

As the question of accounting prices was discussed in Section 5.3, the discussion of the corrections to be made can be brief. For *Land*, the accounting value is to be calculated in the manner discussed in Section 5.3.2. Item 2, *Construction*, has to be broken down in three components, materials, transport and labour. For materials accounting prices can be estimated on the basis of the suggestions contained in Section 5.2.1, making a distinction

TABLE 5.4.1
Investment Expenditure and Financing

Item	Year				Total
	1	2	3 ...	*n*	
A. Expenditure					
1. Land					
2. Construction					
a. materials					
b. transport					
c. labour					
3. Machinery and Equipment					
4. Engineering					
5. Working Capital					
6. Contingencies and Sundry					
Total (1–6)					
B. Financing					
1. Foreign owned equity					
2. Domestic equity					
3. Foreign Loans					
4. Domestic Loans					

between international and national goods. Transport from the factory to the construction site is a national activity for which the centrally determined accounting price is to be applied. If this is not available, and if moreover transportation costs are small relative to total expenditure, a standard conversion factor could be applied. Labour costs have to be corrected through the accounting price for unskilled labour as defined in Section 5.3.4. to the extent that unskilled labour is employed. For skilled labour market prices may be a sufficiently close approximation for real scarcity. If there are good reasons to expect that there does exist serious disequilibrium in the market for skilled labour, accounting prices as suggested in Section 5.3.5 may be applied. Item 3, *Machinery and Other Equipment*, in principle consists entirely of international goods, which should be valued at their border prices, and transportation costs, which are to be valued in the same way as transportation costs for construction material. However, in many cases, all, or part, of the machinery and equipment is obtained directly from the parent firm, at prices which need not necessarily be equal to those prevailing in the world market. If this is the case the c.i.f. price stated in the proposal should be used. Import duties, if any, are never to be treated as a cost item in a national economic appraisal. Item 4, *Engineering Expenses*, consists of payments to expatriate and domestic staff, as well as ot other expenses, most of them for services rendered by consulting engineers. The foreign exchange costs involved are also national economic costs. Expenses incurred on behalf of domestic staff as well as other domestic costs are more difficult to treat, but can in first instance be treated as approximating their scarcity value.

For item 5, *Working Capital*, the correction from commercial costs to national economic costs involves an investigation concerning the physical stock to be financed with the working capital. Although this can never be done with great accuracy, some insight can normally be obtained in this matter. The national economic costs of working capital is equal to the value (at accounting prices) of the stocks it finances.

Finally an adjustment has to be made for item 6, *Contingencies and Sundry Expenses*, which cannot easily be broken down into physical terms. The solution here is to value this item for the national economic appraisal through multiplication of the commercial item by the ratio of national economic to commercial costs for the project in total.

Addition of the different cost items valued at accounting prices would give the total investment costs incurred in any one year if the project was a domestic one. In the case of foreign investment projects, however, at least part of the investment funds will be provided from abroad, in the form of equity investment, and perhaps also in the form of loan capital. These amounts have to be subtracted from the investment costs in order to obtain the net national investment costs of the project. In some cases this may lead to a situation where the net national investment costs are negative, indicating a national economic benefit during the investment period. Finally it should be stressed that since they are defined as the difference between investment expenditure valued at accounting prices and investment funds provided from abroad, the net national investment costs are not necessarily equal to the sum of domestic equity participation and loan capital.

5.4.2. *Benefits and Costs During the Operation Period*

For the calculation of the national economic profitability of a proposed foreign investment project during its operation period a basis can again be found in the commercial appraisal of the project by the foreign investor.A typical scheme for the income and expenditure account is presented in Table 5.4.2. For the calculation of the national economic benefits and costs one has to correct the values contained in such a presentation for differences between market prices and national economic opportunity costs. Again this is to be done through accounting prices, as discussed in Section 5.3. The discussion on the different items in the commercial Income and Expenditure account and their relevance for a calculation of the national economic benefits and costs, can in the light of what was said earlier be rather brief.

Gross national economic benefits in any particular year equal the sum of items 1, 2 and 3, all evaluated at proper accounting prices. For item 1, *Gross value of sales*, no particular problems arise in this respect. Item 2, *Recoupment of working capital* and item 3, *Scrap value of plant*, will only be of relevance in the final year of the projects existence. The social worth of these items can again be estimated through the application of accounting prices. Part of the benefits of these last two items will be appropriated by the foreign

TABLE 5.4.2

Income and Expenditure Account (operation period)

Item	Years						
	1	2	3	4	...	$n-1$	n
Income							
1. Gross value of sales							
2. Recoupment of working capital							
3. Scrap value of plant							
4. (1–3) Total income							
Expenditure							
5. Raw materials and intermediate goods							
6. Energy							
7. Wages and salaries							
8. Repairs and maintenance							
9. Fees and other payments							
10. Interest payments							
11. Depreciation							
12. (5–11) Total expenditure							
13. (4–12) Net profits before taxes							
14. Taxes on profits							
15. Net profits after taxes							
16. Repayments of loan capital							
17. Profits accruing to foreign investors							
18. Profits accruing to domestic shareholders							

investor. Since the scheme takes care of this at another place, no separate attention need be given to this aspect, however. Items 5 up to and including 11 are the current production costs at commercial prices. To translate them into accounting prices is not a serious problem for items 5, 6 and 8, as for these cases the procedure outlined in Section 5.3.1 can be applied. Some complications arise, however, with the other items.

For *Wages and salaries*, item 7, accounting prices for unskilled labour as outlined in Section 5.3 and accounting prices for skilled labour as outlined in Section 5.3 should be applied to the extent that expenses are due to the employment of domestic staff. In addition there will also be payments of salaries of expatriate staff included in this item, for which separate treatment is required. In theory this would imply a detailed investigation in order to determine which percentage of the salaries earned by expatriates is transferred abroad and which percentage is spent on consumption expenditure. For this latter part it should then again be established what the social opportunity cost is of the goods and services consumed. Such an approach is, of course, out of reach for practical work. Therefore, a simpler method should be used, even if this means that this can only be an approximation. This can also be justified on the ground that salaries for expatriate staff are often only a minor item in the total current operation costs. It is, therefore, suggested that all payments of salaries, with the exception of any direct taxes paid, to expatriate staff are fully treated as national economic cost.

Item 9, *Fees and other payments*, has to be broken down into payments to abroad and domestic fees and payments. Payments to abroad will consist mainly of licence fees, management fees, etc., and are to be treated fully as national economic costs. Domestic fees and other payments will, if they occur at all, mainly consist of payments to the Government, in the nature of implicit taxes, such as operation fees, which are not costs in a national economic sense, and perhaps also for services rendered by the host government or other domestic parties, in which case they have to be valued at their opportunity costs for the national economic appraisal of the project.

Item 10, *Interest payments*, constitutes a national economic cost item only insofar the interest is paid to foreign lenders. Interest payments to domestic lenders do not constitute a national economic cost.

The treatment of item 11, *Depreciation*, requires careful investigation. In economic terms the relation between depreciation allowances and the decline in value of equipment is generally a weak one. Therefore the general practice in social cost-benefit analysis is not to deduct depreciation allowances from the benefits, but instead to discount the benefits of the project over a period equal to the expected lifetime of the project. (If depreciation is treated as a cost item, the project gets, because of the implicit assumption that replacement investments equal depreciation, an infinite life). In the case of a social cost-benefit analysis of a private foreign investment, this rule can no longer be applied since the foreign investor is entitled to expatriate the depreciation allowances. The best procedure would therefore seem to be to include all depreciation allowances accruing to the foreign investor under costs of production, without, however, attaching an infinite life to the project, as the depreciation allowances are assumed to be transferred abroad and not to be used for replacement investments. In cases where the project is partly owned by domestic investors (joint ventures) this procedure would imply that only a proportion equal to the foreign share in equity capital is treated as operating costs.

In the case of domestically owned and financed projects net benefits in any particular year of a project are equal to gross benefits in the form of sales minus current operation expenditure, both expressed in accounting prices, and no further attention would have to be given to the destination of the benefits. For foreign investment projects this is not the case, however. To the extent that benefits accrue to the parent firm or other foreign parties these have to be treated as national costs. With reference to the Income and Expenditure Account presented before, this means that in the case of item 16, *Repayment of loans*, this has to be deducted from the benefits to the extent that it refers to repayment of principal to foreign lenders. Repayment on account of domestic loans does not, of course, belong to national economic costs. Likewise, item 17, *Profits accruing to the foreign investor*, is a cost item in a national economic sense. Here one might argue that this item only constitutes a liability to the extent that it is transferred, and that consequently reinvested earnings should not be treated as a national economic cost item. Although there is a point in this argument, there are good reasons, as will be explained in Chapter VI, to treat all profits accruing to the foreign investor as costs in a national economic sense, and not only that part of profits that is transferred to the parent company.

5.5. PRIVATE FOREIGN INVESTMENT AND POSSIBLE ALTERNATIVES

Having established the annual benefits and costs of the proposed foreign investment project in the way outlined in Sections 5.4.1 and 5.4.2 the calculation of the present value of the proposed project is simple and straightforward, as the present value is nothing but the future stream of benefits and costs properly discounted. In Section 5.3.3 the question of estimating the appropriate discount rate was discussed. If the stream of future benefits and costs discounted at the discount rate established by the central planning authorities leads to a negative present value the project should be rejected, if its present value is positive the project should be accepted in all those cases where there is no domestic alternative to the project. However, in cases where there is an alternative to the proposed project a positive present value, although a necessary condition, is no longer a sufficient reason for accepting the project[7]. In this case a comparison has to be made between the present value of the foreign investment project and the present value of the alternative. This means that in addition to the estimation of the present value of the foreign investment project the present value of the alternative has to be estimated. This latter can be done following the lines of the discussion in Section 5.4.1 and 5.4.2. If the outcome of this analysis is that the domestic alternative has a higher present value than the proposed foreign investment than this latter should be rejected. Only if the foreign investment project has a higher present value than the domestic alternative, and if it is also positive, should the foreign investment project be accepted.

5.6. CONCLUDING REMARKS

In this chapter a scheme for the appraisal of private foreign investment was presented. In presenting this scheme strong emphasis was given to the practical applicability of the method, leaving aside considerations of a theoretical nature which would complicate the method, and could in some cases make the application of the scheme unfeasible. It is due to this bias that the scheme presented is a rather simple one. Even then, however, the application of the scheme may sometimes be less simple than is suggested. Major problems may arise in the accurate measurement of the different cost and benefit items. For certain items this may indeed be troublesome. Although in principle all items should be measured as accurately as possible, the project evaluator may find himself occasionally in a situation where he has to accept rough approximations. There is no easy way in which to establish for which items detailed information is required and for which items more or less rough guesses can be accepted. Indeed project analysis is an art in the sense that the project evaluator has to make a judgment concerning which factors are important and therefore have to be estimated with great accuracy and which factors are less important and for which in the absense of reliable detailed information in-

7 For a discussion of possible alternatives to a foreign investment project see Section 3.4.

formed guesses may be sufficient. Only experience in project appraisal may develop the required skills for this art!

The system as developed above leaves a number of problems undiscussed, which cannot in reality be neglected. For instance, it was tacitly assumed in Section 5.4 that the future transfers to the foreign parent company in the form of dividends and other payments are known. This need not necessarily be the case, and consequently some further investigations may be required. This will be done in Chapter VI, where also some further refinements and complications are discussed.

CHAPTER VI

SOME REFINEMENTS AND COMPLICATIONS

6.1. INTRODUCTION

As was noticed at the end of Chapter V, the basic scheme presented there leaves a few open questions concerning the payments to the foreign investor and expatriate staff which deserve more attention than they have been given in Chapter V. These questions relate to the estimation of profits, the treatment of reinvested earnings, the payment of fees and the treatment of salaries paid to expatriate staff. These questions are discussed in Section 6.2. In addition attention is paid in this chapter to a limited number of other issues. Section 6.3 discusses the effects of a new investment project on existing plants, and the way this can be taken into account in a social cost-benefit scheme. In Section 6.4 attention is given to the treatment of complementary projects, such as for infrastructure.

6.2. PAYMENTS TO THE FOREIGN INVESTOR AND EXPATRIATE STAFF

In Section 5.4.2 we noticed that a properly prepared commercial analysis of a foreign investment includes an estimate of the profits to be derived from the project, which estimate we took over as basis for deriving the national economic costs involved in the repatriation of profits. The profit data contained in the commercial evaluation refer to anticipated earnings, which need not necessarily be equal to realized profits. For that reason the procedure suggested in Section 5.4.2 is occasionally objected to, the argument being that the projected profits need not be an appropriate approximation of realized profits. This objection is correct in the sense that the data are subject to uncertainty and should therefore be interpreted carefully. It does not follow, however, that the estimated earnings are not a proper basis for estimating future costs of the project in the form of dividend payments to abroad. The uncertainty concerning the outcome of the project affects all data, not only profit data, and therefore all data entering the social cost-benefit scheme have to be assessed as carefully as possible, in such a way that in the end the results of the analysis reflect the most likely situation. Provided this is done, the appropriate starting point for estimating costs involved in transfer of profits is the estimate of commercial profits, after taxes. If the private foreign investment project is fully foreign owned than all of this has to be treated as social costs. If on the other hand, part of the profits accrue to domestic participants in the project, the profits accruing to these domestic shareholders should be deducted from total after tax profits in order to obtain the national economic costs involved in the separation of profits.

If all profits made by the foreign investor were actually transferred the treatment of profits would be simple. However, sometimes only part of the profits made is transferred, the remainder being reinvested. This leads to the question of how to treat reinvested earnings. If it could be estimated beforehand which proportion of profits accruing to the foreign investor is to be transferred to the parent company, the problem could be solved by including only that proportion in the national economic cost estimate. If this procedure were followed, some further problems would arise, however, because reinvested profits will lead to higher production and profits in the future, and consequently also to higher future profit remittances. In reality it will be next to impossible to estimate beforehand which proportion of profits will be reinvested. This is left, within the limits of the laws regulating private foreign investment, to the discretion of the parent firm, which may take decisions regarding profit transfers on the basis of considerations concerning the interests of the consolidated operations of the firm. As will be understood this interest may well be different from the interest of the private foreign investment project concerned, and therefore, unless specific binding agreements have been made, the project dossier does not contain information on which as estimate of reinvested earnings can be made. For this, and other, reasons the only feasible procedure is to treat all profits accruing to the parent firm as a cost item. Reinvested earnings may then, if and when they occur, be treated as new foreign investments, and perhaps be subjected to a separate cost-benefit analysis.

A few comments should be added about the treatment of salaries paid to expatriate staff. If complete information were available, the correct procedure would be to make a distinction between salaries, net of direct taxes, transferred to abroad as savings of the salary earner, and salary consumed. The first item would fully qualify as national economic costs; for the second item the consumption by the foreign employee would have to be expressed in accounting prices, in order to establish its true costs. In reality no such information will be available, and consequently rough estimates have to be made. In general salaries to expatriate staff will be a minor item only, and it is therefore normally acceptable to treat salaries paid to expatriates fully as costs in a national economic sense. Only in exceptional cases will a more precise dtermination of the costs involved be desirable.

6.3. EFFECTS ON EXISTING PLANTS

A further factor to be taken into account is that the proposed private foreign investment may have negative effects on already existing plants. The argument here is that, due to a superior technology, the private foreign investment project, or for that matter any new project, is able to produce goods either of a higher quality, or at lower prices than existing plants, and is therefore able to compete existing firms producing products of the same type as the new project out of the market.

The possibility that new firms will negatively affect the competiveness of existing firms is in many cases a real one, and consequently has to be taken serious. The proper way to take this factor into account is to estimate the losses in national benefits arising in existing firms, valued at accounting prices, and to deduct them from the benefits of the project proposal under scrutiny. In this way a penalty is given to new projects just equal to the damage done to existing plants, which, moreover, assures that, given the aims of economic policy, the project appraisal is not unduly biased in favour of or against new technologies.

Perhaps it should be mentioned seperately that the adjustment for effects on existing plants is not specifically limited to the analysis of private foreign investment projects. Indeed, although not much attention is given to the problem in existing methods for social cost-benefit analysis, this type of adjustment may be relevant for any project.

6.4. INDIRECT EFFECTS AND COMPLEMENTARY INVESTMENTS IN INFRASTRUCTURE

No specific attention has been paid in this paper to the benefits and costs arising from so-called indirect effects, and the question could be raised whether the social cost-benefit scheme presented is not incomplete in this respect. However, although indirect effects were not covered explicitly, they were taken into account in an implicit way through means of the accounting prices. In this way it was possible to take care of indirect effects, to the extent that this was relevant. For international goods and services the question of indirect effects can, assuming rational economic policies, be neglected, since here one has the opportunity to export or import. This is expressed also in the way accounting prices for these goods and services are determined. For national goods and services the trade possibility is, by definition, absent, but here the accounting prices are expressing the real costs of producing them, in terms of foreign exchange, labour and capital, and consequently the question of indirect effects is properly taken care of.

The same reasoning applies to the question of infrastructural and other investments undertaken by domestic agents, generally, but not always, the government, on behalf of a foreign owned enterprise. Also in this case the costs involved should, in principle, be reflected in the accounting prices for transportation and other services. An exception to this could be made in cases where these complementary projects are captive, in the sense that they are used only by the foreign investor. In this latter case the investment costs have to be added to the investment item in the present value formula. In other words, the project to be appraised now consists of the foreign investment plus complementary investments in infrastructure.

CHAPTER VII

SOCIAL COST-BENEFIT ANALYSIS AS A TOOL IN NEGOTIATING WITH FOREIGN FIRMS

7.1. INTRODUCTION

Generally, before an agreement on the establishment of a foreign firm is reached, a long and often tedious process of negotiating takes place between the host country and one or more potential investors, in which the foreign firms will try to maximize the concessions to be obtained in the form of tax exemption, import duty exemptions, tariff protection, cheap land, etc. The host country, on the other hand, should try to limit the extent to which concessions are granted. The outcome of these negotiations depends primarily on the bargaining strength of the parties concerned, and in this respect social cost-benefit analysis can be of little assistance in strengthening the bargaining power of the host country. However, concessions are often granted on an *ad hoc* basis without carefully scrutinizing its consequences. Here social cost-benefit analysis may prove an effective tool for preventing too liberal concessions to the potential investor. Moreover, this analysis may give insight into the question which type of concessions have little impact on the host country's gains from the project and can, therefore, be granted without much reluctance, and on the other hand, which types of concessions are very costly and should for that reason be avoided to the maximum extent possible.

In this final chapter, some suggestions are given as to how social cost-benefit analysis may be useful in the process of negotiating with potential foreign investors. In Section 7.2 we deal with a situation in which several foreign firms are competing for an investment licence. Section 7.3 deals with a situation in which a foreign investor puts forward alternative proposals for a specific investment. Section 7.4 finally deals with bargaining on the specific terms of a specific investment.

7.2. COMPETITION BETWEEN FOREIGN FIRMS

A common experience of less developed countries engaged in attracting foreign investors is, that for certain sectors it requires considerable activity on behalf of the host country to attract foreign investors, whereas in certain other sectors foreign investors are very eager to obtain permission to start a project. In this latter case not only is there no need for active promotion, but also the potential eagerness to invest may lead to a significant number of applications by competing firms. As is obvious, in those cases the bargaining strength of the host country *vis-à-vis* the foreign companies is a strong one, and consequently the host country should be able to negotiate an agreement in which the social profitability of the proposed foreign investment is substantial. Among other things this means that concessions given to the foreign company should be kept very limited.

In order to ensure that the host country chooses the best project, or if there is scope for a few projects, the best projects from the competing proposals, a first step is to make a comparison between the different proposals. Some of these might prove, even on first inspection, to be not attractive and can be discarded right away. The other proposals have then to be appraised in detail, along the lines presented in Chapter V, in order to determine which proposal has the highest present value. This project is obviously the most attractive, and the government might decide to accept this project, rejecting all other proposals. In doing this the authorities would in any case choose the best alternative from among those presented.

It might be questioned, however, whether in such a situation, a host country should not go further, through an active bargaining process. The fact that a number of companies are competing for the permission to invest would seem to indicate possibilities for obtaining an agreement on terms superior, to the host country, than those offered originally. Moreover, since the foreign firm concerned knows that it has competitors for the requested permission, it should not be too difficult to induce him to accept a permission on terms superior to the host country than those offered originally.

The normal procedure for host countries engaged in active negotiation in a situation of competition between foreign firms, is to choose from among the applications for an investment licence those which seem promising, and try to improve the terms suggested. This can be done by negotiating with these firms more or less simultaneously, stressing all the time that, although the authorities are in principle not unfavourable towards granting the permission requested, they can only do so if the benefits accruing from it for the host country are higher than those to be obtained from granting permission to competing firms. If this is done with sufficient vigour, the host country may be in a position to increase the benefits from a particular foreign investment considerably by way of promoting competition between applicants for a foreign investment project.

7.3. SEVERAL ALTERNATIVE PROPOSALS BY ONE FOREIGN FIRM

In a situation where several foreign firms try to obtain permission for a particular investment the bargaining position of the host country is generally rather strongh. This is much less the case if only one foreign firm has asked for permission to invest. But also in such a situation the host country is not necessarily in a position where it has either to accept or to reject the proposal. Often the foreign firm will present a number of alternative draft agreements for the proposed investment, which differ in the combination of terms asked from the host country. Here again, the host country should, by means of project appraisal, determine which of the alternatives proposed is most profitable from a national economic point. By applying social cost-benefit analysis, in other words, the most attractive alternative can be identified. Depending upon the bargaining position of the host country, the authorities can then, as a next step, try to improve the specific terms on which permission is to be granted, in a way consistent with what is said in Section 7.4.

7.4. NEGOTIATION ON THE SPECIFIC TERMS OF A CONTRACT

Before an agreement is reached between a foreign firm and the host country's authorities on a specific investment project a long and often tedious negotiation process generally takes place, in which the foreign firm tries to maximize the number of concessions granted and in which the host country tries to maximize national economic benefits to be derived from the foreign investment. As was mentioned before, the outcome of these negotiations depends primarily on the bargaining strength of the parties concerned, and social cost-benefit analysis can be of little help in improving the bargaining strength of the host country. However, it is a particularly strong instrument for calculating the economic consequences of different types of concessions.

Negotiations on the terms of a specific investment project generally focus on questions of tax holidays, depreciation allowances, import duty exemptions, tariff protection, subsidies in the form of cheap land, permission to borrow funds from domestic sources and domestic equity participation. All of these questions affect the commercial as well as the national economic profitability of the proposed project, and consequently the impact of these possible concessions should be determined through checking, with the aid of the scheme presented in Chapter V, what the consequences of a particular concession are. Note that in many cases, the exercise requires first of all to determine the commercial effects of a concession, with the national economic profitability being effected only indirectly as a consequence of changes in net profits accruing to the foreign investor.

AUTHOR INDEX

SUBJECT INDEX